RACE

TO THE

POLE

RACE
TO THE
POLE

TRAGEDY, HEROISM, AND
SCOTT'S ANTARCTIC QUEST

Sir Ranulph Fiennes

NEW YORK

Library of Congress Cataloging-in-Publication Data

Fiennes, Ranulph, Sir
    Race to the pole : tragedy, heroism, and Scott's Antarctic quest / Sir Ranulph Fiennes.—
1st ed.
        p. cm.
    Includes bibliographical references and index.
    ISBN 0-4013-0047-2
    1. Scott, Robert Falcon, 1868–1912.   2. Explorers—Great Britain—Biography.
3. Antarctica—Discovery and exploration—British.   4. Scott, Robert Falcon, 1868–1912—
Travel—Antarctica.   5. British National Antarctic Expedition (1901–1904)
6. British Antarctic ("Terra Nova") Expedition (1910–1913)   I. Title.

    G875.S35F54 2004
    919.8'904'092—dc22
[B]
                                                                              2004047491

Hyperion books are available for special promotions and premiums. For details contact Michael Rentas, Manager, Inventory and Premium Sales, Hyperion, 77 West 66th Street, 11th floor, New York, New York 10023, or call 212-456-0133.

FIRST EDITION

10 9 8 7 6 5 4 3 2 1

To the families of the defamed dead

❦ CONTENTS ❦

❧ MAPS ❧

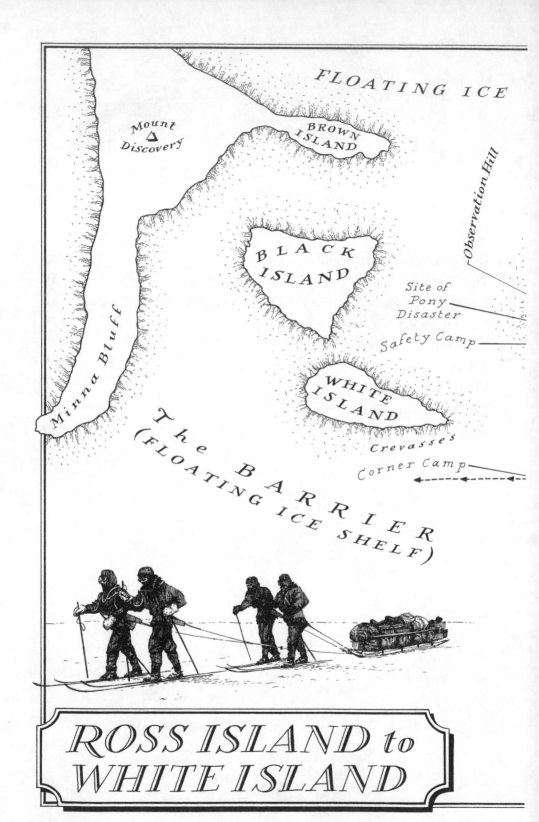

FLOATING ICE

Mount
Discovery

BROWN
ISLAND

Observation Hill

BLACK
ISLAND

Site of
Pony
Disaster

Safety Camp

WHITE
ISLAND

Minna Bluff

The BARRIER
(FLOATING ICE SHELF)

Crevasses

Corner Camp

ROSS ISLAND to WHITE ISLAND

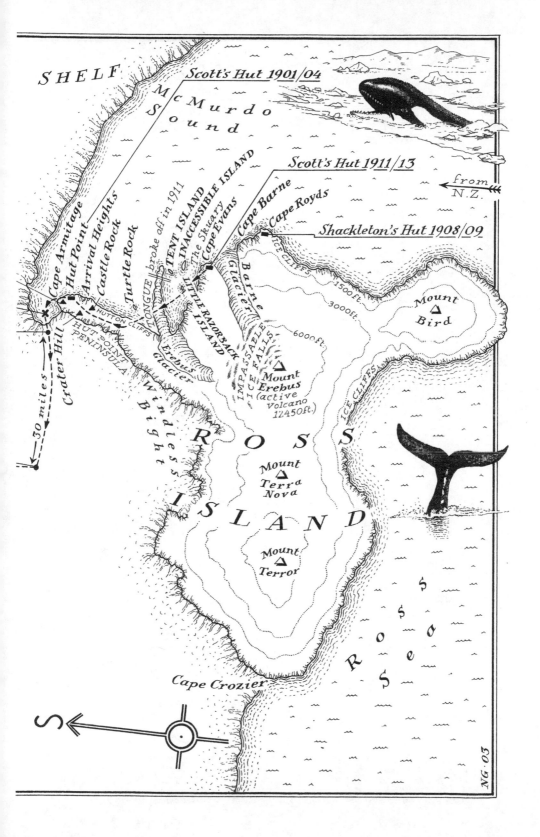

SHELF

McMurdo Sound

Scott's Hut 1901/04

Scott's Hut 1911/13

from N.Z.

TENT ISLAND *broke off in 1911*

INACCESSIBLE ISLAND

The Skuary

Cape Evans

Cape Barne

Cape Royds

Shackleton's Hut 1908/09

Cape Armitage

Hut Point

Arrival Heights

Castle Rock

Turtle Rock

GLACIER TONGUE

LITTLE RAZORBACK ISLAND

Barne Glacier

ICE CLIFFS

1500 ft.

3000 ft.

6000 ft.

Mount Bird

Erebus Glacier

HUTTON CLIFFS

HUT POINT PENINSULA

Crater Hill

30 miles

IMPASSABLE ICE FALLS

Mount Erebus
(active volcano
12450 ft.)

ICE CLIFFS

Windless Bight

R O S S

Mount Terra Nova

I S L A N D

Mount Terror

Ross Sea

Cape Crozier

S

NG·03

✥ INTRODUCTION ✥

IN THE SHORT POLAR summer of 1911–1912, five Britons and five Norwegians raced each other to the bottom of the world. Only the Norwegians returned. What happened to the British? We *should* know, since over fifty biographies have since been written about their leader. But there were no witnesses, so a few biographers without experience of the realities have played many tunes, invented many twists to the tragedy, and told many lies. In this book, I have done what my predecessors could not do; I have put myself in the place of the British explorers and used logic based on personal experience to reconstruct the events. No previous Scott biographer has man-hauled a heavy sledge load through the great crevasse fields of the Beardmore Glacier, explored ice fields never seen by man, or walked a thousand miles on poisoned feet. To write about Hell, it helps if you have been there.

I do not in any way identify with Scott, nor favor him over his two brave and brilliant contemporaries, the Norwegian Amundsen and the Irishman Shackleton. All three made deadly errors, had grave character flaws, and, at some point in their careers, caused other men to die. All that remains by way of evidence as to why the British died are the diaries of the dead and the writings of their surviving friends who described the way things went on journeys under Scott. Some of the writers, for a time, loved or hated Scott, and they often made their feelings clear. I have used their words and my experience to give an unbiased account of the way Scott and his men made history.

RACE

TO THE

POLE

MARKHAM'S GRAND DESIGN

THREE MEN WERE CLOSE to death on an ice plain in Antarctica in March 1912. They had all reached the South Pole with Robert Scott but were failing on the return journey. Lawrence Edward Grace Oates, known to his expedition colleagues as "Titus," soon to become an archetypal hero of his century, died slowly over many days and nights of intense pain, finally choosing the moment of his end by going outside the tent, where Antarctica killed him in minutes. Oates once said of his leader: "I dislike Scott intensely . . . he is not straight, it is himself first, the rest nowhere, and when he has got what he can out of you, it is shift for yourself." So Oates shifted for himself.

A few dire days later, two other members of Scott's polar team joined Oates in death. One, Scotsman Henry Bowers, had said of Scott: "I am Captain Scott's man and shall stick by him right through." And, "he is one of the best and behaved up to our best traditions at a time when his own outlook must have been the blackness of darkness." And in a letter to his mother: "The Captain is a splendid leader and one for whom I have the greatest admiration." The other, doctor and chief scientist Edward Wilson, the most respected man on the expedition, had written: "There is nothing that I would not do for him. He is a really good man." "He is thoughtful for each individual and does little kindnesses which show it . . . I have never known him to be unfair." "I have known him now for ten years, and I believe in him so firmly that I am often sorry when he lays himself open to misunderstanding. I am sure that you will come to know him and believe in him as I do, and none the less because he is sometimes difficult."

Slowly freezing and starving to death beside Bowers and Wilson, Scott also died, and a controversial legend was born that, ninety years on, still retains the fascination and power to spark bitter debate and raise hackles. Scott remains an enigma, and Wilson's hope that "you will come to know him and believe in him" has not been realized, despite some four dozen biographies.

Through two world wars, the Scott story was used as a heroic example of how to live and how to face death when fighting for your country. Since the 1980s, Britain has looked more askance at her past and, led by a different type of biographer, the modern cynical version of the popular Scott story has become one of failure: a failure caused by typical British imperialist qualities at a time when the empire was beginning to wane.

I have read all the pertinent literature and correspondence about Scott and his men, but, unlike his previous biographers, I have shared Scott's experiences over many years and so can the better comment on his decisions and his behavior, bringing a sympathy for and practical understanding of the severe problems Scott actually faced. When Robert Scott, an unknown lieutenant in the Royal Navy, came, in the early part of the twentieth century, to lead two of Britain's attempts to unravel the mysteries of Antarctica, nobody even knew if the icy South Pole was on land or at sea.

Scott, born in 1868, no rebel or liberal, had experienced little of life beyond full-time immersion in naval training schools since his early teens. He was very much a product of his age and nation. British coal, steam, and steel, driven by the British genius for invention, had powered an unprecedented Industrial Revolution. During the nineteenth century, the Royal Navy and a network of institutions such as the East India and Hudson's Bay Companies controlled one-third of all world trade. British technology (using other countries' raw materials) produced goods that were considered the best and the most reliable in the world. Half of all the ships on the oceans were British. At the turn of the century, the empire spread over ten and a half million square miles, 26 percent of the earth's land surface. Over 400 million people were ruled by the British, and, thanks to the imperial invention gutta-percha, 83,500 miles of rubberized undersea cable linked most of these (in Africa, Canada, India, and Australia) to the mother country by telegraph, another British invention. The language of Victoria's tiny island was already creeping over the world, as were British fashions, customs and sports, insurance, and the use of postage stamps.

By the end of the nineteenth century, Scott and his contemporaries really did live in Great Britain, not little England. "To have been born English," said Cecil Rhodes, "was to have won first prize in the lottery of life." He went on to state that: "we happen to be the best people in the world" and "Ask any man what nationality he would prefer to be, and ninety-nine out of a hundred will tell you that they would prefer to be Englishmen." He even considered that Britain could and should recolonize the United States. At the height of empire, the British exhibited both a healthy confidence and sometimes an unhealthy arrogance. Although it didn't feel like that to my grandfather, who worked for Rhodes and was a typical empire builder of his time. He would have been shocked and hurt if anyone called him arrogant or narrow-minded just because he believed deeply that the British way was the best way.

One field where for three centuries Britain and the Royal Navy had held undisputed sway against all comers was that of polar exploration. Already, for the last quarter of the century, Clements Markham, president of the Royal Geographical Society, had been an ardent campaigner for another polar push. In the south, James Cook from Yorkshire and James Clark Ross from Scotland had pioneered the way, while up north in the Arctic, successive naval expeditions held the "farthest north" record, ensuring Britain's priority of geographical arrival and thus, by unwritten law, of tenure. The common British view, which today sounds somewhat extreme, was that if nobody lives there, the empire rules. *Terra incognita* was really *terra pax britannica.*

What little was known about Antarctica came largely from the early Royal Navy excursions. In 1773, Cook's ship, HMS *Resolution*, achieved the first crossing of 66°33'S, the Antarctic Circle. Four years later, on his third attempt to penetrate the Antarctic pack ice, he reached 71°S, some 1,100 miles from the South Pole and 300 miles south of the Antarctic Circle. Unimpressed by what he saw there, Cook wrote: "Should anyone possess the resolution and the fortitude to [push] yet further south than I have done . . . I make bold to declare that the world will derive no benefit from it." Although Cook would not live to know it, the ice and bad visibility on both his voyages halted him a mere day's sailing from the coast of Antarctica. He always believed in the existence of a hidden ice-bound continent, but in 1779 he was killed by Hawaiians, and for forty years the admiralty sent no more ships south to pursue his discoveries.

One of Cook's many achievements involved reports of seal colonies on the island of South Georgia. Seal fur was greatly in demand, and, since Britain's cities were burgeoning at the time, they needed oil to fuel the increased street lighting. Oil from the blubber of whales and seals supplied this key necessity, but, although great "blubber fleets" sailed every year to Greenland, demand was fast outstripping dwindling supplies. Cook's report of South Georgian seal colonies was greeted with all the joy of a twentieth-century oil strike, and the fleets headed south. Some skippers, seeking ever-new seal colonies to slaughter, discovered islands and spotted fleeting glimpses of mainland Antarctica, not that they recognized it as such.

Fifty years after Cook and seventy years before Scott, a naval officer, James Clark Ross, made his name by being the first to reach the north magnetic pole, in 1831. The Royal Society then persuaded the admiralty to send Ross south to bag the other magnetic pole, the position of which was important for navigation. But when he reached Tasmania to set up a magnetic observatory and to take on supplies, he learned that French and United States ships were just ahead of him on the same quest, so instead of following them due south he headed southeast into seas where no vessels had previously sailed. When his ships, *Erebus* and *Terror*, reached the pack ice, he simply kept going, for both were strongly built "bomb vessels," strengthened to fight and survive in pack ice. After only four days, the pack suddenly vanished and Ross sailed on south and into an open sea.

Ross carried on toward the magnetic pole with growing excitement, as his dip-circle needle pointed to 85°, suggesting that the magnetic pole could not be far although the geographic one was still more than a thousand miles away. Then land was spotted, high mountain peaks some 280 miles south of the Antarctic Circle. Ross called the promontory ahead of him Cape Adare and, landing on a nearby island, claimed the region for Britain, naming it Victoria Land. He then followed the mountainous icebound coast a farther 360 miles south, until an entirely new and formidable feature, which he called the Great Ice Barrier, barred his way, for it ran east-west across his path, a solid wall of ice up to two hundred feet high.

Ross's subsequent reports highlighted two geographical features that all future explorers seized upon: At that point in his voyage, where he first ran up against the barrier, he described a 12,400-feet-high active volcano, Mount Erebus, and a deep bay in the Ross Sea, which he named McMurdo Sound. Four hundred miles farther along the barrier and east of the volcano, where Ross ended his exploration that season and turned back, he reported briefly seeing the appearance of land at 71°40'S. Two years later, by the time Ross finally headed home, in 1843, he and his men had opened the way to the Pole.

Her majesty's admirals next dispatched HMS *Erebus* and HMS *Terror* north to complete the discovery of the Northwest Passage (the long-sought but illusory quicker passage to the Indies) under an already celebrated but aging Captain Sir John Franklin. Franklin's two illustrious vessels, which had achieved so much under Ross down south, headed north in 1845 and vanished into thin air, along with their complement of 129 naval officers and men. Over a period of fifteen years, some thirty expeditions were dispatched to search the treacherous seas north of Canada and "find Franklin." These failed forays helped to solve the mystery of the Northwest Passage, and they surveyed much of the Arctic archipelago with a hundred sledge trips covering eighty thousand kilometers. Canada's sovereignty over the region is based on this achievement. But the last of the Franklin searches also saw the end of Royal Navy activities in the region.

In 1875, the admiralty sent HMS *Alert* and *Discovery*, under Captain Sir George Nares, to reach the North Pole. *Alert* achieved a new "farthest north" record of 83°20' (four hundred miles from the Pole), but Nares returned home to semidisgrace, for four of his men had died of scurvy. Once again the admirals turned their backs on polar exploration.

A generation before Scott's, there was thus a twenty-five-year blip in the admiralty's ongoing policy of nudging the north, and, when Scott was a boy in Devon, eminent individuals in London were deeply worried that Britain had left "the North" to pioneers from other lands for far too long. Britain's supremacy at polar exploration was under threat from foreigners. By 1881, when Scott left school and was sent to the HMS *Britannia* training ship in Plymouth, it was clear that those foreigners most threatening as north-polar rivals were Americans and Scandinavians, including Robert Peary of the U.S. Army Engineers and Fridtjof Nansen, a young Norwegian scholar.

Scott's destiny as an explorer lay in the hands of the eminent geographer Clements Markham, born in 1830, and the grandson of the archbishop of York. At the age of thirteen, Markham left Westminster School and joined the Royal Navy. As a midshipman aboard HMS *Resolute* in 1851, he searched for Franklin alongside Lieutenant Leopold McClintock, who devised the man-haul sledging techniques that impressed Markham and convinced him that fit and disciplined men were far more reliable for long, arduous journeys through the broken pack ice of the Canadian Arctic than were the dogs used by the Inuit, or Eskimos, as they were called at the time and so also in this book. Ironically, McClintock was later to use dog teams successfully on long polar journeys.

It is fair to say that there were two schools of opinion among the Franklin search veterans, and quite a few favored dogs. Admiral Sir George Richards, a famous long-distance sledger of the 1850s, considered that sledges "dragged like ploughs" and wrote: "There will never be any more Arctic Sledge travelling . . . I would confirm anyone who proposed such a thing in a Lunatic Asylum."

After his Arctic experience, Markham resigned from the navy, partly because he disliked the excessive punishments inflicted on bluejackets by way of maintaining discipline. Joining the India Office, he smuggled seeds of the cinchona tree, jealously guarded but ruthlessly exploited by the Peruvians, into India to provide a source of quinine in the first major step toward the control of malaria there. This led to his appointment as private secretary to the secretary of state for India, and, in 1863, five years before Scott's birth, he became honorary secretary of the Royal Geographical Society (RGS), where he worked doggedly to encourage British involvement in polar exploration. He also launched a campaign, which was eventually successful, to end all flogging in the navy. On becoming president of the RGS, he announced unequivocally and unsurprisingly that the main aim of his term would be the mounting and execution of a British Antarctic expedition. He attacked both the admiralty and the treasury with zeal for the support and funds needed for his project. Two years later, he helped organize the Sixth International Geographical Congress in London, which passed a unanimous resolution that the signatory countries, including most of the major powers in Europe, should do their utmost to conduct scientific exploration of the unknown region of Antarctica. Although pleased with the outcome, Markham is likely to have felt uncomfortable that the first two expeditions to take up his challenge were led by a young Norwegian named Carsten Borchgrevink, with some British money in tow, and a Belgian naval officer, Adrien de Gerlache de Gomery.

Rebuffed in his fund raising overtures to the treasury, Markham fretted and plotted and decided to appeal to public sentiment and purses. His fundraising appeal was two-pronged. He aimed at scientists who, in an age of burgeoning scientific research, were eager for knowledge of a region about which so little was known, and by 1898, Markham had won over the scientific establishment and presided over an august joint committee of the RGS and the Royal Society. With such an organizing body at its very core, the expedition could hardly avoid major involvement in scientific research. And Markham aimed at patriots.

Patriotic fervor was alive and kicking with the queen's forthcoming Diamond Jubilee. The public, Markham knew, clamored for sensational achievement from its own national heroes. To be first at the South Pole was a tantalizing dream and one calculated to shake pennies from pockets, but Markham was at heart a would-be scientist and knew his expedition must be a three-in-one entity involving the Royal Navy, geographical exploration, and the collection of scientific data. This would satisfy all that Markham held most dear—his love of country, his geographical hobby horse, and, above all, his belief that the naval way was the best way. Markham wanted more than mere static studies conducted from a polar base. He thirsted for a geographic quest, the finding and mapping of new lands, and, ideally, a new "farthest south" record.

Markham was very much a man of his era, and many of the Victorian ideals that he held were contradictory to today's commonsense views, such as "any fool can be uncomfortable." Struggle is no longer an end in itself, even if fitness manuals still proclaim the "no gain without pain" mantra. But in Markham's day, the very act of a good fight well fought against adversity, or even merely against the elements, was greatly admired throughout most levels of society and most religions. Markham was not, as has been suggested, old-fashioned, hidebound, narrow-minded, or even traditional in his admiration for the naval methods of exploration. The navy patrolled the seas and was responsible for almost all polar knowledge. He was simply normal, a man of his times.

By 1899, Markham's appeal had netted a mere £14,000 (£658,000 in today's money) and things were looking far from rosy, when out of the blue came a £25,000 (now £1.2 million) check from a rich Hull businessman and fellow of the Royal Geographical Society, Llewellyn Longstaff, who told Markham he wished to contribute to the advancement of knowledge of our planet. The government unexpectedly chipped in £45,000 (£2.1 million) on condition that a like amount be raised elsewhere. The RGS added £7,500 (£352,500) to Markham's existing total so, with £90,000 (£4.2 million) in the coffers, Markham was at last adequately financed.

Not a moment too soon. The Norwegian Borchgrevink was already en route back to New Zealand after an uneventful and static winter spent in a prefabricated hut at Cape Adare. He had not explored the interior and had undertaken very little scientific work of note, although he had been the first to spend an entire winter in Antarctica. But while Borchgrevink was no longer a threat to Markham's plans, the Germans planned a scientific expedition, under Professor Erich von Drygalski, underwritten with £50,000 (£2.3 million) by their government. Drygalski was well ahead in organizing his expedition with an impressive custom-built vessel, *Gauss*. By 1901, when this and Markham's expedition were to finally set off, a Swedish venture had been announced, led by explorer Otto Nordenskjöld. In Edinburgh, the scientist William S. Bruce was organizing a Scottish National Antarctic expedition.

In the face of so much competition and with no time to lose, the moment his £90,000 was ascertained, Markham advertised for a suitable leader to handle the Markham polar enterprise under his guidance and using methods of his choosing. In particular, Markham required maximum Royal Navy participation, Royal Navy discipline, and Royal Navy methods of travel in polar terrain. Since he also wanted the best scientific results, his leader could either be a scientist or a navy man, but his strong preference lay with the latter. Markham was seventy years old at the turn of the century, a manipulative spider with a web that radiated from his RGS headquarters. He was charming, but uncompromising, crusty, dictatorial, and devious.

The main charge leveled by Markham critics was his preference for men rather than dogs to haul sledges. The Royal Navy expeditions, which for three centuries had opened up the north (without help from Eskimos, Scandinavians, Americans, or, except in a few cases, dogs), had progressed through often nightmarish sea-ice conditions by a well-tried man-haul system. Once their ships became icebound, foot parties of hardy bluejackets would sometimes haul their tents and stores over ice floes, using lifeboats as crude sledges. Whenever stretches of open ocean separated the floes, they simply launched their boats and carried on. As time went by, runners were devised to help this process, or sledges were carried for use where fewer open-water obstacles were expected. Markham had been greatly impressed by this system during the search for Franklin aboard *Resolute* in 1851.

While Markham admired and wished to emulate the McClintock man-haul system, another school of polar travel based on Eskimo skills had also developed in the 1850s, largely pioneered by employees of the Hudson's Bay Company in Canada, such as the Orkney man Dr. John Rae, who led various survey expeditions and decided to copy, where useful, the ways of native North Americans who lived and traveled in the polar wastes. Rae's results were spectacular. He surveyed over 870 miles of new terrain and led one of the more successful Franklin searches, but his report on the fate of the vanished expedition included indications of cannibalism that the British public found difficult to accept.

Americans Charles Hall, Elisha Kane, Francis Schwatka, and Robert Peary all followed various Eskimo or Lapp practices, including travel with skis, dogs, and light sledges. Fur clothing and footwear, igloos and seal-hunting were all employed in the Americans' race toward the North Pole, and those Europeans most accustomed to snow and ice in their own backyard, the Scandinavians, were not slow to join in. Fridtjof Nansen and Otto

Sverdrup developed native methods in their own different ways, as did Roald Amundsen. Unlike the British, the Americans and Scandinavians had no entrenched methodology. They were able to look around and experiment without bucking an existing system, since they had none.

As a result, today the likes of Peary and Amundsen are considered versatile, whereas their British rivals, the Markham school, are castigated as arrogant and unwilling to learn from other cultures. Such criticisms were wrong. However, Markham knew that Eskimos could survive in those same desolate regions where Franklin's men had died; indeed, he wrote learned articles extolling Eskimo skills at survival. But he did not believe Eskimo ways were applicable to polar explorations. Eskimos, he pointed out, had no need to extend their geographical knowledge. Their fishing, trapping, hunting, and meat storage skills depended upon a stable base, or bases, from which to operate. Applying such Eskimo skills to ship-based expeditions in search of a 2,600-mile-long marine passage or new territory was not as straightforward as modern critics often suggest.

When, early in 1899, Markham advertised for an expedition leader in both Royal Navy and scientific circles, he also had his own secret short list of favored navy officers drawn up over a period of a dozen years or more. Markham is often accused of being stuck in a rut, but, far from favoring the old-school polar maestros from among his old Franklin-search buddies, his essentials for leadership demanded youth rather than experience. Elderly men, he asserted, were not amenable to new ideas and lacked the energy to meet emergencies. Since he wanted someone with technical ability and a generally scientific turn of mind, he directed his search to regular gunnery or torpedo lieutenants. His list started:

Captain George Egerton, 46 years, "the very best man for it, but too late."

Commander John De Robeck, 38 years, "hard as nails, lots of nerve, an excellent messmate."

Commander Murray J. Park, 37 years, "keen sportsman, hard as nails, very energetic."

Commander Owen Gillett, 37 years, "overflowing with energy."

Commander James W. Combe, "clever and full of resource."

Robert Scott, thirty-one, with no comments attached, was listed in sixth place out of eleven officers.

Markham had first noticed Scott, one of twelve midshipmen on *Rover*, in the West Indies back in 1887, during a race between two navy ships' cutters. "I was much struck by his intelligence, information, and the charm of his manner." Ten years later, Scott was a torpedo officer aboard *Empress of India,* training off the Spanish coast, when he again bumped into Clements Markham, who inquired about Scott from Captain, later Admiral, Sir George Egerton (once Markham's favorite for the leadership spot), who knew Scott's command abilities well. Egerton sent Markham a list of officers he recommended, with Scott as his preferred choice.

In June 1899, Markham posted an official advertisement for a leader, and only two days later, quite by chance, he met Scott, who was in London on leave. They chatted and Scott learned two things: A national expedition to Antarctica was planned and a leader was being sought. Doubtless with Markham's overt encouragement, Scott duly applied for the post and then returned to his job aboard HMS *Majestic*. He was thirty-one years old and supporting his mother and two sisters on his pay packet. He needed promotion, and leading polar expeditions, he had heard, was a quick way up the ladder.

Who was he? An obscure torpedo specialist destined to die in fearful circumstances but, in doing so, to become a hero of the British empire.

❧ 2 ❧

TORPEDO LIEUTENANT SCOTT

THERE IS NO CONCRETE evidence as to Scott's family origins, but all known clues point to the lowlands of Scotland, possibly the village of Haddington in East Lothian. In 1908, the garter king at arms told Scott's sister that her family was descended from the House of Buccleuch and a Jacobite rebel hanged by the duke of Cumberland's men. One of this rebel's sons or nephews, a Robert Scott, born in Leith in 1745, fled to France, but later settled in Devon, not far from Plymouth, as a schoolmaster. His four sons joined the navy and fought Napoleon. Two of them, Robert and Edward, retired as naval paymasters, bought the Hoegate Brewery in Plymouth and an attractive property called Outlands, near Devonport, the naval section of Plymouth.

Edward's sons included an engineer, who designed and supervised the building of the Royal Albert Hall, while Robert sired eight children, the youngest of whom, John, a delicate boy, was trained to take over the family brewery while his four sturdier brothers all served abroad in the forces. In 1862, John married Hannah Cumming, the daughter of a Lloyd's surveyor, who produced four daughters and two sons, one of whom, the future polar explorer Robert Falcon, was born in Devonport on June 6, 1868, and known in the family as Con.

Including a maid, a nanny, and various aging Scott relatives, Outlands housed seventeen people and bulged at the seams. One of Robert Scott's sisters described their childhood as happy but simple. They never traveled outside Devon and their one annual outing was to the Plymouth Theatre pantomime. A neighbor said later: "We frequently robbed orchards just for the fun and excitement of being chased by a fat farmer with a long whip . . . Con was very unselfish. He had a pony and I had not so he shared him with me." Scott went to the village school, riding there and back on his pony Beppo. William Hands, the brother of the Outlands lady's maid, remembered years later how he and Con would catch eels and go boating on the Outlands pond. "His temper never lasted for very long and he was always out for fun and games. He was a very good friend and when you were around him you were never without a laugh."

Like his father, John, Scott was born delicate, weak chested, moody, quick tempered, and inclined to laziness. Although hard exercise later toughened him physically, he was to die still fighting his inherited blights of depression, temper, and indolence. His hatred of human or animal suffering, a natural squeamishness at the sight of blood, and a tendency to seasickness would have had little consequence if Scott had taken over the family brewery. But mainly due to parental pressures, and influenced perhaps by tales of derring-do from their four brave uncles, Scott and his younger brother, Archie, both accepted careers in the forces.

John Scott was a pillar of the local establishment, a magistrate, churchwarden, and chairman of the regional Conservative Association. But Outlands' expenses slowly outstripped the brewery income, and when invited to stand for Parliament, Scott senior sadly had to decline for want of funds. He was a frustrated if not embittered man with an explosive temper, not improved when he sold his ailing brewery and retired on the invested funds to tend the Outlands garden.

Scott adored his mother, loved his sisters, and enjoyed a close friendship with his only brother. From his father, he learned the consequences of a quick temper and its poor effect on others, so he fought to squash his own irascible tendencies from an early age. John Scott was ambitious for his children and disappointed when Con obtained less than excellent school reports. Freud would doubtless deduce a strong motive here for Scott's subsequent struggle to forge his own way to success. One reason for the initial appearance of Scott as the runt of the Outlands litter, in addition to his inherited physical frailty, was a marked ability to daydream. His father called him Old Mooney, and, although his surviving relatives failed to recall the subject matter of his many daydreams, they all stressed his tendency to switch off into a dream world both at home and, more seriously, at school.

From his cozy family nest and local village school, the eleven-year-old Scott was thrust into the harsh reality of a naval cramming school at Fareham called Foster's, or Stubbington House. There he remained until, at thirteen, after holidays spent with further cramming to counter the daydreaming, he passed the exam to be a naval cadet and joined the training ship *Britannia*, moored in the River Dart. Temporarily shocked out of indolence and abstraction, Scott learned the realities of discipline, sparse conditions, conformity, punctuality, and, above all, the Royal Navy way of life. Since his innate moodiness, quick temper, and shyness were clearly adverse traits in his new surroundings, Scott learned to suppress or at least hide them. Four years earlier, the family doctor had predicted Scott's inability to join the navy due to his narrow-shouldered, pigeon-chested physique, but life onboard *Britannia* slowly wrought physical changes in the frail cadet. He learned to work the rigging a hundred feet above the deck in high winds; sleep in a hammock; compete at numerous drills; and survive on salted meat, cabbage, and hardtack.

Plymouth was both the birthplace of the navy and the fount of the empire. From her sturdy womb had issued forth the likes of Richard Grenville, John Hawkins, Walter Raleigh, Martin Frobisher, and Francis Drake, to name but a few. But now, although Britannia's Royal Navy still ruled the waves, the navy was living in the past, forever recalling the glories of Nelson and Trafalgar, and by the time the fifteen-year-old Scott joined his first seagoing ship, HMS *Boadicea*, as a midshipman in 1883, Prussian victories over France had begun to frighten the Royal Navy's smug and cobwebbed admirals into abandoning their yacht-club ways to peer nervously at changing naval technology.

Warships in 1883 Britain were still equipped with obsolete muzzle-loading guns. This and other such embarrassments had to change, and an already accelerating process of modernization coincided with Scott's naval apprenticeship. The First World War was still thirty years away, but German and British naval technological rivalry was already under discussion by a group of long-sighted officers, including the great modernizer "Jacky" Fisher, even as the young midshipman Robert Scott learned the traditional rudiments of running a warship alongside the 450 other inmates of *Boadicea,* the flagship of the Channel Squadron.

Like the majority of mankind, Scott was not a so-called natural leader of men. Asserting himself over others did not come easily, so he had to learn the process as he might any other naval skill. Likewise, confidence and decisiveness rather than introspective dalliance were expected, so Scott learned to acquire a new persona. At this time, he also learned to live off his annual pay, which was £30 (now £1,400), and, after two years on *Boadicea,* he moved to the smaller brig *Liberty,* where his commander described him as a "zealous and painstaking young officer." Three months later, on the battleship HMS *Monarch,* he was described as "promising," which boded well for his eventual promotion prospects. As a midshipman, or snottie, in a warship, Scott was a teenage pupil learning to become a teacher. His four-year apprenticeship would lead, if he survived, to acceptance as a sub-lieutenant, the lowest grade of officer, and entry to the Royal Naval College at Greenwich for the studies required to be a full officer.

Scott learned to work with his sailors and slowly discovered how best to control them. Often enough he would find himself a teenage duty officer in charge of shore-leave parties, boisterous at best but frequently surly and drunkenly aggressive. Not a job for a weak character, and one made easier by learning the lore and the ways of the lower deck.

In December 1886, at age eighteen, Scott was posted to HMS *Rover* of the training squadron, where his report summarized him as "intelligent and capable." He worked hard in the knowledge that, as he had heard through the grapevine, promotion came either through genuine merit or through family connections. Lacking the latter, he focused on the hard grind and discovered in passing that he possessed a steel-like determination. After his year at Greenwich, he emerged near the top of his class with four out of a possible five first-class exam results.

There is no record of Sub-Lieutenant Scott showing any interest in exploration. His short but fateful meeting on *Rover* with Clements Markham had registered in the older man's expedition-recruitment diary, but not in the younger man's career dreams as he moved on from Greenwich to active service on a cruiser, HMS *Amphion,* based near Vancouver.

En route to his new appointment in Canada, Scott joined an old tramp steamer in San Francisco bound for Alaska via Vancouver. A violent storm lasting several days caused chaos. Heavy seas swept the decks and poured into the galley, where terrified women and children, sick and freezing, crammed the floor space. Many of the California miner passengers, drinking heavily, began to brawl. Screaming, squalid chaos reigned, with no food or hot drinks to alleviate the misery, and the crew concerned only with the ship's survival. Unable to call on Royal Navy discipline, the twenty-year-old Scott acted off the cuff. He took charge, organizing some of the passengers into groups to nurse the sick, swab the filth, find and dole out food, and generally alleviate the nightmare. He used his fists and his presence to sort out those miners who failed to stop fighting. Scott did not need the disciplinary framework of the naval hierarchy to enforce his way, merely the strength of his personality. His years as a snottie had obviously taught him that, although the navy system might be the best way, it was not the only way.

While based in North America, Scott was briefly posted to another ship, HMS *Caroline,* but was soon back in San Francisco, where he fell for a married American girl, the daughter of an ambassador, and flirted briefly with the daughter of a Canadian judge. He also began what was to become the lifelong habit of recording his thoughts and his worries in a diary. One entry at that time shows that the dark, depressive moods of his childhood, a medical condition perhaps, were still with him: "This slow sickness that holds one for weeks. How can I bear it? I write of the future; of the hopes of being more worthy; but shall I ever be? . . . No one will ever see these words, therefore I may freely write, 'What does it all mean?' "

He returned to Britain as a full lieutenant in 1891, keen to specialize as a torpedo officer. His boss on *Amphion* had given him a good report as "a young officer of promise who has tact and patience in the handling of men. He is quiet and intelligent and I think likely to develop into a useful torpedo officer." Scott's decision to specialize, in a technical branch of the navy then growing in importance, made good sense from a promotional viewpoint. Torpedo warfare tactics were increasingly important to the rival German and British navies, and the latter, waking up rather late in the day to their vanishing superiority, had quickly built two hundred torpedo boats and ordered seventy new warships in the 1890s, so torpedo specialists were in great demand. Since Scott had no family connections to help him in the rat race of promotion, technical expertise must have seemed like an excellent alternative route, so Scott spent the next two years in an old wooden torpedo training ship, HMS *Vernon,* in Portsmouth, where his annual salary rose to £182 10s (£8,554) a year (from which all uniform costs were deducted).

He studied torpedo sea launching, harbor attack, and defense systems, and advanced electricity on *Vernon,* at the same time enjoying himself when on leave at Outlands. The Scotts were a loyal and close clan. His best friends were clearly his brother, Archie, with whom he rode and played golf absent-mindedly, and their sisters, with whom they sailed along Devon's rivers. Asked about her brother's girlfriends, his sister Grace said: "his romantic nature caused him to idolise women . . . His affections were easily caught though not easily held."

By now Scott's pigeon chest and physical frailty had been replaced by a strong, lean figure and a determined athleticism. He was proud of his fitness. His first cousin Bertie Scott remembered meeting him in London "on a bitter March morning, the only person I saw that day who wasn't muffled up to the eyes. He hadn't even an overcoat on." Scott told him, "I don't feel the cold." The same cousin recounted how Con had forced himself to visit the local slaughterhouse in a (futile) attempt to cure his innate horror at the sight of blood.

In naval terms, Scott was doing well, gaining the highest marks of the year for seamanship at his rank and coming first out of nineteen other contenders in the practical exams at the Royal Naval College, Greenwich. Scott's time on *Vernon* was a success, the naval records showing only favorable comments.

HMS *Vulcan,* his first specialist posting, was technically the most advanced cruiser in any navy, uniquely combining the roles of warship, torpedo depot, and floating dockyard. Six torpedo boats gleamed on upper deck davits alongside a fearsome array of torpedoes and gun batteries. Torpedo Lieutenant Scott was no longer a graduate, but an acting naval officer in the world's most powerful navy. Scott was pleased as punch with the *Vulcan* job. He was, he wrote to his father, "precisely in the same position to gain experience as if on board a battleship. To fall back on the torpedo work again at which I have worked exceedingly hard, I look upon the ship as the best practical experience that could possibly befall an officer; in fact I look upon myself now as an authority on the only modern way of working a minefield and such like exercises." The records show that his captain agreed with this assessment, so Scott's future prospects in his chosen career looked rosy.

He wrote to an old girlfriend in British Columbia: "At present I have neither rest nor peace to pursue anything but promotion." But Fate interfered with his plans when, going home on Christmas leave in 1894, he heard that the family was bankrupt, his father's retirement investments all gone. He and his brother, Archie, agreed to put their careers on hold to help their family in this hour of need. Archie gave up his job as a Royal Artillery subaltern and joined a Nigerian regiment with better pay and lower expenses. Scott applied for a transfer to HMS *Defiance,* a torpedo training ship at Devonport, close to home. Of their sisters, Rose became a nurse, Ettie an actress, and the other two learned the trade of dressmaking.

The brothers' contribution allowed their parents to weather the storm. Their sixty-three-year-old father rented their beloved Outlands to a wealthy linen draper and then found a job as a brewery manager near Shepton Mallet. Once the family was safely resettled, Scott focused again on his favorite subject, the development of torpedoes and mines. By now he was recognized as an expert and was tasked to produce the section on mining for the Royal Navy's torpedo manual. He was also well versed in the principles of surveying, magnetism, and electricity.

In 1896, at the age of twenty-eight, Scott applied for a seagoing post and joined HMS *Empress of India,* a Channel Squadron battleship. Clements Markham happened to be a guest aboard a sister warship and, eleven years after their first meeting, the two men met again, briefly, in the Spanish port of Vigo. Scott again made his mark on the older man, who remembered him despite the many hundreds of other naval officers he had checked out over the intervening years. "I was more than ever impressed by his evident vocation for command," Markham recorded. A year later, he asked Scott's then captain, George Egerton, for his opinion of the lieutenant as a potential polar leader. "He is just the fellow for it," was the reply, "strong, steady, genial, scientific, a good head on his shoulders, and a very good naval officer."

By now, Scott ruled the roost in HMS *Empress of India*'s torpedo department. The 1896 admiral's inspection gave his unit a flattering report. Scott's sixty sailors responded well to his command. For fifteen long years, he had worked the navy system with British bluejackets and no single complaint about his man management was ever recorded. It is safe to assume that his men liked him and that he liked them. The Royal Navy way worked for Scott. Later, in Antarctica, when he had the choice to abandon it, he saw no reason to do so.

In the summer of 1897, Scott was promoted to torpedo lieutenant on *Majestic,* the Channel Squadron's flagship, a crack warship far superior to any other ship afloat at the time, with a crew of seven hundred under the command of Prince Louis Battenburg, Queen Victoria's grandson. Two of Scott's brother officers, Michael Barne and Reginald Skelton, were destined to join him in Antarctica, as would three of the crew, James Dellbridge, David Allan, and Edgar "Taff" Evans.

In October 1897, only four months after Scott joined *Majestic,* his father, John Scott, died of heart disease at the age of sixty-six. Workers from the Holcombe Brewery, which he had managed for the previous three years, carried his coffin to the local churchyard, followed by a long procession of mourners. The old man had been popular in the parish. Con and Archie moved their mother to London, along with their two dressmaking sisters, to start a small business in Beauchamp Place. They further agreed to find £200 (£14,000) a year between them to help their mother in her widowhood. A year later, Archie died of typhoid, and Scott, at the age of thirty, became the sole support of his mother and unmarried sisters. He had always lived frugally, but now he pared his expenses to the absolute minimum.

Six months after Archie's death, Scott was on leave in London visiting his family at the dress shop. Heading down Buckingham Palace Road, on his way out of Victoria Station on June 5, 1899, he spotted Sir Clements Markham and greeted him. They walked together to the old man's home in Eccleston Square, where Markham told him about his polar-expedition plans. That very week and after years of negative response, the British government had promised Markham enough funds to launch the expedition as soon as he could mount it. So Markham was on the lookout for a suitable man to command the venture and, for anyone with a tendency toward superstition, Scott's coincidental appearance at that auspicious time would suggest a powerful nudge by the Fates. Whether or not either man was influenced by this thought will never be known, nor will the content of their conversation, but two days later, Scott applied by letter for the post of expedition leader. Markham's journal, penned many years later, stated: "I was just sitting down to write to my old friend Captain Egerton of the *Majestic* about him, when he was announced. He came to volunteer to command the Expedition. I believed him to be the best man for so great a trust."

Maybe Markham's memory was muddled, or perhaps Scott did go to see him after sending off his written application. Either way, the burning question is why, out of the blue, did Scott decide to change the whole direction of his promising career only two days after hearing about this expedition to an area about which he knew nothing? He admitted later that he had no predilection for polar exploration, and his sister Ettie, with whom he was in constant touch at the time, said he "had no urge toward snow, ice, or that kind of adventure."

In thirty years of reading about explorers and their motives for choosing their way of life, I have grown to suspect that there is usually a great difference between the explanation they choose to give (especially in autobiographies) and the truth. My own motive for leading expeditions has always been to make a living, but the financial sponsors who have made my journeys possible have shown distinct disapproval of such a commercial response to the media question: "Why do you do it?" They would prefer a more romantic rationale along the lines of Mallory's ageless "Because it is there." I have always stuck to my guns, but I can sympathize with explorers who have at least adjusted their memory of the why and the wherefore for public consumption.

Scott, like Shackleton, had spent many years on ships listening to the romantic escapades of older naval officers, tales of action, war, and remote regions, yet all he experienced day after day, year after year, was an endless series of textbook exercises. Markham offered adventure. The great climber Edmund Hillary said of the Antarctic explorer Vivian Fuchs: "I felt that the underlying urge . . . came more from an honest love of adventure and the pride and prestige that he felt would accrue to his country and himself if he were the first to succeed in such a long and hazardous undertaking." Robert Swan, who attempted to follow Scott's footsteps in the 1980s, wrote: "I have to feel that life is worthwhile. If or when we pull this [journey] off, I will have done something extraordinary which will give me the opportunity I long for." And Reinhold Messner, who crossed Antarctica in 1989, said: "I undertook the expedition because I was curious and was seeking adventure again. Moreover I was a person with a hunger for recognition, with ambition and the need for enhancement."

Scott may have responded to any or all of such general urges: fame and fortune, love of country, a craving for excitement, the hope for promotion and respect, the curiosity of the amateur scientist. All these, mixed with more mundane personal reasons, probably passed through Scott's mind during the brief two days between his learning of the unique opportunity and the penning of his application. He had always felt a deep responsibility toward his mother and sisters and would have considered the implications of being away from them for a likely minimum of two years, but by then his sister Ettie had married an ambitious politician who had already helped their mother financially and who, Scott knew, would look after the family in his absence.

Scott must have been flattered by the approval of a prestigious personality like Sir Clements Markham, president of the Royal Geographical Society, one-time searcher for Franklin, and friend of many admirals. To fail to apply for the leadership post after Markham had shown enthusiasm and possibly even urged his application would have seemed churlish and, after all, the project might never actually come to fruition, with or without Scott as leader.

It is tempting to imagine that Scott's career was in the doldrums and his main motive was merely to climb the ranking ladder. But it wasn't, and Scott was not a taker of wild risks. The expedition might not succeed. He might prove inadequate in the as-yet-unknown skills required to organize and execute such a venture, whereas he was already well on his way to achieving specialist success through his chosen field of torpedo and mine warfare. Why throw this all away? Viscount Goschen, a first lord of the admiralty, was indeed soon to deplore the possibility that Scott would be "relinquishing a brilliant navy career." Markham's polar project was not a miracle failsafe passage to promotion and glory.

His application duly lodged with Markham and his shore leave over, Scott returned to *Majestic* and concentrated on the down-to-earth business of naval warfare. From time to time, Markham wrote to keep him posted on his chances of selection as expedition leader. These appeared minimal because the expedition committee had thirty-two argumentative members, only seven of whom were naval officers, and many of whom wanted a scientist, not an officer, to lead the venture.

Scott's application was strongly supported by his commander, Captain Egerton of HMS *Majestic,* by his admiral, by the first lord, and the first sea lord of the admiralty, but it took a year before his supporters finally won the day, when it became clear that the scientists had found no other willing and suitable candidate. Scott had meanwhile continued to shine at sea and his only comment about the Antarctic opportunity in letters to his mother was: "I have my eye on another thing which I fear is a bit out of my reach." Well within his reach, however, thanks to his service record, was promotion to commander in the navy lists to be published in June 1900. How would Robert Falcon Scott have appeared to an observer meeting him for the first time in those days? On the plus side, he was charming, intelligent, observant, businesslike, straightforward, kindly, reserved, and confident in his ability to command by example and not by mere naval rote. He was genuinely fascinated by all things scientific and technical. He inspired the great majority of his men to love and respect him, as years later a close study of their diaries and letters would reveal. Scott's negative traits included a tendency to periods of depression and self-doubt, a quick temper, and natural impatience. There have been as many contradictory summaries of Scott's character by his various biographers over the past century as there are ways of describing a controversial work of architecture. But most objective records would agree with his salient pros and cons as listed above.

The world must have seemed a wonderful place for the thirty-two-year-old Scott when, on June 9 that year, Markham signed his appointment as leader of the national Antarctic expedition, and on June 30 he received promotion. He was now Commander Scott. In August 1900, his posting to *Majestic* ended and his work as Britain's great hope for priority in polar exploration began. His learning curve would not be steady; it would be viciously precipitous.

ORDER OUT OF CHAOS

IMAGINE A FLOATING OFFICE worker, for such Scott had been since a teenager, being faced with the task of organizing in only fourteen months one of the most ambitious scientific expeditions ever mounted. Since the work was to take place in an entirely unknown region, to whom could he go for sound advice on what skills and knowledge to obtain?

In the 1970s, I wanted to organize and lead the first expedition to circumnavigate the world on its polar axis. Working flat out with a dozen helpers and modern communications, it took my wife and me seven long years of full-time work to mount the project. Scott, completely untrained in any polar skill, without knowledge of what problems would confront him in Antarctica, without even an efficient telephone system in his office, had exactly one year and two months in which to build Clements Markham's brainchild into the reality of a suitable ship, crew, and equipment. To fit in with the Southern Ocean's narrow window of navigable summer ice, his ship must leave Britain in the month of August. A host of reasons dictated departure in August 1901 and no later. Scott started work in June 1900.

Markham must have loomed like a colossus in the young man's esteem.

At that time, Markham defined the very terms of British polar exploration, and without him there would have been no expedition. He had taken twelve long years to force the Antarctic expedition to become a reality. Single-handedly he had raised the funds required to build a suitable ship and single-handedly he was responsible for Scott's leadership appointment. However, the reason ten months had passed between Scott's application and final appointment as leader in April 1900 was the existence of various committees Markham had found it necessary to form, mainly from the RGS and the Royal Society "men of influence." Without such committees, Markham could neither have persuaded his sponsors, especially the treasury, to part with the huge sum of £90,000, nor the admiralty to lend the paid services of Scott and others to the expedition.

Markham recognized that his committees were a necessary evil, "wild professors" and "howling cads," he called them, and a millstone around his neck. He seldom ceased to rail about them to Scott. Many of these "wild professors" from the Royal Society faction had only voted for Scott when their own leadership contenders had proved unsuitable or unwilling, and, even a year after Scott's appointment, they were still making progress anything but smooth for him. A critical difference between Markham's faction and his mainly Royal Society opponents was the basic issue of the expedition's chief aim. Should it be a wide array of scientific research programs, including oceanography, magnetic studies, and geology, or should its main thrust be geographical exploration and survey? Markham and the RGS faction favored the latter.

Five months before Scott's appointment as overall leader, the committees had voted a geologist with sound expedition experience, one Professor J. W. Gregory, as director of scientific staff for the expedition. The general idea was that Gregory and his scientists would be landed at a suitable spot on the Antarctic coast, where he would set up a base hut from which to send out research forays. Once the expedition ship had dropped off the Gregory team, it would sail off to conduct coastal survey and dredging work. In the eyes of the Royal Society, the ship's captain might hold the title of leader, but in reality he would merely provide a taxi service for Gregory.

Markham's group, on the other hand, saw their Royal Navy commander both as ship's captain and overall expedition leader, in charge of all operations, including overseeing the work of the director of scientific staff. Scott made his own position clear to the joint committee only a month after he became the active leader. He sent them a list of five conditions on which his continued acceptance of the leadership role would depend.

1. I must have complete command of the ship and landing parties. There cannot be two heads.
2. I must be consulted on all matters affecting the equipment of the landing parties.
3. The executive officers must not number less than four, exclusive of myself.
4. I must be consulted in all future appointments, both civilian and others, especially the Doctors.
5. It must be understood that the Doctors are first medical men, and secondly members of the scientific staff, not *vice versa*.
   I am ready to insist upon these conditions to the point of resignation if, in my opinion, their refusal imperils the success of the undertaking.

That Scott needed to insist, as leader of the expedition, that he was to be consulted about the makeup of those he was to lead shows how serious the committee problem was.

Scott would have to perform a number of miracles, and quickly. Six days a week he left his mother's flat early to walk to Green Park, then jog to the expedition's rented office at Burlington House, in Savile Row. There he joined the affable twenty-one-year-old Cyril Longhurst, who had already acted as Markham's expedition secretary for over a year, time spent largely recording the minutes of endless subcommittee meetings. Markham had persuaded the Royal Navy to lend the expedition three other officers. He personally selected Lieutenant Charles Royds to be Scott's first lieutenant, while Scott chose two of his old messmates from HMS *Majestic*, Lieutenant Michael Barne and Engineer Reginald Skelton.

The expedition ship was under construction in Scotland, and Scott went there whenever he could find time. But he knew that this was not enough, so he sent Skelton and Barne to the Dundee dockyard to watch over the ongoing work. No major scientific expedition, such as Markham envisaged and Scott was to organize, had left Britain for a quarter of a century. Its exact aims were still being argued over by the committee members who controlled it some five weeks before its launch date. This could have been hopelessly confusing and distracting for Scott, but he concentrated on those things he knew would be needed whatever the committee's eventual decisions. His ship must travel through the tropics and through the roughest seas in the world to reach Antarctica. It must withstand huge pressures from the ice pack and be able to serve, if need be, as a floating or icebound base for two or even three years. From the ship, Scott's men, sailors and scientists, must have the equipment and transportation to take them over unknown regions of land or sea ice.

Professor Gregory, chief scientist designate of the expedition, complained about Scott's general organization, suggesting that he was casual and generally ignorant about the correct equipment. Worse still, he seemed unaware of these failings. Such words from a man naturally annoyed that his own leadership position had been clumsily handled by the committee and usurped by Scott were understandable, but Scott was both aware of and openly honest about his ignorance and did intend to make up for it. He read a great deal, in what spare time he could find, about previous polar journeys and was much helped in this by the librarian of the RGS, Hugh Robert Mill, a normally critical person, who described Scott as having a most sympathetic character, "and we were friends at once." Mill said that Scott "if anyone, could bring order out of the chaos which had overtaken the plans and preparations." Mill also recorded Scott's speed in grasping the essentials of oceanography and meteorology, as well as his industry in reading and absorbing everything that had been written about the Antarctic.

Several sea routes could be followed to reach previously reported geographical features on the known outer edge of Antarctica, but Markham favored McMurdo Bay, which Ross had discovered sixty years before, on the principle always followed in Arctic exploration that "in going to the unknown, they should start from the known." On reaching McMurdo Bay (now McMurdo Sound), Scott should, in Markham's opinion, but not that of his opponents, anchor his ship and winter aboard, in readiness for patrols

into the interior the following spring. Such forays would be leaps into the
unknown territory to the south and west of McMurdo Sound. Markham
wrote: "The main object of the expedition, then, would be to explore this
Antarctic continent by land, to ascertain its physical features, and above all
to discover the character of its rocks, and to find fossils throwing light on its
geological history . . . everything else should be left to the discretion of Captain Scott." Various versions of the "Expedition's Aims" reached Scott from
the committee as time went by and none of them mentioned a race to reach
the Pole. On the other hand, there was an unwritten understanding that
Britain must be first if polar contention should arise.

On the supplies front, Cadbury's gave the expedition 3,500 pounds of
chocolate. Birds produced generous amounts of custard powder. Nine tons
of flour came from Coleman, butter from Denmark. Space to move inside
Scott's office was soon at a premium. Scott was later criticized for shipping
quantities of Danish butter through the tropics when, surely, he could have
used butter from New Zealand, his launch point for the last leg to Antarctica. We too, in the 1970s, used Danish not New Zealand butter simply because, like Scott's, it was freely given in great quantities.

A key item on Scott's list was sledging gear. Adapting many Eskimo
travel techniques, Parry, James Clark Ross, and McClintock had gradually
increased the length of their man-haul sledge journeys to the point where
they could cover 1,175 miles in seventy days. Their sledges were modifications of native models and James Ross made several of his pioneer journeys
together with Eskimos, thereby enabling him to attain the north magnetic
pole.

Scott noted that, since then, "England has not maintained her reputation
in the sledging world," and "it is abroad therefore that the modern traveller
must look for all that is latest and best in this respect." Scott was referring to
Oslo, known then as Christiania, and the great Norwegian polar explorer
Fridtjof Nansen, whom he visited personally for advice.

Nansen was also advising Professor Erich von Drygalski, the leader of
the German Antarctic expedition, whose voyage was due to start at the same
time as Scott's. After leaving Nansen, Scott visited Drygalski in Berlin and
was shocked by the efficiency and the advanced state of the German prepa-

rations. Back in London, he impressed Markham with his description of the German chain of command and, as a result, was given full independent powers, answerable only to Markham himself.

Markham also introduced Scott to a Merchant Navy officer and Arctic veteran, Lieutenant Albert Armitage, whom Markham wanted Scott to take on as his ice pilot and second-in-command. Armitage was in reality a would-be expedition commander himself, a wanna-be Nansen. He was later to say, "What a wonderful pair of men were Nansen and Peary. Together they might have conquered the world. But two such men would never hold together for long; their wills would clash." He may well have recognized this tendency in himself. Armitage met Scott and impressed him with his firsthand experience of polar work for, only three years earlier, he had explored Franz Josef Land, north of Russia, as the second-in-command of the Jackson-Harmsworth expedition. Armitage was in turn charmed by Scott and agreed to serve under him. He took over all matters relating to sledging equipment.

Armitage favored ponies for hauling, arguing that ponies can be eaten by humans and Siberian ponies can stand the severest cold and drag heavier loads in proportion to their own food needs than can dogs. Their meat is also tastier than dog. The argument that ponies need grass, of which there would be none in Antarctica, whereas dogs could feed off the abundant seal and penguin harvest, was specious since any travel in Antarctica's interior would be quickly out of reach of the sea and into regions as meatless as they were grassless. Fodder bales or seal-meat caches would have to be prepositioned whichever animal was used. Though Armitage favored ponies, the question was wide open. Should men haul the sledges, as Markham and the veteran McClintock clearly expected, or dogs, which Nansen had encouraged both Scott and Drygalski to use? Perhaps someone from a land where one particular method of snow travel had already been successfully developed would have had no trouble making the choice. But to Scott, all options must have appeared confusingly open. He clearly wished to go for whichever travel mode was most likely to prove successful. At times, he seemed to waver between dogs and ponies, but then some champion of man-haul would step in and further muddy the waters. With hindsight, it seems that dogs must have been the obvious choice, but Scott had no crystal ball and knew as many good reasons for dogs proving to be a disastrous choice as might have pointed in their favor.

Scott noted that Nansen's famous first crossing of the Greenland ice cap in 1889 had been completed by man-haul alone, but Russian and Canadian backwoodsmen used dogs to pull sledges in mostly flat tundra country, and in the 1890s, Nansen and Robert Peary of the United States had started to emulate them with some success, so the messages were mixed. Scott knew that he could not count on smooth ice down south. In the unknown region, he might face rough surfaces over which Nansen had agreed that dogs were not much use. Men, Scott knew, could cope with the rough or the smooth. Armitage, with experience of both dogs and ponies, but a preference for the latter, was eventually given the job of obtaining two dozen suitable dogs.

With Armitage handling sledging gear and dogs, Scott could spend more time worrying about his ship. By the end of the year 1900, he was personally involved in decisions affecting the ship's design, decisions not made any easier by the many different functions required of the vessel, nor by the fact that the expedition's ship committee had decided what type of ship was needed long before Scott had appeared on the scene.

Markham had invited tenders for building the ship back in 1899. A Barrow-in-Furness yard sent back a cost estimate of £90,000 (£4.2 million) and the Dundee Shipbuilding Company a better offer of £66,000 (£3.1 million). Markham haggled the Scots down to £45,000 (£2.1 million). They were, he knew, the only firm left in Britain with the knowledge and the craftsmen to construct a large wooden sailing ship. To cope with the immense crushing power of sea ice, a thick wooden hull was imperative, so the Dundee shipwrights ordered wood for an inner lining of Riga pine, a framework of Scottish oak, an internal skin of pitch pine, Honduras mahogany, and oak, and an outer skin of elm and greenheart.

The resulting hull thickness averaged twenty-six inches and, in the bows, eleven feet of solid wood. Her design was based on the lines of Scottish whalers well used to working polar ice, but she was to be one of the very last wooden three-masted ships to be built in Britain. Equally, she was the first to be custom-designed for the purpose of scientific exploration since a 1694 vessel built for the scientist Halley, of comet fame. Her engines and boilers could be easily drained of water to prevent freezing, she had no portholes or unnecessary protuberances below the waterline, and both her rudder and propeller could be jacked up and removed from the deck. Asbestos lining between structural layers was included as insulation, and no iron was used within thirty feet of the deck-mounted magnetic observatory. The final cost of the fully modified *Discovery* was £51,000 (£2.4 million) including the engine.

Fifty years earlier, coal-powered steamers were already competing for cargo with sailing ships, but they were far slower and limited by their coal endurance. The risk of running out of coal was high for long voyages into the unknown, so both sail and steam must power Markham's vessel. Scott's copious correspondence with Reginald Skelton, his old *Majestic* colleague and chief engineer designate of *Discovery*, shows that they spent many hours discussing and dealing with flaws they spotted in the design. Scott's first team members, Albert Armitage, Charles Royds, and Michael Barne, worked hard supervising the modifications and the additional requirements necessitated by newly planned oceanographic or magnetic research work.

Nonetheless, as was hardly surprising for a ship built after its era, the finished article was less than perfect. She leaked in spectacular fashion, her bilge pumps were unreliable (not good on a leaky ship), she consumed coal greedily, and some of her sailing responses were snail-like. Skelton, a critical man who spoke his mind openly on all things, wrote that the shipbuilders had "performed their contract in a most scandalous manner" and he found their iron and steel work "perfectly disgraceful."

Scott's other major task was recruiting the crew. Scott was clear in his own mind about the way he wanted to run his expedition and therefore the type of man required. "From a very early date I had set my mind on obtaining a naval crew. I felt sure that their sense of discipline would be an immense acquisition." He had grave doubts as to his ability to deal with a different class of men. Only three months before the launch date, the admiralty agreed to a maximum of some twenty warrant officers, petty officers, and sailors.

Legally, Scott was not entitled to run *Discovery* as a Royal Navy unit under the Naval Discipline Act and everyone onboard knew this. However, each new volunteer, whether sailor, officer, or scientist, signed on under

Captain Scott as master and voluntarily accepted Royal Navy conditions. Scientists were to be treated as officers and were to eat their meals in the ship's saloon, dubbed the wardroom, rather than on the mess deck. Other expeditions of the period, run on more democratic lines, often suffered from insurrection or outright mutiny from one or more members. These included expeditions under Amundsen, Shackleton, Mawson, Borchgrevink, and de Gerlache. Scott led two major polar expeditions involving over sixty often highly critical and difficult characters without a whiff of mutiny. For complex and demanding ventures by groups of disparate individuals, such as accompanied Scott, discipline could be a highly useful and healthy basis of operations.

Some of Scott's scientists on both his expeditions found the navy system extremely difficult to accept. A later colleague of Scott's, Canadian Sir Charles Wright, expressed his surprise at how British naval captains were cut off from the crewmen in their own little cabins and passed down orders second- or third-hand through their officers and petty officers. And how their orders would be obeyed without question, whereas, as a scientist, he was accustomed to questioning things. Scott faced another potential source of division, especially on the mess deck, because of the admiralty limits on navy volunteers. Scott had been forced to fill the gap by accepting Merchant Navy seamen, and there was a deal of historic antagonism and scorn between the two services.

One common myth current today is that the Merchant Navy ran on some form of democratic consensus system, and that discipline depended on officers with strong personalities or big biceps. In fact, Merchant Navy crews had strict hierarchies and rules of their own and apprentice cadets were not supposed to mix with their social inferiors from the lower deck. There was even a marked social coolness between Merchant Navy engineering and nonengineering officers. Scott's team of volunteers came together gradually. In the light of the violent personal clashes later rumored to have scarred the expedition, it is important to understand the key characters' backgrounds.

Charles Royds, from a Hampshire family, was accepted to join the expedition even before Scott. He was a protégé of Markham, who had great respect for his uncle, Wyatt Rawson. Tall, handsome, and strong, Scott's first lieutenant proved both efficient and popular with everyone. Scott, recognizing Royds's capacity for hard work, was inclined to overwork him, but Royds seldom complained.

Reginald Skelton was Scott's first choice for the key post of *Discovery*'s chief engineer. They knew each other from service on *Majestic*, and Scott showed sound judgment in his selection. Scott also asked him to keep a photographic record of the expedition, so he became a first-class photographer.

Michael Barne, another of Scott's messmates from *Majestic*, volunteered as soon as Scott approached him. His position on *Discovery* was that of second lieutenant under Royds.

Neither Markham nor Scott selected the next two volunteers. News magnate Alfred Harmsworth (later Viscount Northcliffe), the owner of the *Daily Mail*, gave the expedition £5,000 (£235,000) on the condition that he could put forward two experienced polar men as his nominees. The committee had little choice but to accept. Dr. Reginald Koettlitz had been the doctor on a three-year-long Arctic expedition led by Captain Frederick Jackson and sponsored by Harmsworth. He was trained in London, and was a keen botanist and a specialist in the treatment of scurvy, which at the time was still not fully understood and an ever-present threat to isolated polar ventures. Harmsworth's other nominee, Lieutenant Albert Armitage, has already been mentioned. Merchant Navy man, Arctic veteran, and friend of Nansen, Armitage was, polar-wise, the most experienced man on *Discovery*. He wrote many years later about the nature of his appointment:

> I went to see Scott, and dined with his mother and sister and him. I was charmed by him from the first. He said to me, "You *will* come with me, won't you? I cannot do without you." I felt that we would be friends; I wanted to see the Antarctic . . . Scott had no experience of the work that he was undertaking; I had three years' knowledge of it. I was to be his adviser, a sort of dry-nurse, and knew enough of human nature to fear the result. I threw my reasoning aside. I will say at once that I never met a more delightful man than Scott to work with during our

collaboration in the preparation of all matters in connexion with
the expedition.

Armitage became known as the pilot and was to be responsible for navigating *Discovery* through the Antarctic ice. Many years later, embittered
perhaps, he was to claim he had been asked by Markham to lead the expedition long before Scott was appointed.

With Armitage as his navigator and second-in-command, Charles Royds
as first, and Michael Barne as second lieutenant, Scott then had a powerful
personality thrust upon him as third lieutenant, the last posting to be filled.
Ernest Shackleton was born in Kildare in 1874 and lived in Ireland until he
was ten, when his father took up a doctor's practice in Croydon, near London, and packed young Ernest off to Dulwich College public school where
he excelled at boxing and poetry. At the age of sixteen, he was apprenticed
to a Merchant Navy ship, joining as ship's boy and rising to the rank of
third officer on the Union Castle line by the age of twenty-five. Shackleton
was first mate on *Gaika* late in 1900, taking troops to Cape Town for Boer
War duty, when he met Cedric Longstaff, the son of the businessman whose
£25,000 (£1.1 million) had recently saved Markham's expedition. Cedric,
charmed by Shackleton, who had already applied to join and been turned
down by the expedition, persuaded his father to pressure Markham into accepting him. So Markham passed Shackleton to Scott in March 1901 with
his full backing.

It is not difficult to imagine the two officers meeting in Scott's cluttered
little headquarters. At that first meeting, both men wore tweed suits, highly
polished boots, and uncomfortably high stiff white collars. They were both
strong, ambitious characters, magnetically charming when they wished and
stubborn if pushed. Neither had any particular desire to explore or even visit
Antarctica for the joy of the great unknown, but both hoped the venture
would lead them on to greater things.

How did Scott appear to Shackleton at that first meeting? He was a few
inches shorter, but well built and broad chested, with strong, firm features
and steady blue eyes. Recently promoted to commander, full of newly acquired knowledge from Norway and the confidence born of having dealt
firmly with most of the committee problems, Scott did not need a uniform

to exude an aura of authority. But he did need an experienced third lieutenant and the Royal Navy would supply no more officers. So he asked Armitage to check the background of his fellow Merchant Navy officer and, not surprisingly, Armitage returned a glowing report on the Irishman.

Fate dealt Scott a decidedly dubious card on this occasion, for Ernest Shackleton was to become Scott's nemesis and rival, at least in the opinion of four generations of journalists and the numerous biographers of both men. Jealousy, duplicity, and even hatred were the ingredients of this ever-popular myth.

Scott now had a full complement of officers, but the hunt for scientific staff continued. One of the committee, the president of the Zoological Society, was searching for an assistant doctor to help Koettlitz with his zoological work and noticed Dr. Edward Wilson drawing birds at the London Zoo. Impressed by his artistic talents and likely ability as a scientific illustrator, he asked Wilson to apply for the expedition. At twenty-nine, Wilson, who had worked at St. George's Hospital in London, seemed at loose ends, for his heart was not in medicine and his passion was nature, all aspects of which he illustrated with great skill. Scott so took to the affable bird artist that he ignored a medical report that declared Wilson unfit owing to tubercular scars on one lung, common enough at that time. He was taken on as *Discovery*'s assistant surgeon in December 1900, another fine example of Scott's good judgment of character.

The scientific complement was rounded off with marine biologist Thomas Hodgson from Plymouth Museum, Cambridge geologist and palaeontologist Hartley Ferrar, and Australian Louis Bernacchi, a physicist and expert researcher on magnetism who had been to Antarctica with Borchgrevink in 1899, and who summarized his experience with the words: "No living thing walks or creeps or flies there."

For a ship of *Discovery*'s size and accommodation space, she would be overcrowded. They had settled for a company of forty-seven, including five scientists and thirty salaried navy officers and men, more than the navy had originally promised. As it turned out, when scientific shore parties were out sledging and *Discovery* was exploring the coast, every man would be needed and kept at full stretch. There is a detailed crew list at the end of this book.

Scott's enemies meanwhile had been preparing a last-gasp confrontation. Their champion, Professor Gregory, the prospective science director, fiercely opposed Markham's intention that *Discovery* should winter in Antarctica since that would mean Scott would command at the base camp. That being so, Gregory feared that he would be unable to keep his important science program on track, because journeys of geographical discovery, or mere adventuring, as he saw it, would take precedence. For a while, Scott and Gregory coexisted, but in March 1901, Gregory placed a formal complaint to the committee that Scott had ordered some item of scientific gear without consulting him.

Refusing to accept a position subsidiary to Scott (or presumably *any* ship's captain of Royal Navy origin), Gregory resigned in May 1901 and a new science director, Dr. George Murray, head of the botanical department of the British Museum, agreed to take over the job of training the various scientists until *Discovery* reached Australia, at which time he would return to Britain, leaving Scott as de facto science director. Scott and Gregory in fact parted on good terms. Scott was still writing to Gregory in a friendly vein after the return of the expedition, and Gregory's review of Scott's book contained no criticism.

Scott would then become not merely ship's captain but unchallenged leader of all aspects of the expedition. It could be said that Markham's committee machinations had finally won the day for his man and averted the pitfalls of dual command that had beset earlier expeditions.

The aims of the *Discovery* expedition can be summarized as coastal exploration to the west and east of McMurdo Sound with inland sledge journeys to include geological and magnetic work on land and at sea where possible. The 1902 winter was to be spent in the ice, and a second winter, if funds were available by then, to be spent at sea in the deep south. In an unknown region, plans that allow for flexibility are sensible plans. *Discovery* was launched in Dundee on March 21, 1901, and engines were fitted; then she sailed under her own steam to a jetty in London's East India Dock, where Scott's team swarmed all over her as instruments, equipment, and cargo began to arrive on the quayside.

Queen Victoria had died earlier in 1901, and the Boer War was going badly for Britain. The *Discovery* expedition was a tonic for Londoners, who crowded the quayside and sometimes the decks, to the disapproval of Scott's men, especially Ernest Shackleton, in charge of all stowage work under the hot summer sun. With weeks, not months, to go, the hectic preparations gathered speed. New construction faults were noted by Skelton, but, still within budget, the stores kept pouring in and each new problem was solved.

In the last week, Scott sent everyone for dental checkups at Guy's Hospital, a sensible precaution. In 1979, I remember visiting a Cape Town dentist along with the rest of our team due to spend eighteen months in Antarctica. To avoid the danger of peritonitis, I also tried to have all our team's appendixes removed, but was turned down on the principle that more people die from a general anesthetic than ever do from appendix troubles. Ninety-two teeth were removed from Scott's men and 170 holes filled at a cost of £62.45 (£3,000). The records fail to list any cost for the hunting down and execution of the thirty-one stray East End cats found onboard.

Discovery sailed from London on the last day of July 1901 to the cheering of crowds and the hooting of Thames boats. The new king and queen came aboard at Cowes and presented Scott with the MVO (Member of the Royal Victorian Order). As *Discovery* disappeared from the view of the cheering populace, Scott reflected that a venture starting off with fanfare might still end in failure. He may well have nursed fears of hazards ahead and his personal ability to deal with them, but he could be justly proud of what he had already accomplished against great odds over the past twelve months.

By way of judging the scale of Scott's achievement, think of the expedition of Vivian Fuchs and Edmund Hillary, the first to cross Antarctica, in the 1950s. Despite Fuchs's own unparalleled experience in Antarctica and full support from the British and New Zealand governments, it still took him five long years of full-time work to launch that expedition.

$\Leftarrow$ 4 $\Rightarrow$

THROUGH THE PACK ICE: 1901–1902

DISCOVERY'S FIRST STOP WAS Funchal, on the island of Madeira. En route, Scott and Chief Engineer Skelton had closely monitored their new ship's coal consumption and they were not impressed. *Discovery* must reach New Zealand, the launch point for Antarctica, by late November if they were safely to penetrate the pack ice in the 1901–1902 summer season. So from Funchal, Scott knew, they must make New Zealand in ninety days. But reaching Funchal from Britain had taken eight days, so a quick calculation showed that more speed was needed. This meant maximum use of engines as well as sail, but as coal storage space was at a premium, Scott had to cut out a majority of the halts planned for oceanographic and magnetic work. Scott desperately wanted to achieve the scientific program entrusted to *Discovery,* but something had to give.

The "Dundee Leak" became ever more troublesome as *Discovery* approached the equator and the wooden-planked hull responded to the heat. Soon, twenty tons of water had to be pumped out of the ship at least once a day. A foul stench invaded the entire ship soon after she entered the tropics and a search in the bilges quickly traced the noxious source. Hungry or cu-

rious workers in the London docks had opened various cans from the expedition's meat supplies and consumed some of the contents. The leftovers had
gone bad floating around in the ship's bilges. Scott gave Shackleton the job
of unloading, cleansing, and then reloading the holds, work that Shackleton
achieved quickly and efficiently, thereby winning Scott's admiration.

Shackleton's previous service in merchant ships was very different, of
course, from the background training of Scott, Royds, Barne, and Skelton,
and the Irish officer's comparatively casual way with the *Discovery* ratings
(non-rank sailors) may have struck them as strange. Able Seaman James Dell
noted that Shackleton was rather an enigma to ratings on the lower deck because he kept a foot in both camps. Shackleton was by nature a hail-fellow-
well-met populist, besides which, he had a genuine knack for getting on
with all people.

Scott's ratings slept on the mess deck in hammocks, warrant officers in
their own quarters, and officers in individual cabins. Everyone ate the same
food, but separately, with a couple of navy stewards serving the officers in
their wardroom on a table laid with linen and napkins. Scott's physicist, the
Australian Bernacchi, was later to observe the way *Discovery*'s naval hierarchy worked and compared it with his experience of the democratic anarchy
of the 1899 *Southern Cross* expedition of the Norwegian Borchgrevink, the
first group ever to spend a winter on the mainland of Antarctica. Without
the framework of an accepted hierarchy, Borchgrevink's ten men had a terrible time. With nobody prepared to take the burden of active command,
dirt, disorder, and inactivity were the order of the day.

On October 3, 1901, eight weeks after leaving home, *Discovery* sailed
into Table Bay, Cape Town's spectacular harbor. The Royal Navy base of Simonstown lay just around the coast and offered Scott full support. At no
cost to the expedition, naval divers scraped the hull, craftsmen modified the
engine room and corrected various faults, while the admiral's administrative
staff provided Scott with virtually all his listed needs, including five Royal
Navy volunteers to bring his crew up to full strength. As leader of a polar
expedition, being a naval commander clearly had its advantages over being
a civilian scientist.

Although Scott's chief of science, George Murray, had agreed to stay onboard all the way to Australia, he now decided he must leave at Cape Town. At the time, no relief ship had been purchased to supply *Discovery* in Antarctica or, if she were to disappear, to search for her. Murray was keen to be involved in organizing such a vessel as soon as possible, and since delay had meant curtailing the planned oceanographic program, it seemed sensible for him to leave from the Cape. Scott's critics later seized on this as proof of some deep grievance, but the records show otherwise. Scott and Murray became good friends, and by the time they had reached Funchal, Scott had written: "Murray is excellent as messmate and as director." He later modified his opinion of Murray's executive ability, but they remained very friendly. As for Murray, he concluded a note to Scott: "Goodbye old chap. Yours affectionately—give Scamp [Scott's terrier] a pat from me."

Scott became fascinated by the tasks of the scientists and increasingly involved himself in their work. Murray's early departure accelerated this involvement which, luckily, did not seem to irritate the scientists. One of the few *Discovery* men who did have previous polar experience, the Australian physicist Louis Bernacchi, was critical of many onboard, including Scott, who sometimes gave him the sharp side of his tongue. Nonetheless, he noticed the captain's increasing interest in the scientific program on the long voyage from Cape Town. "With his quick brain he could analyse statements and theories in a very embarrassing manner, and the scientists on board soon learned to row cautiously in connexion therewith . . . He was interested in every branch of research carried on in *Discovery*, and frequently made original suggestions to the workers."

By now, some expedition members had formed definite opinions about Scott's abilities and personality. They knew they had volunteered for an extremely risky venture and that their chances of survival would depend largely on Scott's competence. They all knew he had no previous polar experience and they watched his every mood, his reactions to small emergencies, and his behavior toward others with close attention. Many kept diaries in which they lodged their feelings. While they felt it best not to let off steam to their captain's face, they could do so safely in their personal diaries. Readers who themselves have not experienced the extreme stresses of enforced togetherness in uncomfortable circumstances usually believe that diary entries, or letters back home, contain only truthful renditions of facts and of the writers' feelings. From my expedition experience, this is certainly not always the case.

On polar expeditions over the past two centuries, those involved have sometimes been driven insane by the conditions and by each other, both on-board ships marooned by ice and in their snowbound bases. In the early twenty-first century, the black moods polar explorers and scientists can experience after spending long stretches in polar bases are generally described as "winteritis." SAD, or seasonal affective disorder, can also affect the mind. On Scott's expedition, the huge uncertainties of what lay ahead, the stresses especially on those responsible for stores, ponies, dogs, prototype motorized sledges, and scientific programs, and above all, the strains on the leader himself, were extreme. Any natural tendency to irritation, depression, pessimism, or worry would have been magnified and, in the absence of loved ones, the natural, indeed the safest, outlets for pent-up feelings were diaries and letters home. That's human nature.

Today I can look back at my own expedition diaries and letters sent to my wife, or mother, and wonder how on earth I could have written such bitter and twisted comments about good people who are now my friends and with whom I can remember having had no open arguments at the time. The thought that such heat-of-the-moment jottings could be served up by some future biographer as history is laughable. In my case, there is no danger of this, but it certainly makes me view critical comments made about past explorers by individuals under stress with great caution. I stress the word "critical" because comments of a favorable nature made in such diaries and letters tend to be rare but accurate. Diaries yield clues but not hard evidence. Some recent biographies of Scott where his warts dwarf the greatness of his achievements seem to have made unbalanced use of his colleagues' diaries and letters.

One man who kept a concise diary and appears to be a reliable judge of character was the doctor, Edward Wilson, who found a special friend in Third Lieutenant Ernest Shackleton, whose enthusiasm for the poetry of Browning hinted at intellectual depths that Wilson found lacking in many of the others onboard. About Scott, Wilson wrote that he admired him greatly: "all but his temper. He is quick-tempered and very impatient."

Clarence Hare, the steward, who saw more of Scott from day to day than did most of the officers, said of his captain that he was not "bad-tempered in the ordinary sense of the term. He was over-sensitive and allowed himself to get worked up if things did not go as planned."

Scott wrestled constantly with the problem of improving *Discovery*'s speed. He wanted speed and brooked no delay. He was used to naval efficiency at all times onboard ship and was easily niggled by the easygoing, less than speedy responses to orders by some of the Merchant Navy men. He aimed straight at the immediate task ahead, dealt with it, and then focused on the next one and he expected the same from his men. As Wilson wrote: "He is very definite about everything; nothing is left vague or indeterminate." Wilson felt that under Scott's leadership there was "no fear of our wandering aimlessly about."

The person on whom Scott was most severe and unrelenting, as can be seen clearly from his own diaries, was himself. When he felt the *Discovery* team had slipped up, he often blamed himself, despite having been miles away from the relevant "error" at the time, unless he genuinely believed things were going wrong through sheer bad luck, in which case he said so. Scott fought hard to cut out the personal weaknesses he had lived with since childhood and which now, as captain of his own ship and leader of his country's most important venture, were deeply embarrassing to him. His natural inclination to be lazy and untidy and his struggle to hide these tendencies were soon noted by Clarence Hare, the steward, who recorded that Scott did his own clothes washing "and made a very poor job of it." Scott smoked heavily but advised Hare not to. "He said that at my age it would stop my growth." Hare also caught the skipper pouring milk over his plate of curry while his mind was off daydreaming. "He was going to add sugar, only I stopped him and changed his plate." The guffaws of those officers who witnessed this gaffe brought Scott back to life with a jolt.

"These 'brown studies,'" Bernacchi wrote, "might be mistaken for the depression, moodiness and even ill-temper hinted at during his second expedition. He certainly could be irritable and impatient." So did the critical Bernacchi learn to dislike the crotchety captain after three years in his company? Apparently not, for he went on to note that Scott's predominant trait was "his sense of right and justice . . . Truth and right and justice were his gods, and these did not come from any religious sense . . . He led a decent human life because he was a decent human being." As the *Discovery* men were to learn during their ninety days of constant rolling and pitching on the jam-packed, hopelessly cramped vessel, their skipper was not by nature tactful; he called a spade a spade with little attempt at subtlety. Bernacchi summarized this unfortunate failing. "One of his weaknesses was his strong likes and dislikes. He had no use for shifty blustering and inept people, and his mind was clear of cant and snobbery . . . pompous people annoyed him."

Some of these comments make Scott sound a cold, humorless sort of fellow, inclined to bursts of aggression, but when Scott's guard was down, he loved a joke and his laugh was as infectious as his smile. In my experience, a good test of a person's personality is to watch them eased by alcohol. Scott seldom drank, but when, at official functions, he did indulge, it "affected him quickly," in Bernacchi's words, "making him very pleasantly and smilingly cheerful." No hint of aggression there. Scott's main pleasures were reading and pipe smoking. He did a great deal of both and his pipe would have helped his social awkwardness when the *Discovery* wardroom became boisterous, as happened fairly frequently. He did not join the frolics but nor did he discourage them. He sat back, and watched and smiled through a veil of protective smoke.

Scott and Armitage kept the ship at maximum feasible speed, for the success of the entire expedition depended upon reaching New Zealand by late November 1901. On October 21, they clocked two hundred miles in twenty-four hours and, better still, some days later, eight hundred miles in four days. Her high, rounded stern allowed *Discovery* to plow through huge forty-foot cresting waves without shortening sail as most cargo sailing ships at that time would have done. The quartermaster once failed to apply the brake to the helm, which, forced over by a sudden monster wave, flung all three helmsmen to the deck. One man who had watched the wave approach described it as towering up to the upper topsail. On the bridge, Barne, Wilson, and Scott were submerged below the cold, green water for many seconds until the ship rolled free. The wardroom was drenched, crockery smashed, science notes sodden, and the polar clothing, just brought up from the hold to hand out, was soaked. Scott noted that the way the ship behaved was a great credit to her designer.

In November 1979, en route to Antarctica, our polar vessel *Benjamin Bowring* carried a brass inclinometer we had borrowed from Scott's *Discovery*. One day a giant roller forced us to keel over 47° both ways, as recorded by the inclinometer's brass arrow. Our ship could manage nine knots when at full steam and with a favorable wind. *Discovery* at best managed ten. We had only one sailor, a deckhand, onboard who had sailed that far south before. Scott had none. I was terrified. He obviously wasn't.

Hundreds of miles south of the shipping lanes, a sudden roll toppled a pile of oilskins over an oil lamp and fire broke out. This was spotted in time by the watch and extinguished. Scott pushed on south toward 65° of latitude to research magnetospheric anomalies in that key region, but *Discovery* ran into pack ice and was forced to slow. As soon as all magnetic readings were completed, and with time against him, Scott steamed toward New Zealand, halting only at remote Macquarie Island to collect rare bird specimens for Wilson.

Scott made the men eat the leftover meat from Wilson's skinned birds, especially the penguin meat, which was disgusting. He wrote: "I had anticipated considerable prejudice on the part of the men to this form of diet which it will so often be essential to enforce and was agreeably surprised to find that they were by no means averse to it. Many pronounced it excellent, and all seemed to appreciate the necessity of cultivating a taste for it. I found no prejudice more difficult to conquer than my own." Some modern biographers wrongly blame Scott for failing to focus on the need for fresh meat to prevent scurvy; the above, however, is proof to the contrary.

Two days west of New Zealand, Scott recorded "as big a sea as one ever comes across" and the inclinometer recorded a record roll of 56°. They dropped anchor off the New Zealand port of Lyttelton on November 28, 1901, just on schedule and proof of highly efficient seamanship.

Discovery could not immediately refuel and rush on south to her Antarctic objective, much as Scott would have wished to do so. Her magnetic foray into the ice had caused suspected damage to the hull and an hour's work with the main pumps was now needed daily to expel leaked water. Another dry-docking was essential. Every item had to be unloaded and Scott chose Shackleton to supervise this key task. Once the leaks were repaired, Shackleton would have to note every single item in every box, with its precise location in the holds, as they were restowed. Manpower would be sorely needed for all this, but the crew, exhausted after their long and commendable voyage, were due shore leave, which, of course, involved relaxation and alcohol. New Zealand hospitality ensured that by three the next morning there was not a single sober crewman onboard. Skelton noted: "there has been a great deal of fighting and drunkenness and I hope two of the seamen will be discharged." He wheeled the miscreants in front of Scott, who merely gave them a dressing down, initially discharging nobody, partly I suspect because he was not sure he could find replacements. To Skelton's eventual satisfaction, one was demoted and another, who deserted, was replaced by an excellent Irishman, Thomas Crean, from the Royal Navy.

After a long delay caused by repeated but unsuccessful attempts to locate the source of the leaks, Scott was reluctantly forced to accept the fact that he would have to set out into the ice pack in a slowly leaking, heavily overladen vessel, hoping that good weather and much pumping would serve to keep the ship afloat. To make matters worse, when the diligent Shackleton had somehow managed to squeeze three years of provisions into the hold, there was no room for the 30 tons of prefabricated huts, 40 tons of coal, and 1,500 gallons of paraffin (kerosene), so this was all lashed on the decks. *Discovery* was dangerously top-heavy and wallowed low in the water.

Just before departure, the twenty-three sledge dogs Scott had ordered from Russia were chained to kennels amidships and soon began to fight each other, just like the sailors, but without the excuse of alcohol. Scott's little terrier, Scamp, was discharged to spend the expedition with New Zealand friends, because Scott feared the twin hazards of extreme cold and hungry huskies. Shackleton had forty-five sheep, a gift from a local farmer, penned up on a bed of coal sacks and out of the huskies' reach. Bales of sheep fodder were stacked between rows of gas cylinders.

When *Discovery* slipped her moorings and edged away from the Lyttelton quay on December 21, 1901, the cheering of thousands of well-wishers mingled with the bleating and the barking onboard. The crew waved from the rigging and, perched on the highest mainmast stay, a deckhand named Charles Bonner slipped and fell. His body cartwheeled down through the rigging and his skull cracked against the winch gear. Although Bonner was probably sober, Skelton noted that he had been clutching a whisky bottle handed to him during his ascent by his crewmate, Robert Sinclair. Greatly distressed, Sinclair ran away when Bonner's body was landed, technically absent without leave, and a sympathetic Scott refrained from reporting him to the police. Bonner was buried with full naval honors and the Christmas Eve festivities that Scott had planned were postponed.

Discovery headed south from New Zealand's friendly shores into a thick sea fog. Scott's men were on their own, heading into a chartless region, where millions of tons of floating ice crushed ships, and where human life did not exist. As the whalers once sang: "Beyond 40° south, is no law. Beyond 50° south, no God."

NUDGING THE GREAT BARRIER: 1902

ON NEW YEAR'S DAY, Scott broke out rations of whisky punch and lime to celebrate, and the following noon, *Discovery* passed her first iceberg. A day later, crossing the Antarctic Circle on January 3, 1902, *Discovery* nosed into loose pack ice. Scott knew that Ross had once taken forty-six days to break through Antarctica's unique protective belt of floating ice and that in the Arctic, other ships had sunk, crushed like eggshells in the billion-ton grip of shifting pack ice.

At Wilson's request, Scott halted the ship amid five-foot-thick floes while ornithological specimens were collected and Scott followed up his plan to obtain and store fresh meat for the coming winter. Six crab-eater seals were shot and hung from the rigging to freeze. All the Lyttelton sheep were also slaughtered, skinned, and frozen. The next day, Scott had his men ax chunks of ice from the floes to be sledged onboard to replenish the water supply. In time, brine drains from sea ice and ice from old floes is almost fresh when melted, so Scott saved his precious coal supplies by avoiding the use of *Discovery*'s steam-driven desalination plant.

On January 5, 1902, still held by the ice, Scott decided to celebrate

1. Robert Falcon Scott in his early twenties. He never planned to become an explorer but was one of the Royal Navy's top torpedo experts. From 1901, his polar destiny lay in the hands of the eminent geographer Clements Markham, who was determined that Britain should be the first to penetrate the unknown land of Antarctica.

2. *Discovery* under sail.

3. Charles Royds, with a penguin for dinner.

4. Jacob Cross on board *Discovery*.

5. Reginald Skelton, chief engineer and expedition-appointed cameraman.

6. Ernest Shackleton on a vitamin C hunt.

7. Collecting eggs —
Frank Plumley (left)
and Arthur Blissett
return from a penguin
egg-hunting foray.

8. The crew of *Discovery*
or the "Antarctic
Theatrical Company"
in *Ticket of Leave*:
(left to right, back row)
Pilbeam, Weller, Cross,
Feather, Allen; (seated)
Buckridge, Wild,
Gilbert Scott.

9. Scott's dog, Scamp.

10. The first occasion
when Antarctica was
photographed from
the air. The balloon
was inflated on the
ice beside *Discovery*
prior to an almost
lethal ascent by Scott.

11. Early man-hauling trials in Antarctica.

12. Dogs helping Royds's sledge party on the first attempt to reach Cape Crozier, on which George Vince (believed nearest of rear pair) lost his life. Others shown in the photograph are: front pair, Royds (far side) and Koettlitz; next pair, Wild (far side) and Quartley; rear pair, Weller (far side) and Vince.

13. Left to right: Ernest Shackleton, Robert Scott, and Edward Wilson at the start of the southern journey, January 1902.

14. A photograph by Shackleton shows Scott or Wilson in the chasm that prevented them from traveling from the barrier to continental Antarctica, December 15, 1902.

15. Blasting with explosives close to *Discovery,* which lies hidden behind Hut Point, cut off from the open sea by twenty miles of pack ice.

16. Thanks largely to ocean swell breaking up the fast ice, *Terra Nova* and *Morning* break through at midnight on February 14, 1904. Further blasting finally released *Discovery* (left) on February 16.

Christmas Day, the original festivity having been postponed when Seaman Bonner fell to his death. Scientists, officers, and men were issued skis and given their first chance to learn how to use them as part of the Christmas fun. Even in Scandinavia, the home of cross-country skiing, only one seven-foot-long ski stick was normally used, with the skier grasping it in both hands in the manner of a Canadian canoeist using a paddle. The skis themselves were wooden "planks" and far heavier than today's models. Surviving photographs of *Discovery*'s crew learning how to ski on that "Christmas" outing are generally hilarious, with as many people dotted about the ice floes on their backs as on their feet. Nevertheless, after an hour or two, some individuals were already becoming quite competent. A prize was given for a two-statute-mile ski race, firecrackers were lit, and a sing-along followed onboard, topped up with a rum-ration handout.

Scott had read everything he could lay his hands on about man-hauling sledges and he knew that all the great polar journeys by his Royal Navy predecessors had been achieved without skis. He knew that learning to ski fast downhill, or the skill of cross-country glide techniques, would be of little or no use to his men, who would have to pull heavy sledges slowly but surely over generally level surfaces. So ski expertise was not pivotal in any way to his plans. Using skis to shift a heavy sledge didn't require skill.

On January 7, the clouds to the south darkened in a way unique to pack-ice skies and caused by the clouds' reflection of dark seawater belts between ice floes. Early the next morning, *Discovery* broke into open water and clear skies. As lucky as Ross had been on his first foray through the pack, Scott passed through the pack-ice zone in only four days and nights. All sails were set, and soon the mountains of Victoria Land blurred the rim of the southern seascape.

They anchored off a second, coastal band of ice floes, some five miles out from the two deserted huts of the Borchgrevink expedition at Cape Adare, where Scott landed with Bernacchi and others, in a row boat, to leave a sealed canister containing a brief summary of his intentions—the first clue laid down in a potentially life-saving paper trail. If Markham's relief ship was ever to reach this and five other prearranged message points, they would with luck be able to locate *Discovery*.

Scott's original exploration orders from the committee instructed him to explore the coast from Cape Adare south to McMurdo Sound and to locate any likely harbors en route. On reaching McMurdo and its volcano, Scott was to sail east along the barrier wall and claim for Britain any landmass he might find there. The most hazardous of passages for a ship like *Discovery,* indeed for any vessel short of a modern icebreaker, is to skirt the Antarctic coast. In the fjords and between offshore islands, even in the wider waters like McMurdo, ice conditions can switch from open sea to millions of tons of fast-invading sea ice that will collide, with enormous power, with cliffs and beaches and crush anything in its way. Yet Scott's duty involved purposefully nosing into every nook and cranny along this hazard-strewn coast. This was asking for trouble and Scott knew it. Extra hands were placed on watch as lookouts, including the scientists.

On January 7, Skelton and Shackleton shot a leopard seal. Wilson, who had been appointed chief butcher, was exultant. "He was near a ton in weight and took the whole watch to hoist him inboard, an enormous beast with a mouth full of teeth and a head bigger than a Polar Bear." In time, Scott noted: "we came thoroughly to enjoy our seal steaks and to revel in the thought of seal liver or kidneys." But not at first.

On January 14, 1902, a seventy-five-mile-per-hour force 11 gale obliged Scott to shelter his ship in the lee of Coulman Island with both boilers at full steam to provide enough power to fight the current that threatened to tear *Discovery* from her cover. Great icebergs rushed by, any one of which could sink the ship in minutes. The following day, when the wind died away, a boat took Captain Scott ashore to a large cove on the island, the second preagreed-upon message point, where a post was positioned and, lashed to it, a red message container.

For two weeks, with many narrow escapes from ice cul-de-sacs, they sailed south, finding two potential harbors en route to McMurdo Sound, which they reached on January 21. In the hope that the twin volcanoes Ross had named after his ships *Erebus* and *Terror* were on an island and that they could sail south between it and the mainland, they plowed on through loose pack deep into McMurdo Sound. High cliffs ahead soon disillusioned them and, at midnight, they headed back north, then east, around the volcanoes. At a northeastern cape, close to where a descending flank of the volcanoes met the western rim of the ice barrier, Scott, Wilson, Royds, and others rowed a boat between lethally teetering icebergs in an attempt to land. This point, Cape Crozier, was an important message point and a potential base from which to make sledge journeys into the interior.

Wilson wrote about this little boat foray: "There was a . . . heavy swell, which broke on the shore with an appalling force and thunder in some places . . . It was a scene one can never forget. [The bergs] had enormous gulf-like caves and arches and tunnels, into which the swell broke with a thunder like an avalanche. The water was full of penguins popping in and out like black rabbits." They somehow managed to land, place their message canister, and collect rock specimens.

Having found two likely harbors thus far, Scott told his men his outline intentions and Stoker Plumley summarized one of them in his diary. "The exploring party reported it [Granite Harbour] suitable for winter quarters, so if we do not find better we shall come back there for the winter." Now everyone knew that the entire ship's crew, and not just a select sledging group, would be staying put with the ship at anchor through the Antarctic winter with a prefabricated hut for use for shore deployment and as an observatory. When each man had originally signed on, he had known this might happen, but some had preferred to hope *Discovery* would go back to New Zealand in between polar summers. Such wishful thinkers were now disillusioned.

By noon on January 29, 1902, *Discovery* at last passed by the limit of Captain James Ross's exploration along the barrier, the point where he reported seeing possible land to the southeast. Soon afterward, Armitage, the ice pilot, calculated the height of the surface of the barrier to the south to be at least five hundred feet above sea level. Some upturned bergs around the ship, floating topsy-turvy, had embedded earth and rock, and the geologist Ferrar rowed a boat over and took samples. Scott and his scientists were convinced this was proof of Ross's "land." Fog closed in, but, late the next day, the watch officers spotted through the gloom the black face of a rocky cliff high above the decks. A hundred miles beyond the farthest point of Ross's exploration they had finally located land and established another fixed point of Antarctica's outline. They named it King Edward VII Land (now Edward VII Peninsula).

The committee's orders to Scott were to settle into winter quarters

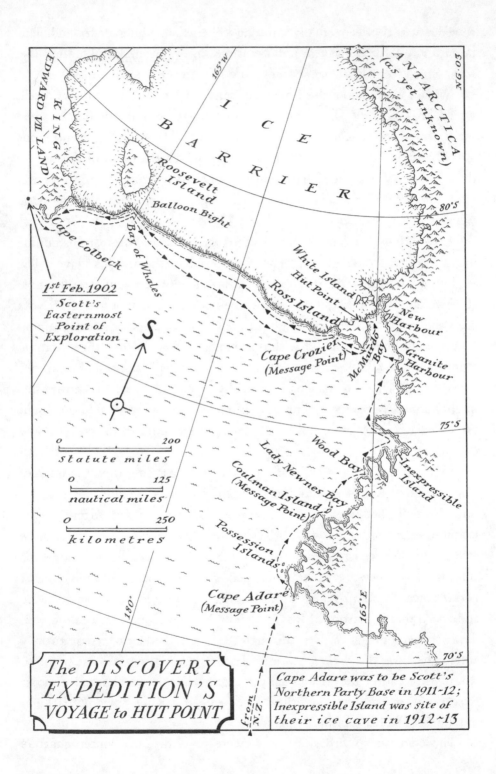

The DISCOVERY EXPEDITION'S VOYAGE to HUT POINT

somewhere along this eastern section of the coast, should he find land and a harbor, but finding none and after becoming comprehensively lost amid the pack ice in the fog, Scott sensibly headed back west, to McMurdo Sound.

The next day, Scott summoned all his officers and told them his intentions. *Discovery* would winter in the most southerly McMurdo harbor they could find, from which, the next summer, two sledging parties would explore the region of the volcanoes and a third would head due south. The relief ship that Markham had promised would, by visiting the message points, locate *Discovery*, pick up Armitage with a fourth sledge team, and drop them off at a coastal point with access to the south magnetic pole. The relief ship would later take this group straight back to New Zealand. *Discovery* would collect the other three groups on their return, explore to the west, and then refit in New Zealand. Further exploration of the new eastern land they had discovered would then be possible in the summer of 1903. Even the critical Royds praised Scott's plan, and Armitage, who had originally agreed to join the expedition on the understanding that he would lead a major sledge journey, was content.

Some hours later, the watch officer spotted an inlet in the wall of the ice barrier, unseen owing to fog on their earlier eastward passage. This channel was two miles wide and ran on for twelve miles, deep into the barrier. Although the containing ice walls were up to 140 feet high, they tapered at the head of this inlet to a mere 12 feet, which allowed the ship to moor and the men to land.

Scott had onboard a hydrogen balloon, with a basket big enough for a single passenger, which he hoped to use to gain a panoramic view of the ice barrier's inner reaches. If the wind changed to the north, floating bergs might easily advance down the inlet, trap *Discovery*, and crush her against the cliffs in minutes, so Scott did not intend to stay long. While Skelton and Shackleton set up the fragile skin, winching gear, and gas cylinders on the ice, Wilson expressed his disapproval: "an exceedingly dangerous amusement," he grumbled, "in the hands of such inexperienced novices."

The first to try *Eva*, as they called the balloon, was Scott, who threw out the wrong amount of ballast and was lucky to survive. At six hundred feet he saw very little through his binoculars, owing to poor visibility and, of course, as was later learned, there was very little to see in the whole featureless vastness, almost the size of France, of the ice barrier. This was unknown territory. Was the feature one giant floating berg or floe? Was it attached to land and, if so, at what point? The *Discovery* balloon did not answer any of these questions, even after Shackleton ascended to eight hundred feet and took aerial photographs with his camera. The wind speed increased, the balloon fabric was torn, and the main hydrogen valve was found to be lethally unreliable. *Eva* was a death trap and further flights were abandoned. This was the first flight by men in the Antarctic.

Scott had enforced a twenty-four-hour limit on the balloon halt not only for fear of entrapment but also because, aware that the short Antarctic summer was ending, he needed to reach the hoped-for safety of McMurdo Sound before the sea froze and cut them off from its sanctuary. As soon as the balloon had been unloaded, two of the three members of the expedition with previous polar experience, Armitage and Bernacchi, had rushed off on skis with four sailors and a sledge to reconnoiter inland and take magnetic readings away from the ship. They had Scott's blessing, but only for twenty-four hours. They soon found that the barrier's coastal zone was riven by shallow valleys with deep cracks to be avoided.

With two hundred pounds on their sledge, Armitage's group traveled at three miles per hour for two or three hours and pitched camp. In the haste of their departure, they had forgotten one of their two tents, so Bernacchi spent the night outside at −17°C, a good test of his polar clothing. The following morning, four of them skied south for eleven miles, wanting to beat the southerly record the *Southern Cross* expedition had made after wintering in their hut at Cape Adare two years previously. Armitage claimed a new record but, as Scott recorded: "At this time we were very prone to exaggerate our walks." Armitage's little trip on February 4, 1902, almost certainly fell short of the *Southern Cross* record.

While the sledging group was away, Scott sent men to kill seals, for he could not be certain they would still be around when winter came and he was desperate to avoid scurvy, the dreaded scourge of any group spending long periods in polar regions. At the time, there were many theories as to how best to prevent scurvy but no proven solution. Fresh meat, fruit, and vegetables were believed to help, as were hygiene and sunlight. Some, including Scott and the senior surgeon, Dr. Koettlitz, also thought that canned food was often spoiled and a cause of the disease. Wilson, as junior surgeon, had the dubious pleasure and task of tasting the cans of food and milk when they were opened, to check for spoilage.

Scott loathed the killing of any animals but closed his mind to this perceived weakness and had his men kill for meat whenever he could. In the inlet, which he named Balloon Bight, a hundred seals lay sunning on their icy beach, showing little interest in the arrival of these first human beings. Their black, limpid eyes expressed no fear and their shiny whiskered muzzles twitched merely with curiosity as Scott's nominated butchers approached them. Scott confessed to his diary his nausea and shame at plundering nature in this unspoiled place: "but necessities are often hideous and man must live."

With the sledgers back onboard, *Discovery* sailed west, to the place of the volcanoes and, edging past Mount Terror, nudged south into McMurdo Sound. Under a clear sky and a shower of ice from the frozen rigging, Armitage, the pilot, pushed the ship through loose pack, probing south until a line of hills ran down from the volcano to form a narrow westerly peninsula with bays on either side. Scott bade Armitage head into the most northerly of the two bays, which he christened Arrival Bay. With Skelton, he walked south for ten miles over fast sea ice and around another peninsula or cape until they could see the ice barrier rolling away, flat and seemingly easygoing, toward the South Pole. The geologist Hartley Ferrar climbed a prominent conical hill beyond the second bay and was able to report that the flanks of the two volcanoes were nowhere joined to the mountain ranges to the south. They were clearly on a volcanic island joined to the distant mountains only by the vast expanse of the ice barrier. They named the conical feature Observation Hill.

Further exploration on foot revealed that the bay immediately to the south of their anchorage was ideally suited as a winter harbor, being shallow enough to protect the ship from invading bergs, a constant threat in such a place. So they maneuvered with care through the rocky shoals and around to the next bay south of Arrival Bay. This, their new home, they called Hut Point. Over the next two weeks, the engineers and the carpenter erected on a gravel ridge above the ship the main thirty-ton hut, two smaller magnetic huts, and kennels for the dogs. Eight months of provisions were also stored ashore in case the ship was forced away from the bay when teams were inland, or in case of fire aboard. Scott was not certain how the ice would behave, nor was Bernacchi, the only man aboard who had wintered in Antarctica before, albeit 370 miles farther north.

In the mid 1980s, an expedition set out from Britain calling itself In the Footsteps of Scott and using a powerful North Sea trawler refitted for pack-ice conditions. They reached McMurdo Sound at the ideal time of the year, midsummer, when U.S. Coast Guard icebreakers were already in the vicinity. An unexpected shift in the pack ice crushed and sank their ship in a matter of hours. That 1985 crew was rescued by a U.S. helicopter but, back in 1902, *Discovery*'s whereabouts were unknown and a single false move or run of bad luck could have cut off her crew with consequences as fatal as those of the Franklin tragedy.

The only other human beings in Antarctica, or even south of the Antarctic Circle, were the Swedish and German expeditions, and they were in no position to rescue anyone. The German expedition of the scientist Professor Drygalski, whose preparations had so impressed Scott, had reached the Antarctic coast only to be dangerously encircled by pack ice. The Germans' 1901–1903 scientific and exploration programs were, therefore, out of reach, and their survival hung in the balance. The *Scotia* expedition (1902–1904), led by another of Britain's most experienced polar scientists, the Scottish oceanographer Dr. William Bruce, had failed to make a landing on the continent and wintered in the pack off the South Orkney Islands. The great Swedish explorer-scientist Otto Nordenskjöld's ship *Antarctic* was crushed in the pack ice off the northern tip of the Antarctic Peninsula on February 12, 1903. The explorer Dr. Jean Charcot, who led the 1903–1905 French national expedition, altered plans for an Arctic voyage that year and diverted south to help rescue the Swedes. He arrived to find that an Argentine gunboat had already found and saved Nordenskjöld. Charcot then set his sights on a southern survey voyage, which he duly completed, but his ship nearly sank and some of his crew almost died of scurvy.

Markham had chosen his leader well, and Scott in turn had put together a fine group of men. As the long polar night of 1902 closed in, Scott wrote:

"Eyes are turned towards the south; the land of promise." But he knew no human could travel far in the terrible cold of an Antarctic winter, so he and his forty-seven men would spend the next ten months crammed together in their ship, the only humans on a continent bigger by far than all of China and India.

DOGS, SKIS, AND MEN

ERNEST SHACKLETON, IN CHARGE of all stores, had to decide what to leave aboard and what to send ashore in case of an emergency. In the hold were three years of provisions for four dozen men, including six thousand pounds of soup, forty-two thousand pounds of meat, seven thousand pounds of fish, and thirty gallons of brandy. Shackleton was riled by the offhand manner of the man most involved in the ship's commissariat, the ship's cook, an Australian named Brett, and, Merchant Navy officer or not, Shackleton took him to Scott and reported his insolence. Brett was equally rude to Scott, who described Brett as "a wretched specimen of humanity," and told the warrant officers to lock him in irons, a standard navy punishment for disobedience. Brett fought his jailers and twice escaped the irons, but after recapture and eight hours of shivering in the fo'c'sle, warmed only by the galley stove below, he was released in a less rebellious state. History does not relate whether or not his cooking or his behavior subsequently improved, but it was a significant event, the only time in a ten-year span of expedition work that Scott ever applied any form of physical punishment to any of his men.

Being clapped in irons was uncomfortable and undignified but not painful. And it was not uncommon. Many sailors, when given the choice, preferred a few hours in irons to the alternative of losing grog, tobacco, or ship-leave allowance. If anything, Scott erred on the side of gentleness in his application of naval discipline. He preferred to use his personality and a good tongue-lashing to enforce discipline, whether with senior officers or ratings. Nor did he judge his men harshly if he could give them the benefit of the doubt.

Discovery's arrival at Hut Point on February 8, 1902, was an anxious time for Scott. Although he had found a reasonable spot from which to unload by holding the ship broadside against a twelve-foot-high ice face, there were constant dangers from floating flotillas of ice, smaller than bergs but able to invade the shallow bay and sink the ship should the wind change. To reach the rim of the ice barrier, the gateway to the south, at any point from their Hut Point cove, Scott's men would have to haul their sledges up steep inclines to the island's plateau above the ship and then over various rocky ridges before descending to the barrier. This overland route could be avoided only if the sea around the island from the ship to the barrier was to freeze solid and provide an easy shortcut for sledge groups. Scott was aware, however, that such sea ice might appear to be safe but, with a slight wind change, could break up in minutes and float out to sea. Any sledges out on such ice might then be lost forever.

The Great Ice Barrier (or the Ross Ice Shelf, as it is known today) was a hugely tempting feature to Scott and his men for it rolled away in a southerly direction and, except where snowdrifts lay deep, looked easy to walk or ski upon. But because the ship could not reach any point with direct access onto the barrier ice, Scott would have to put up with the difficulties of sledging over the foothills and coastal cliffs of the island with bare rock stretches that could ruin sledge runners, and deeply crevassed glaciers that tumbled sheer to the sea. Either that or risk crossing treacherous sea ice after it formed.

Scott's plans for local sledge trials involved immediate action because winter was already closing in on Hut Point. Scott had never worked with sledging equipment before, nor had any of his men save Armitage, Koettlitz, and Bernacchi. These three had scant expertise with sledge dogs and Armitage was openly scathing about their abilities when compared with ponies. Both Armitage and Bernacchi tried hard on the snow slopes around the hut to galvanize the expedition's twenty-three dogs into action. Armitage cracked a whip but could not persuade his charges even to trot, whereas Bernacchi, using only verbal instructions, found that his team shot away, immediately out of control, leaving him cursing back at the starting point.

Scott therefore sent off a small dogless team consisting of Shackleton, Wilson, and Ferrar to head south to a distant rock-topped island out on the barrier, from the summit of which, with luck, they would be able to see many miles farther to the south. In case they found open sea at any time blocking their way to, or back from, the barrier, Scott instructed them to lash a light row boat to their sledge. On February 18, 1902, this boat-sledge was towed eight hundred feet uphill via the snow slope above the ship, between two obvious features, Crater Hill and Observation Hill, then on through a low pass they called the Gap and down to the barrier ice below. A wind sprang up but the three men tramped on toward the distant island for nine hours until, exhausted, they stopped to camp. The extent of their ignorance in contending with low temperatures is illustrated in Wilson's diary: "The ski boots were frozen to the socks . . . and it took us all we knew the next morning to tear the socks out. The sweat of one's feet had lined the boots with ice . . . we began to get our furs on, an awful job in a small tent . . . They dressed me first, as I was constantly getting cramp in the thighs whenever I moved, and having dressed me they put me on the floor and sat on me while they dressed each other. We lay on our jaeger blouses, but the cold of the ice floor crept through."

The next day, they climbed the island (White Island) to its 2,300-foot summit and Wilson sketched the panoramic view. They had established a safe route onto the barrier and south between White Island and its neighbor (Black Island) to a prominent cape (to be called Minna Bluff), some forty miles due south; an ideal location for an initial provisions depot on the barrier.

Meanwhile, to use the fading daylight hours of summer, the men began to learn how to dog-sledge and ski. Only a dozen or so explorers, primarily Nansen, Peary, and Jackson, had used dogs to haul their sledges in the Arctic, and Armitage had been Jackson's second-in-command. So Scott could hardly be said to have no dog advisers. Armitage and Scott, using Nansen's dogs' performance as a model, reckoned they would need twenty-three animals for Antarctica, so this was the number selected for them in Siberia by the man who had supplied Nansen. Unbeknown to Scott, he had selected the *Discovery* dogs from three different canine strains, an error that would lead to even more aggression than is normal between sledge dogs. Another mistake was made when instead of keeping set teams together to cut down the fighting and develop team spirit, the various sledgers who tried their hands with the dogs, owing to their initial lack of experience, used different dogs on different occasions. Another common error was to help the dogs pull by harnessing men alongside them. This merely encouraged the dogs to take it easy and let the humans do the work. Armitage advised against it and Scott eventually agreed with him. During the early days at Hut Point, the *Discovery* dogs proved disappointing but not hopeless. Nonetheless, Scott continued to push his men to keep trying their best at dog driving.

When, in the 1970s, I made plans to cross Antarctica and the Arctic Ocean, I had to decide whether to use motorized sledges or dogs or to manhaul. I asked the European with the then-greatest experience in dog driving, Wally Herbert, the modern equivalent of Nansen, and his response was concise: "Do not even attempt to use dogs unless you and your men train with them for at least two years fulltime before your expedition begins."

Gradually, Scott's twenty or so dogs were welded into workable teams and some of the men became reasonable drivers. Scott's attempts at learning the rudiments of man-hauling progressed equally slowly and with as many errors made through ignorance.

Scott's polar model was Fridtjof Nansen, who in Norway had helped him to put together the best equipment money could buy and had stressed the benefits of using dogs and skis. Scott knew of Nansen's great pioneering journeys in the Arctic, but could not be certain that either dogs or skis would suit the unknown conditions of Antarctica. Nansen's first journey, which had made him famous, was the crossing of the Greenland ice cap and was achieved entirely without dogs. His second, much longer Arctic Ocean traverse, including an attempt on the North Pole, did use dogs, but in conditions unlikely to occur in Antarctica.

Nansen was straightforward about dog usage. "It was undeniable cruelty to the animals from first to last . . . it makes me shudder even now when I think of how we beat them mercilessly with thick ash sticks when, hardly able to move, they stopped from sheer exhaustion . . . I have moments of bitter self-reproach."

Nansen believed that "a combination of horses and dogs might prove advantageous on the Ross Barrier." Today, Britain's most experienced dog driver, who has driven dog teams for thousands of miles, including a 220-day, 3,760-mile Antarctic crossing, is Geoff Somers. His random thoughts on Scott include: "In recent times monumental traverses have been accomplished by teams pulling their own supplies (with no dogs) . . . there have been failed dog sled trips and manhaul treks . . . In Scott's day the greatest dog journeys had only been carried out in the northern hemisphere where dogs were run in their home environment, food was plentiful and the useful sledging seasons longer."

Scott's attitude toward the use of skis or any form of snowshoe was to take them and try them, use them where they work and not where they don't. Before *Discovery* left London, Scott, who had never seen skis in use and whose experience of snow extended to throwing snowballs at his sisters in Devon, had to decide what to do about skis. In 1901, skis were heavy and bulky, weighing an average of twenty pounds per pair and being seven feet in length. Even ten years after the *Discovery* expedition, the British public knew so little about skis that Herbert Ponting, in his popular book about Scott, had to explain what they were. Nansen had told Scott that skis were far superior to any other method of transportation when traveling on snow. Scott had no need to read Nansen's books to appreciate such advice. But, as Scott was to learn, Nansen was as fallible in his opinions as any other polar traveler of his day. Sensibly, Scott did not rely only on Nansen, but listened to others with ski experience.

Another great Norwegian Arctic explorer, Otto Sverdrup, had written: "Polar exploration without ski is extremely awkward." The Norwegian Borchgrevink had used skis in Antarctica for a few miles only and then merely close to the coastline, not really proving their usefulness one way or the other. There were a few individual Britons with considerable ski experience. The chief of these was David Crichton-Somerville, an Englishman who had lived in Norway and skied for over twenty-five years. He had written of the usefulness of skis for light work on soft snow but said that he would not use them if he was hauling anything or the snow was firm. On the other hand, contemporary British ski pundit Martin Conway wrote after a few weeks' skiing on Spitsbergen that he could drag heavy weights over any kind of snow wearing skis.

Scott soon picked up the advantages of ski use. You could move more safely over crevassed areas if you spread your weight on skis, and a man on skis would not sink as deeply in soft snow, so would save energy. Scott appreciated these advantages, but was equally aware he would critically have to add one hundred pounds to the weight of a sledge-load, for the skis of the five man-haulers, wherever the route climbed uphill and skiing was impossible. Skis were easily broken and sledges often overturned. Spare skis were too heavy to take. Such mathematics made it extremely tempting not to take skis at all and that is precisely what Shackleton decided, four years after the *Discovery* expedition, when his turn came to lead a major South Pole attempt.

As with dogs, Scott sensibly decided to assess the usefulness of skis with realistic sledge loads by trial and error. Would a course of Scandinavian instruction beforehand have helped? Even if he had found the time to fit one in, it is unlikely. In Norway and Bavaria in the 1960s, I spent long months learning the technique of *langlauf,* or cross-country skiing, from Norwegian and German instructors. I spent four winter seasons on the Austrian border instructing Scottish soldiers in the sport and competing in army *langlauf* races. I then led expeditions towing heavy sledges over Norwegian glaciers and soon discovered the difference between *langlauf* skiing with and without heavy loads to drag. With loads, the entire business of technique and skill becomes superfluous. The huge advantage of the Scandinavians virtually disappears when the art of gliding and energy conservation is rendered useless by the need to shift a heavy sledge. Anybody, with a few hours' practice, can learn the simple plodding movement needed for heavy man-haul on or off skis.

A few months later, after considerable experience of local man-haul, Scott wrote: "We have been trying once or twice lately to go on ski as the snow is very soft and we sink deeply, but we find that we cannot put the same weight on the traces as we do on foot. On the whole our ski so far have been of little value. They have saved us labour on the rare occasions on which we have not had to pull . . . but the labour thus saved is a doubtful compensation for the extra weight which they add to the load." He added a very valid but often ignored point: "Another thing to be remembered is that one gets used to plodding, even in heavy snow, and, though it is very tiring at first, one's capacity for performance on foot ought not to be judged until one is thoroughly accustomed to the work."

The factor that Scott would learn only after long journeys out on the ice barrier, in changing wind or cloud conditions and varying temperatures, was the incredible difference that these very changes cause to the experience of man-hauling. Within a few meters, differing snow surfaces can change easy haulage into nightmare work. A rise or fall in temperature can have the same effect. One minute a man-hauler will praise his skis, the next curse them, load them onto the sledge and carry on without them. When Nansen advised Scott to take skis, neither he nor the ski makers advised Scott or Armitage to take ski skins and ski wax to help the skis grip the snow when heading uphill. Scott and his men were thrown in at the deep end and their first real test run was to be the apparently simple hundred-mile flat run from Hut Point, around the south of Ross Island, to Cape Crozier, where, the previous month, and from the seaward side, they had established a message point.

Now that they had found their winter quarters, they would have to re-visit Cape Crozier to leave details of their location for the relief ship. It would be their first man-haul journey. Scott himself was hors de combat with a wrenched knee from his skiing efforts, so it was Charles Royds who led the four sledges hauled by twelve men and, at the last minute, eight dogs. Those who favored their use took skis, much to the annoyance of those who felt they were white elephants and merely an additional weight on already heavy sledges.

Royds led with four dogs and five men, sailors Wild, Vince, Weller, and the American Quartley, together with the experienced Dr. Koettlitz. They hauled two sledges, as did the second group, also with four dogs, of Barne, Skelton, Plumley, Heald, the young New Zealander Hare, and the big Welshman Edgar Evans.

Scott waved off this cavalcade on March 4, 1902, and later noted: "I am bound to confess that the sledges when packed presented an appearance of which we should afterwards have been wholly ashamed, and much the same might be said of the clothing worn by the sledgers. But at this time our ignorance was deplorable; we did not know how much or what proportions would be required as regards the food, how to use our cookers, how to put up our tents, or even how to put on our clothes. Not a single article of the outfit had been tested, and amid the general ignorance that prevailed the lack of system was painfully apparent in everything."

Why was this? Was there no precedent for Scott to have learned from? Mostly, the answer is no. This was the first-ever attempt to penetrate Antarctica. There were no existing accounts of travel there. Borchgrevinck's local wanderings around his Cape Adare hut cast no light at all on sound choice or the usage of relevant gear. This Royds-led outing provided Scott and his men with their first lessons in what to do and what not to do. As H. R. Mill recorded, Scott had assiduously read polar literature at the Royal Geographical Society, but none of it referred to Antarctica, only to the Arctic, and as I was to learn in the 1980s, the application of techniques that work well in the Arctic can prove disastrous in Antarctica. What Scott and his men learned the hard way in 1902 provided the knowledge base that Shackleton, Amundsen, and Scott himself, ten years later, used to successfully penetrate Antarctica's secret interior.

Each day out on the trail taught each of these amateurs little lessons on how to make things easier for himself, how to adjust clothing, and how to sleep with socks or mittens close to the body to avoid overnight freezing. This journey, in itself hardly overambitious, was a sound early apprenticeship for a quarter of Scott's men.

In the months ahead, temperatures around the island would drop to −56.5°C but now, early in March, 0°C with little or no wind served as a good level of schooling for the men, enough to teach such novices lessons but not so severe as to cripple them. They suffered painful cramps in their tents, a normal post-man-hauling complaint; one of the cookers broke, probably for lack of a protective box; there were lightly frost-nipped ears and feet; and a lack of sleep due to too-small, three-man sleeping bags and the fearsome intermittent roar of avalanches cascading down the ten-thousand-foot slopes of nearby Mount Erebus.

After four days' travel through deep, soft snow, they had advanced only twenty miles and Royds calculated that their twenty-one days of rations would not last. Sensibly, therefore, he divided the group into two, sending everyone and everything (except Skelton, Koettlitz, himself, and one sledge) back under Michael Barne. Royds suggested that Barne take his group back to the ship by the known outward route, rather than by any easier-looking shortcut he might spot.

Two days later, on March 11, 1902, Barne's group of nine men and eight dogs found themselves camped back on the Great Ice Barrier beneath Castle Rock, an easily recognized feature astride the island's ridgeline and some four miles north of the bay at Hut Point. Barne spotted an easy snow slope leading up to the ridge. The visibility was good and he knew he had only to follow the ridge south until he recognized Crater Hill, at the top of the Hut Point ski slope and leading down eight hundred feet to the ship. This would be an easy enough task in good visibility but, unfortunately, no sooner had Barne's men reached the ridgeline than the fine weather broke with a vengeance and a bitter wind whipped the drift snow into a whiteout.

At this point, Michael Barne made a basic error. Instead of settling down with his eight companions in their two tents and waiting for clear visibility, he decided to risk a quick dash of less than four miles along the ridge top and down the ski slope to safety. He would leave the heavy gear, including the sledge and the tents, on the ridge to collect later under better conditions. Within an hour, he expected they would all be safe aboard *Discovery*. With a little bit of luck, Barne's plan would have worked. They all left their sledge dump wearing ski boots, except for young Clarence Hare and the chirpy Dorset man George Vince, whose boots had frozen so hard the previous night they had to march in their sleeping boots, soft *finnesko* of thick, warm felt. The nine men and their dogs were now stumbling along through the gloom immediately above, but unaware of, sheer ice cliffs that fell away to the sea far below. None wore crampons and, as the slope became steeper, they began to lose their footing, especially Hare and Vince in their smooth-soled *finnesko*.

Without warning, Hare disappeared down the slope and Barne told the others to spread out as they groped their way forward so that when Hare caught up, he would more easily bump into someone. Evans then slid away out of sight, followed by Barne and the American, Quartley. A ledge of soft snow halted their downward plunge and a clear patch in the mist revealed to their horror the cliff top just a few feet below them. Frank Wild had knocked nails through his ski-boot soles and so had slightly more leverage than the others. He rallied the remaining sailors, who were rapidly growing dangerously cold, and led them on in the assumed direction of Hut Point. The slope steepened abruptly and all five men, slipping on the ice, hurtled downward. Wild and three others managed, just, to kick their boots into a patch of snow along the very rim of the precipice, but George Vince's *finnesko* gained no grip and he continued to slide until his flailing body disappeared into the void.

Terrified, and using their sheath knives to gain tenuous holds, the four survivors inched their way back up to the crest of the ridge and at length found the rocky plateau that led to Crater Hill and the ski slope above the ship. George Vince's body was never found and the cross Scott had erected in his memory still stands on the summit at Hut Point. Hare miraculously survived. He had careered down the slope, ending up unconscious in soft snow that covered his body and, forty-eight hours later, he returned to the ship as merry as ever and entirely without frostbite. Scott, overjoyed, cried out: "Thank God one of my boys has returned."

The bad weather that caused this tragedy also nearly killed Charles Royds, Koettlitz, and Skelton, for they were at the time attempting to descend the Cape Crozier cliffs to the message point and, in the whiteout, almost failed to make it back to their camp. As it was, they were low on food and, after two more futile attempts to locate their goal using crampons and a rope, Royds sensibly decided they should head back to the ship, overruling the others' zeal to keep trying. On their return journey, the temperature dropped to −41°C of frost, but they made it back in only four days. All the dogs, but for one, which had slid over the cliff with Vince, were recovered and a great many lessons were learned.

Scott took reports from Royds and the others about the equipment very seriously and quickly ordered modifications for the future. The fact that Hare had survived without tent or sleeping bag for forty-eight hours in his sledge clothes and *finnesko* was hopeful, whereas Skelton's report on the three-man fur sleeping bag his group had used was not. When they first used this bag, it weighed forty-five pounds, but only twenty days later, owing to the accumulated weight of frozen perspiration, it weighed seventy-six pounds.

With Vince's death and the reality all forty-six men now faced of wintering in this stark, unforgiving place, the atmosphere aboard *Discovery* may well have been as gloomy as her bleak surroundings when the sun disappeared altogether for the next five months.

THE FIRST WINTER

ON THE SUNDAY EVENING after the death of George Vince, a service was held onboard in his memory and the sound of the hymns sung by the forty-six men of *Discovery* rose and fell against the flanks of Mount Erebus and above the frozen sea. Scott reminded the ship's company that winter was coming and nobody had ever wintered this far south before, so there could be no knowing what conditions to expect. But one thing was certain—Hut Point was not a place for personal errors: Even a mere one hundred yards away from the ship or the hut a man could be quickly cut off by a blizzard, with no visibility to see his way back to safety and warmth. Never, Scott warned, count on good weather lasting. Koettlitz lectured on the hazards of frostbite and Scott announced one last journey before winter conditions prevented further travel. This was to position further depots to the south, give more men sledging experience, and allow another trial with the dogs.

His knee recovered, Scott set out on April 1, 1902, together with Albert Armitage, Edward Wilson, Reginald Koettlitz, eight sailors, and eighteen dogs. The temperature hovered around −40°C. The dogs managed twenty-three miles on the first day, but, at −44°C and with a stiff headwind, only

notched up a poor ten miles on day two. The extreme cold had made the
snow surface abrasive and the dogs' paws bled. The simplest camping chore
took forever with frozen fingers. Eyelashes froze together. Experiments in
dragging sledges separately were dropped in favor of all the men and all the
dogs hauling all the sledges hitched together in a single train. Most of the
time, the men hauled without their single ski sticks, which certainly helped
avoid the frostbitten fingers that can result from using a stick with both
hands held high; but a disadvantage was that hauling power was diminished.

After three days and nights of purgatory, Scott realized that this first experiment at winter sledging in Antarctica was liable to end in injury, or
worse, to men and dogs. Some twelve miles from the ship, four sledgeloads
with two thousand pounds of provisions were left on the ice barrier as a depot for later journeys and Scott turned back. With light sledges and the
knowledge that they were heading home, the dogs covered the distance back
in only six hours. For their very first lesson at sledging, the eight inexperienced sailors must have suffered a great deal. Even for Antarctic veterans in
modern times, man-hauling in April is a nightmare.

In his diary, Scott wrote of this and subsequent prewinter journeys:
"everything was wrong." Only years later, when writing a book about the
Discovery experiences, did Scott appreciate the very real value of those early
trials. "That we were eventually able to make long and successful sledge
journeys is no doubt due to the mistakes which we made and the experience
gained at that time and the fact that we took our lesson to heart."

Before further thought could be given to sledging, Scott needed to concentrate on the immediate and critical task of organizing life onboard *Discovery* to cope with four dozen humans crammed together in conditions
that by any normal standards would be judged as appalling. The only prece-
dents Scott had were the wintering of de Gerlache's *Belgica,* captive in the
floating pack, and the *Southern Cross* crew of ten in their Cape Adare hut
370 miles farther north of Hut Point. Those experiences had involved quag-
mires of social dissension, an outbreak of insanity, violent hatred, and
scurvy, and Scott resolved to avoid a repeat performance on *Discovery,* despite having four times as many men as were in *Southern Cross* and, therefore, a bigger potential for trouble.

The navy, Scott knew, had a simple formula to avoid trouble: Lay down a basic set of rules for everyone onboard and stick to them. Few folks will admit to enjoying the imposition of discipline in civilian life, and Scott, realizing this, sensibly watered down traditional Royal Navy regulations to a minimum to cope with his mixed-bag crew.

The basis of Scott's discipline system was the standard forces' three-way hierarchy split between officers, noncommissioned officers (petty officers in naval parlance), and ratings. Each group shared separate living quarters and mess tables. Non-naval people, such as the scientists, were classed as officers. The eleven "officers" ate and lived in a communal wardroom, wood-paneled and ten yards long with a table down the center and an often-defective piano at one end. On those occasions when the fingers of its only competent player, Charles Royds, were not frostbitten, after-dinner music was popular. Each officer had his own tiny cabin, of which Scott's was the largest, but coldest, onboard. A good deal of chess was played, each move loudly argued. Hodgson observed that the skipper hated losing, which was true of everything he did, from football to man-hauling. He was highly competitive and would have been a poor choice for leader had he been otherwise. The warmest room, positioned over the main hold, which provided excellent insulation, was the mess deck where the ratings slung their hammocks when they wished to sleep.

The sun, Scott knew, would disappear completely for four months starting in late April and he feared the tales of polar anemia that had followed the *Belgica* experience. Medical science had not in 1901 defined seasonal affective disorder as an existing medical condition, but many doctors did believe that lack of light for long periods could cause depression, aggression, and even insanity. Scott therefore provisioned *Discovery* with great numbers of candles, 1,500 gallons of kerosene for lanterns, and a newfangled windmill to generate an electric lighting circuit to illuminate the ship. Nansen's *Fram* had used a similar apparatus with some success in the Arctic, and Drygalski had a German version in *Gauss*. Chief Engineer Reginald Skelton, a good-natured grumbler who put together many Scott-designed gadgets, nonetheless complained loud and long about Scott's windmill, which needed constant attention by his hard-worked engineers.

On April 23, 1902, the sun dipped below the eastern horizon for the last time, to disappear for 123 days, and, as was expected, crew morale dropped.

When a storm eventually wrecked Scott's windmill on May 2, much to Skelton's delight, even he could not deny that the month of light it had generated had been greatly appreciated by all onboard.

Wilson noted: "Men don't improve when they live together alone." Scott could not read helpful psychological literature on how best to cope in such circumstances, for none was available. The navy answer to keeping the skipper's finger on the communal pulse was through careful maintenance of contact between the junior officers, petty officers, and ratings. Albert Armitage, the senior officer beneath Scott, was under a special contract as ice pilot, so the first officer, Charles Royds, was Scott's conduit to the crew and Royds handled the men with both tact and firmness. He held a fine line of discipline but spent many hours on the mess deck chatting to the men, as did Michael Barne and Ernest Shackleton. They knew from experience that there would be tensions and they hoped, through contact, to defuse them where possible.

Scott has been ridiculed by late-twentieth-century biographers for running his semicivilian expeditions the naval way. Louis Bernacchi, who lived under Scott's *Discovery* regime for two winters and had also experienced the dismal winter with the *Southern Cross* non-naval crew at Cape Adare, was in a good position to be able to compare the two command methods. He was a critical scientist and an Australian with no Royal Navy attachments, but his opinion was straightforward: He stated that Scott's formalities at dinner "helped to preserve an atmosphere of civilized tolerance such as has seldom been found in polar expeditions." In the minutiae of everyday life, Bernacchi added that naval tradition was "of infinite benefit."

Ninety-nine percent of the time, the only "discipline" that Scott relied upon was his quick-tempered reputation and his ability to give a fierce verbal dressing-down, very often in public, whether the target of his wrath was First Lieutenant Charles Royds or the ship's boilerman.

The hut was less than two hundred yards from the ship and a guide-rope covered much of the intervening distance, yet in blizzards there was still a danger of disorientation; one night Bernacchi and Skelton left the hut and failed to find the guide rope, which had been blown down. For an hour and a half, they lost their bearings and their shouts were inaudible mere yards away. A group returning from the hut, by chance and good luck, found both men, but by then they were badly frostbitten on their faces and legs. All this happened on the short, flat, familiar path between hut and ship's gangway.

Wilson wrote: "You can see nothing but white drift and the roar of the wind is utterly bewildering. You cannot consult with anyone because you can't hear him, even if he shouts in your ear. I know nothing so terrifying as these blizzards."

Scott took *Discovery*'s science program as seriously as the safety of his men, even inventing gadgets to help additional research work, such as tide measurement. Wilson recorded: "The Skipper is endlessly planning new theories and new methods of observation. He's an excellent man for this job, full of theories and ingenuity; always thinking."

The scientist most at risk from blizzards was Louis Bernacchi, whose two magnetic huts were a hundred yards farther inland than the main hut and well away from any steel materials. The extremely delicate instruments he monitored daily and for hours on end included one that could measure electricity in the atmosphere, especially useful during aurora displays, and a prototype seismograph. Some of Bernacchi's experiments were timed to the second to coincide with parallel work programmed for the German and Swedish expeditions, the first example of international scientific coordination on the Antarctic continent.

Although research jobs kept the scientists, the officers, and their selected helpers busy through the long winter, as did routine maintenance by the engineers, there were still long slack periods for many, and Scott, well aware that inactivity could lead to discontent, asked Shackleton to edit a magazine, *The South Polar Times,* to which anyone could contribute articles, drawings, cartoons, comments, and quizzes. This proved to be a big success.

For those letting off more private steam, diaries were wastebaskets for hurt feelings, minor dislikes, and petty jealousies. On all expeditions, diaries have traditionally targeted for criticism the person responsible, the leader. On the *Discovery* expedition, every action Scott took, every mood he exhibited, every meaningful comment he made, was recorded in one or a dozen diaries. All that went wrong or was thought to be wrong was his fault. Any item missing or faulty was due to his inefficiency. Discomfort, bad weather, poor morale . . . all, in the diaries, could be blamed on Scott. Some writers tempered and balanced their criticisms. Others just let off steam.

Scott maintained just enough of a framework of traditional naval activities to avoid anyone becoming lazy or dirty owing to the unaccustomed pressures of the polar winter. On Sundays, each man had to change his clothes from his weekly wear and join the others to parade in two ranks. Scott had ordered a custom-made canvas awning to cover much of the deck, where the Sunday services and a weekly inspection were held. This provided excellent protection against the wind and blown snow. Scott, Royds, and Skelton inspected first the mess deck and then the men by the light of a lamp held high by Boatswain Thomas Feather. Such regular inspections served two main purposes: to remind everyone of the basic framework of naval discipline, and to check for any signs of ill health.

The ship's bell was then tolled and a church service held, still on deck, at which attendance was not compulsory. Royds played the piano when it worked and everyone sang rousing hymns like "Eternal Father Strong to Save." Frank Plumley wrote of the weekly church parades, "We are not angels but I think the greater part of us enjoys it." Once, in August, Scott's inspection of the mess deck lasted over an hour while the men waited up on deck. This naturally had the men, or at least the voluble Scots carpenter James Duncan, complaining: "we are treated like children." But it appears to have been a one-time lapse on Scott's part, for there were no other such complaints. Frank Wild, a merchant seaman, found the Sunday parades "somewhat unnecessary in the circumstances," but another shrugged and said, "Oh well, it pleases him and doesn't hurt us."

The long darkness passed slowly by, marked sixty days after the sun's disappearance by a special Midwinter Day celebration on June 22, 1902. Gifts and cards were doled out to every man, after a Christmas lunch of turkey and distinctly alcoholic plum pudding. Hodgson noted that: "the Captain was quite as much excited as was necessary for his dignity." Duncan, who had long grumbled that more entertainment should be planned, built a stage in the main hut for Charles Royds's first play, *Ticket of Leave,* with Frank Wild as the male lead and two sailors as leading ladies. This was so popular that Royds soon began to rehearse a follow-up show.

Immediately after the morale boost of the Christmas festivity transplanted to Midwinter Day came the white nadir of the darkest moonless week and successive blizzards. Clarence Hare, the youngest man on the ship, wrote that there were more fights and quarrels than usual and unnecessary behavior by certain of the crew, but he added: "These little troubles are expected. No expedition has been without them."

Early in June, Scott told everyone they should start full-time preparations for sledging as soon as the hours of twilight began to increase. He did not elaborate on the detail of each planned sledge journey or which men would go where and the resulting uncertainty tended to keep everyone on their toes. Some individuals had already won their spurs the previous autumn and privately favored their chances of selection for one of the sledge teams. Frank Wild, for instance, had probably saved lives by his steadfast action at the time of Vince's death. Wild would, fifteen years later, become Shackleton's right-hand man, and Shackleton himself was to serve his own polar apprenticeship through selection by Scott as a sledger.

Scott realized that three men stood out for their strength, equanimity, and ability to undertake equipment modification, repairs, or even to design new gear suggested by the failure of existing items. They were Edgar Evans, William Lashly, and Tom Crean. Late in June, Wilson suspected that Crean was exhibiting the early scurvy symptoms of swellings on his lower legs. Luckily, a month later, the Irishman's swellings disappeared and scurvy was ruled out. Two months later, careful inspections by both doctors indicated that no cases of scurvy (and, therefore, no vitamin C deficiency) existed onboard, so the increased seal-meat diet had at least prevented the *Discovery* men from suffering the fate of many of their predecessors aboard *Belgica*.

Thanks to the detailed critiques of Royds and the others who had suffered from the defects of the sledging gear on the autumnal trial journeys, Scott knew exactly what modifications were needed and, with two clear months of ever-improving light conditions prior to the first planned sledge outing, Crean and company began their work. Dog harnesses were designed and produced, tents were strengthened, roomier three-man fur sleeping bags were made, sledges were assembled, and their runners were sheathed with German silver (thin nickel-plated steel), food bags were sewn, and wooden sledge boxes were fashioned to avoid the breakage of biscuits and other rations. At one point, more than twenty of the crew were active at this sledge-gear work, especially the sewing of wolf and reindeer skins, using their sail-repair needle skills to full advantage.

All work that could be foreseen was finished in good time for the first spring trial, but Scott, like his Norwegian rival Amundsen after him, was too eager to start his trial journeys as early as possible, not appreciating how vicious the spring weather could be. His first outing and the suffering involved by both men and dogs came as quite a shock.

Some critics (including Scott in his own diary) suggest that he should have started his trials even earlier, perhaps using the winter moonlight, instead of playing football. Bernacchi had been the only person allowed to leave the ship during extreme conditions, since his work in the magnetic huts was critical to the science program, often reaching his hut only by crawling all the way and never letting go of the safety line from the ship. He became blasé and wrote that some sledging rehearsals could have started earlier. But such a course could easily have led to severe frostbite and dead dogs. Starting trials at the end of August, as Scott did, was probably the most sensible timing.

The very first outings merely tested different dog-harnessing systems, including, on September 2, a foray by six men, under Scott, along the Ross Island coast. The overall impression Scott had gained from the first fumbling trials back at the time of Vince's death was that progress over the Great Ice Barrier, when towing heavy weights, was extremely difficult, especially in bad weather, but that dogs made things slightly less difficult than no dogs. Since, contrary to the ever-present myth, he had no built-in preference for man-hauling over any other form of traction, he decided to concentrate first and foremost on dog trials in the hope that the canine way really did prove to be the best way. The main journey for the coming summer, planned to start in mid-October, was intended to go due south as far as terrain and supplies would allow.

The myth that Scott was set in his ways over man-haul, or anything else, was way off mark. He constantly looked for new answers to his problems and sometimes, if none was available, he invented solutions of his own. Navigating in whiteout conditions can be a soul-destroying, confusing business with zero perspective and no aiming mark. Scott tied a shred of wool to a light bamboo pole and steered by the direction of the wind.

Especially in the region of the south magnetic pole, a standard compass was useless or, at best, extremely slow, so Scott prepared a device for steering by the sun, a small wooden dial with a shadow pin. He marked two outer rings, one with the compass points and the other in half-hour stages. Anyone with a reasonable understanding of navigation could use this with ease on the move. He improvised a slightly more complex method of determining the daily change in the sun's declination to allow him to locate latitude when out of sight of land.

He invented a tough and practical trawl net for *Discovery* after all the official nets were broken, as well as an ingenious tide-measurement gauge. To protect the face from frostbite when traveling into the wind, Scott designed a jacket hood with a face funnel into the front rim of which he threaded a hoop of copper wire, soft enough to bend into any shape and stiff enough to retain that shape. This "face-funnel wire" is still used by scientists in Antarctica today. Apsley Cherry-Garrard later recorded that Scott designed tapered sledge runners, wider at the front than the back, which worked well with much less friction involved. Scott also laid the first-ever Antarctic land-line telephone link for communication, between Cape Evans and Hut Point.

Scott was always inclined to observe his men and keep private notes, either highly critical or full of praise, on their ongoing performance. He was quick to forgive and forget, unlike most expedition leaders, including Amundsen and later Shackleton. So a man who was in his disfavor one month might easily redeem himself the next. A record of poor health meant little to Scott if the sick person subsequently completed some admirable sledging feat. This may well have stemmed from Scott's own past as a delicate child. He had taken to Wilson from their first meeting in London and had overruled those who advised him not to take someone on the expedition who had only recently recovered from tuberculosis. Michael Barne had once been Scott's first choice for the southern journey, but after he damaged his fingers on the first spring attempt to lay the Bluff Depot, he had to be relegated to less ambitious projects. Over the long winter, Scott came to trust and admire Wilson to the point where his tubercular history was ignored and he became first choice for the southern journey.

As a disciple of Nansen, whose famed north-polar wanderings had been achieved with only one companion, Scott favored an equally small team. Wilson favored a third person, on the grounds that, with only two, a single injury would be a disaster. Seeing the sense in this, Scott chose Ernest Shackleton, whom he had grown to trust and clearly saw as extremely capable. He also appreciated that the Irishman was powerfully built, ideal for man-hauling, and a good friend of Wilson.

If, as biographers with no personal experience of polar travel have sub-sequently suggested, Shackleton had shown Scott signs of rivalry, actual or psychological, Scott would not have selected him for a major role on the southern journey. Scott favored the competent at all times: He had chosen Shackleton for sledging trials from the very first Antarctic outing and had appointed him editor of the *South Polar Times,* not a position to hand to a potential rival in a small community.

When selecting team members for my own polar expeditions, I choose confident, highly capable individuals who are not yes men but will not threaten my status as leader. Shackleton was to become a rival to Scott in the years that followed the *Discovery* expedition, but that was all very much in the future. Two strong people chasing the same goal will always be rivals and gossip will often invent personal ill will between them. Scott and Shack-leton were no exception, and unsubstantiated rumors of a bitter feud be-tween them rumbled on for years, stoked every so often by successive biographies of both men.

Shackleton was overjoyed when Scott asked him to become the third man for the great trek south. If he or others had believed that Scott would se-lect only Royal Navy men for the plum jobs, they were surely surprised when the final choices were Wilson, a civilian, and Shackleton, from the Merchant Navy.

Scott's plan was straightforward. The three men would set out in mid-October with all twenty-two dogs. Shackleton would, during the preceding weeks, train and learn to handle the teams; a tall order perhaps, but he had Armitage on hand for advice. To conserve the dogs' energy at the outset, Michael Barne would lead a man-haul depot-laying group to leave provi-sions at Bluff Depot and at 79°30'S. To reach the Pole (90°) would entail a round trip of 1,480 miles and this was just attainable, assuming that flat bar-rier ice stretched unhindered all the way there. Such conditions would make an average of sixteen miles per day for a hundred travel days feasible, a rate achieved by Nansen on his Greenland crossing. Scott himself at no point mentioned the possibility of getting all the way to the Pole on this first major journey into the interior although Wilson was more hopeful: "We will go as far south in a straight line on the Barrier as we can, reach the Pole if possible, or find some new land."

When the sun returned to Hut Point early in September, hunting parties were sent out to kill seals to restock *Discovery* with fresh meat. At the same time, experiments took place on the sea ice with four sledges and sixteen dogs. The results confirmed that, rather than attach four dogs to each sledge, the best method was for all the dogs to haul all the sledges hitched together. This avoided factional fighting.

After a thirty-seven-mile journey, which traced the edge of the firm sea ice to the north of Hut Point, Scott's group returned, pleased with Shackleton's dogs and with the bicycle-wheel meters Skelton had cobbled together to record distances traveled. At the same time, various other local outings by small groups suffered due to simple carelessness—a sleeping bag being allowed to blow away, or a tent not securely anchored. Scott blamed himself for not having practiced the basic skills of camping during the long, dark winter months in the immediate vicinity of the ship, but it is easy to be wise after the event and, in my experience of Antarctic winters, dress rehearsals carried out close by a base camp are no substitute for the real thing and can serve merely to give false confidence.

On September 11, Armitage set out with five men to find a route to the magnetic pole. Locating the position of the magnetic pole was crucial to the updating of magnetic maps of the Southern Hemisphere and thus to marine navigation. And if they could beat Drygalski to it, so much the better. As the most experienced polar traveler aboard *Discovery*, Armitage's adverse opinion on the use of skis for man-hauling was well known, so eyebrows were raised when his men, on skis, were each seen to wield a ski stick in unison as they pulled away from Hut Point. Scott recorded: "I am inclined to reserve my opinion of the innovation."

Armitage led his men by a zigzag coastal route to the inlet named New Harbour, where he discovered the beginning of an inland route at the mouth of a great glacier that looked hopeful, and which he named after Ferrar. A blizzard then pinned him down and attempts to reconnoiter on foot soon proved dangerous in poor visibility and high winds. Worst of all, two of his men, Ferrar and Heald, became weak with symptoms that Armitage recognized as scurvy. He knew he must turn back at once lest he and the others also succumb. Back aboard *Discovery,* Wilson confirmed that all of Armitage's group were showing symptoms of the much-feared affliction.

Royds was astounded, "when one thinks of the fresh meat which has been constantly provided throughout the winter." He, Wilson, and Armitage decided in Scott's absence on another provisioning trip to increase the seal-meat diet at once. They also double-checked the daily availability of lime juice, jams, bottled fruits, potatoes, and other vegetables. Hunting sorties were increased and Armitage, aware that some men often avoided rancid-tasting seal meat, which was due to the cook's slackness and failure to remove all the blubber, confronted Henry Brett, the cook, and stressed that his future pay level would depend entirely on how well the food was thenceforward prepared and presented.

Scott, Shackleton, and the boatswain Thomas Feather returned to the ship on October 4 with sixteen dogs after an encouraging journey. They had left provisions sufficient for six weeks for three men and eighteen dogs at the Bluff Depot and, despite Feather's near death in a crevasse, they made the return journey of sixty-seven miles in only three days. Scott was pleased with the dogs and had no complaints about Shackleton, with whom he had chosen to do more sledging than anyone else. On their arrival at the ship, Wilson wrote: "None of them were any the worse, apparently, except Shackleton, who has blistered all his finger tips again with frostbite and is obviously a bit done up. He is very much thinner and has lost pounds in weight."

Scott took the news of the scurvy calmly enough and congratulated Armitage on the measures he had taken to combat the sickness. His southern journey plans, however, all based on a mid-October start, were badly dented. He would have to wait a month, according to contemporary medical theory, to be sure that his own group had no scurvy symptoms. Instead of a hundred days for the southern trip there would now be a mere ten weeks, nowhere near enough to make the Pole at 90° south but, with luck, 85° south might be reached and a huge chunk of unknown terrain explored.

This change of program showed the good sense of Scott's policy of keeping crew briefings about his future intentions to a minimum since, in Antarctica, even the best-laid plans were liable to be altered by last-minute problems. As Professor Drygalski had once advised Scott, theorizing back in Europe was a waste of time.

While anti-scurvy operations were in full swing on *Discovery*, including every effort being made to improve hygiene, dryness, and ventilation, on October 4, Charles Royds took a team to Cape Crozier, where he finally managed to update the message point with the expedition's latest plans for the information of the expected relief ship. A blizzard pinned them in their tents for five days and nights and their thermometer recorded −50°C. From a cliff top near Cape Crozier, Royds's men, Skelton, Frank Wild, and the American stoker Arthur Quartley, spotted a colony of three hundred emperor penguins on an isolated beach, which they suspected might be the emperors' breeding grounds. Foul weather forced Royds to turn back and great was the general relief, when Drs. Wilson and Koettlitz examined them, that all were found to be fit and well. The scurvy outbreak had been checked and, after giving final detailed orders to Armitage and Royds for their own coming journeys, Scott set out for the interior on November 2.

THE SOUTHERN JOURNEY: 1902–1903

SCOTT AND HIS TWO equally inexperienced companions were about to attempt to unravel the mystery of the interior of the last unknown landmass on earth. Was it some floating ice field, punctuated here and there by islands, or a frozen continent? All they could see to their south and east was the limitless Great Ice Barrier, which Scott shrewdly guessed was "all afloat." To their west as they set out lay the distant mountain chain of Victoria Land, which, as far as they knew, was in reality merely an island. Not knowing how difficult the snow surfaces ahead would be, nor the likely frequency of blizzards, fog, crevasses, and other obstacles, Scott could not predict how many miles his group would advance for each day of rations consumed, but they had food for seventy days, so must turn north again after thirty-five.

To pinpoint their progress in an often-featureless terrain, the three men used the mariner's latitudinal measurement system, based on each degree traveled due south being made up of sixty minutes. Each minute is one nautical mile, so each degree is exactly sixty nautical miles. I use nautical miles in this book, unless stated otherwise, which was also Scott's practice. (A nautical mile is 800 feet [244 meters] longer than a statute mile.) Since Hut

Point lay at 77°40'S and the Pole at 90°S, the direct distance between the two, as flown by a freezing crow, was clearly 740 miles. At any point, the direct way south might be blocked by mountains or impassable ice formations. Regions of heavy crevassing and volcanic phenomena had been conjectured and might lie ahead. A leader of great courage and willpower would be needed to press on to the limits of endurance but, when Scott had been chosen as leader, the selecting committee had no idea of his character in this respect. Nor, as they set out, did Shackleton and Wilson.

Before departing, the three men wrote farewell letters to their loved ones: Scott to his widowed mother, Wilson to his young wife, and Shackleton to his fiancée. Scott also wrote orders to his second-in-command, Albert Armitage. "Should I not return before a date at which there is any possibility of the ship being again frozen in, you should take the ship back to New Zealand provisioning the hut and leaving, if you think fit, a search party, which could be recovered the following season." Implicit in these instructions was the possibility that Scott's group might not be seen again, might be swallowed up by terra incognita. Scott was to be the chief navigator but, should he be injured or debilitated by snow blindness, Shackleton had during the winter practiced using the theodolite, introduced by Scott in place of the lighter and easier to handle, but less accurate, sextant. Theodolites need no visible horizon, unlike sextants, and are ideal for survey work in mountainous areas such as the group might well encounter.

Early attempts at skiing when pulling alongside the dogs proved unhelpful, so for the first two days, the three men lashed their skis to the sledges, just as Scott's mentor, the great Nansen, had done during his first crossing of Greenland. After the third day, the snow surface changed and the skis worked well. Each man used a single ski stick, toe-strap ski bindings, and warm Lapp *finnesko* boots, as advised by Nansen. Their wooden skis gripped the snow well enough without ski skins or waxes, since the terrain was wholly flat. For four days, they averaged eleven miles per day, but then blizzards slowed their pace and at length they reached the Bluff Depot on November 10. By the fourth day, Wilson, the doctor, noted: "Shackle started a most persistent and annoying cough in the tent."

For the first two weeks, they were followed by a support team under Michael Barne. Scott noted: "Confident in ourselves, confident in our equip-

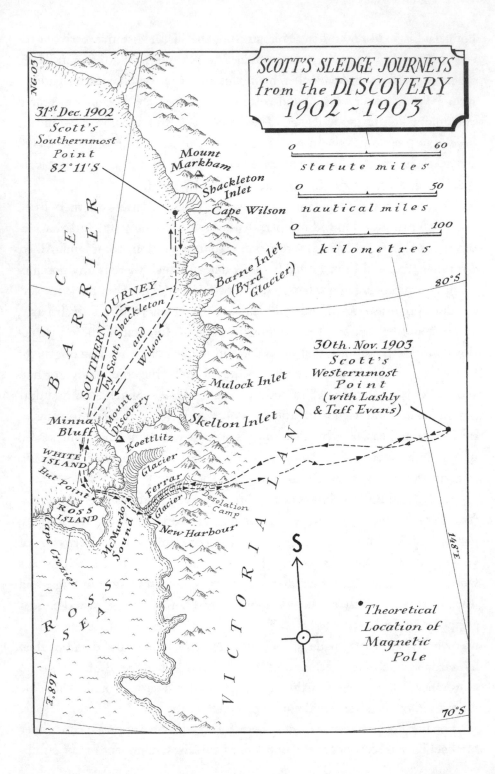

SCOTT'S SLEDGE JOURNEYS
from the DISCOVERY
1902 ~ 1903

31ˢᵗ Dec. 1902
*Scott's
Southernmost
Point
82° 11' S*

Mount
Markham

Shackleton
Inlet

Cape Wilson

0   60
statute miles

0   50
nautical miles

0   100
kilometres

Barne Inlet
(Byrd
Glacier)

80° S

I C E

B A R R I E R

SOUTHERN JOURNEY
by Scott, Shackleton and Wilson

Mulock Inlet

30th. Nov. 1903
*Scott's
Westernmost
Point
(with Lashly
& Taff Evans)*

Skelton Inlet

Minna
Bluff

Mount
Discovery

Koettlitz
Glacier

WHITE
ISLAND

Hut Point

Ferrar
Glacier

Desolation
Camp

V I C T O R I A   L A N D

ROSS
ISLAND

McMurdo
Sound

New Harbour

Cape Crozier

S

R O S S

S E A S

• *Theoretical
Location of
Magnetic
Pole*

168° E

148° E

70° S

ment and confident in our dog team, we can but feel elated with the prospect that is before us." But only one day later, their first full day after Barne had left and their loads were at full weight, their progress slowed dramatically, for the dogs no longer coped with the heavier weights. Soon Scott was writing: "Shackleton in front, with harness slung over his shoulder, was bent forward with his whole weight on the trace; in spite of his breathless work, now and again he would raise and half-turn his head in an effort to cheer on the team."

They agreed that the dogs' rapidly worsening performance was partly due to the absence of any visible object out ahead of the lead dog. There was nothing to aim at in 180° of featureless waste. The obvious answer, frequently noted by Scott, was for one of the group to ski far enough ahead of the lead dog to provide an aiming mark. Unfortunately, the loss of a third of their human pulling power would have made this uneconomical, since there were many other reasons for the dogs' poor performance. The best they could manage was to have one man hauling alongside the lead dogs. Whenever feasible Scott would keep his men traveling in bad weather, since the alternative was the quickest way to use food without gaining mileage.

The wind dropped and the temperature rose to −6.5°C and higher, which made sledge hauling extremely warm work. The harder a sledger, human or canine, hauls a load, the more the heart pumps, the more the body heats up, and the more exhausting the work becomes. Rather than kill the dogs through sheer exhaustion in these new difficult conditions, Scott made the painful decision to divide and relay the load. Thenceforward they would pull three of the six sledges for five miles (or less in bad visibility), depot them, then return for the other three. They would now have to travel three miles to gain a single mile of progress. Scott switched from daytime to nighttime travel to avoid the hottest time of day since, despite twenty-four hours of daylight, the sun was a lot lower at "night."

A phenomenon that frightened men and dogs when first they experienced it was christened the "barrier hush" or "shudder." One man described it as "the most eerie sound you can imagine." The worst such quakes I came across in Antarctica were close to the Pole. When snow builds up into a patch of wind crust several inches thick, whether as big as a sports arena or merely room-sized, the pressure of even a dog's foot can be enough to trigger a sudden collapse of the whole suspended mass. Never more than a few inches, it is enough to spark thunderous sound waves for several seconds.

By early December, after many days of relaying, the men all agreed that the chief reason for the dogs' weakness was their food. The strong recommendation of Nansen, the world's most famous polar traveler, had been the source of the switch in food from Spratt's cod-liver-oil biscuits, which Scott had originally planned for the dogs. These biscuits had been fed to the dogs along with fresh seal meat for much of the previous winter. Nansen, however, had urged the use of Norwegian dried stock fish. Scott and his men surmised that their dried fish food must have become damp and rotted in the tropics. Scott blamed himself in his diary for not discovering this problem in time and, as the leader, he was right to take responsibility. However, it seems odd that rotting fish would not have been apparent through its stench and so noticed by Armitage, who had fed the dogs on dried fish previously, or Shackleton, in charge of all ship's storage, or Dr. Koettlitz, the expert bacteriologist.

After weeks of featureless travel on the floating Great Ice Barrier, they saw slightly to the right of their southerly bearing a dark smudge on the horizon. Another island? They steered for it. Their hunger grew and grew like some living, gnawing creature in the depths of their stomachs. To gain more days for southerly travel, Scott had cut their daily ration to less than twenty-nine ounces each, far too little to replace their caloric expenditure caused by the extreme toil of man-hauling. They were consuming around four thousand calories and probably using more than seven thousand calories daily. Their weight loss would have averaged around ten ounces a day and, since most of their body fat would have disappeared in their first month of travel, their starved bodies were by December metabolizing the very muscle they depended upon.

Their mental drive must have received a valuable boost when on November 25 Scott's theodolite readings placed them at the 80th parallel, the nearest anyone had gotten to the Pole from any part of Antarctica's circumference. This reminder of their unique achievement did nothing to help their hunger pangs: Scott found that his meager daily tobacco ration took the edge off his hunger and when he ran out he noted: "Today I have been try-ing old tea leaves but they are horrid."

The three men's diaries indicate that they were happy together. If Scott's typical impatience flared from time to time, there is no indication of it. After a month or so, Wilson's diary mentions that they had Scott "well in hand." This comment is cryptic enough to allow many interpretations, but to me it merely implies that he and Shackleton were coping well with any aspects of their leader's behavior about which they might previously have been appre-hensive, such as his tendency toward periods of depression.

At times, the land seemed much closer, but then mists would swirl about them and, with nothing at all to steer by, they would attempt to follow a compass bearing, a slow and frustrating task even after weeks of experience. Whenever they halted briefly from exhaustion, they quickly chilled to the core. Then, resuming the haulage, their sweat would again trickle down their necks. The dogs labored on beside them. Wilson wrote: "The amount of shouting and beating the dogs want before they will do any work at all is soul sickening. They feel the heat so much despite the night marching."

By the end of November, individual features to the southwest were sometimes clearly visible. Wilson noted: "The coast we are making for is still about 50 miles away . . . It looks very beautiful though, all snow-covered peaks, bold cliffs and headlands." Then, soon afterward: "Snow grains falling all day. Nothing but 'white silence' all round us."

They depended on their tent for their very lives, as do all polar travelers. At the lunch stop on December 2, Wilson recorded that Scott: "in preparing our hot stuff set the tent alight, luckily just as we came up with the second loads, or the blessed thing would have been burnt. Providentially I was able to grab the thing the moment the flame came through to the outside and put it out, so that the only damage was a hole you could put your head through." That night Shackleton worked hard with needle and thread to repair the damage before the next blizzard.

Early in December, Scott began to worry that the fuel stocks were run-ning low and instituted the economy of chewing frozen, rather than boiled, seal-meat chunks at the midday halts. Halfway through December, the loads had become light enough to pull without relay, a huge relief since every mile marched now meant immediate southerly progress. For the past nightmarish month, only thirty miles had been gained at the mind-numbing rate of one mile a day, despite ninety miles of ground being actually covered. The reason for the lighter loads was that they had finally gotten to within a mile of the land they had crept toward for so long, so could safely leave a depot there for their return in the knowledge it would be easy to relocate. They had tried to reach the nearby land to take rock samples, but a deep chasm, like some giant hinge, separated the floating Great Ice Barrier from the landmass and their attempts to cross this divide proved futile. To reach land, they had been steering southwest, but now they returned to a due-south bearing and, because nighttime now invariably brought long periods of thick fog and slower progress, they returned to daytime travel. Wilson wrote: "Our hunger is very excessive." On December 19, he further noted: "We have decided now to feed up 8 or 9 of the best dogs on the others, and when these dogs have eaten each other up we must pull our own victuals and gear."

Contrary to the written evidence, critics have suggested that Scott would never have premeditated such un-British dog slaughter, even though he knew the Norwegians accepted it as a sound means of polar travel, scorning what they saw as sentimentality. Scott was unable to force himself to drive dogs to death in the manner described by the likes of Fridtjof Nansen but he had always accepted the potential need for dog slaughter. With Wilson the previous winter, he had preplanned the precise mathematics of progress by the dog-eat-dog system, as can be seen in Wilson's diary. They must have hoped they would never have to use it but they were ready for the necessity.

As Scott's men trudged painfully south, two always man-hauling alongside the dogs and one, turn by turn, cracking the whip and shouting from the rear, they slowly grew to loathe the experience and silently to vow never to repeat it. As each dog died or was butchered by Wilson, the men recorded its death in their diaries like the passing of a friend. Scott was in no doubt but that dogs could increase distances to be traveled. His problem was that, for the dogs, it involved torture and slow death. Wilson used his medical scalpel to pierce each new victim's heart, a speedy method of dispatch and, when snow blindness made him incapable, Shackleton took over the gruesome work. Scott was ashamed of his squeamishness and wrote: "It is a moral cowardice of which I am heartily ashamed and I know perfectly well that my companions hate the whole thing as much as I do . . . [Wilson does] all my share of the dirty work."

To cope with burns, snow blindness, cuts, fungal sores, ulcers, diarrhea, teeth broken on frozen meat chunks, gangrene, and a hundred and one other possible ailments, their doctor, Wilson, carried a basic medical pack, which, like everything else on their sledges, was as light as possible. A typical field pack for Scott-era journeys included chalk powder, bismuth, and lead compound (all with opium); and a tonic containing strychnine, sodium lactate, and chlorodyne. Also quinine for fever, cascara for constipation, and calomel for purging; mercuric chloride as an antiseptic and liquid cocaine for stove fumes and snow blindness. A mix of bandages, sticking plasters, and sprain emulsion completed the doctor's armory, along with tweezers and some scalpels.

Snow blindness was the most common affliction. Scott noted: "Poor Wilson has had an attack of snow-blindness, in comparison with which our former attacks may be considered as nothing; we were forced to camp early on account of it, and during the whole afternoon he has been writhing in horrible agony. It is distressing enough to see, knowing that one can do nothing to help. Cocaine has only a very temporary effect, and in the end seems to make matters worse. I have never seen an eye so terribly bloodshot and inflamed as that which is causing the trouble, and the inflammation has spread to the eyelid. He describes the worst part as an almost intolerable stabbing and burning of the eye-ball."

There were times during the journey when two out of the three men were blind and the third had the use of only one eye. As Wilson dragged himself and his load along blindfolded, Scott described to him the view of the landmass to the right of their line of advance. No human eyes had ever seen this unfolding panorama, which included the gleaming black-and-red cliffs of mountains rising to fourteen thousand feet and more. Although they could not know it, they were walking along Antarctica's heavily indented continental coastline, and each wide inlet between successive land features was the snout of a glacier descending to the Great Ice Barrier from the ten-thousand-foot-high inland plateau. Fighting his blindness, Wilson worked, whenever they halted, to sketch each new landscape with commendable accuracy.

Christmas Eve saw an improvement in the surface and the three men found to their relief that they could shift the entire load with no help from the surviving dogs. Shackleton had secreted in his clothes bag a cricket-ball-sized plum pudding and a shriveled sprig of holly in a spare sock, which he produced for their festive Christmas dinner, and Scott broke out triple rations to celebrate. They were within ten miles of 82° south, but their food and fuel stocks would allow for only four more days' outward travel. Despite further snow blindness and bad weather, they reached five miles beyond their unseen goal on December 28. This put them in the mouth of a wide west-running inlet between two sets of mountains. They realized that, with just a few more miles of southerly toil, they might be able to see sufficiently far into this great inlet to learn whether it was merely a bay or a channel cutting off the coast that they had followed for so long from the new land rising ahead of them.

Neither Wilson nor Shackleton at any point suggested in their diaries or elsewhere that they were continuing too far for safety. Scott used the word "argued" but not in the sense that later detractors used to support a quarrel between the men as to when they should turn back. Scott's words were clear: "We argued, however, that one never knows what may turn up, and we determined, in spite of the unpromising outlook, to push on to our utmost limit. As events proved, we argued most wisely, for had we turned at this point we should have missed one of the most important features of the whole coastline."

Explorers who turn back a touch before they really must may be lauded as responsible or branded as craven. In my opinion, and, it seems, in the judgment of men like Wilson and Lashly, who volunteered again and again to follow him, Scott was bold and ever prepared to take a calculated risk, but never foolhardy. Wilson was clearly pleased. On December 28, he wrote: "we have had the unlooked for, hardly expected, interest of a long new coast line with very gigantic mountain ranges to survey and sketch."

The next day unfortunately brought next to no visibility, but on the thirtieth, the three men pushed on toward the mouth of the mystery inlet through dense fog. Scott and Wilson skied on with the specific intent of interpreting the nature of the inlet, rather than due south in an effort to add distance to their "farthest south" record. On the last day of 1902, the fog and the clouds dispersed, confirming that, since there was no visible end to it, the twenty-mile-wide inlet must be a strait between two islands. Wilson sketched all the features visible as far as 83° south and Scott named two of them the Shackleton Inlet and Cape Wilson. Knowing the importance of obtaining geological proof to help identify the origins of their new land, they determined to collect rocks before heading back toward *Discovery*, but despite cutting steps in the ice, they were thwarted by unpassable crevasses.

Back at the tent and famished, they made soup, but Shackleton knocked the pot over so they scraped the mess off the floorcloth and recooked it. Not an angry word was spoken nor even diarized but, having experienced the embarrassment of my own in-tent clumsiness many times, I can imagine the wretched Shackleton's thoughts. Scott noted: "luckily it all remained on our waterproof floorcloth and by the time we had done scraping, I do not think that any was wasted."

On New Year's Day, having discovered and mapped nearly three hundred miles of virgin coast, the three men turned their eleven surviving dogs homeward from their most southerly point, which is likely to have been 82°11'S. They now faced the classic race against time that is the anticipated risk of all such finely tuned return journeys. Speed of travel set against rate of food expenditure equals an outcome of either death by starvation or just reaching base. The explorer who makes it back with plenty of food and fuel will realize that he could have gone farther and could have discovered more unknown land. On the other hand, his counterpart who cannot travel fast enough or suffers unexpected bad luck will die regretting he did not turn back earlier.

When in the 1990s Mike Stroud and I planned the rations necessary to man-haul across the entire continent in a hundred days, we took an additional ten days of emergency food. In 1902, for a seventy-day journey, Scott took five days' worth of emergency rations and, by spending that one day rock hunting, cut his bad luck/bad weather reserve down to four days. One of the purposes, perhaps the main aim, of Scott's southern journey was to determine the nature of Antarctica, and the obtaining of rock samples could help establish the existence or otherwise of a southern continent. Detractors mutter that this was reckless, but they forget that Scott's men could yet cut their food intake to half rations and so spin out their survival, desperately hungry maybe but still able to progress.

For four days, the exhausted little group averaged eight miles a day, just enough if they were to reach their next depot without cutting into emergency rations. But the dogs were dying one by one and from January 5 the men did nearly all the work with most of the dogs walking behind, an all but useless canine caravan surviving on cannibalism as their numbers dwindled. At midnight on January 13 Scott scanned the horizon through the telescope of his theodolite and thrilled at the sight of a tiny black spot in 360° of whiteness. He had found the depot.

"I sprang up," he wrote, "and shouted 'Boys, there's the depot.' We are not a demonstrative party, but I think we excused ourselves for the wild cheer that greeted this announcement." They camped at the depot, and agreed to prune their gear to absolute minimal requirements and to kill the last two dogs. Of the dead dogs, Scott noted: "I think we could all have wept . . . [at] the finale to a tale of tragedy; I scarcely like to write of it." Neither he nor Shackleton would ever forget what they had been forced to do to their dogs. They would remain determined never to repeat the experience.

Although all written records of the journey are devoid of any reference to any argument between Scott and his two colleagues, a story first told by Armitage twenty-five years later sparked a legend of a tiff between Scott and Shackleton. The passage of time has long since buried the truth but the myth created by Armitage's tale has blossomed and grown in the telling. "No smoke without fire" is the standard reaction by most people on digesting the story and neither Scott nor Shackleton is around to deny the whole saga as a groundless lie. The bare facts are as follows. Shackleton's health broke down badly during the return journey and he was still in a bad way after a month of rest and good food onboard *Discovery*. At that time, Scott had to decide who to send back home in the relief ship and both doctors, Wilson quite clearly and Koettlitz waveringly, advised him that Shackleton should go.

Two years later, Scott's one-time rival for leadership of the *Discovery*

expedition, Albert Armitage, wrote his book about the expedition in which
no mention is made of any rift between Scott and Shackleton. But Armitage
grew bitter with the passage of years, a terrible marriage, and the strains of
service at sea through the long years of the First World War. In 1925, he
wrote his autobiography and, twenty-two years after the event, he suggested
that Scott (who, in his eyes, had usurped his own position as expedition
leader) had tried to rid *Discovery* of all Merchant Navy officers by sending
both himself and Shackleton back in the relief ship in that February of
1903. Armitage also wrote a letter to H. R. Mill (who had left *Discovery* in
Madeira back in 1901 and was in 1922 writing a biography of Shackleton).
In this fateful letter, Armitage produced a bombshell from out of the blue:

> Shortly after their return from the Southern Journey,
> Shackleton told me that Scott was sending him home, and asked
> me if I could do anything about it. He was in great distress, and
> could not understand it. I consulted Koettlitz and he informed me
> that Scott was in a worse condition than Shackleton. I then went
> to Scott, and asked him why he was sending [Shackleton] back. I
> told him there was no necessity from a health point of view, so
> after beating about the bush he said: "If he does not go back sick
> he will go back in disgrace." I told Shackleton, and promised to
> look after his interests.

Armitage then added another ancient "memory," also told for the first
time.

> During the winter, Wilson told me the following story, which
> Shackleton confirmed later. On the Southern Journey, Wilson and
> Shackleton were packing their sledges after breakfast one
> morning. Suddenly they heard Scott shout to them: "Come here
> you BFs." They went to him, and Wilson quietly said: "Were you
> speaking to me?" "No Bill," said Scott. "Then it must have been
> me," said Shackleton. He received no answer. He then said:
> "Right, you are the worst BF of the lot, and every time that you

dare to speak to me like that you will get it back." Before Shackleton left he told me that he meant to return to prove to Scott that he—Shackleton—was a better man than Scott.

Would Wilson, Scott's great friend and known for his loyalty, have told such a story to Armitage, with whom he was never close? The polar historian David Wilson, Edward Wilson's great-nephew, has no doubt that Armitage, embittered by the passage of two difficult decades, invented the conversation between himself and Wilson.

Why should Armitage have invented such a story? *Discovery*'s chief engineer Skelton's personal shipboard notes record: "Armitage is a peculiar chap, especially with regard to his arguments . . . His methods are not always genuine." After Armitage's death Skelton wrote:

> I think Armitage's character was often rather soured—he did not think he got enough credit for his work—he is not popular in our Expedition nor in his own Service, the P & O. Scott was tactful with him and none of us had rows. He had that silly inferiority complex of the Merchant Navy for the Royal Navy. In his private life he had much misfortune, his brother in the RN, who I knew well, committed suicide rather than face a Court-Martial for a nasty crime. His wife was "a hell of a woman" and poor old Armitage whom she made penniless was far too kind to her. The last ten years of his life after leaving the P&O found him very impecunious and embittered by lack of appreciation by others . . . Personally I never had a row with him but never corresponded or got near to him and that goes for all of us in the *Discovery*. His books are not always accurate, and rather poor stuff . . . he is inclined to claim too much.

What did Scott himself give away at the time he sent Shackleton back home? A private letter to his mother was later unearthed in which he wrote: "All the crocks I am sending away, and am much relieved to get rid of. Except Shackleton, who is a very good fellow and only fails from the constitutional point of view."

Shackleton's diary made it crystal clear that relations on the journey back were good, but nevertheless the Armitage tale has been seized upon by successive generations of biographers. Here is the record from Shackleton's diary:

> On January 15 I broke down owing to overstrain, and haemorrhage started, which was naturally a rather serious matter, as the party was a hundred and seventy miles from the ship. I was, however, able to march the nine or ten miles a day that the party made . . . Captain Scott and Dr. Wilson could not have done more for me than they did. They were bearing the brunt of the work, and throughout the difficulties and anxieties of such a time showed ever cheery faces.

The acid test of how men have fared with each other on such a long and nightmarish journey comes, in my own experience, at the journey's end when it is at last possible to escape from each other's company. The night after the three men returned to their cabins on *Discovery*, Gerald Doorly, one of the officers from the relief ship, which had arrived during their absence, was passing by the neighboring cabins of Scott and Shackleton. He heard Scott calling out: "I say Shackles, how would you fancy some sardines on toast?" This hardly supports the rumors of any estrangement let alone hostility between the two men.

At the time Scott sent Shackleton home, the seventy or so men on *Discovery* and the relief ship were mingling and gossiping, as expedition members do, and finding out from one another the inside story. Those team members due to stay in Antarctica for another year were also writing their experiences to their loved ones back home for mailing on the relief ship. Many of the men's diaries and many of those letters (including fifty-six letters written by the garrulous Charles Royds) have been scrutinized again and again in later years by Scott biographers searching for the least mention of the rumored rift with Shackleton. No single shred of evidence has yet come to light.

Another myth encouraged if not invented by the embittered Armitage some ten years after the expedition was his "memory" that Wilson once told him he "had it out with Scott" during their southern journey and that "it" involved Scott's treatment of Shackleton. In 1933, the author George Seaver quoted, apparently from papers that Wilson's widow let him see before she destroyed them, the same single sentence from Edward Wilson: "Had it out with Scott." Some Scott biographers have used this ambiguous Wilson quote, of which no written source exists, to show that Wilson confronted Scott about his treatment of Shackleton. There is no evidence that this was so. And, because of this, Scott is now believed to have behaved badly toward Shackleton and been called to account by Wilson.

There is no mention in any of Wilson's meticulous diaries or anywhere else of any incident that this could conceivably have referred to. Yet this single tale of Seaver has been seized upon by generations of polar historians as evidence that Wilson, acting in his habitual role of peacemaker among all men, attacked Scott over some specific incident that occurred between Scott and Shackleton or, perhaps, warned Scott against aspects of his behavior. Maybe Scott's often-confessed bad moods, impatience, and quick temper were the topic of this tête-à-tête? No one will ever know, they can only speculate.

What needs no speculation, since Wilson's diary and subsequent letters are all available to the public, are his opinions about Scott. On January 23, he wrote: "The Captain and I had long talks on every subject imaginable and indeed he is a most interesting talker when he starts." In a letter Wilson sent to Scott's mother when he was back on *Discovery*, he wrote: "during these three months we naturally saw a good deal of each other. I am sure he will bear me out in saying that although we got to know each other very well, we were better friends at the end of the journey even than before. He stood the journey better than either Shackleton or myself, indeed he seems as strong as any here, and fit for any amount of exertion and exposure."

On January 25, with ragged clothes, raw lips, swollen scorbutic gums, and ravenous with hunger, they saw the smoking stack of volcanic Erebus still a hundred miles away but a welcome signpost to Hut Point. Nine days later, at the barrier's edge, the three men were met by Skelton and Bernacchi. Wilson wrote of their homecoming on February 3: "the relief ship, *Morning*, had arrived a week or more before and . . . All the news was good except that the *Discovery* was still blocked in by over eight miles of sea ice. But that didn't trouble us too much . . . we saw the ship decorated from top to toe with flags and all the ship's company up the rigging round the gangway ready to cheer us . . . as we came on board . . . Then came the time for a bath, and clothes off that had been on since November the second of the year before and then a huge dinner."

At dinner, there were riotous toasts to everyone, according to Skelton, who raised a toast to all who had died in the cause of science, including the dogs. Shackleton did not attend the dinner. He wrote: "I turned in at once when I got on board, not being up to the mark, after having had a nice bath—that is the first for ninety-four days. It is very nice to be back again, but it was a good time."

Scott wrote of the southern journey: "we had plodded with ever-varying fortune over a vast snow-field . . . [and] covered 960 statute miles, with a combination of success and failure." This modestly summed up man's first great penetration of the unknown southern continent.

The idea of sending a ship to Antarctica in the southern summer of 1903 to relieve Scott (as and where he might need such relief) was that of Clements Markham. As early as May 1901, the expedition's chief sponsor, Llewellyn Longstaff, had donated £5,000 (£235,000) toward such a vessel, aware that if *Discovery* should founder in Antarctica, all Scott's men, benighted perhaps on some remote and barren coast, would be at ever-increasing risk of a Franklin-type tragedy. Markham's fund gradually mounted and he had long promised Scott that a relief ship would materialize to bring provisions and mail, take back any invalids, and, should *Discovery* have foundered, all the surviving ship's company, too.

Markham purchased a tough little wooden whaler, *Morgenen*, in Norway for £3,800 (£178,000), renamed her *Morning*, and recruited Captain William Colbeck from the Merchant Navy as skipper. Colbeck was ideal for the job for he had served as surveyor in Borchgrevink's *Southern Cross* and had wintered at Cape Adare. The Royal Navy allowed two of its officers to join Colbeck's crew. One was George Mulock, a skilled surveyor, and the other a Welsh sub-lieutenant named Edward "Teddy" Evans (later Lord

Mountevans). Both officers were only twenty-one years old. Other officers, including Gerald Doorly, were chosen by Colbeck from the Merchant Navy. Royds commented: "Evans I thought an ass, and not a good representative of the senior service. Apparently he had been causing a great deal of trouble there by want of tact."

The question now was whether the natural ice breakup would reach Hut Point in time to release *Discovery* before *Morning* had to leave. Early attempts by Armitage and Royds to blast *Discovery* free with explosives were ineffective and when, by February 10, there was no sign at all of further breakup, Scott agreed that all winter provisions should be sledged over to *Discovery* just in case she really did remain icebound at Hut Point. The two captains also agreed that *Morning*, far less powerful in ice than *Discovery*, should depart well before any danger of her being caught down south might threaten. If, after she had gone, the ice did break out, then *Discovery* could follow her north after completing any coastal surveying that might prove possible.

Colbeck's provisions were greatly welcomed by Scott's men, especially the fruit, vegetables, and mutton. Scott estimated that his crew could now easily survive another two years stuck at Hut Point, but only if enough local meat was obtained; a total kill in Wilson's reckoning of two hundred seals.

An earlier error had been overcome during Scott's absence. *Discovery*'s lifeboats had all been stored beside the ship, as was the custom on previous naval expeditions to the Arctic when lifeboats were removed to make room for canvas deck awnings. But placing *Discovery*'s boats on the sea ice proved inadvisable. Since Scott had merely been following a well-tried naval custom by stacking the boats on a floe, he had not taken it kindly when the civilian physicist Louis Bernacchi had warned him the previous autumn that the boats might be lost. He told Bernacchi in no uncertain terms to mind his own business. However confident he clearly was that long-established Arctic practices of boat stowage would work at Hut Point, Scott should surely have listened to Bernacchi's warning at least in terms of checking the boats' well-being on a periodic basis. The boats were, thanks to Royds and his men, ready to go but *Discovery* looked increasingly like a firm Antarctic fixture for another twelve months.

The moment had come for Scott to determine who should go home with *Morning*. The party of ten included two sent back on health grounds. Dr. Koettlitz recommended that Royal Navy petty officer William MacFarlane should leave, despite his specific request to stay on. MacFarlane was one of Scott's chosen sledgers, but on Armitage's western journey, while Scott was away, the petty officer had been stricken by a suspected heart attack. He seemed to have recovered, but Scott could not risk any recurrent attack on a journey the following year and so MacFarlane was to be sent home. Mac-Farlane, popular and Royal Navy, was not the only one to be sent back on health grounds and against his will, for Scott decided that Shackleton was also too sick to take on the coming year's sledge journeys. Wilson agreed, for he too had witnessed his friend's rapid and alarming deterioration during their recent journey south. Wilson stated that Shackleton's throat and breathing passages had been affected and that his attacks of dyspnea, coughing, and blood spitting made it inadvisable for him to risk a second winter.

Koettlitz examined Shackleton and, finding no permanent damage and perhaps responding to the patient's clear desire to stay, told Scott that he felt Shackleton need not go. Scott pressed him for a definite opinion on whether Shackleton was fit to lead a sledging journey or not. Koettlitz then wrote: "Mr Shackleton's breakdown during the southern sledge journey was undoubtedly, in Dr Wilson's opinion, due in great part to scurvy taint. I certainly agree with him; he has now practically recovered from it, but referring to your memo: as to the duties of an executive officer, I cannot say that he would be fit to undergo hardships and exposure in this climate."

Koettlitz could not have taken kindly to Scott pressing him for an official medical report on Shackleton, rather than his initial vague diagnosis. Subsequent disgruntled comments to his fellow scientist, Hodgson, resulted in the latter writing: "I hear it is true, as I suspected, that personal feeling is the real reason for Shackleton's departure." This is the only comment from any of the participants to this effect. Clarence Hare, the steward, who was close to all the officers and scientists and kept an observant diary, mentions no bad blood between Scott and Shackleton, nor does the prolific and critical letter writer Charles Royds. Remember too Scott's personal regret expressed in his letter to his mother. In his official report, he wrote: "It is with great reluctance that I order his return and trust that it will be made evident that I do so solely on account of his health and that his future prospects may not suffer."

Shackleton's lungs and heart were clearly susceptible to some ailment unconnected to scurvy. Subsequent sicknesses and eventually his death proved this, but at the time, both Wilson and Scott, the two men who actually witnessed Shackleton's physical problems, were both clearly against trusting his health on future journeys. No other rationale was needed, however regretfully, to send both MacFarlane and Shackleton home.

Scott inadvertently fueled the rivalry myth by asking his dour second-in-command, Albert Armitage, if he too wanted to leave on *Morning*. Before joining *Discovery* the latter had told Scott that he must have his wife's agreement. Scott had now been given by Colbeck a confidential instruction from the admiralty via Markham that he should try to persuade Armitage to return. The reason was not fully spelled out but involved Mrs. Armitage's young child and a brewing scandal with some third party. Scott's attempts to put this tactfully to his second-in-command misfired badly and Armitage decided he was to be purged merely because he, like Shackleton, was Merchant Navy. "Fortunately my appointment was independent of him. I absolutely refused."

Scott relied on Shackleton to present as good a picture as possible of the expedition when back home in Britain. Had he suspected bad blood existed between them he would hardly have written as he did to his Royal Society mentors: "Mr E. H. Shackleton, who returns much to my regret should be of the greatest use in explaining the details of our position and our requirements for the future." Back in Britain, Shackleton was to write a twelve-hundred-word report on the southern journey with no note of blame, resentment, or victimization. This is equally true of his personal diaries.

By the time *Morning* left Hut Point on March 2, Shackleton had rested and eaten well for over a month but, as Michael Barne noted when he accompanied his friend over the ice to say farewell: "we went on very slowly as poor old Shackles is still very shaky." Scott had given the proud Anglo-Irishman a taste for polar adventure and had selected him as a star player, but then had seemingly cast him aside. Shackleton wept openly as *Morning* sailed north. Scott and his three dozen remaining men waved from the ice edge. Shackleton must have recognized his physical problems. He was a proud man and the ambitions that had seen him join *Discovery* were now redoubled, for he knew he must prove himself to the world. By choosing Shackleton as his companion for the southern journey and then sending him home as unhealthy, Scott had inadvertently ensured that the two men would become lifelong rivals for the same prize.

LOST ON THE PLATEAU: 1903–1904

As Scott's men prepared for a second season's work in August 1903, what of the German expedition of Professor Drygalski? His ship, *Gauss,* had survived twelve months' captivity in sea ice many miles from the region the Germans had intended to explore. They had tried to sledge inland, but crevasses and rough ice soon reduced their activities to building an icehouse laboratory four days' travel from the ship; when that proved unworkable, they set out their magnetic equipment on the floe beside the ship. Their on-deck windmill blew down, as had Scott's, so all lighting was by oil and blubber lamps. Most attempts at scientific work in the vicinity were blighted by blizzards, poor equipment, reluctant dogs, and broken sledges.

When, at about the time Scott returned from his southern journey, the ice about *Gauss* showed signs of breakup, the Germans tried to shatter the floes with explosives and large ice saws. These were ineffective, but on February 8 a gale broke up the ice and allowed them to escape to the north. Drygalski later tried to head south again, but storms and a shortage of coal frustrated him. Near mutiny onboard was narrowly averted and Berlin ordered the ship home, as funds were exhausted. A great deal of coastal magnetic and oceanographic work had been done, an ice shelf and an extinct volcano, the Gaussberg, discovered, but no inland exploration or southern journeys were carried out, nor was the existence of a southern continent confirmed.

Scott's other contemporary, Otto Nordenskjöld, had fared little better. The Swedes managed some fine mapping work of the coast of the Antarctic Peninsula and South Georgia before their ship was lost; the Scots under William Bruce achieved fine scientific results but could not penetrate far to the south. The *Discovery* expedition, by the time the men braced themselves for their second winter at Hut Point, had proved by far the most effective and efficient geographical exploration unit in Antarctica. In addition to the research and survey work carried out on or near Ross Island and the various inland forays prior to the southern journey, major journeys from *Discovery* had also been led by Barne and Armitage.

Armitage had discovered a complex route to a great glacier named after Ferrar, a route that led through the ramparts of the western mountains and up to Victoria Land's inland plateau. En route he conducted magnetic readings, which would later help to establish the position of the south magnetic pole. Had he been able to extend his travels west over the nine-thousand-foot-high plateau at the head of the Ferrar Glacier, he might have proved Victoria Land was indeed part of a continent and not just an island. The last chance that year to find such proof was left to Michael Barne's group.

While Scott was beginning his southern journey and Armitage was pioneering a route through the western mountains, Barne's six-man team had headed out from the Minna Bluff Depot and aimed for the most southerly point of land they could see. By January 3, 1903, they had come across a whole new stretch of coastline. Over the next week, in between spells of thick, freezing fog, Barne had surveyed parts of the landmass, including the mouths of three great inlets that lay between the regions then being explored to the east by Scott and to the west by Armitage.

At the outset of the second winter, Scott had studied the detailed reports of Barne and Armitage and praised them both for their considerable success in difficult, often dangerous conditions. With expert surveyor George Mulock, left behind by *Morning* as Shackleton's replacement, he had then carefully worked out a map of the coastline from the survey data, photographs, and sketches resulting from all three journeys. The resulting chart defined some 326 miles of the coastline south and west of Ross Island and gave Scott the information he needed to work out critical plans for the coming summer's exploration work.

Scott knew his career would suffer if *Discovery* remained icebound yet again in twelve months' time. The admiralty would blame him, not the sea ice. He determined to use a giant ice saw and explosives to prepare for a breakout as early as feasible, probably mid-December 1903. Since major sledging journeys to the interior were impractical in the extreme temperatures before October, there would only be ten weeks available to solve the continental mystery. Also, to sledge in October, depots would need prepositioning in the cold month of September. Too few dogs were left, so all journeys would involve man-haul. By midwinter Scott was ready to outline his plans.

First, he would ascend the Ferrar Glacier, taking eleven men all or part of the way, and then traverse the high inland plateau that Armitage had discovered, in the hope of delineating Victoria Land's western limits. Second, Michael Barne and George Mulock would take seven men to survey the region south and east of Minna Bluff where Barne's previous journey and Scott's had failed to define the nature of the great inlets. Third, Wilson and two others would work at Cape Crozier to unravel the mystery of the emperor penguins' breeding habits, which many international scientists then believed to be the key to solving an evolutionary conundrum: Did birds and penguins descend from flightless dinosaurs? Wilson wrote in 1911, "if vestiges of teeth are ever to be found in present day birds, it would most likely be in the Emperor embryo." These scientific journeys would account for all but thirteen of Scott's men and leave only two officers, Royds and Armitage, one of whom, along with a minimal crew of seven, would have to stay with the ship.

With advice from Bernacchi, the magnetic expert, Scott determined that the fourth and last journey, using the available remnant of six men and one officer, should head southeast over the barrier and well away from any known land. There were two aims to this. Bernacchi and his specialist instruments would measure the local magnetic forces in parallel with related plotting to be done by appointed magnetic personnel on Scott's western team. The north and south magnetic poles are the two points on the earth's surface where the terrestrial magnetic field has only a vertical component and a zero horizontal component. At these points, a dip needle points vertically downward. The two resulting sets of readings from Scott's men should help to pinpoint the location of the south magnetic pole, even if Scott, on the inland plateau, did not actually reach it.

Faced with the thorny problem of whether Royds or Armitage should lead this last journey, Scott plumped for Royds for two reasons. It was his turn to lead a journey, for Armitage had already completed the lion's share of sledging and discovery. Second, Scott, knowing Skelton to be a sound and fair judge of character, was worried by his account of Armitage's behavior during the Ferrar Glacier journey. There is no record of what Skelton actually told Scott, but his diary attacked Armitage for overdue caution and slow progress, for his hectoring attitude to the young scientist Ferrar, and for his failure to inspire his men, some of whom grumbled constantly behind his back. Armitage had his own plans to lead a major push due south and was very upset when Scott said no and explained why he should stay with *Discovery*. Scott did slightly soften the blow by asking him to lead a minor journey to the southwest area of McMurdo Sound, but Armitage was to nurse an anti-Scott grudge from then on.

Charles Royds said of the Armitage plan to lead a trip south: "in my opinion his sole wish is to beat the Captain's record."

Wilson also noted: "Armitage applied to the Captain to be allowed to try and get farther south than we did last year, with men only to pull and I think that he was quite rightly refused. The Captain worked the possibilities out on paper and showed them to me and I agreed with him in thinking it was far better to apply all our sledging energies and equipment to new work, rather than to covering old ground to that extent, with the chance of doing so little at the end of it. The upshot of it all is that Armitage is now off the list of sledging for this year altogether though whether this is due to himself or any one else I cannot say."

There were clearly not enough men or sledges to mount another southern journey or even the relevant depot-laying preparation work. From Armitage's viewpoint, he saw Scott gaining the glory of mapping the high Victoria Land plateau, which he, not Scott, had discovered. Yet he was not

allowed to go south. At the end of the *Discovery* expedition, he appeared
to part with Scott on friendly terms and his book about the expedition,
very complimentary to his leader, enjoyed good sales. For many years after
Captain Scott's death, Armitage gave no hint of any latent hostility but, a
quarter of a century after the event, his autobiography appeared and a long-
suppressed resentment poured out. Since many biographers have used the
Armitage papers to brand Scott with various accusations, it is worth a brief
look at them.

Contractual niggles still rankled:

> My appointment was independent of Scott, although of course
> I was under his command. I was to be landed, if possible, with a
> hut and equipment sufficient for two years; eight men, including
> one of the surgeons, and a team of dogs. There was to be no
> restriction put on my sledging. My expedition pay was to be not
> more than fifty pounds per annum less than Scott's. It was to
> commence when I left my P. & O. ship, and continue until I
> rejoined a P. & O. ship.
>
> With the exception of the expedition pay, not one of these
> conditions was fulfilled. I was not put on the pay-sheet until two
> weeks had elapsed after leaving my ship. I was taken off it at the
> end of the month of our return to England although I was nine
> months without a ship. On arrival at our Antarctic base Scott
> implored me to forgo the other conditions, although they were
> quite feasible. He put forward the plea, not only that it would
> cripple his own efforts to a great extent, but that he could not do
> without me. Naturally I consented to stay with the main party.

Armitage summarized his feelings about Scott, by then dead for over a
decade, by asserting that he found much that was lovable in Scott's character
but was quite aware that he would allow nothing to stand in his way and
was of a most suspicious nature; also that Scott would make a great friend
of a man and use him, only to throw him aside. Nor could he be trusted to
keep his word-of-honor promises. Armitage wrote:

I was told off to find a pass between the lofty mountain peaks of South Victoria Land, to the west, and gain the inland plateau if such existed. I did so, although he did not believe that I would find it, as a subsequent letter will prove. But he would not allow me to carry on my work: he did it himself, and refused to allow me or anyone else to attempt a further southern journey, saying that there was no use in it. In the years to come he again attempted it, succeeded in reaching the coveted South Pole, but, alas! only to find that he had been forestalled.

All hard-hitting stuff about a long-dead colleague.

At the end of the *Discovery* expedition, Scott wrote a reference for Armitage: "I received valuable assistance from him in the equipment of the Expedition and formed a high opinion of his loyalty. I found him to be most capable in all his duties and an excellent Navigator. I can confidently recommend him to anyone requiring his services."

Armitage expected promotion and when it was not forthcoming:

[I] did not allow the matter to rest, for I considered that, when Scott had been promoted to Captain R.N. for his Antarctic services, it was an invidious distinction to leave me out in the cold: . . . When my old leader met with his tragic end . . . Mr. Churchill was First Lord . . . So I wrote to Mr. Churchill and pointed this out, saying that I had always heard of him as a fair-minded man, and requested that I should receive the pay I considered myself entitled to.

The admiralty was unmoved.

During the second long winter of 1903 on *Discovery,* according to Skelton, Armitage did not fit in well with the rest. He was unpopular and felt unappreciated. His main associate, with whom he worked at local surveying, was George Mulock, another loner.

The winter months passed with none of the disasters or emergencies of the previous year, for the hazards of extreme cold were now familiar, even though by May record temperatures ranging down to −55°C were being recorded and mercury froze in most of the thermometers. Probably owing to the more aggressive types having left on *Morning* there were fewer if any fights on the mess deck and a more cheerful atmosphere throughout the ship. The former cook, Brett, had been replaced by his assistant Clark, a professional baker, and everyone noticed the improvement. He served up fresh seal or skua meat every day and Royds thought the skua tasted like duckling. Skelton and his engineers fixed up an acetylene lighting system throughout the inhabited parts of the ship, a great improvement over smoky lamps and candles.

Wilson sometimes felt homesick and his diary waxed romantic. He wrote of sheets of flame bursting into the night above Erebus and how it was "Two years now since Ory and I were married and we have had three weeks of it together." There was bridge and chess with often recurring bust-ups between Scott, who as always loved to win, and Koettlitz, whose lack of a sense of humor was famous. Hodgson taught mathematics to three of the ratings and Bernacchi tried to explain the mechanics of the aurora.

All day and every day, the scientists went about their work in all weathers: Michael Barne usually alone with his sounding gear on a sledge, Mulock with his charts, and Bernacchi away in his huts or out on the ice with Koettlitz. Hodgson had to be rescued when a floe from which he was shrimping drifted out of Hut Point cove and Wilson, who sometimes helped him to haul up his fish trap, wrote: "Hundreds of thousands of amphipods come up swarming on the seal scraps like a mass of shrimpy maggots." Royds kept the men busy through the winter repairing and modifying the existing sledging gear and making new equipment where needed. Taff Evans, Crean, and Lashly were as handy as ever with their skills at improvisation and, of course, their newly acquired polar knowledge.

August arrived with wondrous displays of auroral fireworks. The bloodred rim of the sun edged back to lighten briefly the world of Scott's men, turning from black to gold the smoke plume of Erebus. The temperature plummeted to new lows and on August 15, Wilson found one of the dogs, Tin-tacks, too young to have gone south the previous summer, in obvious distress. "On looking at her today," he wrote, "I found she had lost the whole of her tongue . . . She must have got her tongue against some fixed metal and stuck to it . . . then after pulling and struggling till the tongue was dragged far out of her mouth she must have bitten it off . . . it is a most piteous thing to see her hanging her head over food and water . . . Having lost the whole tongue, she can only swallow when her head is held up and we pour something down." They eventually had to shoot Tin-tacks and, when Hodgson requested her body as bait for his fish trap, a sailor who had befriended her indignantly and secretly buried her remains.

Wilson wrote: "Every Tuesday for dinner we have skua, half a bird to a man, enough for a meal and very good indeed. One day in the week we have stuffed seal's heart, another seal steak and kidney pie, another seal steak and onions, and so on. For breakfast we have the best dish of all—seal's liver, twice a week, other days stewed seal meat or curried. Thursday is known to everyone as 'Scurvy Day,' being the only day in the week on which we have tinned meat."

Despite unpleasant memories of man-hauling in early spring the previous year, Scott was determined to start just as early in September 1903. There would, he was confident, be no repetitions of poor Vince's accident, for the men were no longer novices. On September 7, the Cape Crozier penguin foray set out, led by Charles Royds. They slept, or rather shivered, in two three-man bags. Wilson noted: "I can imagine nothing more uncomfortable. One is constantly waking up the others, through restlessness . . . one cannot lie long on one side. Therefore one finds oneself breathing another man's breath for all one is worth half a dozen times in the night." They needed eggs with living embryos to help scientists and their evolutionary questions. Sadly all the eggs at the colony were "dead," but the fact that there were live chicks around showed Wilson that he must come back in midwinter if he was to obtain live eggs.

Michael Barne, at the same time, took sledges out to the barrier to lay a depot southeast of White Island, while on September 9, Scott, with Skelton, Taff Evans, Bill Lashly, Dailey, and Handsley, left to lay a depot to the west and quickly found a far faster route onto the Ferrar Glacier than Armitage's of the year before. They left their most southerly depot two thousand feet up the glacier and averaged twenty miles a day on the return journey, despite the long hours of darkness and temperatures of −45.5°C. Even experienced Norwegian skiers using dog teams would have been highly impressed.

With all the officers and men back from their ordeals, all depots in position, and no serious injuries, the main journeys began on schedule, Barne's on October 6 and Scott's on the twelfth.

Scott's western team consisted of three sledge groups. He took his old depot-laying team but substituted Thomas Feather in place of Dailey. Ferrar and two sailors with a second sledge were to concentrate on the geology of the glacier, and Dailey, with Thomas Williamson and Frank Plumley, would take a third sledge to lay more depots.

Scott's men each hauled 205 pounds but still managed to advance an average of thirteen miles a day through difficult terrain. By avoiding his perilous pioneering route, they reached a point on the lower reaches of the glacier in only six days, instead of Armitage's twenty-seven. However, by scouting out a new, more direct route, their sledge runners unfortunately broke up on the rough ice and proved impossible to repair.

Scott bit the bullet and returned to Hut Point, but in impressive style. Bernacchi, the most experienced Antarctic hand on *Discovery*, wrote: "Their return journey over some ninety miles, on half rations, was a record in Antarctic travel and proved what could be done by fit men, light loads and no dogs. Eighty-seven miles in three days." Lashly said of Scott's sledging: "If he can do it I don't see why I can't, my legs are as long as his."

Their new sledge was cobbled together from the broken ones, and in a few days and with grim determination, they were back on the glacier again. The sledge runners continued to cause delays for running repairs by Lashly, Evans, and the carpenter, Dailey. On reaching their most westerly depot, they found that high winds had in their absence loosened the lid of Scott's navigation box and his key nautical logarithms had been blown away. Scott summed up the problem he now faced:

> The gravity of this loss can scarcely be exaggerated; but whilst
> I realised the blow I felt that nothing would induce me to return to
> the ship a second time; I thought it fair, however, to put the case

to the others, and I am, as I expected, fortified by their willing
consent to take the risks of pushing on.

I must here explain what this loss signified. In travelling to the
west we expected to be, as indeed we were, for some weeks out of
sight of landmarks. In such a case as this the sledge traveller is in
precisely the same position as a ship or boat at sea: he can only
obtain a knowledge of his whereabouts by observations of the sun
or stars, and with the help of these observations he finds his
latitude and longitude. To find the latitude from an observation of
a heavenly body, however, it is necessary to know the declination
of that body, and to find the longitude one must have not only the
declination, but certain logarithmic tables. In other words, to find
either latitude or longitude, a certain amount of data is required.
Now, all these necessary data are supplied in an excellent little
publication issued by the Royal Geographical Society and called
"Hints to Travellers," and it was on this book that I was relying to
be able to work out my sights and accurately fix the position of
my party.

When this book was lost, therefore, the reader will see how we
were placed; if we did not return to the ship to make good our
loss, we should be obliged to take the risk of marching away into
the unknown without exactly knowing where we were or how to
get back.

In 1981, I traveled to the Pole and worried myself silly trying to locate
the uppermost features of the Scott Glacier, which my party needed to descend quickly. I used the same type of theodolite and nautical tables as Scott
had and found the calculations bad enough, even with the key astronomical
data. I remain full of admiration at Scott's ingenuity in devising what he
called "a rule of thumb" method for ascertaining the daily change in the
sun's declination.

He commented on his navigation system:

the prospect which lay before us of wandering over this great
snowplain without knowing exactly where we were . . . had

naturally been much in my thoughts . . . it occurred to me that
we might gather some idea of our latitude if I could improvise
some method of ascertaining the daily change in the sun's
declination.

   With this idea I carefully ruled out a sheet of my note-book
into squares with the intention of making a curve of the sun's
declination. I found on reflection that I had some data for this
curve, for I could calculate the declination for certain fixed days,
such as the day when the sun had returned to us . . . other points
were given by observations taken at known latitudes on the
glacier . . . I plotted all these points on my squared paper, and
joined them with a freehand curve of which I have some reason to
be proud, for on my return to the ship I found it nowhere more
than 4' in error.

Not everyone had complete trust in Scott's ability to navigate over the
white oceanlike wastes of the high plateau without a tried and trustworthy
system of position fixing. Skelton, probably the most mathematically capable of Scott's colleagues, worried that they were likely to be lost forever.

   However, Scott's three sledge groups, sometimes quite far apart, but always camping together, crept up the frozen valley. Lashly and Skelton
needed their skills to repair a number of runner breakages and Thomas
Feather had to fix many of their crampons, which received a battering on
long stretches of bare blue ice. On November 4, at seven thousand feet, a
sudden windstorm caught them all on a surface so hard they could not anchor their tents to the ice nor find snow blocks to place on the valances. Fortunately, Thomas Feather somehow solved the problem before they were
numbed by exposure.

   For seven long days and nights, fierce katabatic winds pinned the men
down in their tents. They called the place Desolation Camp and shared a
single book, Darwin's *Voyage of the Beagle,* between them. They escaped
during a storm lull on the eighth day and continued the climb. Ferrar and
his two "assistant geologists" left at this point on their own mission to collect rocks and fossils.

   Less than half a mile from Desolation Camp, both sledge groups crossed a snow bridge that spanned a mammoth crevasse. Scott noted: "We as nearly as possible walked into an enormous chasm but none of us really cared much as our sole thought was to get away from that miserable spot." Setting a breakneck pace, as was his wont, Scott reached the head of the glacier at 8,900 feet on November 13 and saw ahead "a great snow plain with a level horizon all about." Before leaving the glacier's upper rock features behind, Scott was able to note these carefully, for the weather was briefly clear. These pinpricks of rock might prove vital weeks later in relocating the Ferrar's upper reaches and thus their depot lifeline back home.

When Armitage had reached this point the year before and discovered the plateau, the first man to do so, he had been forced to turn back, but Scott had arrived with five weeks' worth of rations. He hoped this would allow him, if he could move fast and thus far enough, to find out if this high tableland was merely the summit plateau of an island, the island of Victoria Land.

Feather and Handsley were not as fit or as powerful as Scott's other men, so, regretfully, he told them to turn back some seven days out on the plateau. He could not send any group back without a navigator, so Skelton had to go, too. Skelton always recorded his daily grumbles and, during the ascent from Desolation Camp, he had noted that Scott could get very impatient under such delays and say unkind things but that it didn't mean anything, and the ongoing bad weather was enough, Skelton thought, to get on anyone's nerves. Ferrar wrote in a private letter after the western trip: "We all know each other much better and it is entirely due to the Captain for his friendliness and the example he sets of how to pull together."

Scott tried in his diaries at that time to describe some of the detailed privations involved with man-hauling and camping in extreme cold:

> The worst time for sledging is the coldest time . . . the human
> body is always giving off moisture . . . much issuing through the
> pores of the skin . . . a small quantity will remain as ice on one's
> garments . . . [increasing] until one is completely enclosed in it.
> There is ice everywhere . . . and all these things which on board
> the ship were so caressingly soft to the touch will have become as
> hard as boards. Worse still, this ice will be found plastered as
> thickly on everything that makes for comfort at night: sleeping-

bag, night-jacket, and night foot-gear will have grown equally
hard and chill.

Toward the end of a sledging day:

   the sledges have grown decidedly heavier, and legs and back
are already giving warning that the camping hour ought to be at
hand. Breath is now coming gustily; it has frozen thick under the
windguards and hangs in long icicles from the unshaven chins;
eyelashes are thickly encrusted with it, and now and again a bared
hand has to thaw out a sealed eyelid and restore the sense of
vision to its owner.

When they reached the campsite: "There must be no standing about in
this weather; we must be constantly active until we can creep into the shelter
of our thin tent." The gloom of the tent was lit only by a flickering candle
that hung from a tent pole. Any incautious move was likely to send this flying. While the cook made supper, the rest of the party changed footgear, sodden *finnesko* and ice-covered socks. Night socks were retrieved from warm
breast pockets. It was always likely that someone's leg might shoot out dangerously near the Primus and they would exclaim loudly as cramp hit them.

   Once the hoosh boils, off comes the pot's lid and all is hidden
in a cloud of steam as the cook fills the pannikins . . . This is a
moment to be lived for . . . The *hoosh* is followed by an equally
delightful drink of boiling hot cocoa, but even as we gulp it down
we feel that pleasure is drawing to an end, for the Primus is now
out, the steam of cooking that has not passed away through the
ventilator has frozen in glistening crystals on the side of the tent,
and the chill of the outer air is again finding its way through the
thin canvas . . .
   Meanwhile the sleeping bag is dragged to the door of the tent,
and by dint of much coaxing it is eventually got inside . . . it
crackles as it is forced open, and has to be flattened out with the
full weight of the body. What was once the soft covering flap will

now stand erect and rigid, so stiffened is it with ice. Inside [it is] so hard in places that under the raps of one's knuckles it resounds like a wooden door. Could any bed be more uninviting?

Before we enter it we must have a look round . . . Are we in for a blizzard? . . . a last look at the thermometer shows that the temperature has fallen to −48° . . . It is breathless work this . . . we lift the flap of the sleeping-bag and step inside . . . this is the time for diaries, meteorological records, casual repairs, *and pipes.* The last-named, being the only attractive part of this programme . . . Experience soon teaches that a pipe must be kept in a very warm place, otherwise the stem will be found choked with ice . . .

As these tasks are finished, one by one the inhabitants of the sleeping-bag wriggle down into its horny depths. The last to lower himself is the centre man . . . he laboriously wrestles with the fastenings of the bag over their heads . . . and works himself down as best he can between his companions, and finally seals the opening above his own head . . .

The last squirm brought the wind-guard of our helmet across our face. It is crusted with the ice of the day's march: this is now gently thawing, and presently a drop trickles down our nose. Our thoughts become fixed on that drop. It is very irritating; we long to wipe it away, but that means taking out one hand and disarranging the whole scheme of defence against the cold. We are debating the question when a second drop descends. Flesh and blood cannot stand this: out comes our hand, and for the next quarter of an hour we are pitching and tossing about to try to regain the old position.

The morning ordeal was putting on their marching boots:

It is very trying work. With a caution born of experience we took immense care last night in freezing them to conform as nearly as possible to the shape of our feet. After the march they had been wet through, and came off in a soft and flabby condition; we knew that this would only last for a few minutes, and as they froze we had carefully supported and kneaded them into the required shape. Half an hour later they were so hard that we could throw them about without risk of altering it; they are still in this condition, and we are about to test the result of our labours. They clatter like wooden sabots as they are deposited on the floorcloth.

We squat down and withdraw one foot from its night-clothing, grope in our breast for our day-socks, produce one of them still very wet but moderately warm, jam our foot into it, and with many gasps proceed to wedge it into a wooden finnesko. The finnesko has been prepared by placing in it a sole cut from reindeer-skin and a little padding of *sennegrœs*. This grass is soft, but the sole is as wooden as the boot, and has needed much pushing to get it in place. We are lucky if our foot gets half-way into its rocky cover at the first attempt. We leave it at that for the moment, and proceed with the other; by the time it is in a similar position, an inch can be gained on the first, and so inch by inch these tiresome boots are pulled on. Meanwhile our feet have got alarmingly cold, and with a groan we are obliged to start up and stamp about.

Once Skelton's little group had departed on November 23, Scott was left with two sailors, Taff Evans, whom he knew well from his *Majestic* days, and Stoker William Lashly. Evans weighed 178 pounds, Lashly 190 pounds, and Scott 160 pounds. Each towed well over 200 pounds, but they worked extremely well as a team. Scott wrote: "With these two men behind me our sledge seemed to become a living thing, and the days of slow progress were numbered."

Constantly checking his course by a simple neck-slung sundial when there was the faintest hint of the sun's position or by compass when there was not, Scott led the way at first west and later southwest over the rolling white snowfields. For twenty-one days they crawled on over this featureless tundra, ever hoping that some landmark would eventually reward their toil. Ranks of parallel ice ridges called sastrugi, like deeply plowed field furrows, some two feet high and more, slowed their advance and caused capsizes.

Their breath came in gasps of rarefied air at the polar equivalent of fifteen thousand feet in the Alps or the Himalayas. Constant capsizes resulted in slow leakage from the cap seals of their kerosene cans and Scott took a calculated risk by continuing south and west until the last day of November, the date he had set as "turn-back day" when they had left Desolation Camp. On reaching the last horizon that day, they saw only the ongoing "immensity of this vast plain" and no end to Victoria Land.

A week into the return journey, having averaged sixteen miles daily, Scott asked the others if they were prepared to march an extra hour each day, forgo a midday halt for hot food, and reduce their daily rations. They agreed. There were soon no traces of their outward tracks to follow, for snowdrifts had covered them and, with no nautical tables or features to help, doubts crept in. On December 10, Evans glimpsed a faint black dot that hour by hour grew into one and then several rock features, none of which Scott recognized. In such a situation, it would have been very easy to panic, for, if, as they so easily could, they missed the entry to the Ferrar Glacier, and their depots, no other route could save their lives.

Eventually they found a smooth crevasse-free slope and set out down it wearing crampons, with Scott up front and the other two holding the rear of the sledge to keep it from sliding downhill. Lashly lost his footing and the others, jerked forward by the runaway sledge, followed suit. Tumbling over and over, they shot downward, bouncing off ice blocks and cartwheeling through the air. Some three hundred feet below, they came to a halt, much shaken but alive. Not only were no limbs broken, but immediately they knew where they were. The sky was bright and clear and they could see as far as Erebus. Scott wrote: "Half an hour before we had been lost . . . Now in this extraordinary manner the curtain had been raised; we found that our rule-of-thumb methods had accomplished the most accurate 'land fall.'" Some miles below them, they could see the rocks that marked their first depot and, restacking their miraculously unbroken sledge, they set off at once across the next plateau.

With no warning at all, Scott and Evans broke through a snow bridge and plunged into the void of a hidden crevasse. By good luck, the sledge jammed by the narrowest of margins between the lips of this abyss, and Lashly did his best to hold it there against the swinging motion of the two bodies down below, suspended from their harnesses in the dark, cold air. With infinite care, he maneuvered two skis as wedges to anchor the sledge so that the men below could move without fear of dislodging it.

Scott somehow managed to swing his feet onto a little ledge protruding from one sheer blue wall of the crevasse. Once he could stand up on this icy platform, he helped Taff Evans across to join him. There they stood some twelve feet below the thin ribbon of sky and the outline of their sledge. Soon they would lose all feeling in their hands in that dark deep freeze, so the lighter Scott hauled himself up his harness with his numb and blistered hands, a performance needing considerable strength, to the point where Lashly could help him. Then, together, they hauled Evans to the surface, where the dazed Welshman, according to Scott, exclaimed, "Well, I'm blowed!"

They soon reached their depot, and, two days later, the tireless Scott decided they had sufficient rations to spend a day exploring a series of side valleys branching off the Ferrar Glacier. This excursion on December 7, 1903, resulted in the discovery of a network of narrow rock valleys containing lakes and running streams with no ice or snow in sight but for the ends of retreating glaciers high up the valley's canyon walls. Scott wrote: "It is certainly a valley of the dead: even the great glacier which once pushed through it has withered away." He had discovered one of Antarctica's rare dry valleys, as they are known today.

Observing all the alluvial mud on the valley floor, the practical Lashly commented: "What a splendid place for growing spuds!"

On December 20, the three men topped a rise and saw to their dismay that McMurdo Sound was still blocked with sea ice for many miles to the north of Hut Point. *Discovery*, they feared, might have to spend yet another year in Antarctica. Four days later, on December 24, 1903, they were back onboard to learn that the edge of the sea ice was still twenty miles to the north and, as instructed previously, Armitage had set up a camp out on the floes with a giant ice saw to cut a route through the sea ice in readiness for the anticipated arrival of Colbeck on *Morning*. A report from Armitage soon reached the ship with an optimistic assessment of the cutting operations, so Scott and his men took a few days off to recover and reflect on their expedition's accomplishments.

Scott's first priority was to check the accuracy of his watch, upon which depended the longitudes of all his theodolite sightings and, therefore, the exact route of his recent journey. The resulting mathematics were startling. The three men had for eighty-one days, in all weathers and snow conditions, man-hauled 827 miles, including climbs of 19,800 feet. In 1949, the director of the Scott Polar Research Institute in Cambridge summarized this feat: "Few dog parties, working under plateau conditions, have ever exceeded Scott's best, when on foot when returning from their plateau journey of 1903." Charles Royds noted of Scott: "He takes the cake for being a hard nut. His total is 197 days for two seasons."

On a personal level, the expedition had worked well, too. Scott's affection for Taff Evans and Bill Lashly was evident in his diaries. Scott enjoyed the company of his men, living, eating, and suffering cheek by jowl with them, sharing a sleeping bag month after month, laughing, joking, and singing together. "Few of our camping hours," he wrote, "go by without a laugh from Evans and a song from Lashly." And he added, "no class of men are so eminently adapted by training to cope with the troubles and tricks of sledging life as sailors." With Evans, Lashly, and the third sailor, Crean, as much as with Skelton or Wilson, Scott experienced true comradeship. They also understood and forgave his brief outbursts of impatience and periods of depression. After the western journey, Scott never again sledged without at least one of these three beside him: the Welshman Evans, his fellow West Countryman Bill Lashly, or Irishman Tom Crean.

During Scott's absence, the other journeys had enjoyed mixed results. Repeated visits were made to the Cape Crozier penguins, as Wilson was increasingly convinced that an embryo would confirm that the emperor was the missing link between birds and their possible Jurassic progenitors. But they never managed to bring back an unbroken egg containing stages of developed embryos.

On Michael Barne's expeditions to the southwest in the spring of 1903, his colleague George Mulock surveyed more than two hundred mountains and consolidated the intricate data needed to map three hundred miles of coast to the south and southwest of Hut Point. During this journey, Barne collected key geological specimens that would later help prove Antarctica's continental nature.

Charles Royds and Louis Bernacchi had sledged over the southeast sector of the Great Ice Barrier never visited before and proved that it continued as an entirely level shelf. Their magnetic observations were later to yield key data about the region's magnetic characteristics.

Returning from the Ferrar Glacier before Scott, Skelton had obtained a unique set of half-plate panoramas of the southwestern mountains and Hartley Ferrar had collected fossils that, when finally broken open (in 1928) at the Natural History Museum, provided crucial additional evidence of Antarctica's former position in the supercontinent of Gondwana 300 million years ago.

Although, as with most successful scientific projects, the findings of the *Discovery* expedition would take many years of specialized work to analyze, it was already clear that Scott's scientists had been hugely successful, especially during this second season. In the fields of meteorology, magnetic research, geography, biology, geology, and glaciology, extensive new data had been collated, the first long-distance penetration of the continent achieved, and the high inland plateau discovered. Armitage, in locating and ascending the Ferrar Glacier, had also identified the then-largest-known valley glacier in the world. Scott's *Discovery* achievements far outweigh those of his contemporary scientific leaders Nordenskjöld in 1901 and Drygalski in 1902.

The only enterprise that was making no progress was Albert Armitage's attempts to break through the sea ice with saws and explosives. Scott inspected the work and called it off. They would have to wait for nature to do it for them. Meanwhile, they looked out for the return of the relief ship *Morning*.

When, on January 5, 1904, the ship duly arrived, they were all astonished to spot another bigger vessel, *Terra Nova*, close behind her, and Scott was shattered soon after boarding *Morning* to find that his mail included an envelope containing orders from his employers at the admiralty instructing him that, if *Discovery* could not be retrieved as soon as possible, she was to be abandoned and all her crew must return north with the two relief ships. Scott summoned all *Discovery*'s men to a meeting aboard and, with tears glistening from the emotion of the events, he explained the admiralty's ultimatum after thanking everyone for their years of loyal service to the venture.

Charles Ford noted that the men gave Scott three cheers, which Ford thought were well deserved.

Scott did not need a "rescue." Just one item was in short supply, coal, and that needed only a single ship, *Morning*, to provide. Relief by one ship was useful. Relief by two was unwanted. Even before the two ships' arrival, Scott had begun plans for another winter, since he could plainly see that the ice was more extensive than the previous year when they had remained icebound. He knew they had up to five years of supplies onboard and had conquered the scurvy threat. So why the sudden order to abandon ship? As he opened all his mail, the background to the fiasco became clear.

After raising funds for the 1903 voyage of *Morning*, Markham had to find more money to send her back south in 1904, so he applied to the government for a grant. The treasury, fearing that this expedition was a bottomless pit that might long continue to devour government money, took matters out of the hands of Markham and the societies and agreed to fund one last relief voyage large enough to extract the entire crew of *Discovery*, should that ship still remain icebound. Clements Markham was furious but powerless, since he had no funds. A letter from Markham's expedition secretary, Scott's London colleague, Cyril Longhurst, lamented: "I feel more disgusted about this than I can say . . . you will probably be sick at having the *Terra Nova* down there."

Scott expressed his private thoughts to a friend:

> the utterly unnecessary efforts that were made and the frightful waste of money makes me terribly sore. I had to write a lot in a hurry last year and I wrack my brain to think if there was an excuse, for none of us felt any alarm or even that the situation was serious . . . The second winter was passed in the greatest comfort without a sign of sickness or discontent . . .
>
> [I] suppose anyone would object to being moved in such a position however much they might appreciate the motive!—to crown it all, the ships brought tons of stores which we had no use for at all and of coal, which was the one thing I DID especially ask for, they could only spare a miserable 75 tons when it came to the point . . .

I fear I shall not be very popular at the Admiralty after giving so much trouble, but I do hope they will be prepared to deal handsomely with the other officers and men for if ever people deserved it, they have.

To avoid any risk of *Morning* and *Terra Nova* becoming icebound themselves, all three captains agreed, Scott doubtless reluctantly, that *Discovery* be abandoned if not free by February 25 at the latest. A major attack began at once on the seaward edge of the ice with explosives, saws, and all available manpower. By February 5, the ice edge was a mere six miles from Hut Point and Wilson wrote: "Guncotton explosions were going on all day, the Captain superintending." By the evening of the fourteenth, Scott recorded: "A glorious sight met our view. The ice was breaking up right across the strait, and with a rapidity which we had not thought possible. No sooner was one great floe borne away than a dark streak cut its way into the solid sheet that remained and carved out another, to feed the broad stream of pack which was hurrying away to the north-west."

At dawn on February 16, Scott set off two further explosions and the ship broke free. The crews of all three ships went wild and a party was held onboard to thank Harry McKay of *Terra Nova* and his men from Dundee. William Colbeck of *Morning* wrote: "Scott was terribly excited. He came on board as soon as I got alongside the ice face and could hardly speak. It meant all the difference of complete and comparative success to him and there was not a happier man living than Scott on that night." Before departure, all the men gathered hatless around a cross raised in memory of George Vince and Scott said a prayer for his expedition's only Antarctic victim.

That midnight a gale blew up and the relief ships stood out to sea. *Discovery*'s engines were made ready and the mainsail raised because loose pack ice approaching from the south had begun to look threatening. The wind increased to storm strength and blew *Discovery* onto one of the shallow shoals that had made the bay at Hut Point so attractive two years before by fending off drifting bergs. Now these shoals proved a double-edged sword as *Discovery*'s hull pounded against their rocks and the condenser valves on the ship's bottom went aground. The engines then stopped, to the horror of all onboard. Wilson noted: "Soundings were taken all along the ship and from the end of the jib-boom, which showed that there was no possibility of running *over* the shoal. We must go back to get off." An agonizing period of waiting followed.

"About lunch time," wrote Wilson, "the Captain said to me he was afraid she was done for . . . The seamen too said she was there to stay and when six o'clock came and we sat down to dinner, we were about as glum a party as could well be got together." Some of the crew acted as though nothing had happened and Bernacchi recalled the steward sweeping out the wardroom and polishing the silver. Wilson continued: "Mulock was on watch and when we were half through dinner he came down and surprized us by saying the wind was going down and the ship had begun to swing round and work off the shoal astern . . . The engines were immediately tried . . . they were put hard astern. All hands were called on deck and immediately set to 'sallying' the ship i.e. running from side to side to make her roll . . . for half an hour we rushed backwards and forwards to roll the ship, and the engines plodded on . . ."

At length Scott was able to give Skelton "Full Astern," and *Discovery* slid away from the shoal bank and joined *Terra Nova* out in the open bay. Even then Scott was still eager to trace more coastline, but with a damaged rudder, limited coal, and the winds against them, *Discovery* eventually set course for New Zealand. Only George Vince stayed behind to watch over the empty huts.

⊰᯽⊱ 10 ⊰᯽⊱

A PROMISE BROKEN

DISCOVERY ARRIVED BACK AT Spithead on September 10, 1904, to a warm welcome by the nation. In the two years and three months of their absence, the Boer War had ended, removing from the national consciousness, at least for a while, a sense of diminishing greatness. What had looked at the time of *Discovery*'s departure in 1901 like an inevitable defeat by the puny yet frustratingly invincible Boers had by 1904 ended up as an honorable peace. Nevertheless, to help boost national morale, the British media made great play in early 1904 of the daring and Kiplingesque expedition of Major Francis Younghusband to the Forbidden City of Lhasa, in Tibet. With the nation's appetite for derring-do thus whetted, Scott's return in September of that year from unknown Antarctica was timed to perfection from a public relations point of view, not that anyone, even Clements Markham, had planned it that way.

At thirty-six years of age, Scott became a national hero. One of the first to greet *Discovery*'s return was Ernest Shackleton, who, since his own return a year before, had done his utmost to fight in Scott's corner against hos-

tile elements in the admiralty. Knowing that Scott would not need or welcome "rescue," he had turned down an offer to command *Terra Nova*. Had
he felt bitter personally toward Scott for sending him back home halfway
through the expedition, he would undoubtedly have seized this chance to
score over him. He left Scott a note:

> *My dear Captain Scott,*
>
> *Just a line to welcome you safely back again after your long
> anxious time . . . I am so glad that the whole show has been such
> a complete success, and that you will now for a time be able to
> enjoy a rest from your work. As you no doubt know, I am
> married and settled down as Secretary to the Royal Scottish Geo-
> graphical Society (RSGS). The pay is only £200 [£9,400] a year,
> but it is better than going to sea . . . I had thought of trying to go
> on another expedition sometime but have given up the idea now
> as there seems to be no money about, and besides I am settled so I
> now have to make money.*

Shackleton later joined Scott and Markham for "a very jolly evening."
The RSGS voted that Scott be awarded their most prestigious medal. The
king invited him to stay at Balmoral, and previously hostile elements at the
admiralty were soon converted, at least superficially, and lauded the success
of the expedition.

Scott praised his officers and men loud and long in a series of lectures
that he gave countrywide to enthusiastic audiences. Shackleton attended
many of the celebratory events and clearly had no ax to grind with Scott. Armitage was much involved with the opening of *Discovery* as an exhibition
for the general public after she returned to London and, at the inaugural
dinner, he toasted Scott as a companion and leader for whom all the *Discovery* men "felt they could do anything at any sacrifice."

Late that year, a reporter from the *Daily Mail*, present at a lecture given
by Scott to an audience of seven thousand in the Royal Albert Hall, suggested in an article that Scott had accused Shackleton of malingering. Scott
indignantly wrote back to the editor:

The inference is that after Mr. Shackleton broke down on our southern sledge journey he had to be carried on the sledge for 150 miles. The facts were that though Mr. Shackleton was extremely ill, and caused us great anxiety, he displayed the [most] extraordinary pluck and endurance, and managed to struggle on beside the sledge without adding his weight to our burden.

The struggle over those wearisome miles was bad enough for Dr. Wilson and myself, but it was infinitely worse for a sick man who under ordinary conditions would have been sent straight to bed.

I assume you will see the reason why in remembering the courage and spirit shown by Mr. Shackleton, I am anxious to correct the statement made in the report.

Scott could rebut the *Daily Mail*'s allegations, unlike Armitage's, which were made public only after his death.

Granted admiralty leave for nine months, Scott now concentrated on writing his book about the *Discovery* years. He was as unsure of his ability as are most first-time authors. Nevertheless, he finished the task by the summer of 1905 and in October of that year, his two-volume *The Voyage of the "Discovery,"* containing an impressive array of Wilson's drawings and Skelton's photographs, was published to glowing reviews. Today a single original Wilson drawing can sell for £6,000, but at the time, when Scott offered Wilson £100 (£4,700) for all his work, Wilson refused to accept a fee. Scott paid him anyway.

Scott's evocative book may well have served to kindle existing plans by three of his *Discovery* expedition colleagues to launch their own Antarctic ventures. Michael Barne, Teddy Evans (one of *Morning*'s officers), and Ernest Shackleton were all keen to return to the south. The magical lure of the polar wastes, known to the Norwegians as *polarhüller,* will draw an explorer back again and again to the extreme latitudes. An additional factor urging Shackleton to seek polar glory was his personal pride. He would show the world at large, and his *Discovery* colleagues in particular, that he was an invalid no longer.

Once Scott escaped from his self-imposed book-writing seclusion, he began to accept some of the many social invitations with which, as a well-known and colorful figure, he was now showered. He became friends with literati like James Barrie, the Scottish playwright of *Peter Pan* fame, and the artist Aubrey Beardsley, whose sister Mabel gave a lunch party at which Scott noticed an attractive sculptor named Kathleen Bruce. He followed her away from the party at a discreet distance but did not pluck up enough courage to ask her out. A year later, at another Beardsley party, they finally became acquainted and Scott began to court her with determination, entranced by her forthright manner.

Kathleen, thirteen years younger than Scott, was as wild and eccentric as he was formal and reserved. She was, like him, of Scottish extraction, her father a Wiltshire vicar descended from Robert the Bruce. She had until recently lived in *rive gauche* Paris, where she had studied sculpture under Rodin and become friends with the wild-child Isadora Duncan and other such bohemians. She mingled with equal ease among the upper classes and the Paris poor whom she painted, caring little what others thought of her. She shrugged off numerous would-be lovers. Not unusual for the period, she was a determined virgin and nursed a dream that the man to whom she would give herself would father her child and must therefore be ideal.

Quite why she eventually returned first Scott's interest and much later his love is not really clear, even from her diary. What is known is that they made each other happy and were essentially natural together. Kathleen admitted to being an intellectual snob, yet she never behaved in a socially superior manner. She had never experienced poverty and therefore money meant as little to her as it was important to Scott, who had spent much of his life learning to penny-pinch. He was to write to her some months after his eventual proposal: "I want to marry you very badly but it is absurd to pretend I can do so without facing great difficulty . . . My mother is 67, only a strand of life remains. She has had a hard life in many respects. I set myself to make her last years free from anxiety."

Scott did not see how they could afford to marry, since half of his modest income went to his mother. He sent Kathleen a plan he had worked out as though deciding on the feasibility of an expedition, a plan for a marriage budget—£25 laundry, £15 coal, £5 stationery, papers, etc., £45 for a maid, 10 shillings per head, per week, for food and drink: total £329 (£15,450) per year. Worries over financial viability and their character differences plagued Scott but did not prevent their eventual agreement on a wedding date and Scott's leasing a house in Buckingham Palace Road, his favorite part of London and where the Victoria Coach Terminal now stands.

Not many of Scott's expedition colleagues, even Wilson, found Kathleen easygoing: She could be frightening, confrontational, and blunt. Her diary included her thoughts on government grandee Lord Birkenhead: "I suppose the world does not hold a more repugnant individual . . . He should die. I have always known he is a drunkard and libertine, but I did not know he had such an evil tongue." Of Winston Churchill she commented more mildly: "He may be a genius but he disguises it very well."

During Scott's years of courtship and engagement, he flirted very little with ideas of further polar expedition. His *Discovery* book had sparked Michael Barne into asking Shackleton to join him to "go South." The two met up with Clements Markham to discuss their joint plans in October 1905, only a month after the publication of Scott's book, but soon afterward they were rebuffed by the Royal Geographical Society and dropped the project.

The following September 1906, Scott must himself have started to nurse polar dreams, for he began to discuss another expedition with Markham and then asked Barne if he would join as first lieutenant should he go ahead. Strangely enough, this invitation crossed in the post with a letter Barne had just sent Scott urging him to explore again. This correspondence was kept completely confidential by the three men, so everyone, including Shackleton, remained ignorant of Scott's still-nebulous plans until February 18 of the following year. Scott and Barne had a clear vision: The best way to travel would not be man-haul or dogs but by inventing a motor car capable of snow travel. Scott promptly put Barne in charge of looking into the viability of such a machine because he, Scott, had to spend a year back at sea if he was to stay in the new deadly serious navy of Admiral Jacky Fisher, a navy where promotion to the upper echelons would go to serious naval executives, not to explorers. By Christmas 1906, Scott had broached his still vague idea of a new Antarctic venture to another *Discovery* man, the surveyor George Mulock, who agreed to join. Scott had also taken the big step of confidentially alerting the president of the RGS, Sir George Goldie, and the secretary, Dr. John Keltie, as to his plans to go south again.

All this time, Scott believed he had a clear field in which to operate. The great contemporary polar pundits, such as Admiral Peary and Dr. Frederick Cook of the United States, and the latter's good friend the Norwegian Roald Amundsen, were all firmly focused on the North Pole, and Shackleton, at the time of Scott's 1904 return to Britain, had written, clearly telling Scott that he was not contemplating further exploration anywhere. So Scott was not in a hurry to publicize his own still-uncertain aims when, in early 1907, he went back to sea to follow his naval career. Keltie, Barne, and Mulock told nobody of Scott's plans.

Shackleton, equally unaware that his old leader, Scott, was planning a further expedition, had given up his job with the RSGS and unsuccessfully tried a career as a politician. He kept his ear at all times to the RGS grapevine and heard a rumor in late January 1907 that a South Pole attempt by a Belgium-based Pole, Henryk Arctowski, using snow machines, was under discussion and intending to follow the route from McMurdo Sound pioneered by Scott's southern journey. Shackleton approached his then employer, a rich Clydeside industrialist named William Beardmore, who agreed to sponsor him. He then rushed to the RGS to tell the secretary, John Keltie, of his intention to go south. Keltie did not tell Shackleton about Scott's plans, as they were confidential, and, as a result, Shackleton believed the field was clear for him to announce his plans in public. That same day, February 11, 1907, at the RGS, Shackleton bumped into Arctowski, who informed him of his intention to announce his South Pole plan that very night at an RGS dinner. Shackleton reacted with lightning speed. He announced his own plans at the dinner minutes before Arctowski could do likewise and, after dinner, contacted *The Times* to describe his project as a national venture to beat off a foreign rival.

This sensational Shackleton news reached Scott at sea on his ship, HMS *Albemarle,* a week later at a very bad time, when, due to a serious collision in the Atlantic, Scott felt his whole career to be suddenly in jeopardy. On New Year's Day 1907, Scott had proudly taken command of the battleship *Albemarle* and six weeks later, just before Shackleton's press release, was practicing a dangerous and highly skilled line of battle tactics in the Atlantic, west of Portugal, on a pitch-dark night. Steaming at high speed, eight multiton steel warships sped through the darkness without lights in a staggered line with only 220 yards between each ship. Scott left the bridge to take a signal message to the admiral, in his cabin, and suddenly felt the engines stop, then go astern. Then came the horrific impact as *Albemarle*'s bows struck another ship.

News of the accident, linked with Scott's name, was soon front-page news and Scott wrote to his mother explaining the likelihood of an official inquiry. This subsequently cleared him of all blame, but prior to that outcome, he was under severe stress, fearing court-martial and disgrace. It was in the midst of this that Scott first heard of Shackleton's polar intentions. On February 18, 1907, Scott wrote:

> *My Dear Shackleton,*
>
> *I see by the Times of Feb. 12th that you are organising an expedition to go on our old tracks; and this is the first I have heard of it. The situation is awkward for me as I have already announced my intention to try again in the old place, and have been in treaty concerning the matter. As a matter of fact I have always intended to try again but as I am dependent on the Navy I was forced to reinstate myself and get some experience before I again asked for leave, meanwhile I thought it best to keep my plans dark—but I have already commenced fresh preparations and Michael Barne is in London seeing to things in preparation for August when I shall be free to begin work myself. You see therefore that your announcement cuts right across my plans and to an extent which it would not have done two months ago when I first intimated them to the Geographical Society and others.*
>
> *I needn't tell you that I don't wish to hurt you and your plans but in one way I feel I have a sort of right to my own field of work in the same way as Peary claimed Smith's Sound and many African travellers their particular locality. I am sure you will agree with me in this and I am equally sure that only your entire*

ignorance of my plan could have made you settle on the Discovery *route without a word to me . . . I was going to delay my attempt [until] later as I don't want to take anything that is not well tested.*

He added as a postscript: "I feel sure with a little discussion we can work in accord rather than in opposition. I don't believe the foreigners will do anything much. The whole area is ours to attack."

In a second long letter that day, Scott explained to Shackleton his deeper feelings, intentions, and worries:

I don't want to be selfish at anyone's expense and least of all at that of one of my own people, but still I think anyone who has had to do with exploration will regard this region primarily as mine . . . The question now is what you intend to do? . . . If you go to McMurdo Sound you go to winter quarters which are clearly mine, and I must either abandon my plans or go elsewhere . . . I do not like to remind you that it was I who took you to the South or of the loyalty with which we all stuck to one another . . .

I think at present that there are quite a number of ways in which a compromise could be arrived at . . . My dear fellow it would be a thousand pities to rush this effort that should crown the Discovery *work . . . I am writing these main facts to Wilson— he is a person I think who commands our respect and who could not be otherwise than straight. I shall ask his advice and ask him to communicate with you . . .*

Well goodbye for the present, the subject is very close to my heart so please write openly and freely.

Shackleton's response took fifteen days to reach Scott, for he sent it via Wilson to forward if he approved the contents. Wilson became the middle-man between his two friends and wrote back to Shackleton: "I think you ought to offer to retire from McMurdo Sound as a base . . . I do wholly agree with the right lying with Scott to use that base before anyone else." Letters shot backward and forward and a compromise approved by all parties appeared to be on the horizon. Shackleton went ahead with the detailed preparations and recruitment for his journey while assuring Scott that he had known nothing of his plans and, now that he did, he would of course conduct his journey away from Scott's work area of McMurdo Sound. He then wrote, on March 8, to Clements Markham confirming this:

> *I had always a wish to go to our old quarters though it is only a short time ago since I saw a real chance. How even now things may be altered as I have heard from Captain Scott that he intends to go again . . . I had not the most remote idea that he ever intended to go again: indeed he told us down South that he could not again go because of the Navy . . . He has written me on the subject and so he really means to go. I have advised him that of course I will give up the McMurdo Sound Base . . .*
>
> *I hope Scott will get a good fund and be able to do a really good show. I expect he really would like to do the Pole and I myself have not hidden that idea of mine; yet think that in doing that one can make sense of solving the secret of the Barrier.*

On March 16, Scott sent Shackleton a friendly letter thanking him for agreeing to alter his plans in a very honorable manner and for "the sacrifice you are making." Despite the mutually friendly words, from about this time the relationship between Scott and Shackleton slowly but surely altered. Although they never lost their basic mutual respect for one another, they began to treat each other as rivals for the same great goal. As such, they were open to mutual misunderstanding and the mischievous machinations of the press.

The two men met on May 17 and Shackleton summarized their agreement. "To make everything clear as regards our arrangements and plans for the two expeditions to the Ross Quadrant of the Antarctic, I am following your suggestion and writing it down . . . I am leaving the McMurdo Sound base to you, and will land either at the place known as Barrier Inlet or at King Edward VII Land . . . I shall not touch the coast of Victoria Land at all. If I find it impracticable to land at King Edward VII Land or at Barrier Inlet or further to the N.E., I may possibly [try to land elsewhere]. I think this outlines my plan, which I shall rigidly adhere to."

Three days after Shackleton sent this letter off, the U.S. explorer Dr. Frederick Cook announced his own plan to reach the South Pole from Ross Island. Shackleton accelerated his preparations, purchased *Nimrod*, a Dundee sealer, and in July 1907 set sail for the Ross Sea with a crew that included Frank Wild and Ernest Joyce from *Discovery*. None of *Discovery*'s officers were available to join *Nimrod* and Wilson had to turn down Shackleton's offer because of existing commitments.

While negotiations proceeded and Shackleton was bringing forward his plans, Scott stayed another seven months as the *Albemarle*'s skipper before being relieved by Captain John Jellicoe, later admiral of the Fleet, 1st Earl Jellicoe. From *Albemarle* Scott moved on to command HMS *Bulwark*, flagship of the Nore Division, part of the Home Fleet, and had to rely on Michael Barne, existing on half pay from the navy, to continue development work on a prototype motorized sledge, the key to south polar success, as Scott saw it. He was not alone in this, for France's great explorer, Dr. Jean Charcot, like Michael Barne, was having a snow machine manufactured by De Dion Bouton, near Paris. These two models, plus a third developed in Finchley that used the novel idea of a continuous looped track instead of wheels, all proved highly unreliable during trials, but Scott decided to be patient in the hope the engineers would make a breakthrough sooner rather than later. The Pole would not wait forever, even if Shackleton failed.

In January 1908, Shackleton's little sealer *Nimrod* reached the eastern end of the Great Ice Barrier, which, well away from Scott's McMurdo Sound preserves, was where he had promised Scott he would make his base. Unfortunately, Shackleton fell out in a big way with *Nimrod*'s skipper, Captain Rupert England, a cautious Yorkshireman who considered Shackleton rash and likely to endanger *Nimrod* by entering inlets that he considered to be lethal traps. The new land, confirmed at the eastern limit of the barrier by Scott in 1901 and christened by him King Edward VII Land, appeared to be devoid of any suitable landing spot, so *Nimrod* turned west and nosed along the edge of the barrier searching for an inlet, such as the bay where Scott and Shackleton had once made their balloon ascents.

Since then, huge chunks of the barrier's frontage had calved away, removing many inlets that had existed at the time of *Discovery*'s visit and during those of Ross's *Erebus* and *Terror* and Borchgrevink's *Southern Cross*.

Two of these inlets, known as Borchgrevink's Bight and Barrier Inlet, had been replaced by a single much larger bay, which the *Nimrod* men called the Bay of Whales. Shackleton deemed it to be folly to establish himself in it because there was no guarantee that further calving would not send any base camp placed there out to sea on a giant new berg. He began to feel he had little option but to establish his base in the only known available bay, McMurdo Sound, precisely where he had promised Scott he would not winter.

Nimrod's chief surgeon, Dr. Eric Marshall, ever ready to criticize Shackleton, reckoned that the Bay of Whales would have been viable and noted that, if indeed Shackleton was aiming to land at McMurdo, "he hasn't got the guts of a louse, in spite of what he may say to the world on his return." Soon afterward *Nimrod* narrowly escaped being crushed between bergs during a final desperate attempt to locate an alternative landing spot to McMurdo. Finally accepting the inevitable need to break his written agreement with Scott or abandon the expedition, Shackleton headed for McMurdo Sound with a heavy heart. He wrote to his wife, Emily: "I have been through a sort of Hell . . . I have had to break my word to Scott [due to] the overwhelming forces of Nature."

When, thousands of miles away, frustrated that he could not even launch his own project until his motorized sledge was much improved, Scott heard that Shackleton had disregarded their agreement, he kept his annoyance private; he never indulged in any recriminations with Shackleton or spoke to anyone in public, confining his expressions of anger to correspondence with his family.

Shackleton, whose introduction to Antarctica had been as Scott's right-hand man, was now all set to head for the South Pole using Scott's own unofficially patented route. At that time, nearly a century ago, there was still a generally accepted code of manners in which a person's promise was not lightly broken. When Shackleton eventually returned to England, his old friend and polar comrade Edward Wilson made it clear that he saw his broken promise as inexcusable and never spoke to Shackleton again.

Jean Charcot, the Frenchman also experimenting with motorized transport, stated: "There can be no doubt that the best way to the Pole is by way of the Great Ice Barrier, but this we regard as belonging to the English explorers, and I do not propose to trespass on other people's grounds."

Amundsen, Scott's later rival, clearly agreed with this, for he wrote to Nansen: "it is my intention not to dog the Englishmen's footsteps. They have naturally the first right. We must make do with what they discard."

There are those in polar circles today who support Eric Marshall's view and suspect that Shackleton may have planned all along to base himself in McMurdo Sound and ignore his private agreement with Scott. I do not subscribe to this theory, and recent research by Robert Headland, archivist of the Scott Polar Research Institute, would support my belief. He pointed to a philatelic project set up by Shackleton prior to the *Nimrod*'s arrival in Antarctica, an overprint of one-penny New Zealand stamps with the words "King Edward VII Land." In New Zealand, Shackleton was sworn in by the prime minister as official postmaster and officially opened a branch of the New Zealand Post Office when *Nimrod* was off the Bay of Whales. It is very unlikely that Shackleton would have gone to such trouble if he was never intending to land at or near King Edward VII Land. My personal belief is that Shackleton was basically honest but that circumstances forced his McMurdo landing, much to his distress.

Shackleton was undoubtedly under duress during *Nimrod*'s time in McMurdo Sound. A wide expanse of ice barred any access to Hut Point, attempts to land and use a motor car with wheels slightly modified for ice failed dismally, and an unloading accident resulted in Dr. Marshall having to operate on and remove an eye from one of the crew. Eventually Shackleton had everything successfully unloaded at a bay some ten miles north of Cape Evans, next to Cape Royds, but not before he had fallen out with Captain England, with tension spreading through the rest of the ship's company. At one point, off Cape Royds, Shackleton seized the speaking tube from Captain England and shouted, "Full ahead," to the engine room, whereupon the skipper seized it back and ordered, "Full speed astern."

While Shackleton spent the winter of 1908 at Cape Royds, Scott continued in his naval career, commanding *Bulwark*, encouraged Michael Barne's polar preparations, made ready for marriage, and perused the emerging reviews of the *Discovery* scientific results. It was a hectic time. "I am very, very busy," he wrote, "from 6.30 when I rise to 11.30 when I seek my bed. You can imagine how much is to be done—new ship, new officers, new men."

Some three years after Scott's *Discovery* scientists first handed their results to the research bodies who would analyze and use them, reviews of their work started to emerge. Bernacchi later observed that no funds were made available to enable the *Discovery* scientists to analyze and publish their results themselves so "this comprehensive and important work had to be undertaken chiefly by scientists in Government departments." The work of both Bernacchi, the physicist, and Royds, the painstaking trainee meteorologist, was criticized. Scott studied the reports and discovered that the Meteorological Office's criticisms were themselves heavily flawed. They had, for instance, wrongly transposed expedition data, such as daily camp locations, and even applied magnetic variation backward in their interpretation of the sledge parties' wind-direction reports. Scott and his scientists were rightly incensed and Scott asked the Royal Society for an official inquiry. This was refused, as it might prove embarrassing to the scientific establishment. Scott's erstwhile opponent in the admiralty, Admiral Mostyn Field, who had strongly opposed his leadership appointment in 1901, was now the hydrographer of the navy and equally opposed to an inquiry. He did, however, try to placate Scott by focusing all the blame on the scientists and not the leader. This incensed Scott still further but he was powerless to force a fair and timely reappraisal of the report. When the reappraisal finally came, exonerating the *Discovery* scientists completely, it was not published until 1913, so Scott was never to see it.

Much of the analysis of *Discovery*'s work took decades to complete and it wasn't until the 1960s, when that analysis was finally completed, that its overall success, set against any other polar expedition of the early twentieth century, became self-evident. And, from a southerly penetration viewpoint, four other national expeditions (those of Drygalski, Bruce, Nordenskjöld, and Charcot) that went south at the dawn of the century hardly gained even a toehold on the continent.

The *Discovery* men made the first Antarctic flight (in a balloon) and took the first aerial photographs. Thomas Hodgson remains the pioneer of Antarctic marine biology and thirty-two marine specialists wrote up his phenomenal results in five volumes. Many of his discoveries were of hitherto-unknown marine species. Edward Wilson discovered new bird species, and conducted original studies into their polar lives and behavior, including, for the first time, that of the breeding colonies of the emperor penguin. His superb watercolor panoramas are now collectors' items all over the world. Charles Royds and his helpers maintained continuous meteorological records for two years and identified the phenomenon of the Antarctic coreless winter, when temperatures stay more or less the same throughout that fearful season, a feature of great significance to meteorologists worldwide. Scott, Evans, and Lashly visited the unique dry valleys of Victoria Land during just one of twenty-eight sledging journeys carried out under the severest of conditions. Louis Bernacchi kept magnetic records, often synchronized with those of Drygalski's German team, which, when added to the observations of Armitage and Mulock, located the precise position of the south magnetic pole as accurately as if they had reached it. Their results, together with those of Drygalski, enabled the construction of a magnetic map of the Southern Hemisphere, which had been the Anglo-German aim and which proved key to the navigation of the southern trade routes until the evolution of satellite navigation.

King Edward VII Land was discovered, the coast of which proved to be the eastern limit of the Great Ice Barrier. This was the first Antarctic discovery of the twentieth century. The nature of the Great Ice Barrier was correctly defined as a floating entity, a vast mobile "shelf" hinged to the mainland. An immense new range, the Transantarctic Mountains, was glimpsed and charted for 320 miles, up to 83° south. The southern journey did not reach the Pole but pioneered a route toward it as far as 82°11' south. Hartley Ferrar, the pioneer of Antarctic geology, collected a wide range of rock samples, including a leaf fossil that defined Antarctica's position in the 300-million-year-old Gondwana supercontinent with a once-tropical climate. His samples also confirmed the findings of other *Discovery* scientists, that Antarctica must be a continent rather than merely a collection of islands.

Discovery's scientific program was uniquely successful despite the disputes among its London-based organizers, the extremes of its work environment, and the inexperience of some of those involved with the research, including Scott, the deeply involved director of the program.

In May 1908, Scott wrote to Kathleen telling her proudly that he was the most junior captain in command of a battleship at an annual pay packet of

£832 (£39,000 today). On September 2, 1908, Scott married his Kathleen in the Chapel Royal at Hampton Court during a thunderstorm and in the presence of a 150-strong congregation, including Kathleen's former art teacher, Rodin, from Paris. After a honeymoon in France, which Kathleen described as having passed as "confusedly and insecurely as most honeymoons," she settled into their terraced house in Victoria while Scott went back to his ship *Bulwark*. Scott needed to watch his back, like all navy officers at the time, because Admiral Sir John Fisher, first sea lord, was ruthlessly scrapping any warships and officers he considered obsolete. Scott was proud of his 750-man crew's performance, reporting to Kathleen: "we grow to better understanding to a stronger mutual confidence and so to ordered efficiency. We shall be a man-of-war soon."

Scott's expedition work at this stage crept along slowly, for he knew that the South Pole prize might soon be Shackleton's. Michael Barne called often at *Bulwark* to see how plans were progressing and Scott wrote: "he was full of enthusiasm for the cause but, alas! poor chap, there was little to tell him." Times of doubt and uncertainty had always sparked Scott's "black dog," the phrase his sisters used to describe his dark mood of self-loathing and doubt, quite possibly a medical condition of melancholic depression, which nowadays might be alleviated with daily pills. Scott was famous and successful, his naval career was looking good, and he had secured the woman he loved. So why did he brood and rate himself so low? He wrote to Kathleen: "I'm obstinate, despondent, pigheaded, dejected . . . You're so exalted somehow, I can't reach up."

Good news from the Finchley motorized-sledge engineers would have helped, but there was none. Scott's very best man-haul effort on the *Discovery* expedition had ended less than halfway to the Pole so he attached great importance to the motorized sledge. Shackleton, he knew, had taken a "polarized" motor car and eight Manchurian ponies. Perhaps these would prove the answer? Neither Scott nor Shackleton wanted a repetition of their harrowing dog experience on the southern journey.

Husband and wife rarely saw each other through the first six months of married life owing to Scott's work at sea. As was fashionable at the time, a fortune-teller visited the couple when Scott was on weekend leave and commented on his "laziness, untidiness, touchiness and tendency to gloom."

Kathleen readily agreed with this summary. In January 1909, however, she put her man in a very good mood by announcing that she was pregnant. He temporarily forgot his command status when he heard the news and rolled one of his subordinate officers around on the deck in his happiness and pride.

Two months later, things took a major turn for the better when the commander-in-chief of the Home Fleet, appointed second sea lord, decided he would need a naval assistant at the admiralty. He asked for Scott, who immediately accepted. He could now live at home and spend his spare time on his polar plans. On March 26, 1909, the very day Scott took up his new post, he was walking past a railway station with his old *Discovery* colleague Tom Crean when he saw on a hoarding the news of Shackleton's narrow failure to make the Pole. "I think," he said to Crean, "we'd better have a shot next." He sent a telegram off at once to Shackleton in New Zealand: "Unqualified congratulations on magnificent success."

Because Scott had never made public his correspondence with Shackleton about the use of Hut Point, nor about Shackleton's breaking of their private agreement, nobody but a few of the polar cognoscenti and Scott's friends and family knew of the matter, nor, following Shackleton's triumphant return to Britain that June, did the two men discuss it further. They had never been openly unfriendly. Latterly they may well have nursed the mutually hostile thoughts that come naturally to ambitious individuals chasing the same goal; however, there is no evidence that they were anything but friendly and polite to one another, and managed to compromise whenever their respective aims were likely to clash.

When, on June 14, 1909, Shackleton reached London, a great, cheering throng greeted him getting off the train at Charing Cross. Scott's *Discovery* return five years before had been a muted affair by comparison with the public acclaim for Shackleton's triumph; the public mood was changing. The country, far more aware now of the German menace, was accordingly eager for any boosting of self-esteem. Shackleton's epic journey fit the bill perfectly and reached a much wider audience than had Scott's exploits, thanks to the increased printing and distribution capabilities of the new popular press. Shackleton had even made a movie film of his polar experiences.

At first Scott could not make up his mind whether or not it would be appropriate for him to attend Shackleton's triumphant return. Shackleton's Royal Geographical Society mentor, Dr. Hugh Mill, briefly with *Discovery*, encouraged Scott and they went off together. At Charing Cross, they fought their way through the cheering crowds and Scott was able to grasp Shackleton's hand and shout "Bravo!" in his ear. Then Shackleton, with his wife and children, ignoring the new preponderance of motorized taxis, climbed into an open carriage that made its way past the cheering crowds that lined their route along the Strand and through Trafalgar Square. Hugh Robert Mill, later Shackleton's official biographer, wrote: "I never saw anyone enjoy success with such gusto." But he added, Shackleton "cared nothing for science nor for the Antarctic, and would just as soon have sought buried treasure on the Spanish Main."

Scott went away unrecognized, acknowledging that this was Shackleton's hour and, over the next few weeks, went out of his way to ensure that Shackleton's great feat was fully recognized in all the right places. At the official welcoming dinner, held at the Savage Club, Scott chaired the event and spoke warmly of Shackleton's great achievement. He also announced his own intention to ensure that foreign explorers did not take advantage of the path to the Pole opened by the two of them. "In the immediate future," he said, "and before other countries can step in to take the credit of the results of these great works of Mr. Shackleton, this country should come to the fore and organize another expedition." He was clearly referring to himself.

Shackleton's return and the resulting renewal of public interest in the South Pole spurred on Scott's own plans. First he was keen to learn any lessons he could from Shackleton's experiences. Shackleton's *Nimrod* had been forced by the sea ice to drop the expedition at Cape Royds, twenty-three miles farther north than Hut Point from the Barrier and, therefore, from the Pole. Winter in their hut had been uneventful and more comfortable than had been the cold confines of *Discovery*. Five of the group, none of them experienced climbers, had managed the first ascent of the 12,450-foot-high Mount Erebus. The prototype polarized car proved useless, except on smooth ice floes, so Shackleton concentrated on man-haul and ponies.

Shackleton split his men into three groups. One, including Mawson, made an epic journey to claim the south magnetic pole successfully for the empire. Another group, led by Raymond Priestley, carried out geological exploration work in the western mountains.

Shackleton's main journey was led by him and had but a single aim, to bag the South Pole. His companions were Frank Wild from the *Discovery* crew, a rough-mannered naval lieutenant named Jameson Boyd Adams, and the expedition's surgeon, Eric Marshall, a rugby-playing, public school Cambridge graduate who was powerfully built and arrogant.

Much is made of the fact that Shackleton never compartmentalized his winter quarters on "officers and men" lines as had Scott, but even the quickest glance at the mainly middle-class and civilian bunch of characters Shackleton had selected soon reveals why he could not have done so even if he had wanted to. Shackleton alone had his own room. The others divided the hut into compartments by using sheets. The hierarchical divide was between the leader and the others, rather than between the different classes of expedition members.

Toward the end of the winter of 1908, Shackleton took a small team away to test the polar car and the ever-critical Marshall noted: "A general feeling of relief at absence of Shackleton freely experienced by many, All in excellent spirits and no ill will. Easy to see where cause of all trouble lies." Marshall does not specify the nature of the "trouble" and Shackleton apparently failed to notice Marshall's hostility, since Shackleton selected him to go south as doctor and chief navigator.

The dogs he had brought south were left at base when the group set out for the Pole on the last day of October 1908. The four ponies that had survived the winter coped infinitely better than the dogs Shackleton had trained and led on Scott's 1903 southern journey. The last pony died in a crevasse 1,700 feet up the glacier. As was later confirmed, Shackleton suffered all his adult life from intermittent lung and heart troubles, but was otherwise fit and strong as an ox. He devised a ration based on biscuits and pemmican weighing twenty-four ounces per man-day, almost the same as the *Discovery* allowance. As an example of his vitality, he led his group over the first twenty-three miles of sea ice to the barrier, slept for four hours, then completed the next thirty-nine miles in twenty-four hours. At no stage of his Pole attempt did he or his men wear skis, nor did his ponies have snow shoes. Whereas on the 1903 southern journey the inadequacy of their dogs had led Scott, Shackleton, and Wilson to relay their loads, thereby tripling the mileage to be covered, Shackleton in 1909, not having to relay thanks to his ponies, did the same distance over the ice shelf in half the time.

When they reached that point on their chosen route over the barrier where mountains barred their way south, Shackleton spotted the mouth of a majestic glacier that appeared like a highway to the south. Without hesitation he found and negotiated an access route over the crevasses, which barred the way between the barrier and this glacier. Then, by way of a convenient pass he called the Gateway, he began a nine-thousand-foot climb up this crevasse-ridden 120-mile-long ice ramp. He named it the Beardmore Glacier after his sponsor.

The diary of Shackleton's man Marshall, unlike those of Scott's 1904 colleagues, was filled with hostility and tension, but the group eventually reached the upper plateau and, amazingly, persevered to within only ninety-seven nautical miles of the Pole before turning back. Their farthest south beat that of Scott's 1902 record by 366 miles. The return journey was a classic of narrow escapes and hunger, but they made it back by the skin of their teeth thanks to Shackleton's decision to turn back when he did. He later described this moment of truth to his wife with the now famous phrase: "I thought you would like a living donkey better than a dead lion."

The hard facts behind his turn-back decision were very simple. He and his men knew that one more day's march would end in their deaths by starvation. They knew that if they were tempted to continue, they would die. So the decision was surely that which any leader capable of working out basic mathematics and not palpably insane would have made in the circumstances. Three years later, when Scott traveled to the Pole, he never had to face such a decision because he reached the Pole before his rations dropped to such a turn-around-or-you-die point. On their respective return journeys, both Shackleton and Scott often reached their depots with a mere half-day's food and fuel left. Neither group suffered from starvation merely because they failed to turn around earlier than they did. Yet Scott critics often suggest otherwise.

Shackleton and his men made a journey of 1,613 nautical miles, more than half over virgin terrain, in just over four months. They nearly made the

Pole by man-hauling, with only four ponies, no skis, and no dogs. This was a lesson, the key lesson surely, for Scott to observe in his own planning.

The *Nimrod* expedition was rightly acclaimed at home and abroad for its boldness, the success of its scientists, and, above all, the ascent of the Beardmore Glacier. Shackleton received medals, awards, and praise from many countries. In 1909, he was knighted by the monarch for, unlike Scott, he had not upset the treasury or the admiralty or gained enemies in high places. His expedition's debt was dealt with by a government grant of £20,000 (£940,000), and his fame, at least for a while, eclipsed that of his former leader Robert Scott.

Roald Amundsen wrote to the RGS: "The English nation has by the deeds of Shackleton won a victory in Antarctic exploration, which can never be surpassed. What Nansen is in the North, so is Shackleton in the South." Amundsen could not fail to notice, of course, the inviting highway to the Pole opened up by the *Discovery* and *Nimrod* expeditions. Nor could certain other foreign aspirants, any one of whom could steal a march on Scott, who had no backing this time, no Clements Markham, no funds, and no admiralty acceptance.

Unconfirmed rumors of a Japanese Antarctic expedition to be led by one Lieutenant Nobu Shirase were rife, but nobody took the Japanese very seriously. The Belgians, with memories of *Belgica*, were muttering darkly of south polar intentions, but they, like the Japanese, were largely ignored. Norwegians would have been a different matter, for they were the undisputed world masters of snow and ice travel, but their major protagonist, Roald Amundsen, was known to be focused on the North Pole.

Shackleton was soon in the news again, announcing Antarctic plans for 1911, but he wrote to Scott assuring him that the Pole and the Great Ice Barrier were not involved, and this time Scott trusted him without asking for any private contract.

What Scott did not know was that the man who might nowadays be described as the Dark Avenger had suddenly begun to plot, in great secrecy and with ruthless efficiency, to beat him to the Pole. The chronology of which explorer was doing what at that time is confusing and has been used by anti-Scott, pro-Amundsen biographers to suggest that, when Amundsen originally decided to be the first to the South Pole, he did not know of Scott's plans. To clarify the picture and show that Amundsen's head must have been buried in sand for him not to have heard of Scott's plans, I have listed key dates.

January 1908	News of Scott's trials of motorized sledges in Lauteret, France, is given in *Le Monde*, Paris.
September 1908	Scott marries. News reports mention his general plans for another Antarctic expedition.
March 1909	Scott sees news that Shackleton has narrowly missed claiming the South Pole.
1st week Sept. 1909	Press rumors of American intention to claim the South Pole emerge at same time as the claims of both Cook and Peary to have reached the North Pole (in 1908 and 1909 respectively). The controversy that followed concentrated public attention worldwide on the South Pole.
September 13, 1909	Scott officially announces his South Pole aim. This is in the Norwegian press by September 18. (Amundsen blocked any attempt by Scott to obtain the best Greenland sledge dogs by ordering a hundred himself and writing to the Danish minister responsible for Greenland's interior affairs, firmly reminding him that he was first in the line if the minister should receive orders for dogs from anyone else.)
September 15, 1909	Peary announces from Newfoundland his intention of claiming the South Pole. By this date the German Filchner had already announced his South Pole aims. (Peary's challenge came to naught.)

Meanwhile, in 1907, Amundsen had stated his aim to prepare for an Arctic scientific voyage. He tried to hide his real aim—to reach the North Pole first—from the likes of Peary, and when, on September 15, 1909, he heard of Peary's claim, he immediately switched his plans from the North

17. Some of the *Terra Nova* crew (not officers or scientists), and the ship's cat, right.

18. Unloading the last of the three caterpillar tractors, shortly before it sank through weak sea ice and was lost forever, January 8, 1911.

20. *Discovery* scientists Griffith Taylor and Charles Wright in an iceberg grotto, January 1911.

19. Captain Scott with skis, October 1911. His loose-fitting clothes, bulky boots, and headwear are very similar to those in which we man-hauled over the Antarctic continent in 1993.

21. The Cape Evans hut in December 1911. The hut remains much the same to this day.

22. Oates in the stables beside the hut, with three of the ten ponies he nursed diligently through the long winter months of 1911. Of the nineteen ponies brought to Antarctica, nine had died during the first year.

23. Lawrence "Titus" Oates and his friend Cecil Meares outside the Cape Evans hut in June 1911, midwinter, when the sun disappeared for twenty-four hours a day. Note that Oates was still using just one ski stick, as did the *Discovery* team six years before.

24. George Simpson (later Director of the UK Meteorological Office) at work in the Cape Evans magnetic hut, January 1912.

25. Herbert Ponting with camera gear at Hut Point in 1910.

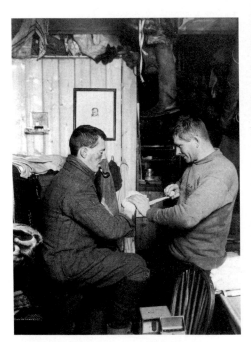

26. Edgar Evans dressing Dr. George Atkinson's frostbitten hand.

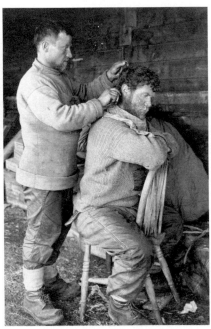

27. Dog driver Anton Omelchenko cutting the hair of Petty Officer Patrick Keohane, a tough and reliable Irish sledger.

28. Apsley Cherry-Garrard, the youngest member of the expedition and trainee zoologist assistant, November 1911.

29. Robert Forde, crew member and sledger, who suffered badly from frostbite, November 1911.

30. Petty Officers Edgar "Taff" Evans and Irishman Thomas Crean, April 1911. The expedition's sledging equipment and clothing was diligently and ingeniously modified by both men.

31. The Canadian Charles Wright, expedition physicist, April 1911.

32–33. Scott's birthday dinner at winter quarters, Cape Evans, June 6, 1911. At the same time, a hundred miles to the east, Amundsen's camp was established on the precarious seaward edge of the Ross Ice Shelf. This base might easily have broken off the mother shelf and floated out to sea, as indeed happened in May 2000.

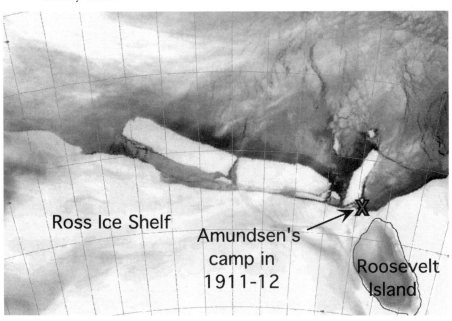

Ross Ice Shelf

Amundsen's
camp in
1911-12

Roosevelt
Island

34. The return of a sledge party to Cape Evans (led by Atkinson), using for a sail a tent floorcloth and a Heath Robinson improvisation of a mast. Wind power was used whenever possible by all the early Antarctic expeditions.

35. Lieutenant Tryggve Gran, the expedition's Norwegian ski trainer. Contrary to the myth created by some of Scott's critics, Gran trained a number of the expedition sledgers to ski cross-country very adequately and, in Scott's case, "as well as the average Norwegian," October 1911.

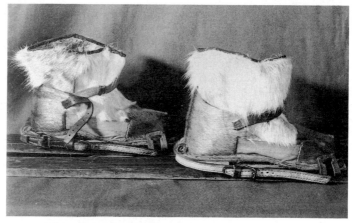

36. Scott's modification for attaching *finnesko* to skis. The finished British version was considerably more effective than the Norwegian boots, which were more prone to giving their wearers frostbitten heels.

37. Chief Stoker William Lashly acted as one of the mechanics for Scott's caterpillar tractors. Contrary to the popular myth, these vehicles were extremely helpful over the first heavily laden key miles of the Pole journey in 1911–1912.

38. Six decades later, Scott's pioneer snow vehicles had pointed the way to tracked snowmobiles, here being driven by Charles Burton towing a 900-pound sledge during the bipolar transglobe expedition, 1979–1982.

Pole to the South Pole and, within two days, had already placed his crucial order for fifty good Greenland dogs, an extremely scarce commodity. By so doing, he was ensuring that no other rival planning to reach the South Pole would have what he considered to be by far the best means of getting there.

Like most polar travelers of the late twentieth century, I was brought up on the tales of the so-called Heroic Age of the Antarctic pioneers, chiefly Scott, Shackleton, and Amundsen. I admired them all and still do, but each had characteristics that, judged from the ethical point of view of their contemporaries, were looked upon very differently than would be the case in the present day. What Roald Amundsen did in 1910 was rated by most of his own countrymen and by those in the know elsewhere as the deceitful machinations of somebody with no sense of honor. Today, the reaction to his behavior would more likely be "Cunning old devil . . . good for him. Why shouldn't he have kept his plans secret and laid false trails if it gave him an advantage over his rivals?" Amundsen's motive in acting as he did was clear. His driving aim, as soon as Peary claimed the North Pole, was to be the first to reach the South Pole. He knew his only rival was Scott. He knew Scott's plans involved cumbersome scientific work in addition to the mere goal of polar priority. He must do nothing to alert Scott that he, Amundsen, the world's most effective polar traveler, was hell-bent on reaching the South Pole first. To hell with the ethics of the day; he would deceive everyone, even his own great patron, Nansen, and his own expedition colleagues if that's what was needed.

So what exactly did he do?

Two days after Scott's own South Pole announcement, Amundsen switched his plans secretly, told nobody but his brother, and, later, said he did not know that Scott had any South Pole plans at the time. Despite being a highly observant, intelligent man with no work or focus but his polar activities, he expected the public to believe that he had heard nothing of the plans Scott had been making for nearly two years. Scott dealt with many manufacturers of polar equipment also used by Amundsen. The polar grapevine, especially in London and Oslo, buzzed with rumor and gossip, then as now, about who was planning what.

The press had leaked Scott's plans and details of his snow-vehicle trials as far back as January 1908, and in March 1909, Scott had conducted further snow-vehicle trials, covered by the local Norwegian press, in the Lille-hammer district, not far from Oslo. Protestations that Amundsen did not know of Scott's South Pole intentions at the time he switched his own plans from north to south are absurd and transparent.

Amundsen proved to be a master of deceit. He told nobody of his decision except his business partner, his brother Leon. He knew that there were various likely rivals for the South Pole, including Scott, and was keen not to alert them as to any challenge from him. He would deceive them into believing he was still focused on the Arctic. He also knew that all his sponsorship and the ship he had "borrowed" from Nansen would be forfeit if he publicly announced this change of plan. He was heavily in debt, which did not help, but he proved as masterful at the subtleties of deceit as the intricacies of polar travel.

Scott's plans, made in ignorance of Roald Amundsen's, involved a major science program in addition to an attempt on the Pole. If at this stage, or indeed at any point prior to his departure from Britain, Scott had contemplated a race with the Norwegians, he would have approached his good friend Fridtjof Nansen for advice. That advice would have been to take the best sledge-trained dogs in the world and a team of the best Norwegian skiers with years of experience of driving dogs . . . or forget it. Otherwise, in race terms Scott would stand as little chance of winning as Amundsen would of competing with Scott in the skills needed to command a battleship involved in torpedo warfare.

Scott's preparations received a boost by the addition to his fledgling team of Teddy Evans, erstwhile second-in-command of *Morning*, now twenty-eight years old and a naval lieutenant. At one point, excited by Shackleton's accounts of the *Nimrod* expedition, Evans had nursed plans for an Antarctic expedition of his own and had begun to raise funds. Clements Markham had encouraged him to join Scott's team instead, and he had agreed at once. "There was not room for two British expeditions, nor was there any man, not even Shackleton, then in our country equal to Scott as a scientific organizer and leader. I willingly stood aside and got many of my supporters to give their assistance to Captain Scott."

But Evans's participation on the Scott team came at a cost. He must be Scott's second-in-command. Clements Markham put this to Scott, causing him a considerable dilemma, for he had already approached his old friend, the chief engineer of *Discovery*, Reginald Skelton, to join the expedition. Evans objected to his presence on the grounds that Skelton had a senior rank. The original suggestion to modify motor cars for use in Antarctica had been Skelton's. Although Shackleton had not succeeded with his motor-car version, Scott and Barne had persevered with theirs and Skelton had agreed to lend his considerable engineering design skills to the project. By the time of Evans's approach to Markham, Skelton had already spent a great deal of his valuable free time working on the motorized sledge at Finchley and abroad, and Scott did not want to drop him from his as-yet-unannounced, unfunded venture. Skelton was loyal to Scott, whom he knew very well and, despite his own career prospects and the needs of his family, he was fully prepared to spend another two years in Antarctica under Scott's command. Teddy Evans had a wealth of support, useful funds, boundless energy, and enormous enthusiasm. He was a highly skilled naval navigator and surveyor with Antarctic experience and, if not subsumed into Scott's expedition, a loose cannon likely to go his own way and drain potential funds from the limited national reservoir.

Scott hoped that there could be some compromise, but Evans declared that he could not accept the invidious position of number two, where another officer with a senior rank (Skelton was a commander) was expected to follow his orders. This despite the clear agreement by Skelton to do just that and numerous examples of expedition ships' companies where such a hierarchy had worked perfectly well. Evans was adamant, so Scott asked Skelton to "write or speak to him . . . quietly and try to remove his objection to yourself." Unfortunately Evans did not remove his objection. Skelton's granddaughter, Judy, an ardent student of Skelton's copious diaries, is uncertain as to the real reason for Evans's refusal to coexist with her grandfather, but she has copies of correspondence between Skelton and Scott over the three years following her grandfather's eventual withdrawal from Scott's last expedition. It is clear that both men retained their respect and friendship for one another despite the problem caused by Evans's arrival on the scene.

Evans was to play a major part in the coming events and, I believe, if Scott had owned a crystal ball back in the spring of 1909, he would have turned down Teddy Evans, whatever the downside of so doing, for Evans was a closet troublemaker, one of three or four that Scott unknowingly took onboard that year. With his *Discovery* people Scott had been fortunate, for Albert Armitage had been the only natural grudge bearer.

In mid-September 1909, Scott opened an office for his British Antarctic Expedition in Victoria Street, manned by Teddy Evans plus a £4 (£188) per week secretary. He was helped rather than hindered this time by an eight-man advisory committee that included Clements Markham. Scott's own name did not appear on the expedition stationery, a true sign of modesty. Scott's old friend Wilson had agreed to join as chief scientist. He had written to Markham, "with him [Scott], it will be an honour to drop down any crevasse in the world. I am really very fond of him."

That month was an interesting time for Scott. His wife, who was eight months pregnant, had introduced him to the new world of flying machines and taken him to an international gathering of aircraft designers and owners, where the fascinated Scott compiled a meticulous report for the admiralty on all the different flying machines with their various pros and cons, as seen from a naval torpedo officer's viewpoint.

In the autumn of 1909, the United States equivalent of the Royal Geographical Society, the American Geographical Society, also announced an expedition to reach the Pole, from the Weddell Sea coast, and its appointed leader, Robert Peary, wrote to Scott to ask if he had any objections. There were none and both men agreed to cooperate over their scientific work. Scott and Peary were never to meet, but Scott's erstwhile second-in-command, Albert Armitage, said of Peary, "He was a splendid specimen of a man physically and seemed to be surrounded by an aura of energy, determination and force such as I have never seen equaled . . . He had the finest belief in his destiny." Scott allowed his correspondence with Peary to be published, adding his own footnote that rivalry to reach the Pole would be "entirely friendly," but that each group would naturally wish to be first. Peary then published his own intentions in Washington and promised that "the race for the South Pole between the Americans and the British would be the most exciting and nerve-wracking race the world has ever seen." At the time, Peary was engaged in a bitter public wrangle with Dr. Cook as to which of the two had reached the North Pole first. Scott's publicly stated aim was simple: "The main objective is to reach the

South Pole and to secure that objective for the British Empire." He did not immediately admit the ambitious scientific program that he envisaged since the aim of his announcement was to raise funds by appealing to the public's craving for national achievements (a trait by no means unique to the British then or now).

He specified a public appeal for £40,000 (£1.8 million). He outlined his intention of completing the great journey by means of motorized sledges, Manchurian ponies, and dogs. Man-haul, like science, was not mentioned. The *Times* summarized Scott's appeal the following day: "£40,000 is needed. The work begun by Captain Cook in the 18th century has been continuously carried forward by British explorers in the face of desperate difficulties and should not be dropped now that the goal seems attainable."

The very next day, September 14, 1909, Kathleen produced Scott's first and only child, a son named Peter, so named because of Scott's friendship with James Barrie, author of *Peter Pan*.

Two months later, Scott resigned from his admiralty post, went on half pay, and left his wife and baby son to tour the country to raise money through lectures and appeals to businessmen. Teddy Evans proved a more successful beggar than Scott. He actually enjoyed fund-raising: "It's no good talking to business men," he opined, "about magnetism, geology, meteorology or any of that scientific stuff" and set about exciting Welsh magnates with tales of unbelievable mineral wealth and whaling profits waiting to be plucked from down among the glaciers.

Everyone in Britain was eager for Scott to claim the Pole so long as somebody else paid for it. Scott was often heckled by worthy socialists demanding to know what possible benefit was to be had from another expensive polar jaunt when in Britain folk were unemployed and starving. This was a time when Lloyd George announced a People's Budget, which aimed to raise vast funds for social welfare through taxing the rich with ever-increasing levies on unearned and investment income. The wealthy were in no mood to give easy handouts to Scott. Miners and dockers were threatening national strikes and workers everywhere were flexing newfound muscles.

Scott and Evans worked on doggedly and learned to reduce the cash needed, where equipment could be obtained free or well discounted. Sir Arthur Conan Doyle, at the height of his Sherlock Holmes fame, gave a well-publicized appeal to the nation, stressing that only one Pole was left to claim and that Scott must be enabled for Britain, and by Britain, to be the claimant. The government eventually relented and gave Scott £20,000 (£940,000).

Scott knew he must aim to leave England by June 1910 to gain the most from seasonal ice movements and set up a base by early 1911. This gave him seven months to find his ship, all necessary manpower, and a lot more funding. His scientific program meant planning for a complement of thirty-three officers, scientists, and other men living ashore, and, depending on the size of the ship, some thirty more to stay aboard, because this time Scott did not intend his ship to winter.

Scott found preparing for his second expedition easier, in that he was the originator and leader, without committee delays. He was now a veteran polar leader with many contacts and a respected name. This was as well, for seven months is not long when organizing such an ambitious venture. The empire's response to Scott's advertisement for volunteers was overwhelming and immediate. Eight thousand applicants flocked to Victoria Street in person or penned eloquent letters explaining why they should be considered.

Scott's French explorer friend, Jean Charcot, wrote on his return from the south that he had lost all confidence in motors for polar work. This hardly worried Scott, who was by now basing his plans on a commonsense combination of *Discovery* and *Nimrod* travel methods. These he summarized as having three stages between the winter base and the Pole—the barrier, the Beardmore Glacier, and the high plateau. If no suitable transportation could be found to climb the glacier, Scott, like Shackleton, would use manpower alone.

Since Shackleton had been forced to turn back only ninety-seven miles short of the Pole, entirely owing to food and fuel shortages, it followed that Scott must reach that latitude correspondingly better provisioned, which would be possible merely by having more men reach that point with more supplies. The same applied down on the barrier: Where Shackleton used four ponies, Scott must take at least eight. Although neither dogs nor skis had been featured on the *Nimrod* sledging journeys, Scott decided to cover his options by taking both.

In March 1910, some three months before his departure deadline, Scott telephoned Roald Amundsen, whom he had never met, to request specific scientific cooperation between himself in the south and the Norwegian up north. Amundsen, desperate to avoid being forced into admitting his real intentions to beat Scott to the South Pole at all costs, would not take the call. He was "unavailable." He continued successfully to deceive his patron, Nansen; his government, whose ship he was using; all his sponsors; and, more important, Robert Falcon Scott.

THE RACE BEGINS: 1910

DISCOVERY HAD BEEN ACQUIRED by the Hudson's Bay Company, who refused to give her up to Scott for this second voyage at any reasonable price. Six decades later, I was sponsored by the HBC with Russian wolf skins to turn into parkas and, by then, their directors were expressing regret at their predecessors' hardheaded treatment of Scott—"We missed a good PR opportunity there."

Scott had objected to the rescue mission of *Terra Nova* back in 1904, but he had not forgotten how well she had handled the ice so he made an offer to her owners, Bowring Brothers of Newfoundland. He went to inspect her with his second-in-command, Teddy Evans, who was to command her. Evans noted:

> She was the largest and strongest of the old Scotch whalers, had proved herself in the Antarctic pack-ice and acquitted herself magnificently in . . . sealing voyages extending over a period of twenty years. In spite of her age she had considerable power . . .
> I shall never forget the day I first visited the *Terra Nova* in the

West India Docks: she looked so small and out of place
surrounded by great liners and cargo-carrying ships, but I loved
her from the day I saw her, because she was my first command.
Poor little ship, she looked so dirty and uncared for and yet her
name will be remembered for ever in the story of the sea, which
one can hardly say in the case of the stately liners which dwarfed
her in the docks. I often blushed when admirals came down to see
our ship, she was so very dirty. To begin with, her hold contained
large blubber tanks, the stench of whale oil and seal blubber being
overpowering, and the remarks of those who insisted on going all
over the ship need not be here set down. However, the blubber
tanks were withdrawn, the hold spaces got the thorough cleansing
and whitewashing that they so badly needed. The bilges were
washed out, the ship disinfected fore and aft, and a gang of men
employed for some time to sweeten her up. Then came the fitting
out, which was much more pleasant work.

Scott wangled the asking price down to £12,500 (£590,000), which was
not difficult, for Bowring was a family firm favorably disposed to British
polar pioneering and even donated £500 (£23,500) to Scott's funds. He
made an immediate down payment without knowing if and how he would
ever find the balance.

Using an early November start date, and after consulting with meteorological experts who had studied the *Discovery* met reports, Scott estimated
that the entire journey to the Pole would last 144 days, returning to base on
March 27, long after his pick-up ship would have had to depart from Mc-
Murdo Sound. This did not worry him, as he had already planned enough
supplies for a second year down south and had initially made unpublicized
plans for a hugely ambitious scientific program.

All his meticulous planning was based on reaching the Pole in his own
good time. If Scott had known before he set out from Britain in 1910 that he
would face a direct race for the Pole in 1911 against one of the greatest
snow and ice travelers in the world, he would of course either have amended
his plans or concentrated on his beloved science program alone (if funds
could have been raised). Believing that he had no immediate rival, he laid out

his travel plans. He would use four types of transport at the start of his journey and discard any that didn't work as he went along. He would try using
his experimental motorized sledges, but, since they were likely to break
down, he would not rely on them. If they worked, even for a short while, at
the beginning, that would be a bonus, nothing more. So all his calculations
for moving his loads were based on the possibility of zero machine usage.

Scott objected to plans that relied upon animals suffering, but he did
not object to animals being shot and used as food, either for dogs or for humans, observing: "There is no real reason why the life of a dog should be
considered more than that of a sheep, and no one would pause to consider
the cruelty of driving a diminishing flock of sheep to supply the wants and
aid the movement of travellers in more temperate climes." He carefully
weighed the pros and the cons. In favor of dogs he listed McClintock's findings: Two dogs need the food weight of one man to go 25 percent farther
with the same load. They require no heavy kit like a tent, sleeping bag,
cooker, clothing, or skis. Against these advantages, Scott had found dogs unreliable compared with men on long journeys with heavy loads over bad terrain. His own best journeys in Antarctica had been achieved without dogs.
Dogs, Scott concluded, could be counted upon to drag loads farther than
men, provided you did not mind their very considerable suffering in the process. So, this time, he would take dogs but only use them for as long as they
could cope without the need of ill-usage. They would not be relied upon as
the main haulage means.

This left two transport systems that would be critical to the Scott plan,
ponies and men. This combination had worked for Shackleton to reach
within a mere ninety-seven miles of the Pole. Calculations showed that
Shackleton's shortfall, a 194-mile round trip, could be covered by the simple
expedient of setting out with more ponies, more men, and more supplies.
Shackleton had learned from Scott in 1903 and had gone on to achieve great
results. Scott would now improve on Shackleton enough to cope with the
extra distance.

There was one imponderable that did not escape Scott's notice—the
plateau. "Shackleton was five weeks there and was nearly done, while our
Pole party will have to spend ten weeks on the plateau—if we have bad
weather, no one can stick it." Scott was referring of course to the effects of

high altitude. Eighty years later, man-hauling close to the Pole, I recorded in my diary:

> We had reached 8500 above sea-level and I was feeling increasingly tight-chested. I eased off my shoulder straps as much as possible but *any* constriction of lungs led to heavy breathing and the noise in my ears of blood rushing to my head. It became difficult to eat chocolate squares on the move because any interruption to the breathing process had me gasping for air. Even to bend over to tighten a ski-binding made me breathless and weak. At night I experienced mild panic from time to time when I woke with air hunger.

The pros and cons of ponies were obvious to Scott. They would be too heavy to manhandle if, for instance, they dropped into a crevasse. Their ground pressure was far greater than a dog's or a man's, so they sank deeper into soft snow and broke through snow bridges more often. They were not as adaptable to extreme polar weather as were dogs and, being herbivores, would need fodder in a land with no grass; nor could they eat each other's meat.

The fact that neither Scott nor his colleagues (other than Lawrence Oates, who was in India until the last minute) were natural "horsey" folk did not help, yet Shackleton had been equally handicapped in this respect and ponies had been key to his success. He had shown that, on mixed snow-and-ice surfaces, ponies could haul heavier loads, pound for pound, than could dogs and that Siberian or Manchurian ponies could withstand the barrier weather, provided no move was attempted before early November (about three weeks later than would be possible with dogs). In any race for the Pole, dogs would therefore be absolutely critical to any chance of winning, but Scott, as noted, was not expecting to race.

Scott took on a self-proclaimed dog-sledging expert named Cecil Meares to procure both dogs and ponies. He had heard about Meares through Herbert Ponting, a forty-year-old professional photographer and cinematographer who had already signed on with the expedition. Ponting had highly recommended Meares, who was the son of an army major. He had failed to obtain a commission but had signed on anyway and fought in the Boer War. He had then become a free spirit, working for no known employer, but most folks assumed he was connected to British Intelligence. At some point, he had spent time in the far north of India involved in the cold war between Britain and Russia, both of whom wooed the tribesmen of the Himalayas, the northern gateway to India. Meares had also traded furs by dog sledge in the Okotz and Kamchatka regions of eastern Siberia, fought in the Russo-Japanese War, and spoke fluent Russian, Chinese, and Hindustani. Meares was summed up by Scott as having "no happiness but in the wild places of the earth." He must have appeared as a godsend, for here was a man with years of experience at driving dogs in Siberia, who knew the exact areas where not only the best dogs but also the best ponies were to be purchased. On top of that, he knew how to horse-trade in the local language and so was unlikely to have cranky beasts be fobbed off on him.

Meares personally checked out and purchased thirty-one dogs and nineteen ponies that he then accompanied to New Zealand on schedule. He also hired two eighteen-year-old Russians, a dog driver, Demetri Gerof, and a groom, Anton Omelchenko, to help with the animals throughout the expedition. Scott later took on horse expert Oates, but he appeared on the scene far too late to help Meares select ponies in Manchuria, since he obtained leave from his cavalry regiment in India only in March 1910 and reached *Terra Nova* in London in May, three weeks before her voyage began.

A myth has been created that Scott instructed Meares to buy only white ponies because they looked charming in a snowy environment. In reality, Scott had studied the history of Shackleton's ponies, four of which had died at Cape Royds, leaving four to make the journey south. The majority of those that died were dark colored, so Scott decided to favor light-colored animals.

Scott sent his brother-in-law, Wilfred Bruce, a Royal Naval Reserve officer who had joined the *Terra Nova* crew, to Vladivostok to help Meares on the voyage to New Zealand, but the two men soon fell out. Bruce was an easygoing bear of a man who Meares considered idle, but then Meares was by nature ever ready to criticize. "We got sick of each other," Bruce wrote to his sister. "He wasn't a bit my style."

While Teddy Evans and Scott set about cutting their list of eight thou-

sand volunteers down to size, Wilson concentrated on the scientists to ensure Scott's wish to take the largest, most professional, and best equipped
scientific team ever assembled to Antarctica. He had, like Scott, smarted under the Meteorological Office's flawed report on the *Discovery*'s weather reports. He was now determined to make sure that such a scurrilous slur
would not be repeated, so he cast a wide net to recruit the very best men in
the Commonwealth.

Back in 1901, Scott had turned down George Simpson, a physicist from
the Indian Weather Bureau, who had failed his medical exam. Scott had then
written: "I am very disappointed as I thought him an exceedingly nice fellow . . . [he] would have been in every way fitted for the work." This time
Simpson's renewed application was welcomed with open arms, his medical
condition notwithstanding, and he brought with him unparalleled knowledge and an impressive array of instruments. His results this time would
render him the father of Antarctic meteorology, and, in the years to come,
the director of the British Meteorological Office. "Simpson," wrote Wilson,
"is our only real socialist, anti everything and a firm believer in the *Manchester Guardian.*"

Simpson's assistant was Charles Wright, a twenty-three-year-old Canadian physicist from Cambridge University. The two men achieved very valuable results down south and the dry, fairly humorless Simpson, ironically
nicknamed "Sunny Jim," was to praise Scott as a great scientific leader. He
noted early on: "One thing which never fails to excite my wonder is Capt.
Scott's versatile mind. There is no specialist here who is not pleased to discuss his problems with him and although he is constantly asserting that he is
only a layman, yet there is no one here who sees so clearly the essentials of
a problem."

Scott tried to recruit Douglas Mawson, the famous Australian geologist
who had reached the south magnetic pole on the *Nimrod* expedition. Mawson was later to fall out with many of his colleagues and, when interviewed
in London for *Terra Nova*, he noted: "I did not like Dr. Wilson," which may
have had something to do with the fact that he also wrote: "I would go in no
other capacity than as Chief Scientist and as Wilson had been appointed to
that position I would not . . . henceforth accept a post on the expedition."

Undeterred, Wilson found three professional geologists: Frank Debenham and Griffith Taylor from Australia and Raymond Priestley, who had been on *Nimrod*, from Cambridge. He also recruited two biologists, both from Plymouth Marine Laboratory: Dennis Lillie, a frail twenty-six-year-old from Birmingham who Scott had his doubts about from the first, and Edward Nelson, a wealthy rake from Cambridge who Kathleen Scott once said "spends all his time on shore being a man about town, which makes him look exceedingly tired."

The scientists were to be classified on *Terra Nova*, just as on *Discovery*, as "officers" and two nonscientists were added to their number. One was Bernard Day, the motor mechanic from Arrol Johnston Motors who had engineered both Shackleton's polarized car and Scott's motor sledge. On the *Nimrod* expedition, the car had proved useful only on firm sea ice, but this time, since Scott's prototype had tracks instead of wheels, Day was hopeful. (Barne, the original motorized-sledge enthusiast, had dropped out to get married.) The other nonscientist was a friend of Wilson from a wealthy estate-owning family, Apsley Cherry-Garrard, who offered £1,000 (£47,000) to the expedition but was still turned down. When he heard this, he asked Scott to keep the money anyway. Scott was so impressed he interviewed him again and, this time, he was appointed as the zoologist's assistant. The scientists' fellow inmates of the *Terra Nova*'s wardroom were mostly from the Royal Navy.

Two characters who appeared onboard during the last few months of loading in London were Henry Bowers and Lawrence Oates. Both were to affect the outcome of the expedition and to suffer dreadfully beside Scott. Henry Bowers yearned from childhood to follow his father to sea and, at fourteen, there not being enough money for regular training at Dartmouth, he entered the Merchant Marine via HMS *Worcester*, a training ship at Greenhithe. After eight years with the Merchant Navy, he transferred to the Royal Indian Marine Service as a sub-lieutenant on river-patrol boats up the fast and tricky waters of the Irrawaddy. He learned Hindustani but was posted to catch pirates in the Persian Gulf. Always hungry for adventure, he read Scott's *Discovery* and Shackleton's *Nimrod* books and wrote home: "If only they will leave the South Pole itself alone for a bit they may give me a chance. Don't laugh!" Clements Markham, who had met and been impressed by Bowers as a cadet years before, put his name forward forcefully to Scott in 1909 and had him accepted sight unseen.

This was perhaps just as well because when Scott did first set eyes on Bowers, he was as startled as most people. Frank Debenham described him as: "a fat little man with a perfectly immense nose and red bristly hair, unquenchable spirits and energy." *Terra Nova* wits soon christened him Birdie. He was twenty-seven on joining the expedition and arrived six weeks before the departure date. His work rate was as phenomenal as his strength. Quasimodo springs to mind. Teddy Evans was not impressed when, soon after his arrival, Bowers fell through the main hatch, a nineteen-foot drop, onto a bed of pig iron. "What a silly ass!" Evans exclaimed when he heard. The mate, Victor Campbell, then reported with amazement that Bowers had walked away unhurt. "What a splendid fellow!" Evans retorted. The legend of the indestructible Bowers was born.

Lawrence Oates, three years older than Bowers, was a very different character in most ways and his background was Essex landed gentry. Lawrence, or Titus, as he was nicknamed after a notorious seventeenth-century conspirator, was outwardly a languid country squire with all the self-confidence and ready arrogance of his class. But Oates was also dyslexic and spoke as he thought, very slowly. He specialized in failing exams and blaming his superiors. I find myself much mirrored in him and empathize with many of his reactions to life. We both lost our fathers when we were young and were blessed with loving mothers. We came from old English families without financial worries. We could not pass exams, nor understand basic mathematics. We went to Eton and failed to enter university. We both desperately wanted to be career officers in the same cavalry regiment, the Royal Scots Greys. We saw action in wild countries against our country's enemies but we never made it to promotion beyond captain and ended up in the polar wastes. Like Oates, I always wanted to be boss in my own fiefdom and have always been wont to castigate my senior officers when they interfered with what I perceived as the best way forward.

Oates's letters home to his doting mother did just that. Although his family was wealthy, she carefully regulated his allowance, which kept him in close correspondence with her and taught him not to be a spendthrift. Given my empathy with the instincts prompting Oates's letters and my great admiration for Scott, I feel doubly sad when I see how Oates, in his kneejerk carping at Scott, just another boss to blame, ends up unwittingly providing the lion's share of ammunition for the serious damage caused to Scott's reputation from 1979 onward.

When in 1909 Oates first heard about the *Terra Nova* expedition, his thirtieth birthday was coming up and his determination to leave the army was peaking. He had moved with his regiment to India where his frustrations and complaints against life in general and his immediate superiors in particular continued to feature in the ongoing stream of letters to his mother. His latest gripe was at a push by the War Office to recruit officers with brains from the working classes. A "man with brains," Oates growled, "knows too much to join the Service."

Oates did not want to join any expeditions as an also-ran. He told a friend soon after his interview at the polar office: "I told Scott I had no intention of being left at the base and that I should want to be in the party to make the dash for the Pole." To his mother he added: "The job is most suitable to my tastes. Scott is almost certain to get to the Pole and it is something to say you were with the first party."

There is no record of how Scott reacted to Oates stressing his aversion to "being left at the base." Oates might be thought to be in no position to stress anything to his prospective leader, being merely one of eight thousand applicants, but he did offer £1,000 (£47,000 today) to expedition funds, which Scott would not have sneezed at, and he did, above all, have great experience in dealing with horses, something that Scott sorely needed. Oatès was the first soldier to join a British polar expedition. He was entering a world of naval customs and naval discipline and when he first climbed up the *Terra Nova*'s gangplank at the dockside, Scott's team was expecting a mustached army caricature. Oates may have been shrewd enough to foresee the danger inherent in his status since he turned up in shabby clothes with a battered bowler. This worked well, for Tom Crean, back again working for Scott and one of the first to meet Oates, remembers his introducing himself very simply to the sailors. "I'm Oates," he said. Crean also noted: "we never for a moment thought he was an officer . . . We made up our minds that he

was a farmer, he was always so nice and friendly, just like one of ourselves . . . and always a gentleman."

Oates settled down happily to menial deck work. As a practiced yachts-
man, he was at home high up in the rigging and could turn his hand to most
things. Teddy Evans and the mate, Victor Campbell, himself an old Etonian,
found Oates an excellent and diligent worker and asked Scott to keep him
onboard during the vital preparations of the last month before departure.
Scott agreed and signed him on as a midshipman for one shilling a month
since little could be achieved at this late stage by sending him out to help
Meares with the ponies long since purchased in Manchuria.

In March 1910, while his team came together, Scott took Kathleen to
Fefor in Norway for the final field trials of his latest motorized sledge. He
was on the lookout for any gadget, old or new, that would help him toward
success and, in 1910, there were plenty of new gadgets about, since electri-
cal propulsion had just begun to take over from steam power and sub-
marines and aircraft were becoming ever more sophisticated, although
neither had reached a stage likely to help his plans. Wireless telegraphy involved too much bulky gear, but the forerunner of British Telecom provided
Scott with a landline that did prove useful.

Scott's latest motorized sledge was made by Wolseley Motors of Birmingham, powered by a gas engine and equipped with a looped track of links,
and was the forerunner of the Snocats that, forty years on, would complete
the first crossing of Antarctica under Vivian Fuchs and Edmund Hillary.
Scott's trials in Fefor, watched by Fridtjof Nansen and presided over by
Bernard Day (who was to go south) and Skelton (who wasn't), progressed
most impressively on good hard snow surfaces. A three-thousand-pound
load of local Norwegian passengers clinging to four sledges in tandem was
dragged with ease up a long one-in-five slope.

Scott and Kathleen were delighted and Day was optimistic, but Skelton
feared that the machine's performance did not bode well for further trials,
which were due to be held in soft-snow conditions. Nansen, if at all impressed, did not show it. He merely congratulated Scott on the fifty pairs of
locally made skis Scott had recently bought and pointed out that he must
now take on a first-class ski instructor to instruct his fifty skiers. He sug-

gested a twenty-one-year-old Norwegian ski champion called Tryggve Gran and introduced this protégé to the Scotts forthwith.

Halfway through the Fefor trials, the motorized sledge's axle broke and Gran skied ten miles down the valley to Bernard Day's store dump to bring back a twenty-five-pound spare axle. He did the round trip in five hours and Scott was highly impressed, not only by Gran's skill but by modifications to his gear, including the use of two sticks, better boots, and clever ski bindings that were all new since the *Discovery* days. Scott did not hesitate to offer Gran the position of ski adviser to the expedition.

Before Scott left Norway, Gran agreed to put him in touch with Amundsen because Scott was still trying to contact the great Arctic explorer to suggest liaising over a north/south science project. The two men traveled to Amundsen's home at Bundefjord where they met one of his brothers, Gustav, who said he had told Roald that Scott was due that day and it was strange he wasn't there. "We waited," said Gran, "a good hour, but not a sign of life from the conqueror of the North-West Passage." Gran went away "ashamed" and Scott disappointed. Amundsen, hiding from his unwelcome visitors, who could not suspect the true reason for his evasiveness, was answering no telephone calls since he needed to deceive his government, his sponsors, all his team, and, above all, his patron Nansen, who was an honorable man and would surely be against any secretive switch by Amundsen from his well-publicized north-polar plan, rich in scientific research aims, to a mere race to the South Pole to beat Scott.

Gran later wrote: "Could Scott have beaten Amundsen? I answer without hesitation that, should he have had the possibility of competing fairly under similar circumstances, he would have had to know that Amundsen planned to be the South Pole conqueror well before the winter of 1910, for the battle is won at the preparation stage."

In mid-May, Gran joined *Terra Nova* in the West India Docks. He noted "a hurry and scurry that impressed me almost as much as the traffic in the streets of the metropolis. Men tore about like busy ants. Sailors were crawling over rigging and spars." Among the stores were gifts to keep the men happy, which included 35,000 cigars, half a ton of tobacco, plum puddings, a piano, and an HMV gramophone with assorted records.

There were good men aboard who had served with Scott before and wanted to go again: as well as William Lashly, Taff Evans, and Tom Crean, Petty Officer Thomas Williamson had applied. "Dear Sir, I have heard that you are contemplating another Expedition to the South . . . I hope when the time comes for the selection of your crew you will not omit me. I feel convinced in myself that I can do much more for you than I did before for the simple reason that . . . I am getting older but wiser. Trusting you will . . . let me know if there is any chance of my serving under you again."

Kathleen had taken an ever-increasing interest in Scott's expedition and there were to be many sour comments as to her wearing the family trousers. She spurred his ambition and bolstered his confidence during his "black dog" moods. Once in a letter she wrote: "You shall go to the Pole. Oh Dear me what's the use of having energy and enterprise if a little thing like that can't be done? It's got to be done so hurry up and don't leave a stone unturned." Gran described Kathleen as "a very very clever woman very very pushing . . . very ambitious . . . I don't think Scott would have gone to the Antarctic if it hadn't been for her." Kathleen was considered clever, ambitious, and pushy by many of the expedition members, and they may well have assessed her correctly in all these respects, but there is no evidence that she was the cause of Scott's decision to return to the south.

So why did Scott decide to go back? I would agree with the assessment of his famous biographer Elspeth Huxley, who wrote: "What persuaded these men to seek out hardships so extreme that most ordinary mortals would give all they possess to avoid them? Fame and fortune . . . also love of country, lust for adventure, devotion to a cause, and more obscure forces like an urge toward martyrdom. Certainly there is a curiosity: desire to know what lies over the next hill . . . or the moon and beyond the stars. All such motives are mixed together and the analyst who tries to sort them out and label them is generally wasting his time." In Scott's case, a keen fascination with scientific research may also have played a part.

If Scott had not gone south, his torpedo expertise and command experience would in all probability have meant rapid promotion in the Great War that loomed even as *Terra Nova* was made ready. On the eve of departure, the *Daily Mail* editor told Scott that there was a strong expectation that Germany would be "ready to strike in the summer of 1914." After a moment's reflection, Scott answered: "By then I shall be entitled to command a battle cruiser of the *Invincible* class. The summer of nineteen-fourteen will suit me very well." Another newspaper reported their interview with Scott. "He was not an alarmist, he said, but he had just recently left the Admiralty, and he believed that the time was coming when we should want men who could shoot. The menace which was gradually showing its head abroad was, he thought, very great, and none of us could afford to treat it lightly. He believed the time was coming when the navy would want to be the strongest navy we ever had."

King Edward VII, after whom Scott had named a huge peninsula in Antarctica, died three weeks before *Terra Nova* set sail and Scott recalled that *Discovery*'s departure, nine years before, had been overshadowed by Queen Victoria's death. As he watched the quayside ease away and waved to the many supporters who had given their time and skills free for the past few months, he could see just across the dock a familiar outline from his past, for *Discovery* was berthed there, taking on Hudson's Bay Company stores bound for North America.

En route to Cardiff for coal in June 1910, Scott summoned everyone on deck and appealed to them all to make a will. He also wrote to the admiralty: "If nothing is heard of the ship by the middle of January 1912, it would be well to consider the organisation of a relief Expedition, but no active steps . . . should be taken until the close of the open season of 1911–1912."

At Cardiff, the ship filled the coal holds with free Welsh coal, the lord mayor promised £1,000 (£47,000) to the expedition, and the city gave a banquet. Taff Evans, being well known in his native Wales from his *Discovery* days, was seated between Scott and the lord mayor. In an impromptu speech, he declared: "No one else would have induced me to go there again but if there is a man in the world who will bring this to a successful conclusion, Captain Scott is that man." Later Evans drank too much and had to be dragged aboard *Terra Nova* by six strong men. At about this time, the quasi-Welsh Teddy Evans began to fall out with his lower-deck namesake. It seems the reason for this had to do with Taff spotting an error made by Teddy (over ordering some wrong ski-bindings) and then "sneaking" to Scott. New equipment was ordered and First Officer Evans was promptly replaced as boss of ski gear by Petty Officer Evans. Teddy was not large in stature but significant in terms of pride, so he nurtured this grudge with dedication.

Scott did not leave Britain onboard the ship because the expedition was still £8,000 (£376,000 today) in the red, and by taking a ride on a speedy mail ship to Cape Town, he could use the extra time in Britain to raise funds; fix media contracts for magazine, news, and cinematograph rights; and pay bills. He nevertheless found time to slip away to his childhood home, Outlands, to say good-bye to his memories and to carve his name on a tree he had planted long ago. He put off the moment of parting with Kathleen. She would now stay with him on the mail boat to Cape Town. Wilson's Oriana and Teddy Evans's Hilda would go the same way. They all met at Waterloo Station for a quiet send-off by a few friends, including Ernest Shackleton, who called for "three cheers for Captain and Mrs. Scott" as the train puffed away.

Meanwhile, aboard *Terra Nova*, the men learned about one another in their cramped and often seasick state. Spells spent working shifts on the bilge pumps or stoking the boilers helped break the ice, and Wilson noted: "The bunkers hold about 50 tons each . . . we take it in three hourly spells . . . It is hot work, and in 10 minutes one is streaming with sweat and black as Kaffirs with dust." In one shift, Bowers and Wilson shoveled seven tons, despite the ship's movement being so bad they had trouble avoiding the moving coal in the darkness. Wilson recorded some time later: "the coal is now patent fuel which has a horrible burning action on one's eyes and skin as it is full of pitch and resin. The scalding comes on in an hour or two after one has bathed and lasts for many hours."

Teddy Evans observed: "In this fashion officers, seamen and scientific staff cemented a greater friendship and respect for one another." The scientists learned various new skills, including, according to the Canadian Charles Wright, splicing ropes, coal trimming, paint washing, and, most alarming, sail hauling aloft.

One of Teddy Evans's party tricks consisted of lifting people off the ground by clenching their trouser belts in his teeth. Horseplay was developed to a fine art under his leadership. Oates, who had seen many an officer's mess after-dinner scrum, must have felt at home, but the scientific types, not to mention the sailors, would surely have wondered where such madhouse behavior might lead.

Time was lost in the Doldrums, but the final stretch to Simonstown naval base, just south of Cape Town, treated them to strong westerly winds and they flew along under full sail, arriving on August 15 to the waiting Scott's great relief. A good deal of work was needed in the harbor to prepare for the voyage ahead, but everyone took some time off and Cape Town was as hospitable as ever.

Oates described *Terra Nova* as an extremely dirty ship and he was not at all impressed with her speed. He wrote to his mother: "The Skipper has decided to come on the ship to Melbourne with us, this is not a very popular move but in a way I think it is a good thing as he gets to know the people better and we get to know him." Scott's decision to travel on *Terra Nova* rather than continue on by mail boat with Kathleen for the next leg to Australia was sudden and unexpected. He sent Wilson on to Melbourne in his place, thereby giving him extra time with his own wife, Oriana, on the mail boat. There may well have been speculation that Scott was keen to escape from Kathleen or that he was jealous of Teddy Evans's rapport with the company, but there is no proof at all of either, and, if Evans was upset at being usurped, he certainly never said so, nor do his personal diaries make any such comment. Bowers, whose early Indian diaries were so critical of his skippers, wrote about Scott in Cape Town: "Scott hits it off well everywhere and is certainly a top-hole leader. There is not one of us whom he does not take a personal interest in . . . He will take nothing but a straight answer to his questions . . . He sticks to what he says, knows what he intends to do, and does not change his mind." The most likely reason for Scott's sudden return was that, having done all that he could to raise vital funds in Australia, he was keen to get back to his men. In such circumstances on an expedition, I would be wary of leaving my team under the command of someone else, however briefly. I would not want their natural allegiance and loyalty to be diluted and dispersed, which would be an increasing danger the longer I was away.

Terra Nova left the Cape bound for Australia on September 3 with Scott in command. The horseplay continued but was muted by the leader's pres-

ence. Charles Wright, the Canadian physicist, noted that Scott, whom he admired for his interest in all things scientific, stayed clear of the horseplay but
never disapproved of it. Gran wrote: "If the voyage from Cardiff to Simonstown has been characterized by splendid comradeship the passage from
South Africa to Australia was an even better proof that Scott had well understood how to choose men who get on well together. In Norway I had
learned to know Scott as a cheerful and easy man, and this first impression
was strengthened when I again came close to him. He was short-tempered
and not to be trifled with when angry, but if he had judged someone unfairly
and discovered his mistake, he was quick to make amends."

Four days out of Cape Town, *Terra Nova*'s passage was being secretly
shadowed by Gran's countryman Roald Amundsen, aboard *Fram*. On that
day, September 6, the Norwegians slipped out of Madeira intent on reaching
the Great Ice Barrier with no further stops en route. Amundsen must have
suspected a hostile public reaction to his ongoing deception and decided to
give at least a minimal announcement of his real intentions to the world at
large and to the British in particular. So he addressed a cryptic message to
Scott to await his arrival in Melbourne, by which time it would be too late
for any change of British plans, too late to buy more dogs. The message
read: "Beg leave to inform you Fram proceeding Antarctic. Amundsen."

He also sent a confidential letter to a Norwegian friend: "The *Fram* goes
direct south from Madeira into the Antarctic regions in order to compete
with the Englishmen for the South Pole." Scott sailed on toward Australia,
in happy ignorance of any rival, let alone the immediate threat of the highly
professional ice traveler Roald Amundsen. He continued to work on his
plans for his scientists and for his own slow but sure plod to the Pole based
on the lessons learned by the only journeys yet made toward it, those of the
Discovery and *Nimrod* teams. His aim was not to man-haul to the Pole. His
aim was to reach the Pole by whatever means at his disposal proved most
successful when the time came. His final choice of his travel system would
not have to be calculated with the aim of being first at the Pole, merely of
getting there by a reasonable date.

Soon after *Terra Nova* left Cape Town, the *Cape Times* noted: "While
Captain Scott and his comrades are making their way southwards towards
the unconquered Pole, a Norwegian, Captain Roald Amundsen . . . is set-

ting out to solve some of the unfathomed mysteries of the Great North." So Amundsen had successfully fooled the world's press all the way.

Amundsen had no compunction about poaching on anybody's pre-serves: "I do not belong to that class of explorer who believes that the Polar sea has been created for myself alone . . . First come, first served is an old saying." This philosophy was in line with that of today's assumption of a competitive free-for-all, each for himself and the devil take the hindmost. The behavioral codes and mores of his day, in Norway, as in Britain, were to him a nuisance. He read everything he could about previous Antarctic his-tory and decided from the works of Ross, Borchgrevink, Scott, and Shackle-ton that by far the best place for a winter base from which to race to the Pole must be the Great Ice Barrier near or at the Bay of Whales. The main danger was that any winter-quarters hut built on the barrier's edge might float out to sea. Amundsen, however, unlike Shackleton and Scott, thought the gamble worth taking. If there was any risk, he assumed it to be minimal since the bay had been sighted by Ross and by Shackleton in the same loca-tion over a seventy-year period. Amundsen was taking a big risk (as the aer-ial satellite photo in the second picture section shows), but the risk paid off. He was also trusting to fate that he would find a convenient glacier to lead him onto the plateau. Unlike Scott's plan, Amundsen's depended hugely on geographical luck.

Amundsen knew that Scott was planning a major scientific program in-volving many scientists and cumbersome instruments. There would be sixty-five men with Scott, whereas Amundsen planned to take no scientists and only a tightly knit group of travelers based around the world's best dog sledgers and skiers. His ship's company would total nineteen men, including both land group and crew.

Once *Fram* had cast off from Funchal's quayside on September 6, 1910, Amundsen summoned his men on deck and dropped the bombshell news of the change in their destination. Now they would not end up being merely second to reach the North Pole but they would go to the Arctic via the South Pole in order to be first. Amundsen told them that it was now a matter of trying to beat the English. "Hurrah" was the response of Bjaaland, a cham-pion skier. "That means we'll get there first." Three weeks after *Fram* left Madeira, by which time Scott could not alter his own plans, Leon announced his brother Roald's new aim to the world press. His statement was couched as carefully as possible to minimize accusations of duplicity: "At first glance this will appear to many to be a change in the original plan. This however is not the case. It is only an extension of the Expedition's plan; not an alteration." Scott received Amundsen's curt telegram on his arrival in Melbourne on October 12. He took it to Gran, who noted at once that the message from Oslo was dated October 3, yet *Fram* had left Madeira three weeks earlier. On Gran's advice, Scott later sent a message to Nansen to ask for clarification of the Amundsen telegram. Nansen, whether he knew by then about Amundsen's deceptions or not, sent an enigmatic response to Scott: "Unknown."

To confuse matters further, Scott received messages from Markham, one of which mentioned a press release from *Fram* talking about oceanographic work they planned in the Punta Arenas region. This inferred that Amundsen *was* planning to head for Antarctica but via the Weddell Sea, not the Great Ice Barrier. On the other hand, Markham had also learned that Amundsen had purchased charts from the admiralty of the McMurdo area of the Ross Sea. Amundsen "is going to McMurdo Sound to try to cut out Scott," Markham deduced. ". . . If I were Scott I would not lend them his land, but he is always too good-natured."

Scott, at the very moment he first received the fateful Norwegian telegram in Melbourne, was being introduced to his new geologist, the Australian Frank Debenham (later the founder of the Scott Polar Research Institute in Cambridge), who was about to join *Terra Nova*. Debenham noted that Scott seemed unruffled on reading the Amundsen news. All but one of the *Terra Nova* crew reacted to the Norwegian announcement in a vein similar to Raymond Priestley, who remembered it as "the greatest geographical impertinence ever committed." Back in London, Shackleton expressed his surprise that Amundsen had "so considerably altered his plans without giving a more explicit explanation."

The only member of the *Terra Nova* crew to find Amundsen's behavior aboveboard was Oates, which appears at first to make little sense since he was by nature xenophobic and distrusted all foreigners on principle. Nonetheless, by the time he gave his reaction to the Amundsen news he had already begun his old habit of criticizing his current boss, Scott, and to a lesser extent, Evans. They could do no right. So his attitude was ambivalent. "Bloody Norskies," he muttered, "coming down south is a bit of a shock," and added, "I only hope they don't get there first." Then, his Scott dislike getting the upper hand of his xenophobia, he added, "It will make us look pretty foolish after all the noise we have made . . . They say that Amundsen has been underhand the way he has gone about it, but I personally don't see it as underhand to keep your mouth shut . . . if Scott does anything silly such as underfeeding his ponies he will be beaten as sure as death."

When *Terra Nova* left Melbourne, Teddy Evans was again in command and Wilson back onboard. Scott was forced back on to the fund-raising front, desperately seeking Australian help with the debt he still owed. In Sydney, the lord mayor appealed on his behalf and in due course the New South Wales government stumped up £2,500 (£117,500), which was half what he still needed. Scott must have realized he could easily capitalize on Amundsen's deceit to appeal to Australians and their wallets. But he said nothing and later noted in his diary: "[Amundsen's] proceedings have been very deliberate and success alone can justify them. That this action is outside one's own code of honour is not necessarily to condemn it and under no condition will I be betrayed into a public expression of opinion."

Scott had a thousand and one more immediate problems than Amundsen. The Cape to Melbourne voyage had allowed him the opportunity to reassess many of those he had previously earmarked in his mind as fit to stay in Antarctica with him. Remembering the unloading of *Discovery* at Hut Point and the efficiency of Ernest Shackleton with all the stores, Scott had already provisionally appointed a stores keeper in the person of Lieutenant Henry Rennick, RN, but on the trip to New Zealand, he had observed the outstanding organizing abilities, strength, and memory of Bowers. He now had to inform Henry Rennick, before leaving civilization, of his decision to replace him on the shore party with the chirpy Scotsman. Rennick, who stayed onboard ship for the rest of the expedition, took the decision in good part, bearing no grudge against Scott or Bowers. Scott, like most leaders, rightly promoting very good individuals over the heads of merely good ones, did not enjoy the task. He wrote of Rennick: "He is a good fellow and one feels for him much at such a time—it must be rather dreadful for him."

Scott made the right decision, for Bowers was to prove a superb quartermaster.

When Scott arrived in New Zealand by passenger boat, he learned that his fund-raising in New South Wales had paid off, for a rich Sydney citizen had now decided to match his government's £2,500 donation and so make up Scott's shortfall. One less problem. But journalists also greeted the Scotts' arrival with gleeful queries about the race and the Norwegians and what Scott would do now. Scott kept his calm and, wishing Amundsen luck, assured the media that his own plans would remain unchanged.

Terra Nova, on arrival in the Lyttelton harbor on October 29, 1910, was completely unloaded under Bowers's supervision, then taken into the dry dock where leaks were plugged, pumps cleaned, and bolts tightened. Back in the harbor, the old boat was found to leak a good deal less and the reloading began. Bowers relisted everything and repacked a good deal in light but strong color-coded boxes. Scott's plans involved the splitting of his overwintering group into two separate units, one to work from the Hut Point vicinity and the other, under the mate, Victor Campbell, to land at the far eastern end of the Great Ice Barrier to explore King Edward VII Land, the landmass Scott had discovered there in 1901. This six man group was called the Eastern Party and all their boxes were painted green.

Bowers worked his men day and night, ignoring the constant stream of visitors as politely as he could. Oates found "rather sickening" the way some of these tourists scratched their names on the paintwork. As new stores arrived on deck, so *Terra Nova*'s long-since-painted-over Plimsoll line sank even lower. Scott and the naval element knew this was dangerous, but there was no alternative. Every last item would be needed down south. Some of the heavier, bulkier gear included two and a half tons of gasoline in drums, crates of large but delicate scientific instruments, three motor sledges with all their spares and Bernard Day's tools, 460 tons of coal, and five tons of dog biscuits. Scott commented: "Meares is reluctant to feed the dogs on seal, but I think we ought to do so during the winter."

The nineteen ponies were housed in stables designed by Oates, and placed immediately above the quarters of the sailors, onto whom the horse urine intermittently streamed. Thirty-three sledge dogs, desperate to kill each other when not barking, howling, or fouling the decks, were chained out of reach of each other, which meant the entire deck was spattered with snarling hounds leashed to sacks, crates, or bollards. There was also a ship's black cat, a blue Persian kitten, three rabbits, a pigeon, some squirrels, and a guinea pig that lived in a tobacco container (which was later dropped overboard by mistake). Once the on-deck "icehouse" was made ready, 162 carcasses of mutton were squeezed inside. Two dozen sledges were lashed aboard, followed by thirty-two tons of pony fodder, somehow to be kept dry and soon to be increased by Oates to fifty tons. The deck itself was everywhere invisible.

In New Zealand, Oates became hostile to Scott. Scott had delegated all equine matters to Oates, but Scott was nonetheless prone to question some of the cavalry officer's actions, and Oates did not like this. Scott seemed to consider that Oates's expertise was unquestionable when dealing with the ponies' day-to-day welfare, but doubted that his understanding of the specific challenges of operating Manchurian ponies in Antarctic conditions was any more foolproof than his own.

Oates wanted fifty, not thirty-two, tons of horse food stacked onboard and if there was no space, something would have to be moved. Oates wrote: "Scott has been kicking up another fuss about the forage but I succeeded in defeating him, also we smuggled in an extra two tons." And again: "I have now ordered just a little more which I shall try to get in on the quiet this afternoon." To accommodate Oates, Scott had Bowers remove a like amount of coal and Oates was triumphant. "Dear Mother," he wrote, "I have had a great struggle with Scott about the horse forage. He told me I was a 'something' nuisance but he has given way which shows he is open to reason." Oates's self-confidence about his own judgment and embattled vocabulary with words like "given way" instead of "agreed" again reminds me of my own attitudes whenever I suffered the affliction of having a boss.

Bowers happily colluded with Oates. "Oates was anxious to procure an expensive linseed meal and Scott was keen on the compressed variety. When my opinion was asked (knowing nothing of horse fodder) I got in a wink from Oates and said I was sure nothing could equal the linseed meal, and to O's great delight the motion was carried on the spot." Oates also made a point of registering his adverse attitude to the state of the ponies Meares had brought from Manchuria, a position in which I suspect there was more than a little self-interest.

Seven weeks after Meares and Bruce left Vladivostok, they had reached Lyttelton with all but one of their ponies alive, despite fifty-two days of nonstop standing up, there being no space to lie down. All the ponies and dogs were dropped off on tiny Quail Island, some two miles from Lyttelton, where they were quarantined and rested well before *Terra Nova*'s arrival. When Scott and Oates went to visit Meares's tented camp on Quail Island, they found Bruce with the remains of two black eyes and a swollen nose dealt him by a punchy pony but otherwise well. Scott warmly congratulated Meares, saying he was "greatly pleased" with all the animals.

Oates wrote home. "Dear Mother, *the ponies themselves are first class* but all the feeding I have been stuffing them with has made them fairly festive and there may be trouble." Some of the sailors came to the island to help exercise the festive animals and Oates moved over to the Quail Island camp, where he made friends with the Russians Gerof and Omelchenko. He also began to teach the ponies to drag loads. Despite the favorable judgment Oates had expressed when writing home, he made a point of giving Scott a damning pony report that included the summary:

> Victor . . . Narrow chest, knock knees . . . suffers with his eyes.
>   Aged windsucker.
> Snippets . . . Bad wind sucker. Doubtful back tendons off fore legs.
>   Pigeon toes. Aged.
> James Pigg . . . Sand crack near hind. Aged.
> Bones . . . Aged.
> Snatcher . . . Black marks under eye. Aged.

It is probable that Oates intended this report to impress on Scott and all the team that the ponies were rubbish. That way Oates would not subsequently be blamed should they fail in Antarctica despite all his expertise and his very best efforts at caring for them. He was therefore most upset when Scott continued to express himself "greatly pleased" with the ponies, feeling that Scott had ignored his advice. Although what use this advice was when Scott could hardly react by exchanging them for a new batch is not apparent.

The only other advice Oates gave Scott was to improve and increase the forage and Scott clearly gave in with hardly a whimper on that front.

No sooner had Scott, at least temporarily, placated Oates than trouble brewed from another quarter. In the frenetic period only three days before departure from Lyttelton, the bishop of Christchurch found a narrow perch somewhere on the deck to bless the ship. The navy men wore their best, normally mothballed, uniforms and all was well until, later in the day, Taff Evans, having enjoyed a final binge ashore, fell into the harbor. An alternative version of events, relayed to Cherry-Garrard by Wilfred Bruce, had Taff Evans arriving onboard drunk just as the bishop was coming and being chucked over the side by Lieutenant Evans. Taff, Scott's old southern journey comrade and one of the most experienced men aboard, hardly warranted sacking from the expedition for what would clearly be his last chance to have a few too many for at least two years. But a semblance of naval discipline being a loose pillar of the whole venture, Scott had to be seen to admonish the giant Welsh petty officer. So he ordered him home on the grounds that he had disgraced the whole venture in public. Teddy Evans, who disliked his namesake, was, naturally, pleased. The ship, on leaving Lyttelton, had to take on more coal at Port Chalmers, a short voyage along the coast. The Welshman managed to tag along and, once there, appealed to Scott to reconsider his banishment. Scott, no martinet and inclined to common sense rather than rigid enforcement of all orders, willingly forgave his contrite chief sledge expert and thereby sparked off a major clash with Teddy Evans, who saw the petty officer's reinstatement as very bad for discipline.

Teddy Evans told colleagues privately that he intended to resign unless a clear understanding was reached between him and Scott. Bowers, Oates, and Atkinson decided they would resign in sympathy if Teddy Evans quit, and they asked Cherry-Garrard if he would join them. He refused. He would have been happy to see Teddy Evans go. "From the first," he wrote, "I have never liked Evans." Behind Teddy Evans's relentless high spirits, Cherry-Garrard saw "a shallow man with none of Scott's complexity or Wilson's thoughtful altruism."

Scott himself mentions no rebellion or threat of resignation. He merely refers to Teddy Evans's "vague and wild grievances." Teddy Evans's diary makes no reference to the affair, which relies for its origins entirely on a note in Cherry-Garrard's journals, whose notes add that Scott called Teddy Evans's bluff and that "Teddy Evans climbed down."

Various diaries mention a tense atmosphere between Kathleen Scott and Hilda Evans, which Bowers attributed to mutual jealousy. Bowers adored Hilda Evans as "wildly beautiful" but said of Kathleen, who had questioned him over a store-keeping detail: "Nobody likes her on the expedition and the painful silence when she arrives is the only jarring note of the whole thing. There is no secret that she runs us all just now and what she says is done—through the Owner. Now nobody likes a schemer and she is one undoubtedly . . . We all feel that the sooner we are away the better."

At one point during the last day at Port Chalmers, Kathleen and Hilda, each about to say good-bye to their respective husbands, lost their tempers for no recorded reason. Oates heard about the resulting shouting match and wrote: "Dear Mother, Mrs Scott and Mrs Evans have had a magnificent battle, they tell me it was a draw after fifteen rounds. Mrs Wilson flung herself into the fight after the tenth round and there was more blood and hair flying about the hotel than you see in a Chicargo [sic] slaughter house in a month, the husbands got a bit of the backwash and there is a certain amount of coolness which I hope they won't bring into the hut with them, however it won't hurt me even if they do."

Oates's exaggerated prose sums up the entire rumpus. Scott and Kathleen later went for a last walk in the hills together. Then, on the day before departure, they collected Teddy Evans and drove together to the ship. On departure day, November 29, 1910, Kathleen's diary had one last spit: "Evans' tantrums spoiled the day," she wrote. "He told me a string of lies and hot air." The exact nature of all this was not recorded. Bowers, who seemed to relish the ladies' ups and downs, wrote: "May it never be known how very nearly the *Terra Nova* came to not sailing at the last few hours."

Kathleen did not kiss her man farewell just before departure as she did not want "anyone to see him sad." Mrs. Evans, on the bridge, said she wanted to have hysterics but didn't. Kathleen took her and Oriana Wilson "for tea in the stern and we all chatted gaily." Teddy Evans described his feelings: "personally I had a heart like lead, but, with every one else on board, bent on doing my duty and following Captain Scott to the end. There was work to be done, however, and the crew were glad of the orders that sent them from one rope to another and gave them the chance to hide their feelings, for there is an awful feeling of loneliness at this point in the lives of those who sign on the ships of the 'South Pole trade.' "

Scott sent off his last letters home. To his little niece he wrote:

> *If you could look down through the Earth right under your feet with a great big telescope you would see Auntie Kathleen and me at the other end . . . The dogs are rather fierce and the people who don't know them have to be careful not to go too close or they would get bitten—but wasn't it funny—there was a girl the same age as Phoebe who went up to the fiercest dog of all and put her arms round his neck—and the dog didn't mind at all. When you grow older you will understand that there are lots of animals and lots of people who are like that dog.*
>
> *We are getting ready to sail away and when you are having your Christmas dinner . . . you can imagine the "Terra Nova" all amongst the ice—great big pieces larger than the Mint or even the Tower will be all around her and the sea will be full of seals and penguins . . . I shall be thinking of you all at Christmas and hoping that you are having a very merry time—and that you won't forget,*
>
> > *Your loving, Uncle Con*

On November 29, *Terra Nova* sailed away from Port Chalmers with an apprehensive crew, for she was dreadfully overladen and sluggish. Many a prayer for the weather to hold fair, at least until a good distance was covered and heavy fuel expended, must have reached the Almighty. But would He respond in that region so famed for its violent storms?

Not everyone was worried. The ship's black cat, who could climb ropes and do tricks, was popular and lay for much of the day on cushions in a cat hammock lovingly made by his fans. A year later, he was to fall overboard in midocean and all hands were set to man a lifeboat and save the sodden feline. Back in New Zealand, members of Parliament and their wives were so enchanted by the tales told by successive Scott and Shackleton visitors to

Lyttelton that they had become keen to head south themselves. Thomas Cook & Sons even announced their intention of sending a tourist ship to the Ross Sea the following summer. (At the time of this writing, they have yet to do so.)

As for Kathleen Scott and Oriana Wilson and the families of Taff Evans, Titus Oates, and Birdie Bowers, they would never see their men again.

❧ 12 ❧

NEAR DISASTER: 1911

ON DECEMBER 1, 1910, less than twenty-four hours out of Port Chalmers, Wilson was "wondering what the barometer was falling so quickly to bring us. The one thing we didn't want was this heavy storm—but it came right enough and it came quickly." Everyone, from Scott and Teddy Evans down, understood the dangerous implications of having overloaded *Terra Nova*, but nobody was blamed, for they all knew there had been no alternative. Bowers noted: "risk nothing and do nothing; if funds could not supply another ship, we simply had to overload the one we had or suffer worse things down south." They also knew of the double jeopardy that had lurked throughout the voyage. The ship was prone to leak and the pumps, vital to remove the leaked water from the bilges, although not defective were prone to clog from oily balls of coal filth. Attempts to plug the leaks and modify the pumps had failed in Cardiff, Cape Town, and Lyttelton so they would have to make do.

Cherry-Garrard, checking the barometer on December 1, wrote: "It makes me feel sick just to look at it." Oil was released overboard to still the rising seas about the ship, as was the custom, but this did nothing to lessen the power of the waves that broke with ever-increasing fury over the decks. Ponies began to fall over and chained dogs to float to and fro in the wash of successive waves. Ponting wrote on December 1: "a full gale was howling and shrieking through the rigging, and raging and roaring over the now mountainous waves. The ship rolled and plunged and squirmed as she wallowed in the tremendous seas which boomed and crashed all that night against the weather side, sending tons of water aboard every minute."

All hatches were battened down, but the storm rose and the ship slowly but surely filled with water. On Friday, December 2, Lashly spent hours up to his neck in the bilges clearing the clogged pump valves, but then the water rose too high for him and, once he stopped, the main pumps seized. They tried the secondary pump, but this too clogged up in a short while. A huge wave of filthy water now washed to and fro in the engine room and all about the furnace stokers. The noise and the steam and the roaring rush of water in the lamplight or the furnace glare were terrible. Up on deck, coal bags burst their ties, and, acting like missiles, tore adrift heavy petrol cans, a hazard to any animal or man in their way. One dog's chain snapped and the animal was quickly washed away. Another was thrown into the sea on the surge of a wave then flung aboard again with the very next roll.

Captain Scott, supervising the relashing of cans, said to Bowers: "I am afraid it's a bad business for us—what do you think?" Bowers was as optimistic as ever. As they watched, the lee railings, between one of the heavy motor-sledge crates and the deck edge, were swept away. Scott restrained Bowers from trying to save the petrol cases, telling him that they did not matter.

Down below, the water rose so high that the engineers feared an implosion of steam, so the furnace was drawn and the engines stopped. It now seemed that only hand pumps could save the ship, but they were tried without success, so Scott divided the men into two shifts using buckets. Debenham wrote: "Seems a primitive idea, to bail out a ship." His fellow Australian, geologist Griffith Taylor, noted: "Thus were we driven to a method almost unique with a ship of 750 tons—that of bailing out with buckets!"

Scott knew the main hand pump was key to survival. He, Teddy Evans, Mate Victor Campbell, and First Officer Harry Pennell worked out a possible solution to reach the suction well of the main hand pump by cutting through a steel hatch in a bulkhead. This was eventually done, whereupon Teddy Evans wriggled his way down into the oily bilges beneath the pump, together with the even shorter Bowers. Between them, and over the course of many hours, they passed up bucket after bucket of oil-coal sludge until, at last, the hand pump worked again.

Pennell at one time spotted Scott high up "on the weather rail of the poop, buried to his waist in green sea." Scott wrote: "A dog was drowned last night . . . Occasionally a heavy sea would bear one of them away, and he was only saved by his chain. Meares with some helpers had constantly to be rescuing these wretched creatures from hanging." Evans found Oates, by himself, for the two Russians were both badly seasick, "actually lifting the poor little ponies to their feet as the ship lurched heavily to leeward . . . He himself appeared quite unconscious of any personal suffering, although his hands and feet must have been absolutely numbed with the cold and wet." Oates wrote: "I was drenched all night . . . one pony was down as many as eight times and . . . two killed. One fell and broke its leg and the other got cast so badly . . . it could not be got up." By chance, these two ponies were called Davy and Jones.

Once the exertions of Evans, Bowers, and the engineers had the hand pump working, things gradually improved, the water level fell, and, at length, the boilers were refired. By noon on Saturday, the nightmare was over. Scott, Oates, and others squeezed the bodies of the two dead ponies out through the fo'c'sle hatch and overboard. Scott heaped praise on the crewmen whose quarters, bedding, and possessions were soaked. There was little light, no fresh air, and a constant rain of urine from the stables above. "Not a word has been said; the men living in that part have done their best to fend off the nuisance . . . but without sign of complaint." The scientists and officers had fared a little better but their notebooks, diaries, and belongings floated about their cabin floors. Teddy Evans wrote: "Scott himself working with the best of them and staying with the toughest. It was a sight that one could never forget: everybody saturated . . . every one filthy." Their hair stayed sticky with coal-oil grease for weeks afterward.

Despite the loss of a dog, two ponies, some coal, and some gasoline, the ship had survived and the men had gained a great deal of respect for each

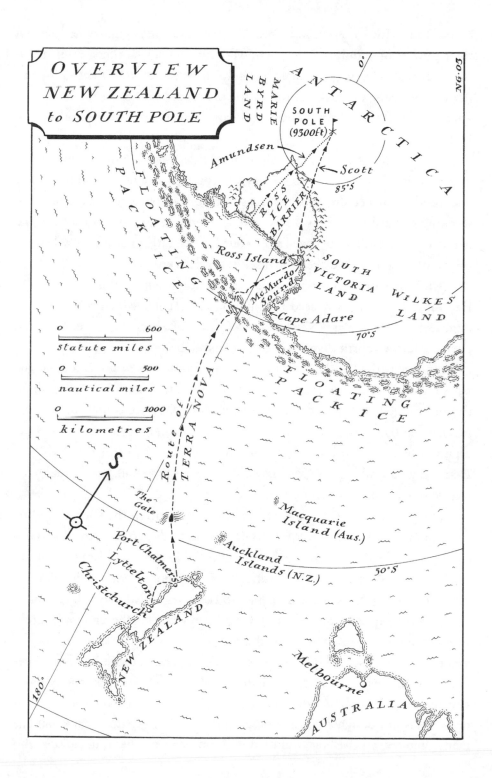

OVERVIEW
NEW ZEALAND
to SOUTH POLE

NG·03

A N T A R C T I C A

MARIE
BYRD
LAND

0°

SOUTH
POLE
(9300ft)

Amundsen

Scott

85°S

ROSS
ICE
BARRIER

FLOATING PACK ICE

Ross Island

McMurdo Sound

SOUTH
VICTORIA
LAND

WILKES
LAND

Cape Adare

70°S

FLOATING PACK ICE

0   600
statute miles

0   500
nautical miles

0   1000
kilometres

Route of TERRA NOVA

S

The Gate

Macquarie
Island (Aus.)

Port Chalmers
Lyttelton
Christchurch

Auckland
Islands (N.Z.)

50°S

NEW ZEALAND

Melbourne

180°

AUSTRALIA

other. Teddy Evans, Bowers, Oates, Meares, and the engineers had shown their powers of endurance and there were no obvious shirkers, a fine comment on Scott as a judge of character in his final selection of the ship's company. Not a single note of criticism for the leader or "Owner," to use his applied and affectionate title, was sounded in any letter or diary, not even by Oates.

Bowers, so critical a week before of Kathleen Scott, noted now: "Captain Scott was simply splendid, he might have been at Cowes, and to do him and Teddy Evans credit, at our worst strait none of our landsmen who were working so hard knew how serious things were . . . take my word for it, he is one of the best, and behaved up to our best traditions at a time when his own outlook must have been the blackness of darkness."

After the storm, *Terra Nova* pushed on south with sail and steam. On December 5, Gran was teased for sighting an iceberg, which turned out to be merely a whale blast. Nevertheless, *Terra Nova* reached the edge of the pack ice farther north than expected, probably because Scott had arrived in the area far earlier in the year than had *Discovery* or *Nimrod* and so the pack had not yet begun its seasonal dispersal. Scott's ongoing worries about the tight schedule had become irrelevant since they were now utterly dependent on the whims of the pack ice. There was no way of knowing how long it would take to break through into the open waters of the Ross Sea. *Discovery* had taken only four days, but other ships had been caught for twelve months or more inside the pack.

The best way to make at least some progress within the pack would be to maintain full engine power twenty-four hours a day to push the floes constantly and always at their weakest point. To do this would involve more coal use than Scott could afford. Patience was the only answer, but Scott, famous for his impatience, was desperate to reach McMurdo Sound, set up his base, and complete major depot-laying forays before the end of March, when travel would become impossible.

The ship was soon jammed between floes and most of the crew were delighted by the welcome rest, the chance to dry out clothing on sunny days, and the novelty of their situation. The ship's freshwater-from-the-sea condenser was not designed for a complement of over sixty thirsty men and as many animals, so the boatswain led a chain gang of chanting sailors who manhandled chunks of ice aboard from old floes where the brine had leached away.

Cherry-Garrard, one of the youngest at twenty-one and fresh from university, was beginning to learn his new job as assistant taxidermist to Wilson by skinning penguins caught on the shipside floes. He waxed delirious: "I have never thought of anything as good as this life . . . the novelty, interest, colour, animal life and good fellowship." The penguins probably did not appreciate Cherry-Garrard as much as he appreciated them. He and Wilson had developed a method of killing them that Debenham described: "Dr. Wilson then 'pithed' the penguins . . . 'Pithing' consists of pushing a needle thro' the back of the head and shoving it about in the brain. A penguin will take half a dozen shots from a gun and any amount of waddling before it will die, yet these were motionless in less than 20 seconds."

Up in the crow's nest, Teddy Evans or Harry Pennell peered ahead for weaknesses in the pack and shouted their orders through a megaphone to the helmsman below. Wild games began again in the wardroom with Oates and Wilson among the most rowdy participants. Gran seized his chance to do what Scott had ordered, the training of the company to become top-rate skiers. The flat floes provided good nursery slopes and Gran did his best. Oates and his friend the navy surgeon, Edward Atkinson, stripped to the waist and goggled, speeding around the floe with no attempt at technique, but most of the sailors shied away from "the planks." Gran had taught the queen of Norway to ski but could never have had so much difficulty as with these fifty or so clumsy Britons on their way to conquer the Pole. Meares and Gerof harnessed a dog team to a sledge and went for a trial run, greatly cheered by the onlookers, most of whom had never seen any sledge in motion before, with or without dogs.

Teddy Evans, unable to coax the ship south faster than a rate of one knot at full power, agreed with Scott to conserve coal and let the furnace die. He wrote, on December 13, as five days of enforced sailing began, that *Terra Nova* "is like a slug crawling across a bucketful of biscuits strewn on the water," and further commented that "our patience was sorely tried." Evans wrote about "penguin stews and 'hooshes' to eke out our fresh provisions . . . Wilson found a new kind of [penguin] tapeworm . . . with a head like a propeller. This worm has since been named after one of us! . . . We are now down to under 300 tons of coal . . . I had no idea that Captain Scott could be so patient. He put the best face on everything, although he certainly was disappointed in the *Terra Nova* and her steaming capacity."

Cherry-Garrard wrote years later, "To Scott any delay was intolerable" and this I am sure was a correct assessment of the man. He must have tried hard not to show his impatience, for he knew it to be his greatest failing, but his diary remained a safe outlet. Near the end of what must have been a nail-biting three weeks in the floes, he wrote:

> I can imagine few things more trying to the patience than the long wasted days of waiting. Exasperating as it is to see the tons of coal melting away with the smallest mileage to our credit . . . It's damnable for them [the ponies] and disgusting for us . . . You can imagine how often and how restlessly we climbed to the crow's nest and studied the outlook.

He described the pack.

> Huge icebergs crept silently towards or past us, and continually we were observing these formidable objects with range finder and compass to determine the relative movement, sometimes with misgiving as to our ability to clear them . . . sometimes we passed through acres of sludgy sodden ice which hissed as it swept along the side, and sometimes the hissing ceased seemingly without rhyme or reason, and we found our screw churning the sea without any effect . . . As a result I have grown strongly attached to the *Terra Nova*. As she bumped the floes with mighty shocks, crushing and grinding a way through some, twisting and turning to avoid others, she seemed like a living thing fighting a great fight.

Christmas Day was celebrated with the ship jammed firmly in the heavy pack and much singing to tunes produced by Ponting on a banjo. Scott, who had listened to many previous polar musical sessions, was unimpressed and noted: "It is rather a surprising circumstance that such an unmusical party should be so keen on singing."

Scott tried to keep his frustration in check by spending many hours in his cabin working on his detailed plans, in readiness for landing. He needed, with as much care and tact as feasible, to designate those men in his opinion best suited for the variety of tasks to be completed as soon as they reached their destination. One such appointment was Priestley as leader of a planned inland journey composed of geologists. Scott chose Priestley as leader on the grounds that he was the most experienced traveler and the oldest of the group. When Scott then told Australian geologist Griffith Taylor that he would be second-in-command, he was visibly upset so, in Scott's words, "we three talked the matter out between us, and Priestley at once disclaimed any right, and announced cheerful agreement with Taylor's leadership." Scott did not find all his people so ready to be understanding. Oates remained determinedly hostile to both Scott and Evans, writing to his mother: "their ignorance is colossal."

I have found on many of my own expeditions over thirty-two years that some individuals are naturally averse to receiving orders. I usually try to avoid confrontation with such types by letting them do their own thing so long as they do not endanger my overall plans. Reading the diaries of Scott and Oates (and of their more reliable colleagues) I detect just such an unfortunate clash of personalities between the two officers, one navy-, the other army-trained. Late in December, Scott noted: "Oates is unremitting in his attention and care of the animals, but I don't think he quite realises that whilst in the pack the ship must remain steady and that, therefore, a certain limited scope for movement and exercise is afforded by the open deck on which the sick animal[s] now [stand]." This was good advice but, for some reason, it appears he never actually suggested it to Oates. Eventually Oates did take the initiative to stretch some ponies' legs and clean their stalls, but not before penning a letter to his mother complaining that Scott had failed to suggest pony exercise on the floes. Scott was very good at his multifaceted, complex job and Oates was without equal at his specific task, but neither could bridge the hostility gap between them because both were natural introverts.

Scott's mood would have deteriorated had he known that Amundsen's *Fram* was to arrive at the northern edge of the pack only a week after *Terra Nova* finally broke into the open water of the Ross Sea on December 29, or that *Fram* would then ease through the pack in only four days, just as Scott had in *Discovery* back in 1901. Frank Debenham noted: "Talking to Capt. Scott about it he told me he thought our slow passage through the pack was due to our starting so early in the season and due to rank bad luck." Scott, expecting a two-hundred-mile band of loose pack, in fact had to deal with double that distance. Anticipating thirty tons of coal consumption, he had used up sixty. Some critics have blamed Scott for bad timing, but he could not possibly have known about the exact seasonal dynamics of the very variable floating pack. We now know from hundreds of subsequent Antarctic voyages, and from satellite photographs, that a very sudden change does occur in the pack in early to mid January, so a single week can make all the difference between meeting heavy pack in December or loose floes in January. Scott had been lucky to enter the pack in January 1902 with *Discovery*, but, in 1910, his natural zeal to make an early landfall resulted only in frustration.

The last of the more solid pack ice was indeed left behind on December 30, and on New Year's Day, the watch sighted Mount Erebus, 115 miles away, and Scott headed straight for his intended base camp, Cape Crozier. Surf pounded the beach at the Cape and bergs jostled one another just offshore, so *Terra Nova* had to nose around the familiar western coast of Ross Island, into McMurdo Sound, and on toward Hut Point. Early on January 4, the ship arrived off two wide bays some ten miles north of Hut Point and Scott called a council with Teddy Evans, Victor Campbell, Harry Pennell, and other officers.

When all were agreed, they steamed directly for a cape baptized back in 1901 as The Skuary, a beach to the north of which would provide excellent winter quarters. Hut Point itself was obviously not a popular destination since the sea ice there had in 1903 and 1904 proved so reluctant to release *Discovery*. The new location of The Skuary, being thirteen miles farther north, should prove far more accessible to ships. In terms of sledging access to and from the Great Ice Barrier, the additional twelve miles of flat sea ice over the two bays that lay between The Skuary and Hut Point was an acceptable nuisance. *Terra Nova* made directly toward the bay to the north of The Skuary, which Scott named Cape Evans in honor of his second-in-command.

Solid bay ice stopped the ship from reaching the beach itself, as was to be expected, but only a mile and a half of smooth, flat going separated the ice edge from the hut site, so the crew, under the experienced boatswain Alf Cheetham, made the ice anchors fast and the unloading process began at once under Bowers's supervision. Two of the three motor sledges were landed, followed by the seventeen surviving ponies, glad to roll on the ice. Meares took the dogs ashore, to the detriment of many overcurious penguins, and within a few hours of arrival a caravan of goods, starting with timber for the base hut, was being sledged to a beach site fully approved of by the entire company. Scott summed up the Cape Evans site as: "Comfortable quarters for the hut, ice for water, snow for the animals, good slopes for ski-ing, vast tracks of rock for walks."

The unloading work continued round the clock with men sleeping briefly when exhausted. The key was speed. At any time, the weather could deteriorate and *Terra Nova* would then have to fire her boilers and move away to open water, thereby losing hours or even days. This Scott could not risk since, after the delay in the pack, time was short in which to lay depots on the Barrier before the beginning of winter, in April. Each day, chunks of sea ice broke off beside the ship and Cheetham's men tightened the anchor chains or repositioned the ice anchors accordingly. Gradually, the distance between the ship and the shore lessened. By the end of January, the bay would be ice free and likely to remain that way for three or four months.

In due course, the third and last of the motor sledges was unloaded and hoisted onto the sea ice where it sat waiting for Day to start the engine. Some thirty minutes later, a message arrived at the ship from Scott warning that the ice was deteriorating rapidly, so no more ponies should be used in rotten areas and the motorized sledge should be taken ashore as soon as possible. Before Mate Victor Campbell's chain gang had managed to drag the machine a hundred yards, the ice beneath it began to give way, tearing the rope out of the men's hands. The bay was over a hundred fathoms deep, so there was no chance of recovering the lost machine. Scott took all the blame for its loss.

I have taken far heavier machines over different thicknesses of sea ice a thousand times over the last twenty-five years but I still find myself unable to predict the weight-bearing behavior of different ice types. If, every time there was a risky patch, I had reacted negatively, my polar career would have stood no chance of success. One day in 1982, wandering around Hut Point after crossing Antarctica, I came across a memorial to one Richard T. Williams, who drove his thirty-ton tractor over the sea ice on January 6, 1956, when the ice gave way and the vehicle sank. Williams was on a standard ice trail used by dozens of heavy U.S. vehicles and close to Cape Evans at the time.

Scott sensibly shrugged and moved on. As Shackleton said: "What the ice gets, the ice keeps." That most critical of writers, Cherry-Garrard, wrote later: "Indefinite conditions always tried Scott most: positive disasters put him in more cheerful spirits than most."

Some days later, the unloading was again interrupted when the wind shifted and Pennell had to move the ship. A few miles offshore, she ran aground. Charles Wright wrote that he was watching the drama beside Scott as the crew of *Terra Nova* struggled to free her. They finally succeeded and Wright was greatly impressed by Scott's equanimity at such a moment of potential disaster. "I mention this because it was the first time I had actually seen Scott suddenly meeting a catastrophe which might have wrecked completely all his plans." Cherry-Garrard, who was with Wright, said: "Scott . . . himself came back into the hut with us and went on bagging provisions for the Depot Journey. At such times of real disaster he was a very philosophical man."

Herbert Ponting was busy with his cameras when not helping with the work. One morning, he walked over the floes close to the ship to film penguins and killer whales. The latter, spotting an opportunity to bag Ponting as well as the penguins, dived deep, then struck upward at Ponting's floe, breaking and tipping it. The photographer fled with his cameras, jumping from floe to floe with the killers in hot pursuit. Sadly, nobody else had a camera to record the event.

The geologist Raymond Priestley was apt to compare everything about *Terra Nova* with his previous experience on Shackleton's *Nimrod,* thereby reminding his colleagues that, unlike them, he was an old hand: "between the way the work was carried out and the way when we were landing stores at Cape Royds . . . there are too many officers superintending and the men never knew when and where to go for orders . . . an Expedition to make a complete success should be entirely away from any Navy ideas . . . in this one particular give me Shackleton's expedition over and over again."

The reality of the two operations was the opposite of Priestley's glib summary. Scott completed his entire operation in eight days despite vastly more complex stores and scientific gear than on *Nimrod*. Shackleton took fourteen days, largely due to a major disagreement with Captain England, who could see the dangers of anchoring against the lee shore selected by Shackleton for his base at Cape Royds. Under Scott's regime, Teddy Evans supervised the erection of the hut, Oates the horse stabling, Meares the dog kennels, and Bowers the exact locating of all stores.

Scott had noted the performance of the different transport systems used to unload the ship, but only over flat, mostly hard, sea-ice surfaces. He proclaimed himself "astonished" by the strength of the ponies who had hauled 1,100-pound loads despite the often slippery ice. "Oates," he wrote, "is splendid with them—I do not know what we should do without him." Eight of Shackleton's ponies had survived his *Nimrod* voyage. Scott, thanks to Oates, now had double that number. Many of the ponies bit, kicked, reared, and refused orders in a committed manner. According to Oates, "a more unpromising lot of ponies to start a journey such as ours it would be almost impossible to conceive." Cherry-Garrard felt that the way Oates handled them "might have proved a model to any governor of a lunatic asylum."

Of the other nonmechanical transport modes, Scott wrote: "The dogs are getting better, but they only take very light loads still and get back from each journey pretty dead beat. In their present state they don't inspire confidence, but the hot weather is much against them." Scott had already accompanied Meares on a short dog-sledge journey, on January 15, 1911, to see if the old Hut Point hut was still in good condition, because it formed a vital part of his plans. He was dismayed by what he found. Wilson later described the scene: "we found the old hut simply filled with hard packed snow drift up to the roof. We had to get in through a window and then we began to dig and clear it out—a long job which we couldn't nearly finish. The last occupants had been Shackleton and his party on their return from the southern journey. His relief and depot parties had also spent a good deal of time there

and had left it in a perfectly filthy condition besides having broken a window open and left it unboarded, so that every blizzard had poured more
snow drift in and filled the hut."

Scott had brought enough ski sticks for all the shore party to use two
each rather than just the single stick per man of the *Discovery* days, noting:
"Everyone declares that the ski sticks greatly help pulling; it is surprising
that we never thought of using them before."

On January 18, the shore party began to move into their new base hut,
which Scott divided into two sections along traditional navy lines. He and
the fifteen other officers and scientists were allotted two-thirds of the space
and the nine sailors had the rest. A shelved wall separated these two living
areas. At no stage was a single voice raised aloud or by way of diary comment against this solid division. Apart from the scientists, almost all of
Scott's men had, since their early teens, been trained and lived with the same
set social structure.

Thanks to his *Discovery* experiences, Scott knew that his South Pole chances
for the following summer would depend on laying out suitable depots on the
barrier, and Bowers, already dog tired but still the most capable of adminis-
trators, was told by Scott to complete the preparations of all sledge loads for
the depot journey as soon as possible. Whatever manpower Bowers needed
to help with these preparations was made available to him and a date was
agreed upon for departure, January 24. Scott made the overall aim of the depot journey clear to all concerned. A series of depots would be laid, starting
at the edge of the barrier and ending at 80° south, 140 miles out on the barrier en route to the Pole. This final dump, the biggest, was to be called One
Ton Depot. No vehicles would be used because the sea ice had already become too risky. Eight of the fittest ponies, out of the seventeen at Cape
Evans, would go, each with a 570-pound sledge load, and two dog teams,
each towing a 490-pound load. Twelve men would be selected to lead the
animals, and it was fairly obvious that Scott's final choice for the main Pole
attempt the following summer would include only men who had experienced this depot journey.

Two days before leaving Cape Evans, Scott noted that he disliked giving
out to the press (or anyone else) "any definite information of details which it

might be advisable to modify at a later date." The scientists who were used to being consulted and to being fully in the picture at all times were hurt by not being told more detail well in advance. Since none but Wilson and Priestley had been south before, they did not appreciate how unpredictable weather and ice changes made Scott's apparent secretiveness advisable to avoid constant modification and plan changes unlikely to inspire confidence in his leadership.

Ten days before departure, on January 14, Scott was ready to draw up a list of those chosen for the depot journey and informed each man accordingly. Cherry-Garrard was a surprise choice as a pony leader and, less of a surprise, Wilson as a dog driver. The cavalcade set out over the sea ice carrying 5,300 pounds, enough food and fuel for fourteen weeks. Apart from Crean, Scott, and Wilson none of the men had traveled in Antarctica before. Some were, Scott believed, prime polar material and this journey would be their testing ground. Atkinson, the naval surgeon, had failed to own up to a blistered heel, no doubt in the hope it would clear up and not be noticed. Within two days, however, the wound was festering and the doctor limping. Like one or two of the others, Atkinson was also soon suffering mild snow-blindness from the glare.

Ponies floundered about in waterlogged patches but the loads were slowly shifted south and around the last capes of Ross Island, toward the barrier. Two days after departure, Scott took a fast dog team hitch back to the ship in order to thank the crew and the two sledge groups of scientists about to head off in different directions. The two Australian geologists, Debenham and Taylor, together with Charles Wright the physicist, Petty Officer Forde, and Taff Evans as their guardian, would be away for six weeks to study three glaciers to the west of Ross Island. *Terra Nova*, under Harry Pennell, was to drop off a six-man group under Victor Campbell at the far eastern end of the Great Ice Barrier to explore King Edward VII Land. Once this group was safely landed with its stores, the ship would head north to New Zealand. Scott thanked everyone aboard and wished them well. He did not expect to see the ship's crew or Campbell's men again for a year.

After four days of ferrying loads over the sea ice, the depot party reached the Great Ice Barrier. Oates had already begun a fresh litany of moans but otherwise all was going well when, a mile or so onto the barrier's

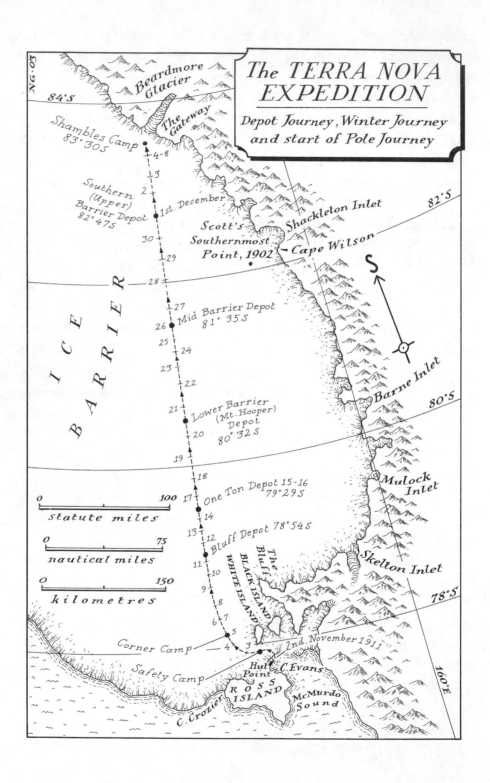

The TERRA NOVA
EXPEDITION

Depot Journey, Winter Journey
and start of Pole Journey

Beardmore Glacier

84°S

The Gateway

Shambles Camp
83°30S

Southern
(Upper)
Barrier Depot
82°47S

Shackleton Inlet

82°S

1st December

Scott's
Southernmost
Point, 1902

Cape Wilson

30

S

29

28

27

Mid Barrier Depot
81° 35S

26

25

24

23

22

Barne Inlet

80°S

21

Lower Barrier
(Mt. Hooper)
Depot
80° 32S

20

19

I C E   B A R R I E R

18

0   100

statute miles

17

One Ton Depot 15-16
79° 29S

14

Mulock
Inlet

0   75

nautical miles

13

12

Bluff Depot 78° 54S

0   150

kilometres

11

10

The Bluff

BLACK ISLAND

WHITE ISLAND

Skelton Inlet

9

8

78°S

6 7

5

Corner Camp   4   3

2nd November 1911

Safety Camp

Hut
Point

C. Evans

160°E

R O S S
ISLAND

McMurdo
Sound

C. Crozier

surface, the ponies hit a soft patch and floundered about, advancing at a snail's pace and only with great difficulty. Scott called a halt a few miles in from the barrier's edge and far enough back that it seemed unlikely their camp site would break off and float away into the Ross Sea. This place was designated as Safety Camp.

Atkinson now admitted that he was in trouble, for his heel had become an open, suppurating sore. Scott was annoyed, for he could not leave the surgeon alone and had to shed Tom Crean to stay with him. This would not be the last time Scott's plans would be thwarted by individuals hiding known weaknesses.

By now Scott had a fair idea of the depot group's travel potential on the barrier's mixed surfaces in autumn temperatures and of how to use ponies as well as dogs with heavy loads. Until now any plan he might have made would have been based entirely on theory, not reality. He unveiled his intentions and kept them simple. There was no frenzied rush, in fact the opposite since they were now on safe "ground" and he no longer feared a sudden breakup of the ice beneath their feet. From Safety Camp, Scott told his men, they would go east in order to avoid the crevasse zone to their immediate south, by White and Black Islands. Once past this danger zone, they would lay another depot named Corner Camp, from whence they would march due south for about ten days to reach 80° south and leave there one ton of supplies ready for the main Pole journey the next summer.

Oates meanwhile had taken against Gran, writing to his mother: "I can't stand this Norwegian chap, he is both dirty and lazy." As for Scott, he "would fifty times sooner stay in the hut seeing how a pair of Foxs spiral puttees suited him than come out and look at the ponies legs or a dogs feet." With Oates, Scott was in a no-win situation since, when he did comment on the pony welfare, it was considered to be fussing or interference.

As Scott saw it, the ponies were the key to success, at least as far as the base of the Beardmore Glacier. Shackleton had proved that with just four ponies. So the fewer ponies that died during the depot journey the better. The ground pressure of an unshod pony hoof is about fifteen pounds per square inch, five times that of a dog, and Scott and Meares had, long before Oates's arrival from India, decided that snowshoes were vital for the ponies' health. They had obtained enough pairs of *hestersko* (Norwegian horse snowshoes) for all the ponies. But the snowshoes were all still sitting at Cape Evans because Oates had no faith in them and had decided to leave them behind, but for a single pair that he might try out en route. Shackleton's ponies had reached the Beardmore without snowshoes, which is perhaps why Oates thought they were unnecessary, but when Scott tried out the sole set of *hestersko* on Gran's pony, a slow coach called Weary Willie, the improvement was "magical." Scott was delighted, but also annoyed with Oates. His diary was fairly restrained given the circumstances. "If we had more of these shoes we could certainly put them on seven out of eight of our ponies . . . It is trying to feel that so great a help to our work has been left behind at the station."

Thirty miles from Hut Point, they laid their Corner Camp Depot. There they were caught by bad weather in the strong winds zone between Minna Bluff and Cape Crozier. Cherry-Garrard described this, his first blizzard, as "raging chaos" and it lasted, as many blizzards do, for three days and nights. They hunkered down in their four-man pyramid tents, smoked their pipes, and waited. Cherry-Garrard decided he was lucky to be sharing the tent of Scott, who knew how to make the best of things. "Scott's tent was a comfortable one to live in, and I was always glad when I was told to join it . . . He was himself extraordinarily quick . . . He was most careful, some said over-careful but I do not think so, that everything should be neat and shipshape." Outside, Cherry-Garrard wrote: "Fight your way a few steps away from the tent and it will be gone. Lose your sense of direction and there is nothing to guide you back."

The dogs curled up in the snow and slept, but the ponies, without their full Arctic seasonal coats, suffered dreadfully. Scott, not Oates, had the idea of building walls out of snow blocks to provide some protection to the windward of each tethered pony and this did seem to help them a great deal. Nonetheless, as Cherry-Garrard added: "all our ponies were weakened [by the blizzard], and two of them became practically useless." This was surely proof that dogs were better suited to the polar cold than even snow-wise Manchurian ponies, but the fact remained that Shackleton held the Antarctic travel record using ponies, not dogs, on this very route.

After the three-day Corner Camp blizzard, they continued south and a week later Scott split the group into two. Teddy Evans, with Robert Forde

and Patrick Keohane, was to take the three weakest ponies slowly and carefully back homeward and try to keep them alive, while the others took the
last five ponies on to the hoped-for goal of 80° south.

On February 14, Gran's pony, Weary Willie, lagged far behind the other
four and at one point lay down to rest. The dog teams were passing at the
time and, seeing a pony in a defenseless position, attacked him in force.
Chaos ensued until Gran, Meares, and Wilson eventually whipped the dogs
off their intended meal. Weary Willie, badly bitten, carried on to the chosen
campsite even more slowly than before and without his load, which Scott
and three others went back to man-haul. Scott recorded with feeling: "It
taught us the nature of the surface more than many hours of pony leading!!"
He noticed that the injured pony's sledge load was a good deal heavier than
the others, which may well have been the responsibility of Oates to check,
although this is not made clear. Scott wrote: "The incident is deplorable and
the blame widespread . . . I blame myself for not supervising these matters
more effectively and for allowing W.W. to get so far behind." Here was another of many examples of Scott's natural tendency to blame himself: an ultimate the-buck-stops-here policy, which does not allow the process of
delegation to provide an excuse.

Throughout this period, Scott and his four remaining companions continuing south with their five ponies used a single four-man tent, as did the
four dog teamsters. At no time did anyone complain about the discomfort of
an extra man in the tent and Scott merely noted: "We are five in a tent yet
fairly comfortable." It was to prove useful knowledge. Three days later,
matters came to a head between Scott and Oates. Watching the suffering of
Weary Willie, Scott had made up his mind. There were two alternatives: either to press on for the remaining thirty miles to 80° south (the geographical and featureless spot that Scott had nominated as the site for his One Ton
Depot), in which case the ponies would almost certainly die, or to dump the
loads where they were and stand a good chance of getting most, perhaps all,
of the ponies back to Hut Point to survive for the main event the next summer, by which time their Arctic winter coats would be fully developed.

On February 17, Scott told his men that he had decided they must cut
their losses, lay the depot thirty-one miles short of 80° south, and head home
to conserve the ponies if possible. Oates was appalled. He pressed Scott to

keep going and to kill each pony as it foundered. The meat could then be dumped in caches for dog or human consumption at a later date.

Many years later, Gran described in his book the conversation he thought took place between the two officers. "Oates proposed to Scott that the animal ('Weary Willie') should be killed and that we should push on with the other ponies, but Scott rejected this suggestion. He had, as he himself put it, felt quite sick on account of the animal's sufferings . . . [Oates said] 'Sir, I'm afraid you'll come to regret not taking my advice.' 'Regret it or not,' replied Scott, 'I have taken my decision, as a Christian gentleman.' "

So that was that. The depot was made not at 80° south but at 79°29' south, some thirty-one miles to the north. A great deal was later to be made of this deficiency of thirty-one miles.

Scott wrote: "It would have been ridiculous to have worked some [of the ponies] out this year as the soldier wished. Even now I feel we went too far with the first three." Scott commented often that Oates was magnificent in his tireless solicitude for each pony, but such care was not everything. He might be the world's expert on horses elsewhere, but on the Great Ice Barrier that was not the only expertise that counted. According to Scott: "Oates is certainly a poor judge of the amount of work which different surfaces entail. He does not show well as a judge of the animals' capacity for covering distance."

They built a six-foot-high cairn at One Ton Depot, inside which was stacked 2,181 pounds of fuel, food, and equipment. Scott knew well that his overall plans were progressing satisfactorily. The thirty-one-mile shortfall in his planned depot line should not prove a serious problem, all things being equal, since the overall reserve fuel and rations allowance could in theory more than cope with such a minor difference. What concerned Scott now was the ever-weakening state of the eight ponies out on the barrier. He bade Oates take Weary Willie and the other four animals back with great care. Their sledges were now lightly laden and the barrier winds would be behind them. More worrying was the state of the three weak ponies Teddy Evans had turned back with the previous week. Scott decided to make his way back with the dogs as quickly as possible to minimize the delay in getting Evans's survivors back to base.

Leaving Oates, Bowers, and Gran with the ponies, Scott joined Meares,

Wilson, and Cherry-Garrard, whose pony had died, with the dogs. Lightly laden, they sped back toward Safety Camp, covering over thirty miles each day. On February 21, the dog teams returned to the region of Corner Camp, the point where the trail turned west at the limit of the White Island crevasse fields. Since the exact edge of this crevassed zone was invisible, Scott, traveling with Cecil Meares, took a chance and cut the corner. Cherry-Garrard, following Scott with the second dog team, wrote: "It was not expected that this would bring us across any badly crevassed area."

Wilson recorded:

> I was running my team abreast of Meares, but about 100 yards on his right, when I suddenly saw his whole team disappear, one dog after another, as they ran down a crevasse in the Barrier surface. Ten out of his 13 dogs disappeared as I watched. They looked exactly like rats running down a hole—only . . . I saw no hole. They simply went into the white surface and disappeared. I saw Scott, who was running alongside, quickly jump on the sledge, and I saw Meares jam the brake on as I fixed my sledge and left Cherry with my dogs and ran over to see what had really happened. I found that they had been running *along* a lidded crevasse, about 6 to 8 ft wide, for quite a distance, and the loaded sledge was still standing on it, while in front was a great blue chasm in which hung the team of dogs in a festoon. The leader, Osman, a very powerful fine dog, had remained on the surface and the 2 dogs next [to] the sledge were also still on the surface.

It was clear to all four men that only Osman's strength, hauling back against the rope's downward pull, was stopping the remaining dogs and the sledge from dropping into the abyss. They managed to haul up all but two of the dogs that had slipped from their harnesses and landed on a ledge sixty-five feet down. Cherry-Garrard described what happened next. "Scott told Meares to go down and get the dogs. Meares refused. I said I often went down the well at home let me go! Scott said to Bill [Wilson] 'What do you think?' Bill said he didn't think anyone ought to go, but if anyone went he would go down. Scott then said he [would go] down; & he went."

Scott was lowered on a rope to rescue the two marooned dogs, but while he was down there, a furious fight broke out between the dogs above. An hour later, the battle over, a freezing Scott and the last two dogs were hauled up. Cherry-Garrard wrote of the crevasse incident: "I feel that a man who never says much in the way of prayers would say one tonight." He added years later: "Up to this day Scott had been talking to Meares of how dogs would go to the Pole. After this, I never heard him say that." Not surprisingly, after seeing the near-terminal effects on an entire dog team of a small barrier crevasse and having read of Shackleton's terrible experiences in the vast chasm fields of the Beardmore Glacier.

They were soon back at Safety Camp, only to find that Teddy Evans, despite great care, had been unable to save two of the three weak ponies. The third, Jimmy Pigg, was greatly recovered. But more bad news awaited Scott in a long letter from Victor Campbell. The news was about as bad as could be. On bidding Scott farewell four weeks before, *Terra Nova* had sailed for the far end of the barrier to drop off Campbell and his five men on the King Edward VII Peninsula coast. But Pennell had found it a hazardous maze of pack, great bergs, and sheer ice cliffs. Threading his way back west, looking for an alternative landing for Campbell's party, Pennell had found none and so decided to try for the Bay of Whales area. Once there, to his shock and dismay, he saw *Fram* and, some three miles from the barrier front, the hut and tents of Amundsen's Norwegians.

When the Norwegians spotted *Terra Nova*, whose arrival the well-informed Amundsen had been expecting sooner or later, one of the *Fram* sailors wrote: "Well, if they are planning something bad (we were constantly asking ourselves in what light the Englishmen would view our competition) the dogs will manage to make them turn back . . . I had better be armed for all eventualities." This indicates that the crew of *Fram* were well aware that Amundsen's behavior might be thought of as deceitful.

Victor Campbell, who had often skied in Norway and spoke the language reasonably well, was duly invited to the camp with others from *Terra Nova*. The two groups visited each other's "properties" and an atmosphere of strained politeness prevailed, mixed with intense mutual curiosity. Campbell learned that *Fram* had sailed nonstop from Madeira, passed through the pack ice in only four days, reached the Bay of Whales on January 9, and that the crew were still unloading her nearly a month later. Amundsen politely offered Campbell the option to make his base at a suitable spot about a mile from the Norwegian camp with unloading help from the Norwegian dog teams. Campbell declined this offer with equal politeness.

Wilfred Bruce wrote that the Norwegians "all seemed charming men, even the perfidious Amundsen," adding that once *Terra Nova* had left the bay, "Curses loud and deep were heard everywhere" and there were "heavy arguments . . . about the rights and wrongs of Amundsen's party and the chances of our being able to beat them. Their experience and number of dogs seem to leave us very little."

Surgeon Levick commented: "It is very unfortunate that Amundsen was not more aboveboard about his coming here . . . Anyhow it is going to be one of the finest races next summer." Priestley added that he and the others were left full of conjecture about the Norwegians and their obvious expertise with polar travel, especially with their great number of dogs.

Once *Terra Nova* had left, the Norwegians completed their unloading and began to lay their own southward depots. Amundsen hoped to place depots as far south as 83°, 180 miles farther south than Scott. Apart from his expertise with dogs and skis, Amundsen's base was sixty miles closer to the Pole. This gave him less far to travel, out and back, and no treacherous sea ice to negotiate between his base and the barrier. Shackleton, in 1908, and Scott that very year could have established their own bases at Amundsen's chosen spot, for they appreciated its obvious advantages. But they had also been well aware of its very real dangers. First, the site was quite liable to break away from the ice shelf at any moment and sail away as an iceberg, and second, it was likely that some huge crevasse field or other unknown obstacle blocked the ice between the Norwegian site and the Pole. Both Scott and Shackleton preferred the far safer locale of McMurdo Sound to the risky Bay of Whales.

The Norwegians set out to lay their depots on February 21: eight men, arguing among themselves, and seven 660-pound sledges, each pulled by six dogs. Amundsen failed to realize how soft his dogs had become during their long voyage on *Fram*. They tired easily, lost weight quickly, and cut their pads, so that their paws became bloody sponges. They reached 81° south on March 1. Somehow they had forgotten to bring the key navigation manual,

The Nautical Almanac, for the year 1912, and only a single copy for the year 1911. One night an oil lamp set fire to this vital copy and burned all but the pages for the summer months September to December 1911. Amundsen decided this was a powerful indicator that he must reach the Pole and return to his base by December 31, 1911. He had neither scientists nor a science program to worry about, so every effort of all his men, save the cook, was focused on the Pole.

He was keen always to explain how he hated any pain suffered by his dogs. On March 6, approaching 82° south, Johansen, Amundsen's deputy, wrote: "16½ miles covered today—the last part of the way terribly slowly. The poor dogs had to be whipped on." And the next day: "did 13 miles with greater difficulty than hitherto, and it goes very sluggishly . . . The Chief's dogs are the worst, they don't take any notice of thrashing any more, just lie down in their tracks, and it is a terrible performance to get them going again." Amundsen, like Scott, was forced by his animals' limitations to set-tle for a final depot farther from the Pole than he had planned. "I have de-cided," he wrote, "only to take the depot to 82° S. It will not pay to push on further."

Shackleton had shown the world that by using pony power on the ice shelf, plus manpower up the glacier and over the plateau, it was possible to reach within ninety-seven miles of the Pole. So, although Scott was well aware of the various apparent attributes of dogs over pony or manpower, he also knew that nobody had ever proved their viability up an Antarctic gla-cier. He chose the proven over the unproven way, accepting that his ponies were less able to cope with the period of extreme cold on either side of the short Antarctic summer. Since dogs were able to travel both earlier and later in the season than ponies, Amundsen carried on well into the month of April, boosting those of his depots closest to his base but at a cost of two dogs lost in a crevasse. With his advance line secured all the way to 82°, able to start out for the Pole at least two weeks earlier than Scott's ponies and with 120 miles less to go, things looked rosy for Amundsen. "We must at all costs get there first," he wrote. "Everything must be staked on that." All should go well so long as his base did not float out to sea and provided that a suitable route to the Pole happened to lie at the end of his Barrier depot line.

When *Terra Nova* left the Bay of Whales, Harry Pennell headed back to Cape Evans so that Campbell could leave news of Amundsen for Scott, then he landed his men on February 18 on the beach at Cape Adare, the original overwintering site of Borchgrevink back in 1899. Scott's Eastern Party had become, owing to events not of their choosing or liking, the Northern Party. *Terra Nova* then left for New Zealand, intending to pick them up the following summer.

Back at Safety Camp, Scott's immediate reaction to Campbell's news about *Fram* was one of shock. Roald Amundsen, the great ice traveler, was not after all aiming for the South Pole via the Weddell Sea. He was just across the barrier, with his base sixty miles closer to the Pole than Cape Evans. Scott wrote: "Every incident of the day pales before the startling contents of the mail bag."

Cherry-Garrard, who was present at the time, noted:

> For an hour or so we were furiously angry, and were possessed with an insane sense that we must go straight to the Bay of Whales and have it out with Amundsen and his men in some undefined fashion or other there and then. Such a mood could not and did not bear a moment's reflection; but it was natural enough. We had just paid the first instalment of the heart-breaking labour of making a path to the Pole; and we felt, however unreasonably, that we had earned the first right of way. Our sense of co-operation and solidarity had been wrought up to an extraordinary pitch; and we had so completely forgotten the spirit of competition that its sudden intrusion jarred frightfully. I do not defend our burst of rage—for such it was—I simply record it as an integral human part of my narrative. It passed harmlessly.

Many years later, Cherry-Garrard, suffering from melancholia and long periods of mental distraction, conferred with his neighbor and longtime friend George Bernard Shaw, who adored Kathleen Scott but, although they had never met, disliked the then long-dead Scott. He helped with Cherry-Garrard's book and Cherry-Garrard told him many a tale that contradicted his initial post-expedition account and included Scott, on hearing the

Amundsen news, leaping out of his bag shouting, "By Jove what a chance we have missed—we might have taken Amundsen and sent him back on the ship." An even later elaboration by the aging Cherry-Garrard added: "Scott in the tent with Wilson and myself said we would go and fight Amundsen. There was no law south of sixty . . . We had hours of it . . . About this time Wilson said to me, 'We had a bad time with Scott on the *Discovery*: but never anything like this.'" These imaginative ramblings of an aging, sick, and unhinged Cherry-Garrard contradict his own clear record written on his return from Antarctica and that of another man present at the time, Teddy Evans, who wrote:

> We spent a very unhappy night, in spite of all attempts to be cheerful. Clearly, there was nothing for us but to abandon science and go for the Pole directly the season for sledging was advanced enough to make travelling possible after the winter. It now became a question of dogs versus ponies, for the main bulk of our stuff must of necessity be pony-drawn unless we could rely on the motor-sledges—nobody believed we could. However, all the arguing in the world wouldn't push Amundsen and his dogs off the Antarctic continent and we had to put the best face on our disappointment. Captain Scott took it very bravely, better than any of us, I think, for he had done already such wonderful work down here. It was he who initiated and founded Antarctic sledge travelling, it was he who had blazed the trail, as it were, and we were very very sorry for him.

Scott summarized his thoughts on Amundsen's situation and his reaction to it: "One thing only fixes itself definitely in my mind. The proper, as well as the wiser, course for us is to proceed exactly as though this had not happened. To go forward and do our best for the honour of the country without fear or panic. There is no doubt that Amundsen's plan is a very serious menace to ours. He has a shorter distance to the Pole by 60 miles—I never thought he could have got so many dogs safely to the ice. His plan of running them seems excellent. But, above and beyond all, he can start his journey early in the season—an impossible condition with ponies." In deciding to follow his existing aims and to ignore the threat of Amundsen, Scott was unknowingly following a George Bernard Shaw adage: "If you have a destination, you will not get to it if you stop to fight people on the way."

When Scott left Cape Evans the following polar spring, he told Simpson, who would take over command at the base, to lend assistance to Amundsen if the Norwegians needed it. Wilson's diary nowhere mentioned any furious reaction by Scott and he was himself ambivalent about Amundsen's chances: "As for Amundsen's prospects of reaching the Pole, I don't think they are very good . . . I don't think he knows how bad an effect the monotony and the hard travelling surface of the Barrier is to animals."

And what of the reaction of others not in Scott's immediate coterie when the news of Amundsen's well-kept secret reached them? Tryggve Gran, according to Bowers, "was so genuinely upset at the behaviour of his countryman that one could not help feeling sorry for him and his awkward position." Gran wrote: "If we reach the Pole, then Amundsen will reach the Pole, and weeks earlier. Our prospects are thus not exactly promising. The only thing that can save Scott is if an accident happens to Amundsen." And elsewhere: "I think Amundsen's enterprise falls far short of what a gentleman would permit: there is nothing like it in polar history."

Back in his homeland, Amundsen's own countrymen, to whom he had earlier ranked as a hero alongside Nansen, now deserted him in shame, and such was their hostility to his behavior that when his backers asked the Norwegian government to request a grant from the Storting (parliament), they were afraid to do so.

When Bowers, Gran, and Oates made it to Safety Camp with the five ponies, the animals were still alive but seriously weak. Scott knew time was of the essence. "Now every effort," he wrote, "must be bent on saving the remaining animals." The only hope was shelter from the extreme conditions on the barrier as quickly as possible and that meant the hut at Hut Point. The best route accessible to ponies lay over the sea ice and that looked hazardous as, although the ice was still in situ, the deep pools that pocked the floes were a sure sign of fragility. Within hours, the pack could crack up and blow out to sea as a thousand rotting floes.

Scott told Wilson, the most experienced man present, with plenty of experience of sea ice, to lead the way over the bay with his own and Meares's dog teams. The total distance to Hut Point was only four miles across the bay. The alternative was to cross the bay, aiming not for Hut Point but for a nearer landing point on Ross Island known as the Gap and then to manhandle each sledge, every item of camp gear, and the dogs in pairs over a three-and-a-half-mile section of slippery rocks. This would be especially difficult for the ponies, which might well break their legs. So since Hut Point was but an hour's trip by pony, or twenty minutes by dog, and since the ice still looked passable, the risk factor to the ponies appeared less by aiming straight across the bay rather than by the Gap.

Wilson, however, voted to go by the Gap and Scott compromised. If Wilson should find the bay route looked dangerous, he should use his initiative and make his own route choice. So Wilson and Meares set off on March 1, aiming for Hut Point. To their right was an area of thick mist or frost smoke, which Wilson knew must come from a zone of open water or thaw pool. Such a pool had existed in the bay even back in January so, at first, Wilson kept going, but then he came to a series of regular thin cracks across his route and found these to be rising and falling with the swell. Should the tide change, he knew, each of these cracks could quickly widen to form myriad separate floes that in a sufficiently strong southerly or easterly wind would blow out to sea. They could well be in imminent danger, so he and Meares turned around and backtracked.

They soon reached a point where Wilson reckoned they could safely aim for the Gap on the island side of the thaw pool. Wilson could see the pony party, led by Bowers, less than half a mile away and heading straight toward him. Shouting loudly at their dogs, Wilson and Meares turned their sledges northward, right in front of the Bowers group, and then headed off toward the Gap, expecting Bowers to follow suit.

At this point, Bowers made the decision to carry straight on toward Hut Point rather than to follow Wilson's dog trail. Since this decision was to lead to tragedy, it seems important to understand Bowers's thinking. Was he following his initiative, as Wilson had done, or had Scott given him instructions? Scott's own diary is clear-cut: "The plan was for the ponies to follow the dog tracks." Wilson wrote, "Meares and I are now to take our dog teams to Hut Point with all our gear and the horse party will follow us. We

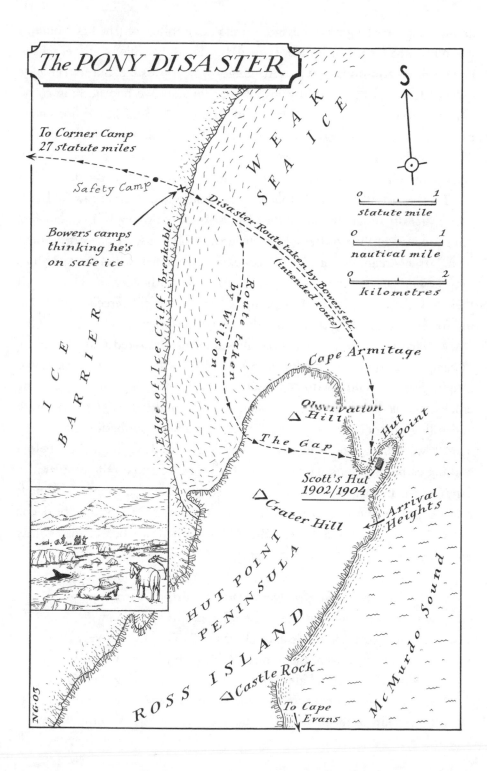

The PONY DISASTER

S

WEAK SEA ICE

To Corner Camp
27 statute miles

Safety Camp

Bowers camps
thinking he's
on safe ice

Disaster Route taken by Bowers etc.
(intended route)

Edge of Ice Cliff: breakable

Route taken by Wilson

ICE BARRIER

0 ——— 1
statute mile

0 ——— 1
nautical mile

0 ——— 2
kilometres

Cape Armitage

Observation
Hill

Hut
Point

The Gap

Scott's Hut
1902/1904

Crater Hill

Arrival
Heights

HUT POINT PENINSULA

McMurdo Sound

ROSS ISLAND

Castle Rock

To Cape
Evans

NG-03

had a somewhat lengthy discussion on the advisability of [the best route]. I was all for the Gap, which point I urged, but I was overruled to the extent of being told to go the direct (Cape Armitage) way, if possible, but to feel quite independent and be guided by my own judgment. We had nothing to do with the ponies as Captain Scott was in charge . . ." Wilson did not know, of course, that Scott was not in fact with Bowers and the ponies due to Weary Willie's breakdown. Bowers himself wrote: "My orders were to push on to Hut Point over the sea ice without delay, and to follow the dogs."

The key to all that sadly follows was that, when Bowers saw Wilson's group veer off suddenly toward the Gap, he decided, wrongly, that they had "misunderstood their orders and, instead of piloting us, dashed off on their own." Tom Crean, one of Scott's most experienced men with many previous journeys on sea ice to his credit, was traveling with Bowers. The two of them and the third man in their group, Cherry-Garrard, agreed to keep going for Hut Point. As with Wilson, the choice was theirs.

At each step, the inexperienced Bowers sensibly asked Crean's advice. "Crean," Bowers wrote, "who had been over the ice recently told me it was alright farther round." After a while, in thick fog, they came to moving cracks, just as Wilson had before them, and wisely also decided to turn back and follow the outward tracks back to firm sea ice close beside the barrier. This Bowers did and he took no risks, continuing to travel for a while before making camp. So, thinking they were off the sea ice and on the comparative safety of the barrier ice, they dug snow walls for their four ponies and made a hot drink. In the semidarkness, Bowers mistook curry powder for cocoa but they were tired and "Crean drank his right down before discovering anything was wrong." He continues:

> It was 2 pm before we were ready to turn in. I went out and
> saw that everything was quiet: the mist still hung to the west, but
> you could see a good mile and all was still. The sky was very dark
> over the Strait though, the unmistakable sign of open water. I
> turned in. Two and a half hours later I awoke, hearing a noise.
> Both my companions were snoring, I thought it was that and was
> on the point of turning in again having seen that it was only 4.30,

when I heard the noise again. I thought—"my pony is at the oats!" and went out.

I cannot describe either the scene or my feelings. I must leave those to your imagination. We were in the middle of a floating pack of broken-up ice. The tops of the hills were visible, but all below was thin mist and as far as the eye could see there was nothing solid; it was all broken up, and heaving up and down with the swell. Long black tongues of water were everywhere. The floe on which we were had split right under our picketing line, and cut poor Guts' wall in half. Guts himself had gone, and a dark streak of water alone showed the place where the ice had opened under him. The two sledges securing the other end of the line were on the next floe and had been pulled right to the edge. Our camp was on a floe not more than 30 yards across. I shouted to Cherry and Crean, and rushed out in my socks to save the two sledges; the two floes were touching farther on and I dragged them to this place and got them on to our floe. At that moment our own floe split in two, but we were all together on one piece. I then got my finnesko on, remarking that we had been in a few tight places, but this was about the limit. I have been told since that I was quixotic not to leave everything and make for safety. You will understand, however, that I never for one moment considered the abandonment of anything.

Meanwhile, on firm ground in the Gap, Wilson and Meares, finding that Bowers had inexplicably not followed them, made camp. Through his binoculars Wilson saw that the others had camped too and turned in.

At 5 am I woke. I was horrified to see that the whole of the sea ice was now on the move and that it had broken up for miles further than when we turned in, and right back past where they had camped, and that the pony party was now, as we could see, adrift on a floe and separated by open water and a lot of drifting ice from the edge of the fast Barrier ice. We could see with the glasses that they were running the ponies and sledges over as quickly as possible from floe to floe whenever they could, trying to get near the safe Barrier ice again. The whole strait was now open water to the north of Cape Armitage with frost smoke rising everywhere from it, and full of pieces of floating ice, all going up north towards the Ross Sea.

❧ 13 ❧

THE WORST JOURNEY: 1911

IN 1982, I SPENT three months with a friend cut off on an ice floe floating for four hundred miles over the Arctic Ocean and constantly fearful that the floe would fracture into pieces. In Antarctica, two British scientists recently died on a floe that broke away from the coastline only a few miles from their permanent base, despite both men's years of experience and ice awareness. Any travel on sea ice is risky, but in many parts of Antarctica, as with Scott's men by Hut Point, there is no reasonable alternative. So, you look at the weather and the state of the ice and, if all looks well, you start out. The weather can sometimes alter without warning, bringing untravelable conditions, so you are forced to pitch camp out on the pack ice just when you know you should be making all speed for land. If your luck is bad, the power of the wind can then fracture the ice into individual floes that may head out to sea. You will then risk death by exposure, starvation, drowning, or killer whales who lurk about the floes and can batter through quite thick ice to grasp their prey.

When Henry Bowers looked out of his tent in the early morning of March 1, 1911, his chances of survival were minimal. They were floating west toward the open sea and he saw that their only hope lay to the south, by moving from floe to floe if and when two floes touched. They found that, luckily, their three surviving ponies were prepared to jump over small water gaps and they made slow but sure progress back toward the barrier edge from which their floe had earlier broken.

"After some hours," Bowers wrote, "we saw fast ice ahead, and thanked God for it." Meanwhile, a further unpleasantness occurred in the arrival of a host of the terrible killer whales.

These were reaping a harvest of seal in the broken-up ice, and cruised among the floes with their immense black fins sticking up, and blowing with a terrific roar. It took us over six hours to get close to the fast ice, which proved to be the Barrier, some immense chunks of which we actually saw break off and join the pack . . . and I made for a big sloping floe which I expected would be touching. We rushed up the slope towards safety, and were little prepared for the scene that met our eyes at the top. All along the Barrier face a broad lane of water from thirty to forty feet wide extended. This was filled with smashed-up brash ice, which was heaving up and down to the swell like the contents of a cauldron. Killers were cruising there with fiendish activity, and the Barrier edge was a sheer cliff of ice on the other side fifteen to twenty feet high. It was a case of so near and yet so far. Suddenly our great sloping floe calved in two, so we beat a hasty retreat . . . to a sound looking floe.

Both Cherry-Garrard and Crean volunteered to fetch help, but because Cherry-Garrard wore glasses and could not see well, Bowers sent Crean. "I sent a note to Captain Scott, and, stuffing Crean's pockets with food, we saw him depart." They watched Crean through the telescope as he jumped from floe to floe and it was some hours later before they saw him up on the barrier. When Crean was later asked about this highly risky journey and the speed with which he managed it, he responded: "Oh I just kept going pretty lively, sorr, them killers wasn't too healthy company."

Meanwhile, Cherry-Garrard and Bowers put up their tent and tethered the ponies close by. Their floe bobbed about close by the barrier edge and they prayed that an offshore wind would not come again from the east or the south before help could reach them. Bowers wrote:

> The Killers were too interested in us to be pleasant. They had a habit of bobbing up and down perpendicularly, so as to see over the edge of a floe, in looking for seals. The huge black and yellow heads with sickening pig eyes only a few yards from us at times, and always around us, are among the most disconcerting recollections I have of that day.

That evening at 7 p.m. Tom Crean appeared at the barrier edge with Scott and Oates: He had taken a great many risks to fetch help. Scott, Bowers wrote, "was too relieved at our safety to be anything but pleased. I said: 'What about the ponies and sledges?' He said: 'I don't care a damn about the ponies and sledges. It's you I want.' I heard later that, when Crean first told Scott of our predicament, he was very angry with me for not abandoning everything and getting away safely myself." Between them they used the sledges as ladders from the floes and up the ice wall to the barrier top.

> Captain Scott was so pleased, that I realized the feeling he must have had all day. He had been blaming himself for our deaths, and here we were very much alive . . . I was all for saving the beasts and sledges, however, so he let us go back . . . Scott knew more about the ice than any of us, and, realizing the danger we didn't, still wanted us to abandon things.

At one point, they were all ready to haul the ponies up the ramp they had made when,

> To my intense disappointment at this juncture the ice started to move again . . . We dug [at the ramp] like fury until Captain Scott peremptorily ordered us up. I ran up on the floe and took the nosebags off the ponies before we got on to the Barrier, and hauled the sledges up. It was only just in time. There was the faintest south-easterly air, but, like a black snake, the lane of water

stretched between the ponies and ourselves. It widened almost imperceptibly, 2 feet, 6 feet, 10 feet, 20 feet, and, sick as we were about the ponies, we were glad to be on the safe side of that.

They pitched tents half a mile back from the barrier edge as new bergs were constantly breaking away from the front. Bowers continued:

> While supper . . . was being cooked, Scott and I walked down again. The wind had gone to the east, and all the ice was under weigh. A lane 70 feet wide extended along the Barrier edge, and Killers were chasing up and down it like racehorses. Our three unfortunate beasts were some way out, sailing parallel to the Barrier. We returned, and if ever one could feel miserable I did then. My feelings were nothing to what poor Captain Scott had had to endure that day . . . He said . . . that he had no confidence whatever in the motors after the way their rollers had become messed up unloading the ship. He had had his confidence in the dogs much shaken on the return journey, and now he had lost the most solid asset—the best of his pony transport. He said: "Of course we shall have a run for our money next season, but as far as the Pole is concerned I have but very little hope."

The next morning, they found that the ponies' floe had floated only a few miles, to another lower part of the barrier edge, so they tried again to save the three animals. Bowers described what happened. His only thoughts were to save the ponies whereas Scott knew that the floes, together with his men and he himself, might drift out to sea at any moment.

> The hardest jump was the first one, but it was nothing to what they had done the day before, so we put Punch at it. Why he hung fire I cannot think, but he did, at the very edge, and the next moment was in the water. I will draw a veil over our struggle to get the plucky little pony out. We could not manage it, and Titus had at last to put an end to his struggle with a pick.
> There was now my pony and Nobby. We abandoned that

route, while Captain Scott looked out another and longer one by
going right out on the sea-floes. This we decided on, if we could
get the animals off their present floe, which necessitated a good
jump on any side. Captain Scott said he would have no repetition
of Punch's misfortune if he could help it. He would rather kill
them on the floe. Anyhow, we rushed old Nobby at the jump, but
he refused. It seemed no good, but I rushed him at it again and
again [and at last he made it] . . . Titus, seizing the opportunity,
ran my pony at it with similar success. We then returned to the
Barrier and worked along westward till a suitable place for getting
up was found. There Scott and Cherry started digging a road,
while Titus and I went out via the sea-ice to get the ponies. We
had an empty sledge as a bridge or ladder, in case of emergency,
and had to negotiate about forty floes to reach the animals. It was
pretty easy going, though, and we brought them along with great
success as far as the two nearest floes. At this place the ice was
jambed.

Nobby cleared the last jump splendidly, when suddenly in the
open water pond on one side a school of over a dozen of the
terrible whales arose. This must have flurried my horse just as he
was jumping, as instead of going straight he jumped [sideways]
and just missed the floe with his hind legs. It was another horrible
situation, but Scott rushed Nobby up on the Barrier, while Titus,
Cherry and I struggled with poor old Uncle Bill. Why the whales
did not come under the ice and attack him I cannot say [but] . . .
we got him safely as far as [the bottom of the Barrier cliff], pulling
him through the thin ice towards a low patch of brash.

Captain Scott was afraid of something happening to us with
those devilish whales so close, and was for abandoning the horse
right away. I had no eyes or ears for anything but the horse just
then, and getting on to the thin brash ice got the Alpine rope fast
to each of the pony's forefeet. Crean was too blind to do anything
but hold the rescued horse on the Barrier, but the other four of us
pulled might and main till we got the old horse out and lying on
his side. The brash ice was so thin that, had a "Killer" come up

then he would have scattered it, and the lot of us into the water like chaff. I was sick with disappointment when I found that my horse could not rise. Titus said "He's done; we shall never get him up alive." . . . In vain I tried to get him to his feet; three times he tried and then fell over backwards into the water again. At that moment a new danger arose. The whole piece of Barrier itself started to subside.

It had evidently been broken before, and the tide was doing the rest. We were ordered up and it certainly was all too necessary; still Titus and I hung over old Uncle Bill's head. I said: "I can't leave him to be eaten alive by those whales." There was a pick lying up on the floe. Titus said: "I shall be sick if I have to kill another horse like I did the last." I had no intention that anybody should kill my own horse but myself, and getting the pick I struck where Titus told me. I made sure of my job before we ran up and jumped the opening in the Barrier, carrying a blood-stained pick-axe instead of leading the pony I had almost considered safe.

Two ponies, Jimmy Pigg and Nobby, out of the original eight used for the depot journey, had survived and were now quartered under cover beside Hut Point hut, which Atkinson and Crean had laboriously emptied of ice and excrement. Over the next few days, the different groups all rendezvoused there.

The bay between Hut Point and the main Cape Evans base was now open sea, so the thirteen men of the depot party would have to live in the hut until the sea refroze in a month or two. It was no paradise. Cherry-Garrard described his first night there: "there was an open blubber fire in the middle of the floor. There was no outlet for the smoke and smuts and it was impossible to see your neighbour, to speak without coughing . . . and to say that the hut was cold is a very mild expression of the reality."

Scott walked to a high point on the ridge above the hut to look north. He was astonished, for half of the Glacier Tongue, a feature that had existed for centuries, had broken off and floated away. Scott realized then the enormous forces of nature that must have caused the recent breakup. By some fateful coincidence, Bowers's group had set out on their disastrous ice crossing, which should normally have lasted an hour at most, at the worst possible moment. Bowers summed up this example of extreme bad luck: "Six hours earlier we could have walked to the Hut on sound sea ice. A few hours later we should have seen open water on arrival at the barrier." Cherry-Garrard wrote: "no one in the world could have foreseen they would break up just in those few hours we were on them."

Nevertheless, Oates wrote, predictably, to his mother: "We lost 6 ponies including mine, which was a long way the best pony we had. I was very upset the more so as I think he could have been saved if Scott had not been fussing to the extent he was, this pony was one of the ones drowned, the loss of the ponies was Scott's fault entirely."

Gran noted on first hearing of the disaster: "Our party is split up and we seemed like a defeated army—dispirited and inconsolable." He added: "Scott was the one with the greatest cause to be discouraged but in fact he tried in every way to cheer us up." Gran described the hut as the "smoke cabin." "Inside it is dark and unpleasant; the fireplace smokes almost unbearably." The usual banter between individuals soon began, as onboard ship. Wilson remarked to Oates one day: "The way thoughts flash through your mind, Titus, reminds me of a snail's climbing a cabbage stalk."

Cherry-Garrard wrote: "We spent . . . our evenings in long discussions which seldom settled anything." Sitting on packing cases, they smoked in the dim glow of candles and the blubber lamp before spreading their reindeer-pelt sleeping bags on the floor. Water dripped on them all night, though after six weeks' hard sledging they were able to sleep for twelve hours at a stretch without any difficulty. "Perhaps this is not everybody's notion of a good time," Cherry-Garrard wrote, "but it was good enough for us."

After two weeks, on March 15, 1911, another sledge group that had spent many weeks geologizing in the western mountains, Ferrar Glacier, and the dry valleys arrived over the ridge above the hut, having followed more or less the same route from the barrier as the original trail pioneered by *Discovery*'s first foray toward Cape Crozier, at about the time of George Vince's death. Griffith Taylor, Charles Wright, Frank Debenham, and Taff Evans made up this party and increased the already cramped Hut Point community to sixteen. Now there was room only to sleep in shifts. Tempers could have flared, but they did not.

Long debates raged about the stove among the ragged, bearded, soot-black figures. Cherry-Garrard noticed: "Scott and Wilson were always in the thick of it . . . Taylor is seldom at a loss and his remarks are often original, if sometimes crude. Rash statements on questions of fact were always dangerous for our small community contained so many specialists that errors were soon exposed." Of his time in the overcrowded, damp hut Griffith Taylor wrote: "I was closer to Scott than at any other time in our association. I was next to him on the floor in our sleeping bags. What discussions we had! Scott was interested in everything. One evening we discussed Mormonism, the medieval ramparts of Aigues Mortes, and the pronunciation of ancient Greek. He and I would talk after all the others had gone to sleep. It was just as well. There was nothing to read: a *Family Herald,* a few reviews, and some copies of *The Girl's Own.*"

Fed up with smarting eyes and oily soot, Wilson, Oates, and Gran experimented with acetylene, but Gran's prototype lamp blew up and nearly killed Meares. "This life," Gran wrote, "is quite interesting despite its monotony. Time goes unbelievably fast and that's the main thing really."

Everyone took their turn at cooking the daily hoosh. Oates, Meares, and Debenham were among the better cooks, or certainly so in Oates's estimation. When some other poor person served up their own exotic effort, Oates commented in a loud voice for all to hear: "Some of our party, who rather fancy themselves as cooks, quite spoil the meals by messing up the food in their attempts to produce original dishes."

There was a nagging worry at the back of all their minds, especially Scott's. Only huge seas, they realized, could have sundered the great Glacier Tongue and, as Wilson wrote: "We wonder what our hut at Cape Evans may have suffered as it is built very low on a shelving northern beach and the swell seems to have been from the N. or N.E." Cherry-Garrard noted, "On top of all the anxieties which had oppressed him lately Scott had a great fear that a swell so phenomenal as to break up Glacier Tongue, a landmark which had probably been there for centuries, might have swept away our hut at Cape Evans."

Scott had every good reason to worry about a possible calamity at Cape Evans, for he had sited his main base there in the light of his previous years' experience of the weather in McMurdo Sound. He had not expected any such cataclysmic events as a storm capable of breaking off an apparently im-movable feature such as the Glacier Tongue. Now he was sorely troubled. His diary notes sought to legitimize to himself his choice of Cape Evans:

> In choosing the site of the hut on our Home Beach I had thought of the possibility of northerly winds bringing a swell, but had argued, first, that no heavy northerly swell had ever been recorded in the Sound; secondly, that a strong northerly wind was bound to bring pack which would damp the swell; thirdly, that the locality was excellently protected by the Barne Glacier; and finally, that the beach itself showed no signs of having been swept by the sea, the rock fragments composing it being completely regular.
>
> When the hut was erected and I found that its foundation was only eleven feet above the level of the sea ice, I had a slight misgiving, but reassured myself again by reconsidering the circumstances that afforded shelter to the beach.

Hut Point is surrounded by sea on every side except for a slope known as Arrival Heights. A devious route to the barrier from this feature, very diffi-cult for heavy loads and ponies, is possible all year round. But progress far-ther north, toward Cape Evans, is cut off for as long as the sea remains unfrozen. Scott and Wilson reconnoitered a possible route north over the slopes of Erebus, but it involved crossing many crevasses and climbing to over five thousand feet, so they gave up the attempt to check up on the fate of the Cape Evans hut (see map on page 234).

With temperatures in late March dropping into the −40°Cs, the sea froze quickly as soon as the wind dropped, but the next breeze soon rippled and dispersed the new ice. Any attempt to travel before truly solid sea ice formed could prove lethal. On March 17, a southerly gale blew against Hut Point with thirty-foot-high breakers crashing against the rock and high-flung spume freezing onto the hut walls. Meares and Wilson had to free the dogs from their picket lines, for their fur was soon covered in frozen-armor plating from the spray. Vince's cross, forty feet farther up the hill, was cov-ered in an inch of ice.

To make the most of their enforced rest, Scott sent another sledge group out to increase the depot at Corner Camp. Teddy Evans led this foray and recorded a temperature of −41°C before returning. Supplies at Hut Point were limited and seals were killed whenever possible. Wilson wrote after five weeks in the hut: "Here we have come to an end of our sugar today. We have also finished the flour . . . [and] our oatmeal, but we have lots of seal meat and biscuit and cocoa. Butter is running out, but we can't starve! And we are a very happy party of bohemians. Our clothes soaked in seal blubber and soot." One day he killed an emperor: "a male, very fat. Half the breast and the liver was a substantial meal for 16 men with nothing else but some pease, cocoa and biscuit. We fried it in butter and it was excellent." Cherry-Garrard described the seal-killing method the party used. A heavy blow on the nose with a large stick stunned the seal, which then felt no further pain as a fourteen-inch knife pierced the heart. The blubber came away with the skin, the meat was sliced away, the entrails removed, and the liver saved. This was all left to freeze, then cut up with an ax when needed.

On April 7, Scott, extremely anxious to know that all was well at Cape Evans, took a small group out on fairly thick ice. Taylor fell through a weak patch, but he quickly levered himself back out. They wisely retreated. That night, a wind blew all the ice out to sea but, four days later, Scott tried again by a new part-land, part-sea route and taking seven others with him. This journey proved successful thanks to Scott's imaginative route-finding abilities. Where a lava rock outcrop at the Hutton Rocks pierced the ice face, he lowered a rope forty feet to the sea ice and then led the group over the truncated Glacier Tongue to the last bay before Cape Evans.

Teddy Evans said of Scott's cliff descent: "It was a good piece of work getting everything down safely, and I admired Scott's decision to go over; a more nervous man would have fought shy because, once down on the sea ice there was little chance of our getting back and we had got to fight our way forward to Cape Evans somehow." Scott asked the seven men if they would prefer to camp where they were, for it was 6:30 p.m., or to attempt the seven-mile trip over the ice to Cape Evans as a night march.

"We gladly started off at 8 o'clock for a night march," Teddy Evans wrote, "picturing to ourselves a supper of all things luxurious." Not a single voice was raised in favor of camping, but Bowers, remembering no doubt his recent experiences of the fickleness of sea ice, later wrote: "it seemed folly to venture upon a piece of untried, newly frozen sea-ice in inky darkness." By 10 p.m., a strong wind had increased to blizzard strength and Scott decided to camp in the lee of a rock islet, Little Razorback Island. Everybody had wanted to press on, including no doubt Scott himself, the hardest and most energetic of sledgers. But, as Cherry-Garrard wrote: "the snow hid everything; in fact we could hardly see the island itself when we were right under it. It was impossible to go wandering on, so we had after all to camp on the sea-ice . . . there was only six or ten inches of precarious ice between you and the black waters beneath. Altogether I decided that I for one would lie awake in such an insecure camp."

Taylor subsequently observed: "If ever there was a reckless stunt, this was it, and I could not admire Scott for it. We had no food. The blizzard was a killer. Instead of a few hours, it took us two days to do those [few] miles and we were lucky to make it. I'd say this was my worst experience in the Antarctic." Debenham, Taylor's fellow Australian geologist, wrote: "Opinions were varied in the camp, I for one wishing to march on in spite of the blizzard and Griff urged it almost too strongly."

Scott would have known, as do all competent outdoor leaders of today, that strong characters who are very cold and very miserable will always opt for carrying on, if only to keep up the warmth of movement. But this natural reaction is not always the most sensible option. Scott knew that the farther north and west he headed toward the mouth of the bay, the greater the chance of floe fracture and open water. Better to stay inland of the island group, including Razorback, at least until visibility improved. This he did, at first camping on the sea ice below the island's cliffs and then, when Bowers located a tiny rock ledge at the base of the cliff, moving to its relative safety. Scott did not lose his sense of humor, commenting to explain this site move that it was "to ensure Taylor's safety."

They stayed on Bowers's ledge for twenty-four hours while the storm raged around them. Gran wrote: "truly awful. I don't dare to take my boots off for fear I shall not get them back on when they stiffen. The sleeping bag is wet through and my teeth chatter as I lie writing this." On April 13, Scott wrote: "I roused the party at 7 a.m. and we were soon under way, with a desperately cold and stiff breeze and frozen clothes." The last bay seemed to go on forever. Gran wrote: "We reached some stranded icebergs, passed them round the point, and before us was the hut . . . soon the people from the hut poured out to meet us. It was 80 days since we had seen each other and we greeted one another with warmth. How wonderful to set foot inside this palace! . . . Soon a bath—and then to bed!" Scott's relief must have been enormous.

Scott was away again in four days to bring more men back from Hut Point. The ponies and dogs, which could not climb down the cliff section, were left at Hut Point, under Meares, with a group of six men to come on only when the sea ice was really solid. The rest raced each other back to Cape Evans, an easy journey with good visibility.

While the depot group was away, the Cape Evans hut had become a place of great comfort for men, dogs, and ponies alike. Music issued from a gramophone and sometimes from the pianola. Acetylene gas jets provided plenty of light around the clock. Adequate hot water was available for baths, and scientific gadgets ticked or purred in many corners, installed by meteorologist Simpson, Bernard Day the engineer, and Edward Nelson the biologist. Scott had his own cubicle full of books, photos of his family, and piles of notebooks to aid his endless planning for the journeys ahead. Ponting had a darkroom. Gran and "the colonials" from Australia and Canada had one section of bunks close by another that housed good friends Cherry-Garrard and Bowers, alongside the close group of Oates, Meares, and Atkinson.

As soon as everyone was well settled into the base, Scott outlined his plan, which, true to his initial reaction when learning of Amundsen's presence on the barrier, completely ignored the Norwegian challenge. His mathematics and his transport system were based entirely and sensibly on the only previous journey to nearly reach the Pole, that of Ernest Shackleton. He would not rely on dogs or motor sledges but, unlike Shackleton, he would take skis and use them wherever they proved an advantage over skiless man-haul, probably at least as far as the Beardmore Glacier.

Scott preferred to choose his sledging groups at the last possible moment, which enabled him, like the leader of an Everest expedition, to select those who were fittest at the key moment rather than have a prenominated group that might entail big disappointments when he made his last-minute and final choice. He announced that he would select men for the Pole team at a later date, but that everyone must understand that a second year at Cape

Evans was already a reality. This had become necessary because of the behavior of the ponies on the depot trip: They could not stand the bitter spring
weather and so would not be able to set out until November 1. This would
mean the Pole party returning to Cape Evans too late to catch *Terra Nova*'s
brief summer call. Those who felt they could not stay on for a second year
would, of course, have to go when she left.

Scott estimated that supplies would have to cover a journey of 144 days,
of which 84 would be spent on the high plateau. Shackleton's men had traveled a lesser distance up there, yet the conditions had affected them badly:
This was Scott's main worry. Shackleton had set out with four ponies, Scott
pointed out, whereas they would have double that number, which, together
with the very considerable amount of stores already laid out in the depots,
would give them the essential extra 200 miles travel ability that Shackleton's
men had lacked.

When Scott had left Britain the year before, his twin aims had been his
scientific program, which was already well underway, and his stated goal to
reach the South Pole. His plan, as announced on May 8, 1911, at Cape
Evans, made good sense to most of those present, but did not remove the
background fear in all their minds that the Norwegians might beat them to
the Pole. Scott knew that he could never hope to compete directly with Norwegian skills on skis and driving dog teams. Scott's team consisted of navy
men and professional scientists, a small proportion of whom had been with
him ten years previously. They were well prepared to follow up their previous scientific work and they had taken great care to learn from their 1903
experiences at man-hauling, dog driving, and skiing. Despite this, they could
not hope to win a race against a group of Norway's best skiers and dog
drivers.

When Teddy Evans and Oates first learned of Amundsen's presence at
the Bay of Whales, they were all for changing plans and making a race of it
by starting out early. But, in Gran's words: "Our expedition to Corner Camp
cured Teddy Evans' desire to leave early." Scott knew he had learned far too
late about the threat from Amundsen to reassess his plans. There was the
faint hope that, even though the Norwegians had 120 miles less far to travel,
they would aim for the Beardmore Glacier, the only known route, which
Shackleton had proved was a bad place for dogs and so could slow them

down. Indeed, Amundsen's successful deceit had reduced Scott's hopes of reaching the Pole first into a mere reliance on the Norwegians suffering a set-back. Scott must have seen that, for he was nobody's fool, but he could not openly say: "Look, we've been fooled. The enemy are at our doorstep. They are the best in the world at traveling on snow. We can only win by default."

So what could he say or do from the moment he learned of the Norwegian presence on the barrier? He could either get on with his science and announce that a Pole attempt was off since it would be futile, or he could hope that Fate would halt or delay the Norwegians. Of these two options, I would have chosen the latter, as did Scott. Any one of a thousand things could go wrong for Amundsen and, if something did, Scott would have cursed himself for not having tried the race option. Amundsen could have suffered an injury. Without him, the Norwegians would have lacked the drive and awareness to make the journey. The Norwegian base could have floated away out to sea, as indeed it later did. The unknown route Amundsen took over the barrier might easily have met with huge geographical obstacles. So, the winter at Cape Evans was to be business as usual, at least on the face of it. Under the surface, however, the personal strain on Scott must have been great.

At the end of Scott's presentation of his plans, he asked for the men's reaction. Gran noted: "The presentation was followed by a long discussion [at the end of which] Scott thanked all his opponents and the discussion ceased after our leader said 'It is easy to make plans when one sits in a good, warm cabin, but to realise them is not so pleasant and simple.'" Charles Wright was impressed both by Scott's presentation and by the round-table discussion that followed it.

On May 14, Cecil Meares and the men who had stayed at Hut Point arrived back at Cape Evans with the two dog teams and the two surviving depot-trip ponies, Jimmy Pigg and Nobby. The sea ice was firm all the way, although still liable to break up because of violent southwesterly storms.

One pony wasted away during the winter and had to be shot. Oates could not identify the cause of the sickness. This left ten ponies in all out of the seventeen landed at Cape Evans. The key to Scott's plan was the health of the ponies and that burden rested squarely on the broad shoulders of Oates. Scott had done well to select him for this purpose. Oates did a truly wonderful job in caring for the ten ponies all that winter, for which Scott was openly fulsome in his praise and his gratitude. Scott must have regretted that Oates had not been available in time to choose the ponies. On May 17, as one of a series of evening lectures in the hut, Oates gave a two-hour talk on horse care. He ended with an amusing story from a sophisticated dinner party he had attended, where a young lady arrived very late and flustered, explaining that "the cab-horse: he wouldn't get on at all. 'Ah, perhaps he was a jibber,' suggested her hostess. 'Oh, no,' smiled the damsel, all un-knowing, 'he was a bugger. I heard the cabby say so several times.'"

Oates was a quiet but powerful character who attracted to his side the equally taciturn Cecil Meares and Edward Atkinson and, to a lesser extent, Frank Debenham.

Debenham, like Oates, wrote letters to his mother as a safety valve for his feelings.

> I am afraid I am very disappointed in him [Scott] . . . There's no doubt he can be very nice and the interest he takes in our scientific work is immense, he is also a fine sledger himself and as organiser is splendid . . . His temper is very uncertain . . . In crises he acts very peculiarly . . . I have been quite disgusted with him. What he decides is often enough the right thing I expect, but he loses all control of his tongue and makes us all feel wild . . . I cannot say he is the least popular, still we are all prepared to follow him . . . the marvellous part is that the Owner is the single exception to a general sense of comradeship and jollity amongst all of us.

Expedition base camps are often hotbeds of small-clique gossip and complaining about the current leadership. Scott was fortunate in ending up with only one such complaints clique and, since their Scott-sniping sessions nearly always took place in the stables around the blubber fire, where Oates prepared bran mash for his charges, the atmosphere inside the hut did not suffer from the hostile murmurings of the disgruntled few. Through the long, dark winter, Oates, Meares, and Atkinson bonded and brooded around the stable stove.

As a result, many of their anti-Scott bickerings did not surface until the bitter dossier of the bereaved Mrs. Caroline Oates (including correspondence between her, Debenham, Atkinson, and Meares), decades after the death of her son, was made available to scholars. Meares told Mrs. Oates that her son had been "disgusted" by Scott's leadership, while Oates stated that there was "no love lost" between Meares and Scott. The occasional snide comment by the stable clique was sometimes overheard. Ponting mentioned that Scott and he both heard Meares tell Oates that Scott should buy himself a "shilling book on transport."

Scott seemed largely unaware of this malignant tumor, which was just as well, as he could have done little about it short of falling in line with every whim that issued from the stable. As it was, he tried to avoid confrontation with Oates whenever he could.

Both Meares and Oates were to an extent outsiders to the norms of Royal Navy and university life. Their hut companions, all quick-witted academic debaters from various universities, included Wilson, Nelson, Wright, and Taylor, all from Cambridge, Cherry-Garrard from Oxford, Debenham from Sydney, and Simpson from Manchester. On many an expedition I have seen how an innate feeling of inferiority can blunt communication between two people. The middle-class Dartmouth midshipman, Scott, probably recognized his social superior in the upper-class Essex squire with his slow Old Etonian drawl, just as Oates may have sensed that his own modest intellectual level and dyslexic disabilities put him at a disadvantage with the quick-thinking, clear-minded Scott.

Oates was supremely and rightly confident in his knowledge of horsemanship and may not have liked to acknowledge that Scott's common sense and razor-sharp powers of observation had sometimes found chinks in his equine armor, as in overbuilding storm shields for the ponies or on the matter of the missing *hesterskos*. During the depot trip, Cherry-Garrard had commented: "One evening we watched Scott digging crumbly blocks of snow out on the Barrier and he built a rough wall windward of his pony. We viewed this with distrust and saw little use in it. But later we were convinced by personal experience what a boon these pony walls could be." Soon everyone, including Oates, was copying Scott. The matter of the snowshoes had registered with both Scott and Oates. Scott saw it as proof that he must watch Oates carefully in future to ensure that such a costly and basic over-sight did not recur and Oates saw Scott as a meddler in *his* fiefdom. He wrote home ". . . I think I have a fairish chance [of inclusion in the final Polar party], that is if Scott and I do not fall out as it will be pretty tough having four months of him, he fusses dreadfully . . ."

Scott's fussing eventually persuaded Oates to take with the pony gear in future two types of snowshoe or *hestersko*, a racket-type for soft snow and a tough canvas hoof bag for ice. Such perceived interference by Scott into Oates's domain provoked many a hostile comment to "Dear Mother."

"From what I see," Oates moaned, "I think it would not be difficult to get to the Pole provided you have proper transport, but with the rubbish we have it will be jolly difficult and means a lot of hard work." And again: "Scott wants me to stay on here another year but I shall clear out if I get back in time for the ship which I hope to goodness will be the case. It will only be a small party to remain next year. Scott pretends at present he is going to stay but I bet myself a fiver he clears out, that is if he gets to the Pole. If he does not and some decent transport animals come down in the ship, I have promised him I will stay to help him have another try but between you and me I think if he fails this time he will have had a pretty good stomach full." Another time he declared: "Myself, I dislike Scott intensely and would chuck the whole thing if it were not that we are a British expedition and must beat these Norwegians. Scott has always been very civil to me and I have the reputation of getting on well with him. But the fact of the matter is that he is not straight, it is himself first, the rest nowhere."

Every now and again, Oates seemed to realize that his tirades might not be entirely fair to the object of his dislike. Then he would add little riders to the effect that he was "having a 'first class' time with the expedition," and "please remember that when a man is having a hard time, he says hard things about other people which he would regret afterwards." He also told his mother not to "think from what I say that Scott is likely to endanger anyone, it is quite the reverse."

Scott, who often wrote letters to the close relatives of many of his men, letters that would be posted home on the next relief ship, clearly remained happily unaware of the depth of Oates's paranoia and wrote many a kind comment to Mrs. Oates about her son. He had no inkling that Oates might not wish to stay on a second year. From the outset in Lyttelton, when Oates had smuggled extra fodder onboard (some at his own expense), to his great bravery, strength, and determination in saving his ponies during the hurricane, to his nonstop focus on and skilled care for each animal through the long, cold winter, he excelled in every way. He organized a personal handler for each pony and taught them how to exercise and cope with their charges' unpredictable, often vicious moods, choosing for himself the most aggressive pony, Christopher, who bit and kicked at anyone who came near him. What a shame that Oates could not sublimate his natural tendency to disloyalty and to carping about his superiors.

Meares, like Oates, would not have enjoyed Scott's comments on his own area of expertise. Scott, soon seeing that the dogs, after some initial working in Antarctica, were not being adequately fed by Meares, made the point at once, adding later: "Meares is excellent to a point, but ignorant of the conditions here. One thing is certain, the dogs will never continue to drag heavy loads with men sitting on the sledges; we must all learn to run with the teams and the Russian custom must be dropped. Meares, I think, rather imagined himself racing to the Pole and back on a dog sledge. This journey has opened his eyes a good deal."

Despite his forthright criticism of Scott, it was, however, Debenham who also wrote that the group's general harmony was due to "the genius of Scott in exercising just the right amount of discipline with a minimum of formality." Even Oates said: "We got on very well together and there was none of the quarrelling which usually accompanies a winter where a number of men are confined together in a dark hut."

Oates was not alone in yielding to the common temptation to complain about a leader. A few hundred miles northwest of Cape Evans, Scott's other science group of six, under the leadership of Lieutenant Victor Campbell, were having their own personality problems. The chief protesters there consisted of navy surgeon George Levick and scientist Raymond Priestley. Levick wrote: "Priestley and I are really good friends. I am, I think establishing an ascendancy over Campbell, which has been a good thing in many ways, as I am gradually getting him out of many of his fads. He is not a bad chap but hopelessly out of place as a leader, being much too self-conscious and lacking most sadly in guts." He added: "I feel rather a beast sometimes when Priestley and I get away together and crab him to each other, whilst all the time he and I remain outwardly friendly."

Meanwhile, a few hundred miles to the east of Cape Evans, Amundsen's men were dividing into two bitter cliques. Bjaaland wrote that his colleagues Johansen and Prestrud were told they would not go to the Pole because they might get together to cause trouble and bring about the failure of the venture.

In the mid 1970s, I carried out a number of polar expeditions with just two companions, Oliver Shepard and Charlie Burton, who were best friends. They could easily have formed a clique and three would have become a crowd. Both were natural leaders of men in their own right, not yes men, and both disliked being told what to do. When they disagreed with my orders, as they frequently did, they did so separately and openly, avoiding the behind-the-back murmurings that constitute the most poisonous ingredient that even a short expedition can suffer. I had been lucky to choose two individuals without malice.

Soldiers are educated to appreciate that the best leaders are those who first learn to accept the principles of loyalty to other leaders. The British Antarctic Survey (BAS) and most other such Antarctic working communities understand the sense of this tenet of leadership. Dr. Phillip Law, the famous director of Australia's DEA Antarctic Division, their equivalent of BAS, wrote, in the 1980s: "Nothing is so important as the appointment of a first-class leader and nowhere are the qualities of leadership subjected to more gruelling tests than at an Antarctic station . . . One quality is fundamentally essential to any team. It is loyalty. A man must be loyal to the expedition, loyal to his leader and loyal to himself. Some men are naturally loyal; some are fundamentally antagonistic, critically outspoken and disloyal." Dr. Law also observed: "It was made clear to all our men that to back up their leader when they agree with him is no test of loyalty. It is when they disagree with him that they must stand behind him."

Oates, Meares, and Atkinson would have scored poorly on Dr. Law's ratings. Atkinson was small and punchy, a keen boxer, like Oates. He became, by seniority of rank, the de facto base leader at Cape Evans during the second winter there. In Scott's absence, he decided to change the routine as little as possible. Meares is a more clearly defined character than Atkinson.

Of him Debenham wrote: "Meares is the wanderer of us all and with all the faults and virtues of such men. China, Siberia, India, anywhere 'ot and un-wholesome' is his hunting ground and he has already tired of this place. He's a good chap, but I liked him more before he got tired of the Antarctic."

On May 22, Scott and five men walked the five miles north to Cape Royds and slept in Shackleton's old hut there. The sea ice was still unsafe in places. They carefully examined everything in the hut and gossiped about each member of Shackleton's group. "It was interesting," Wilson recorded, "to see the remains of this party's life here and their various corners in the hut."

Wilson was, as usual, in charge of the seal cull, as vital as ever in fend-ing off scurvy. His knowledge of anatomy was suited to the task of killing and then flensing the carcasses. Likewise, at the northern party's base five hundred miles to their northwest, surgeon George Levick found himself ap-pointed chief butcher. His comrade Raymond Priestley wrote that they were not yet used to killing the appealing creatures and that even Levick, used to wielding a scalpel, found his first kill unpleasant. "The old bull lay sound asleep, grunting a little as if he was dreaming. I heard him give a sigh of con-tentment as I stole up to him. Raising the iron bar high over my head, I brought it down across his nose, and as he lay stunned, ran in with a grand hunting knife about 10 inches long which I bought in Christchurch, and lift-ing up his flipper, ran it right into his heart. The blood spurted out by the gallon, & I had killed my first seal."

A fortnight later, Scott's birthday was celebrated amid the usual fes-toons of sledge flags, bunting, and good cheer. Outside the hut, two aspirant king dogs, suitably named Peary and Cook, tried to kill each other, and Tryggve Gran, after forcing them apart, settled to discussing his sometimes awkward position in a hut mainly full of Britons while his perfidious coun-tryman Amundsen was parked predatorily just over the horizon. Repairs and modifications of all sledging gear went on throughout the winter. The two motorized sledges had completed many hours of work on hard blue ice between the ship and the hut when unloading, and the wooden rollers of their looped tracks had been shredded, three hundred in all. This would not have happened in soft snow, but Day, not suspecting such damage, had only brought thirty spare rollers. By an ingenious adaptation of the crankshaft of a petrol engine into a makeshift lathe, he managed to manufacture roller re-placements over many hours of hard work. In 1979, unloading our ship in Antarctica prior to our crossing journey, all our steel sledges were cracked through their upright stanchions. Working inside an ice cave over the ensu-ing five months of winter, and remembering Bernard Day, I completed Heath Robinson repairs, which just lasted our own 1,800-mile journey.

Scott noted that, during the winter, Evans and Crean worked on the sledges, Gran on the skis, and that general attention was paid to overhauling *finnesko* boots. "But indeed the whole time we are thinking of devices to make our travelling work easier." While this was going on, Amundsen's men were likewise engaged and, despite their far superior polar expertise and easy access to advanced specialist ski outfitters in Kristiania (Oslo), they were having as many problems as the Cape Evans men. Both Teddy and Taff Evans, over the winter, modified various types of boots for use with skis and crampons with, ironically, a greater degree of success than Amundsen, pos-sibly because of the different demands of man-hauling. Gran tested the new gear. "The ski bindings," he said, "proved to be a success. They held the foot steady in the mukluks without pinching and made it easy to turn." Scott's team used *finnesko* boots made by Lapps, who have tiny feet; so Scott had ordered custom-made boots with quantities of senna grass to pack around the toe end of socks. On taking boots off at night, the senna grass had to be shaken to rid it of ice from frozen perspiration. The long thigh or knee fur boots used by Amundsen's dog drivers were inappropriate for man-haul, owing to the sweat caused by the far greater exertion involved.

Scott had learned on his 1902 expedition that only sleeping bags made from the winter coat of reindeer were reliable. He had obtained in Norway as many of the winter-coat bags as were available. Once wet, summer-coat skins shed their hairs. Three-man bags were very clumsy, but in extreme cold they were warmer than one-man bags.

The tents of green Willesden material had been made by John Edging-ton. These were pyramid shaped, nine feet long, and supported by six poles. In the 1980s, we were still using a slightly modified version of the same model, still the best available anywhere, from the same manufacturer, Black & Edgington of Greenock. Wilson wrote of theirs: "We were using a lined tent which was an invention of Sverdrup's in his last expedition, and we found it a great boon for it undoubtedly made one more comfortable in camp at the low temperatures."

Most of the Cape Evans men took exercise when the weather allowed. Some skied or walked a lot, usually in the immediate vicinity of the hut, and many played football or ice hockey. Taylor noted: "Scott was playing just behind me . . . grinned cheerfully when I said I was too winded! The blizzard nearly blew the ball off the ice." Oates was a keen active player, so an old Boer War leg injury was obviously not then affecting him. Games continued even at −20°C and below, with twenty-five-knot winds. Gran had played for Norway, whereas the Russian Omelchenko had never seen a football before. I well remember playing cricket at the South Pole in 1981 at −42°C and in full polar clothing.

The scientists had their own work by day and by night. Simpson monitored his complex instrument array and sent up balloons attached to instruments, Atkinson searched for parasites and bacteria in his fish-trap victims. Wright studied ice and snow, Nelson took depth soundings, and Taylor studied rock samples taken from the dry valleys, with their original locations plotted on his survey charts. Gran and Debenham spent six days holed up by the weather after a snap visit to Hut Point to collect a fossil collection Debenham had left there. By the hut, they found a dog, lost by Meares a month before, with his jowls covered in seal gore. This husky, Mukaka, gamely helped the two men haul their three-hundred-pound sledge load back to Cape Evans, where he had to be diplomatically reintroduced to the others because any brief absence can turn a dog into a complete stranger to be attacked and mauled by the pack.

The atmosphere in all parts of the hut, the "complaints" clique excepted, was congenial at all times and, according to Cherry-Garrard, there was never any want of conversation. In the main section, Scott sat at the table's head, but everyone else sat where they chose. "If you felt talkative," Cherry-Garrard wrote, "you might always find a listener in Debenham; if inclined to listen yourself, it was only necessary to sit near Taylor or Nelson; if on the other hand, you just wanted to be quiet, Atkinson or Oates would probably give you a congenial atmosphere."

Writing about Scott, Cherry-Garrard observed:

Scott, who always amazed me by the amount of work he got
through without any apparent effort, was essentially the driving
force of the expedition: in the hut quietly organizing, working out
masses of figures, taking the greatest interest in the scientific work
of the station, and perhaps turning out, quite by the way, an
elaborate paper on an abstruse problem in the neighbourhood;
fond of his pipe and a good book.

He was eager to accept suggestions if they were workable, and
always keen to sift even the most unlikely theories if by any means
they could be shaped to the desired end: a quick and modern brain
which he applied with thoroughness to any question or practice or
theory. Essentially an attractive personality, with strong likes and
dislikes, he excelled in making his followers his friends by a few
words of sympathy or praise; I have never known anybody, man or
woman, who could be so attractive when he chose.

Sledging he went harder than any man of whom I have ever
heard. Men never realized Scott until they had gone sledging with
him.

His was a subtle character, full of lights and shades. He was
certainly the most dominating personality in our not uninteresting
community: indeed there is no doubt that he would carry weight in
any gathering of human beings. But few who knew him realized
how shy and reserved the man was, and it is partly for this reason
that he so often laid himself open to misunderstanding.

Cherry-Garrard was well aware that he would be thought to be exagger-
ating. "If then I say that we lived this life for nearly three years, from the day
when we left England until the day we returned to New Zealand, without
any friction of any kind, I shall be supposed to be making a formal statement of somewhat limited truth. May I say that there is really no formality
about it, and nothing but the truth."

One man did strike a different note in his summary of hut life. Scott had
never allowed himself to become one of the lads or part of the family. If
there was to be one big happy family under his wing, he would prefer the

position of amiable but slightly austere patriarch. Frank Debenham expressed this by observing: "We are, with the exception of the Owner, a very happy family." Debenham continues: "Captain Oates is a good friend . . . Griff [Taylor] is not getting on too well . . . He is rather selfish in small matters and his few ungentlemanly habits rather jar on the collection of real gentlemen we have here . . . I shall have to share a cubicle with him and he is not a pleasant cabin mate. Trigger Gran, the Norwegian, is another great disappointment. Very generous and kindhearted he is too youthful in mind . . . In laziness, untidiness, morals and appetite he is a marked contrast to all the rest of us and suffers accordingly."

Scott's opinion of Gran varied from month to month, ranging from noting that he was lazy and guilty of posing during the unloading, to being impatient when pony leading, even regretting that he had brought Gran during the enforced wait at Hut Point. At one stage, Scott grew so exasperated with the young Norwegian that he bawled him out in the hearing of the sailors and wrote of him: "He worries me, since he is only really a boy, and a very nice boy under ordinary conditions, good-natured, good-tempered, helpful. I am inclined to think that the cold and the exceptionally hard conditions of this season's work have affected him mentally as well as physically . . . I feel angry, but extremely glad it is not one of our own people who thus behaves."

Gran asked Wilson why Scott was so upset with him. Was it because he was Norwegian? Wilson said no, the reason was Scott's dislike of laziness. Gran should keep busy or at least look busy and he would have no further trouble. This turned out to be good advice and, once back at Cape Evans, Scott warmed again to his young ski instructor. Gran received his sharpest rebuke from Scott in the early Hut Point days and, if he had not deserved such a dressing down, he would surely have borne an Oates-like grudge against his leader. As it was, he remained intensely loyal to Scott. After the expedition, he said: "Scott was a man. He would always listen to you. Amundsen would listen to nobody. He was only interested in himself. So Amundsen, as a human being, was not worth much, but Scott was worth a lot as a human being. So, you can say Amundsen was a gentleman dressed up, but his mind was not a gentleman's mind. But Scott was a gentleman."

On June 22, Cape Evans came alive with midwinter celebrations. Fol-

lowing a gargantuan dinner, everybody was expected to make a speech and
Gran, in his quaintly accented English, explained how difficult it was to be a
Norwegian member of a British team competing with Norwegians, but that
he was truly pledged to his chosen team and, from his soul, he wished Captain Scott's men all success in the venture ahead. Bowers produced a Christmas tree made from a ski stick with branches of penguin feathers and gifts
for every man in the camp. Scott read aloud from the *South Polar Times,* edited by Cherry-Garrard and illustrated mainly by Wilson. All articles were
anonymous, but bets were taken on the various authors' identities. Currency
was in cigarettes or promissory dinners in posh London restaurants. After
the party, one by one, the men fell asleep. Wilson, watchman of the night,
went outside. The magical waves of aurora australis combined with the faint
refrains of the gramophone to produce a memorable *son et lumière* beneath
the great volcano.

Most nights, through the long months, the hut was quiet by 10 p.m.,
apart from the snoring of some inmates. Bowers was the most acclaimed
snorer and sometimes, it was said, set off the dogs to howl at the moon. The
many scientific instruments ticked through the night or jangled intermittent
bells, ponies kicked at their stalls or their neighbors, and sometimes somebody moaned or spoke in the night. That was all on quiet nights but, when
the storms came, nothing could be heard above the deep roar of the wind.
One blizzard blew with sustained ferocity for six days, hurling pebbles from
the beach against the wooden hut. Sometimes the whole hut shook and the
chimney vibrated with the sound of what might be an iron gate rattled by
prisoners in hell.

Roald Amundsen, that midwinter, did not share Scott's hesitance to an-
nounce plans while they were still tentative. Amundsen was constantly announcing new plans to his men, then changing them. In the words of his
team member Sverre Hassel: "The thought of the English gave him no peace.
For if we were not first at the Pole, we might just as well stay at home." On
July 4, Amundsen told his men he wanted to start out as early as mid-
September, rather than November 1 (the date already firmly fixed by Scott).
But at the end of July, Amundsen suddenly announced his desire to stage a
trial run in August, the day the sun would reappear. His number two, Jo-

hansen, said that was far too early, but Amundsen ignored him. September would turn out to be too cold for reasonable progress: The Norwegians' dogs' feet would be damaged and the men's heels frozen.

On June 25, three days after Midwinter Day, Scott took Wilson aside. For months the two men had discussed a special winter journey to Cape Crozier. Only in the depths of winter, when long sledge journeys were considered suicidal, could the zoological grail of a living emperor penguin embryo be sought. Cape Crozier in winter was a must, therefore, and Wilson had long since persuaded Scott to let him go. Two volunteers, Bowers and Cherry-Garrard, would travel with him. Wilson said of Scott's warning that day: "He also impressed upon me the necessity of bringing back my two companions unhurt from Cape Crozier for the southern journey." This may or may not have indicated Scott's hopes at that time of taking all three men on his Pole team.

Scott was rightly uneasy about losing three of his best men when, in the coldest, darkest time of year, Wilson, Bowers, and Cherry-Garrard set out on their five-week quest to Cape Crozier. But he knew the emperor quest was one of Wilson's main reasons for having joined the *Terra Nova* expedition and both men had intended to have their base at Cape Crozier, close by the emperor colony's site. Wilson thought of the quest, should it succeed, as potentially one of "the biggest scientific breakthroughs of the 20th century, by proving the link between dinosaurs and birds."

Once Scott saw that Wilson's mind was made up, he made the best of it by suggesting the journey also be used as a trial of gear and food, especially the relative merits of different portions of fats, proteins, and carbohydrates when eaten under extreme stress. Scott recorded various equipment modifications. "Another new departure is the decision to carry eiderdown sleeping-bags inside the reindeer ones. With such an arrangement the early part of the journey is bound to be comfortable, but when the bags get iced, difficulties are pretty certain to arise. Day has been devoting his energies to the creation of a blubber stove, much assisted of course by our experience gained at Hut Point."

On June 27, the three men set out into the Stygian darkness for their 140-mile round trip towing two nine-foot sledges, in tandem, with a total load of 750 pounds. Dogs, they had concluded rightly and as Amundsen was soon to discover, would not cope well with midwinter conditions. At the last minute, realizing the enormous weight they would have to haul, they agreed to leave behind the additional weight and bulk of skis. Scott saw them off. "This winter travel," he wrote, "is a new and bold venture but the right men have gone to attempt it. All good luck go with them!"

On the second "day" out, hauling the sledge from the sea ice up to the barrier, Cherry-Garrard took off his mittens briefly to gain a better hold of the ropes. All his fingers were nipped within sixty seconds, causing inch-long blisters full of frozen liquid, a painful condition, which I know well. This was the start of what Cherry-Garrard called "the weirdest bird's-nesting expedition that has ever been." It spurred the writing, some years later, of his book *The Worst Journey in the World,* which, over the twentieth century, was several times voted the best travel book ever written. I will give only a glimpse of the three men's experiences over the thirty-six days of their journey.

At night, Cherry-Garrard's damaged fingers leaked pus, which froze by day. He was in permanent pain, heightened when doing the simplest task, such as tying up a lace or sledge strap. At night, all three men suffered ex-cruciating leg cramps. Their bags collected moisture each time they camped: Cherry-Garrard's bag started out weighing eighteen pounds and ended up at forty-five pounds. Their clothes became less and less insulative as the fibers filled with ice. The tent's inner lining provided warmth but trapped moisture and increased in weight from thirty-five pounds to sixty. They gained more sledge weight in ice than they lost in the rations and fuel they consumed.

The temperature on the barrier, beneath Erebus, dropped to −44°C during their second night out, to −49°C the next night, and to −51°C after a week.

Wilson approved of his companions. "They are the best of our new sledging lot," he recorded. He enjoyed the aurora displays, the mock moons, and the vertical shafts of the lunar cross, caused by temperature inversion. Cherry-Garrard's teeth split from the cold and his spectacles, fogging up, turned him blind. He wrote: "Antarctic exploration is seldom as bad as you imagine, seldom as bad as it sounds but this journey beggared our language. No words could express its horror." But worse was to come. The ther-mometer on July 6 dropped to −60°C, a freezing fog so dense they could

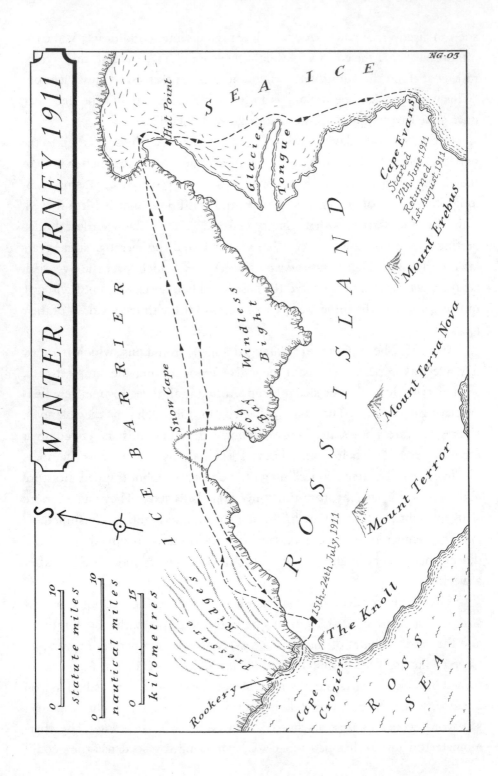

hardly see their ski tips. It took four or five hours in the morning just to dress, cook, pack, and load the sledges.

Their clothes froze like suits of armor as soon as the blubber stove was put out and retained whatever shape they froze in. One morning, just after exiting the tent, Cherry-Garrard stopped to look sideways for some fifteen seconds and when he tried to turn his head back he found the neck of his hood had frozen solid in looking sideways. It took him half an hour of hard man-hauling to get the hood warm enough to unfreeze sufficiently for him to look ahead again. After that, they all made sure to maintain the best posture for hauling as soon as they stepped outside the tent.

Matches, taken from the outside dry cold into the moist atmosphere of the tent with the stove alight, became sodden and useless. The extreme cold, together with new snow blown about by blizzards, produced surface snow crystals as rough and abrasive as sandpaper. Hauling both sledges in tandem became well nigh impossible, so they switched to a relay system, pulling one a certain distance then going back for the other. In this manner, they could shift the loads, but only by slaving away for three miles to gain a single mile of progress. One day they managed only one and a half miles in eight hellish hours of man-haul.

Cherry-Garrard wrote: "I for one had come to that point of suffering at which I did not really care if only I could die without much pain." It was the darkness and the low temperature that made it unbearable. The fog then became so thick that they could no longer relay since they could not see their footprints back from sledge to sledge and so, again, they dragged both sledges together over the gluelike surfaces. At last, after nineteen nightmare days, they came to the gap by the Knoll and pitched their tent in a snowy hollow. Wilson had always known they would need to stay here for some days to locate, reach, and work in the emperor colony and so, as planned, they built a hut from rocks by the light of the waning moon.

Setting off with ice axes, crampons, and an alpine rope, they struggled between ice cliffs and rock outcrops, their route often blocked by gaping crevasses and chaotic masses of tumbled ice boulders. They could hear the distant trumpeting of emperors, but their way to the colony was always barred by some obstacle or other and, fearing the moon's disappearance, they just made it back to their shelter. The next day they zigzagged a perilous new route down the cliffs to the penguins' beach. To be caught there in darkness without shelter would mean likely death by exposure, so they rushed to find warm eggs. Bowers fell through weak sea ice and wet his socks, which froze solid. They wrapped their spoils in their inner clothes and took three fat emperors too for a blubber supply, their only source of light and heat.

Again, they just made it back to their hut before darkness and the arrival of a snowstorm. That night their stove spat burning blubber into Wilson's eye, causing him great pain. Over the next forty-eight hours, the wind rose to force 10 and blew their tent away, along with the mittens, socks, and other gear stowed inside. Their refuge began to fill with snow sucked into the void by the sheer power of the wind. A pipe on their homemade blubber stove melted at the solder joint, rendering it useless, so they had to cook as best they could using their primus lamp. Then their canvas roof was sucked off the hut's rock walls and the three men lay in their freezing bags buried in drift. To eat was impossible, except during a brief lull in the blizzard.

After forty-eight hours of ultimate misery, there was a lull in the storm, and to their huge relief, Bowers located their tent, blown some five hundred yards down the hill. Their situation, with no workable blubber stove and only a single can of primus oil, was still dire so, reluctantly, they gave up further egg collecting and headed back toward Cape Evans. Their route in the darkness took them too far east and into a crevasse field. Bowers, at one point, dangled helplessly down one dark abyss until the others managed to heave his harness up with their blistered hands. The nightmare continued for two weeks with nonstop pain from the raw sores on their fingers, for all their blisters had long since burst and new skin did not grow in the cold.

On August 1, they arrived back at Cape Evans to find that only three of the eggs contained suitable embryos, not enough for useful analysis back in London, so the success of the main aim of the journey remained in doubt. For several weeks, all three men hobbled about on frost-damaged feet, but only a day after their return, Scott noted: "Wilson is very thin, but this morning very much his keen, wiry self—Bowers is quite himself today. Cherry-Garrard . . . still looks worn. It is evident that he has suffered most severely . . . Bowers has come through best . . . Never was such a sturdy, active, undefeatable little man."

Comparing the effects of the three differing ration menus the men had eaten, Scott was able to formulate special rations, with Wilson's help, for the extreme cold expected on the high polar plateau. He called these summit rations and, following the Cape Crozier test, they contained a far greater fat content than any previous polar ration. Cherry-Garrard's menu had proved most effective since, despite his extreme debilitation compared with the other two, he had lost only one pound compared with Bowers's two and a half pounds and Wilson's three and a half pounds. This slight weight loss and the fact that no permanent frost damage occurred even to Cherry-Garrard's fingers was proof that, however uncomfortable in such extreme temperatures, the clothing and bags would be more than adequate for the Pole journey to come. All three men had many suggestions for improving different items of equipment and these were put into effect over the next two months. The journey had proved extremely worthwhile by way of a trial, even though the emperor enigma was to remain unsolved. Their eggs did eventually end up with a specialist at Edinburgh University after many months spent misplaced by indifferent professors at the London Natural History Museum. They did not, however, provide conclusive proof that feathers developed from scales.

Later that winter, Atkinson went out to visit a thermometer screen situated on the sea ice not far from the hut. He became disoriented in a blizzard, wandered about unable to fix his bearings, and was luckily found by a search party with lanterns, by which point he had already been badly damaged in one hand. Atkinson knew that Scott would have been worried sick by his absence and was pleasantly surprised when he did not receive the expected paternally delivered volcano. "It was all my own damned fault," he told Cherry-Garrard, "but Scott never slanged me at all."

In August, the twilit hours gradually increased until, on the twenty-fifth, the sun's rim was first glimpsed, along with an outbreak of champagne, song, and merriment. Debenham noted: "Everyone was out enjoying the return of the light and the Owner I saw, shouting to and playing with the dogs like a 2 year old." Omelchenko, the Russian groom, long convinced that the auroral lights were evil, was overjoyed by their disappearance. He had been leaving precious cigarettes out in the snow to propitiate these spirits of winter. Gran celebrated with a can of wild duck, which he had borrowed from

Shackleton's old supplies at Cape Royds. He placed the can on a primus to unfreeze it, but half an hour later, "suddenly there was an explosion, and millions of particles of tin plate flew round our ears."

With the sun's arrival, Scott at Cape Evans and Amundsen in the Bay of Whales each developed spring fever. Scott forced himself to be patient. A note he penned to a New Zealand friend summed up his feelings. "I am fully alive to the complication of the situation by Amundsen, but as any attempt at a race might have been fatal to our chance of getting to the Pole at all, I decided long ago to do exactly as I should have done had Amundsen not been down here. If he gets to the Pole, he is bound to do it rapidly with dogs, but one guesses that success will justify him, and that our venture will be 'out of it.' If he fails, he ought to hide! Anyway, he is taking a big risk, and perhaps deserves his luck if he gets through—but he is not there yet! Meanwhile, you may be sure we shall be going the best we can to carry out my plan."

39. The brass inclinometer from one of Scott's ships borrowed by my 1979 expedition to Antarctica, which registered 47° swings as we passed through the Roaring Forties. This was child's play compared with the same instrument's violent swings on one of Scott's voyages south, when it registered over 55°.

40. The Bowring Company, who sold *Terra Nova* to the admiralty for Scott's expedition, sixty years later sponsored my expedition with the ice-strengthened *Benjamin Bowring*, which steamed through the Antarctic pack ice to McMurdo Sound at an average speed of six knots, not much faster than the *Terra Nova*.

41. Two members of my 1979 expedition race back toward our ship after being caught out on suddenly fractured floes. Within minutes, these floes had moved a hundred yards out to sea. Bowers, Crean, and Cherry-Garrard were caught out in similar circumstances with their unfortunate ponies.

42–43. Ponting made sure to take good custom-posed shots of Scott's men with sponsors' goods by way of quid pro quo. Nothing had changed by the 1970s, when I had to take photographs of equipment for well over a thousand sponsors against a polar backdrop.

44. This biscuit, currently on a tour of British museums, cost me nearly £4,000 at auction to save it for the nation, only to discover it almost certainly came from Cape Evans, and not from the tent where Scott and his men died, as claimed in its auction provenance.

45. Scott has been heavily criticized for not using Inuit fur clothing. In fact, the wind-proof contemporary clothing with which he equipped his men was infinitely more practical for his purposes. This 1982 photograph shows Charles Burton and me about to depart into the Arctic winter prior to crossing the Arctic Ocean via the North Pole. Charlie favored wearing an Inuit fur jacket, but that year, for the first time, I switched from my normal fur gear to the then-new Gore-Tex material. Because we used open snow scooters to pull our sledges, we needed maximum body protection. Had we been man-hauling, we would have chosen light cotton gear.

46. I am trying to erect a pyramid tent on the Antarctic plateau in a strong wind. The tent was almost exactly the same design used by Scott's men seventy years before, and it is still considered by many governmental scientific institutions worldwide the best model for use in Antarctica.

47–48. Scott's prototype-tracked snow vehicle in 1911 and, in 1982, its descendant, with which we completed the first crossing of Antarctica and the Arctic Ocean via both Poles.

49. Out on the sea ice. Members of the *Terra Nova* expedition in January 1911.
Mount Erebus is active in the background.

50. In 1982, my transglobe expedition reaches McMurdo Sound, under Erebus,
after the first crossing of Antarctica in one coast-to-coast push.

51. Bowers's photograph of the polar party man-hauling their still-heavy load on the polar plateau with about seventy-five nautical miles to go to the Pole.

52. Mike Stroud and I use skis to tow 500-pound loads each at the start of our 2,380-kilometer, ninety-five-day crossing of the Antarctic continent. On many days, we found it easier to travel without skis due to difficult snow/ice conditions.

53. A modern-day man-hauler (Mike Stroud 1993) heads over the plateau toward the South Pole. Since he is treading on his own body shadow, it is safe to assume the local time is midday. Most of the time in Antarctica, we used our body shadows and local time as our main means of navigation.

54. Top right: Oliver Shepard using a standard theodolite in Antarctica in 1979 during our transglobe expedition. Like Scott, I nearly always used a theodolite instead of a sextant, because of the increased accuracy when completing scientific research work.

55. Right: The author, with frostbitten cheek, manufacturing rope crampons in a tent at the top of the Beardmore Glacier in readiness for descending the icefalls below.

56. A modern-day expedition group on the barrier. This photograph shows an area of crevasses and pressured ice in front of the broken line of the shear zone where coastal ice is "hinged" to the continent of Antarctica.

THE DANGEROUS GLACIER

TEDDY EVANS, A MAN small in stature but not in ego, was determined to reach the Pole. He sensibly recognized that man-hauling ability would count highly when Scott came to choose his final team, and Evans believed that skiing ability helped in man-hauling. Gran wrote that the "utmost thing on his mind was to become the expedition's best conditioned skier. Thus every day he wanted to compete with me. Of course he was motivated by a desire to qualify for the last trek to the Pole. Evans was clear that, as the second in command, should he have a chance to be with his leader, he must have better technical and physical qualifications than the others." Evans approached Scott in August 1911 with the suggestion that he, Gran, and Petty Officer Forde make an early spring journey out to Corner Camp to check that the depot was in good order and to clear it of snowdrifts. Scott's response, since he thought the plan unnecessary but presumably could find no good reason for refusing his second-in-command's request, was: "If you people want to suffer, for Heaven's sake, Go!" The trio did in fact perform a useful task, for the depot had drifted over and proved difficult to find. On the way back, the highly competitive Evans pushed them to the limit, covering thirty-four miles in a single twenty-four-hour stretch.

Scott himself wanted to escape from camp on any pretext. He hated inactivity and thrived on physical toil. He chose his companions for his spring outing: the scientist Simpson and two powerful sledgers, his old friend Taff Evans and his rising star Bowers. His stated aim was to check the rate of flow of the Ferrar Glacier by noting the current location of ice stakes placed there by Wright the previous autumn. This group covered 175 miles in ten days dragging 180 pounds each. Temperatures dropped to –40°C, despite coastal rather than barrier conditions. Simpson's face was covered in frost blisters and the last day's travel included twenty-one miles man-hauling into the teeth of a cutting headwind. Bowers described the trip as a picnic, which showed he was already fully recovered from the Crozier penguin journey, and Scott noted that his erstwhile storekeeper was a positive wonder. "I never met such a sledge traveller." If Bowers had not already figured in Scott's mind as one of his prospective Pole sledgers, his choice was now probably assured. Taff Evans, who was as ever a tower of strength on this trip, was another likely choice for the Pole team. Scott described the Ferrar Glacier foray as "a remarkably pleasant and instructive little spring journey."

On September 1, two weeks before Scott's outing, Cecil Meares and Demetri Gerof went to Hut Point with all the dogs, and one week after them, forty miles to the east, Roald Amundsen, too impatient to wait for more suitable temperatures and ignoring the dire warnings of his number two, Hjalmar Johansen, set out for the Pole on September 8, 1911, with seven men and all his best dogs. Only a week later, after sledging at temperatures down to –56°C, he was back at his base with his men in disarray, with serious damage to the feet of both men and dogs and accusations against him of cowardice. Five dogs had frozen to death.

The morning after the Norwegian team's return from this false start, Amundsen wrote: "At the breakfast table . . . Johansen found it suitable to utter unflattering statements about me and my position as leader for our enterprise here. It was not only our return yesterday that he found indefensible in the highest degree, *but* also much else I had taken the liberty of doing as leader in the course of time. The gross and unforgivable part of [Johansen's statements] is that they were made in everybody's hearing. The bull must be taken by the horns; I must make an example immediately." Amundsen quelled his mutiny by banishing the two main troublemakers from his Pole team. Scott was never to suffer from such an internal revolt for three reasons: his selection of personnel; the expedition's basic framework of discipline, which even his non-naval scientists understood; and, mainly, because he never subjected his men or his animals to such plainly foolhardy travel. Wilson had been allowed his winter journey and Teddy Evans had asked to travel on the barrier (at the same time as Amundsen's fiasco) but only for a distance of about fifty miles and hence of very limited real risk.

In the days after Amundsen's false start, he decided to postpone his next attempt to set out until the middle of October. As a result of bad weather, he did not actually start until October 19, only twelve days before the British left their base. The interim month was a time of bitterness and tension in the Norwegian hut.

Six weeks before the British departure date, on September 13, 1911, Scott gave out his sledging plans, the result of many hours closeted with his chief planner and administrator, the ever-cheerful Bowers. Using a hand-drawn map on the supper table, he addressed the crowded room and pointed out the three main stages to the Pole—the barrier, the glacier, and the plateau. "The whole journey there and back," he said, "is about 1,530 geographical miles, longer than any sledge journey ever yet made. Since Shackleton's figures are our best guide, I have laid these prospective plans upon data taken from his book . . . On this calculation the whole journey will be 144 days. I repeat that our plans are laid as though Amundsen does not exist."

Although Scott did not have much confidence in the motorized sledges, he planned that they should set out fully loaded a week before the main party, just in case they proved to be of use. Neither was Scott relying on the ponies or the dogs to be of use after they reached the Beardmore Glacier— he planned on man-hauling alone from that point. Three teams of man-haulers would set out, each comprising three or four men. After a fortnight, one unit would return, and after a further two weeks, the second would leave the last unit alone to make for the Pole.

Across the barrier, the plan was that ten ponies would tow a 550-pound load each and, as they tired, would be shot and used for food. The final two

ponies would be shot on the thirty-fourth day out. Scott was hoping that the
two dog teams would tow their loads as far as the base of the glacier and
that skis might also be useful up to that point. Ten years previously, he,
Evans, and Lashly had lasted for thirty-five days on the plateau with some
difficulty. This time Scott was planning a stay of seventy-five days. "I don't
know whether it is possible for men to last out that time, I almost doubt it."

Scott added many minor details. He also indirectly praised Oates by
mentioning that the ponies were in a much fitter condition than those taken
on the depot trip the previous summer and that the improved fodder had
greatly strengthened them. The man-haul rations, much improved by Bowers and Wilson since the Crozier winter journey, had been divided into standard or summit rations, the latter designed to cope with the greater demands
of the extreme cold haulage expected on the plateau.

If the expedition did not reach the Pole and the Norwegians failed as
well, there would be a second attempt the following year using mules. This
had been recommended by Oates after the previous year's depot-placing trip
and Scott had immediately ordered them from India. The men would not
carry pony whips. If need be, they would use the reins, and the ponies would
wear snowshoes. They would be cleanly shot before they suffered more than
might be expected had they remained in Manchuria as haulage beasts, and
none would spend more than thirty-four days out on the ice. Scott had
learned on the depot trip that his ponies would suffer if they set out on a
date suitable to race the Norwegians so, this summer, they would be traveling only in the sort of weather they could cope with back home in Manchuria.

Scott had already tried dogs in Antarctica, where nobody had ever used
them before for any distance greater than a ten-mile sea-ice trip. On his first
journey in 1903 with Wilson and Shackleton, when their dogs fell by the
wayside, the three men nonetheless covered nearly nine hundred miles. His
next journey, man-hauling with Evans and Lashly, was another huge and
unprecedented success, including thirty-five days spent on the high plateau.
On the *Nimrod* expedition, Shackleton had almost made it to the Pole by
man-haul and with ponies but without a single dog. When Shackleton wrote
about that remarkable journey, he made clear that the horrific crevasses of
the Beardmore Glacier, the same route Scott would have to tackle, were

utterly unsuited for dogs or ponies. Scott had already watched almost his entire dog team drop into a single crevasse. How much worse then for a dog team on this crevasse-ridden, 120-mile-long, 9,000-foot-high glacier that lay ahead? And what did the greatest polar writer of all, Cherry-Garrard, a serious critic of Scott's methods, think of Scott's decision not to use dogs on the Beardmore? "I do not believe it possible to take dogs up and down, and over the ice disturbances at the junction with the plateau . . . but the best thing you could do with dogs in pressure such as we all experienced on our way down would be to drop them into the nearest chasm. If you can avoid such messes well and good: if not, you must not rely on dogs, and the people who talk of these things have no knowledge . . . If Scott was going up the Beardmore he was probably right not to take dogs."

Once Scott knew that man-haul was to be the most likely means to achieve success, he was proud to use it and not afraid to tell the world of his men's man-hauling prowess. Many of today's expeditioners strive for purist achievements that are "unsupported" by modern transportation. Messner's great solo Everest ascent without oxygen or Sherpa aid made him prouder than many of his previous triumphs using all available aids.

So Scott's Pole plan was evolved out of common sense, and, democratically, he asked for a critical response from his men, the majority of whom were scientists with analytical minds and not afraid to speak out. They had, after all, spent the entire winter in heated debate at the same table as Scott. They were neither yes men nor Royal Navy "yes, sirs." Doubtless there must have been incidental queries from the usual quarters, the pessimists and the perfectionists, but given the chance to air their views, not a soul spoke out. The Scott-Bowers planning had been thorough, conservative, and based on the most solid model available, the *Nimrod* journey.

What interested the men most about Scott's plan was the list of participants. Ten pony leaders, including Scott, would set out from Cape Evans on November 1, along with the dogs under Meares and Gerof, a week after the motor party consisting of Bernard Day and Bill Lashly, under Teddy Evans's command. Apart from Day, Meares, and Gerof, any of the others might end up in the final push to the Pole, depending on their fitness at the time. The pony leaders were named as Scott, Wilson, Bowers, Oates, Atkinson, Wright, Cherry-Garrard, Taff Evans, Crean, and Keohane. Scott had spent a great deal of time picking his key men. Throughout the long winter, he had made notes of the good and bad points of each individual to add to his initial impressions from his time on *Terra Nova*. Generally his judgments proved sound, but he was not infallible, as events would soon prove.

Scott could now only wait for November temperatures when he could safely allow the ponies onto the barrier. He knew that Amundsen, his dogs able to face colder, windier conditions, was likely to set out much earlier. Scott's two great personal weaknesses, his impatience and his black-dog moods, attacked him at this time, not helped by a number of minor setbacks. Three of his men were incapacitated, Forde with frostbite, Clissold with various injuries after falling off an iceberg while posing for a Ponting photograph, and Debenham from a football knee injury. One of the dogs died of an unknown sickness, which could easily infect the others, and when the two motor sledges set out on October 24, 1911, an axle casing split. "It is trying," Scott wrote, "but I am past despondency."

It did not help Scott that, whether or not his Pole attempt succeeded, the expedition was deeply in debt. He had raised enough money to reach Antarctica, just, but he knew that debts and the interest on debts were mounting back in London. He had already plowed all his personal savings into the venture. When *Terra Nova* called, he would be away on the ice but she would take his mail back home for him, and to assure his bank manager that he was doing his best, he called everyone together in mid-October and, explaining the expedition's serious deficit, asked if those who could would agree to forgo their pay for a whole year. The response was immediate and generous, enabling Scott to sign a formal indemnity note releasing the expedition office from paying a number of salaries, including his own.

Six days before the Pole team set out, Kathleen, back in London, had a nightmare. "Rather a horrid day today. I woke up having had a bad dream about you, and then Peter came very close to me and said emphatically 'Daddy won't come back,' as though in answer to my silly thoughts."

If Scott was himself having bad dreams, it was probably about the motors. Bernard Day did manage to fix the split axle case and late on October 24, Teddy Evans's two motorized sledge teams set out from Cape Evans towing three tons of stores. "Hooper accompanied Lashly's car," Teddy Evans wrote, "and I worked with Day . . . Many doubts were expressed as to the use of the despised motors—but we heeded not the gibes of our friends." Scott had told Evans that he would be happy enough if the motors could be coaxed at least as far as White Island. The four men were determined to give it their all. The track chains skidded about with little traction on the hard sea ice, averaging only one mile an hour. Evans noted that before the final breakdown, "the motors advanced the necessaries for the Southern journey 51 miles over rough, slippery, and crevassed ice and gave the ponies the chance to march light as far as Corner Camp—this is all that Oates asked for."

Herbert Ponting traveled for some time with the motors to photograph and film Teddy Evans's group. Afterward he wrote: "No praise could be too great for the persistence with which Day and Lashly struggled with these motors. Once, they worked all night—in a temperature of 25°F below zero, in a stiff wind—and, regardless of frostbites and chills, they dismantled one of the engines, and substituted for a broken connecting rod the only spare they had with them." He concluded: "Knowing in what respects Scott's motors failed, and why, it would now be possible to build machines that would work satisfactorily in the Antarctic. To the memory of Scott must therefore be given the honour due to a pioneer of motor traction in the Polar Regions, for he used it with a certain measure of success."

Tryggve Gran later noted that the motor sledges were not regarded as a failure on the expedition but, on the contrary, as a considerable success. Cherry-Garrard, who survived the expedition and went on to serve in the First World War, added: "The general design seemed to be right, all that was now wanted was experience. As an experiment they were successful in the South, but Scott never knew their true possibilities; for they were the direct ancestors of the 'tanks' in France."

Seventy-eight years later, I crossed Antarctica with two friends along the approximate line of the zero meridian, ending up at Hut Point. We used three small open snowmobiles with air-cooled two-stroke engines, each towing a one-thousand-pound sledge load. These were the direct descendants of Scott's prototypes and they enabled us to complete the first crossing of Antarctica that did not approach the Pole from opposite sides of the continent.

When the machines would go no farther, on November 2, 1911, Teddy

Evans and his men repacked 740 pounds of motor-borne supplies onto a man-haul sledge and continued south, laying a trail for the ponies and dog teams that would follow. Every three miles they built snow cairns as markers. Given any sunlight, such markers are highly efficient, as they act as reflectors over many miles and are often more effective than thin black poles. In a whiteout, neither the cairns nor the markers will show up, unless you bump into them by chance.

The main expedition groups set out as planned on November 1. Ten ponies followed Teddy Evans's southerly trail, each led by one man and hauling a sledge load apiece. Halting at Hut Point, someone remembered that they had forgotten to pack the Union Jack donated by the queen, so Scott used the landline telephone he had installed in the winter to call Gran at Cape Evans. The Norwegian skied over the sea ice and gave Scott the flag. Neither man missed the irony involved. They shook hands and Scott said, "You're young, you've got your life before you. Take care of yourself. God bless you."

By November 4, they were onto the barrier, following Teddy Evans's trail, and all went well. In due course they came to first one and then the other motorized sledge, deserted and forlorn in the wide white horizons, but they plodded on through the sunless haze without perspective. The ponies varied in speed, and wide gaps opened between them. In whiteout conditions, no man could even see the trail. Bowers, on one occasion, straining his gaze ahead, thought he saw a herd of black cattle approaching but soon found they were only pony droppings. Attempts to fit the two types of *hestersko* were foiled by the ponies, who found them irksome. Luckily, following the trodden trail, they did not seem to flounder, as had their late colleagues the previous year.

The men wore their warm and smooth-soled *finnesko*, comfortable and effective as long as no great traction was required. Attempts to use skis when leading horses on halters were unsuccessful because the swish of the ski blades spooked the animals and nobody wanted to be run over by a bolting horse or by the heavy sledge that it towed.

No land was visible for days, not even White Island or Minna Bluff, as they plodded on over the barrier where sky and snow merged into a single pall of whiteness. They traveled by night for the benefit of the ponies. The

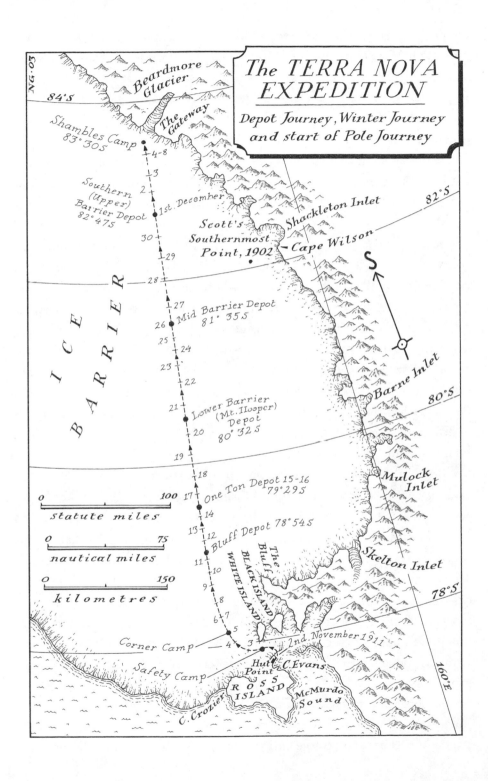

temperature hovered around zero Fahrenheit, for summer had arrived. Bowers noted: "While the sun is shining we have an excellent little sundial—an idea of Captain Scott's. You set the shadow to the time and there you are—it is the simplest device imaginable and useful in many ways besides being the best thing to steer by." But most of the time, the settled weather that was normal at that time stayed away and Bowers added on November 13: "The weather was about as poisonous as one could wish; a fresh breeze and driving snow from the E. with an awful surface . . . I have never seen such snow down here before—large soft flakes; it makes the surface very bad for the sledges."

Scott's moods swung up and down with the weather and the snow surface and he was not the only one. Cherry-Garrard noted: "It is curious to see how depressed all our diaries become when this bad weather obtained, and how quickly we must have cheered up whenever the sun came out. There is no doubt that a similar effect was produced upon the ponies." There was no spare fuel to make water for the ponies but they had all been trained to eat snow during the winter. Scott wrote: "When eating snow he [Chinaman] habitually takes too large a mouthful and swallows it; it is comic to watch him, because when the snow chills his inside he shuffles about with all four legs and wears a most fretful, aggrieved expression: but no sooner has the snow melted than he seizes another mouthful."

Because the ponies had differing speeds, Scott started out from camp each day with the slowest first. On the same principle, Scott had told Meares and Gerof to stay for several days back at Hut Point before coming on to catch up with the ponies. This would save a good deal of dog food and some rations. Meares arrived far earlier than Scott had hoped, on November 7, 1911, having traveled in blizzard conditions that had the pony group camped and tentbound. There were many reasons for this. Huskies' eyes have nictitating eyelids that cope easily with even horizontally blown snow, but ponies have no such mechanism. The dogs could also follow a trail without having to see it, especially one as scent laden as that of Scott's pony group.

Although Scott was annoyed that by arriving a lot earlier than needed, Meares would waste precious dog food, he was also extremely impressed by the dogs' performance, to the extent that he told Cherry-Garrard: "It is satisfactory to find the dogs will pull the loads and can be driven to face such a wind as we have had. It shows that they ought to be able to help us a good deal." He added that his previous attempts at dog driving had obviously not gotten the best from his teams and that, maybe, Meares could be used beyond the base of the Beardmore. At that stage, he saw this as an option should he fall badly behind schedule.

At this time, despite the mostly foul weather, the ponies were all setting a far better pace, some twelve miles a day, than during the depot-laying trip. Oates noted: "Scott told me today he was very pleased with the way the ponies were going and was kind enough to say he owed me a lot for the trouble I had taken. I must say the ponies are going now better than I expected." Oates's pony, Christopher, was a veritable devil and could not be stopped from camp to camp. Only Oates could deal with him and only by keeping going all day without even a lunch halt en route. Scott wrote: "The Soldier thinks Chinaman will last for a good many days yet, which is an extraordinary confession of hope for him . . . if they pull through well, all the thanks will be due to Oates." Oates, more debilitated than the others, thanks to the added exertion required to deal with Christopher, wrote: "if only these wretched old cripples of ours can stick it and we get all the stuff to the glacier I think we shall do the trick . . . Meares said he was surprised how well the ponies were going which is rather amusing considering he was responsible for buying the old screws."

That same day, November 13, 1911, a few hundred miles to the southwest, Amundsen's men came to the southern extent of the barrier and made a "marvellous discovery" right on the axis of his advance. With remarkable good fortune, by heading south from the Bay of Whales, he had chanced directly on the foot of the Axel Heiberg Glacier, which offered a steep pathway south and up to the polar plateau. The gods had smiled doubly on him because this glacier was sixty miles farther south than the Beardmore, which meant 120 miles less to be spent on the dreaded heights of the plateau. Amundsen had set out sixty miles and twelve days ahead and was now some three hundred miles farther south than Scott.

On November 15, Scott's men, knowing nothing of the Norwegians' stroke of luck, pushed on to One Ton Depot, where they rested for a day and lightened the pony loads by dropping off bundles of seal liver for consumption on the return trip. Now the strong ponies towed 580 pounds, the weak ones 400 pounds, and each dog team 800 pounds. Scott was now able to review his plans, based on the performance of the various teams over the 130 miles from Hut Point. In another nine days, the first pony would be shot, Scott told Oates, and the last at the foot of the glacier. No attempt would be made to take horses onto the Beardmore.

Scott was increasingly anxious as the days of bad weather meant lagging behind the key indicator of likely success or failure, the record of Shackleton's journey. Frank Wild, who had been on *Discovery* and *Nimrod*, had given Scott Shackleton's daily progress chart and this became Scott's bible. So long as he could keep ahead, or at least abreast, of the schedule set by Shackleton, there was a chance of success. By late November, in constant fog, they were some six days "in the red" and Scott was not a happy man. For the key last stretch of the barrier, everything depended on the ponies, so Scott was constantly and understandably questioning Oates, who reacted badly to what he considered to be backseat driving. "Scott realises now what awful cripples our ponies are," he wrote, "and carries a face like a tired seaboot in consequence."

Scott acknowledged the ponies' unsuitability in a letter to Kathleen. "Just a note from the Barrier to say that I love you . . . Everything is going pretty well for the present though we had a bad scare about the condition of the ponies last week. The animals are not well selected. I knew this in New Zealand, though I didn't tell you. That they are going well now and bidding fair to carry us through the first stage of our journey is due entirely to Oates. He is another treasure."

On November 21, at 80°32'S, the pony group caught up with Teddy Evans and his three man-haulers, who had laid the trail ever since abandoning their motor sledges. Teddy, always competitive, like Scott, had forced a powerful pace, with the result that he arrived early and had to wait for six days eating up precious food while doing nothing, at the point he had himself stipulated as the rendezvous. To avoid boredom, he and his men had built a fifteen-foot-high cairn beside their camp.

From now on, the expedition advanced toward the Beardmore in five little groups, setting out at intervals from each camp: first the man-haulers under Teddy Evans, the navigator; then the three pony groups; and finally the dogs. Even Scott called the cavalcade a somewhat disorganized procession. On November 24, and according to plan, the first men turned back, a single small sledge with Bernard Day and Frank Hooper. Scott sent with them instructions for Simpson, in charge at the base: "ponies doing fairly well. I hope we shall get through to the Glacier without difficulty but to make sure I am carrying the dog teams further than I intended at first—the teams may be late returning, unfit for further work or non-existant . . . In case [they] are unable to [carry stores to One Ton Camp] it will be necessary to organize a man hauling party to undertake it." This message shows that Scott was fully prepared to be as flexible in changing his original plans as was necessary to adapt them to the ever-changing weather and surface conditions.

With Day and Hooper on their way back to base, everyone else pushed on into a seventeen-mile-per-hour headwind after shooting Jehu, the weakest of the ponies. "Meares," Scott noted, "has just come up to report that Jehu made four feeds for the dogs. He cut up very well and had quite a lot of fat on him. Meares says another pony will carry him to the Glacier." Charles Wright wrote that he and the other pony drivers thenceforward watched Meares with suspicion lest his eyes next alighted meaningfully on their particular charge.

Bowers realized, as did Wright, that the considerable amount of fat revealed on the dead Jehu, the weakest of the ponies, showed that he had been fully capable of working a good deal farther toward the glacier. The ponies were clearly being shot to plan to provide dog food or to maintain plenty of fodder for the survivors and not because they were struggling to keep going. However, Bowers, who so cared for the ponies that he had willingly risked his own life for them the previous summer, was pleased that they now met their ends without suffering. "A year's care," he wrote, "and good feeding, three weeks' work with good treatment, a reasonable load and a good ration, and then a painless end. If anybody can call that cruel I cannot either understand it or agree with them." On November 28, they shot Chinaman. Oates said by way of an obituary: "He was a game little devil and must have been a goodish kind of pony 15 years ago."

The next day the mist banks rolled away. After 370 miles of often featureless barrier gloom and a month of wordless plodding to the crunch of hoof and boot, they were rewarded by a breathtaking panorama. The triple-peaked Mount Markham towered above them, rising 14,000 feet into a clear blue sky. Cutting obliquely across their course, a series of black headland cliffs disappeared into the far distance to the west and east. "Altogether things look much better," Scott wrote, "and everyone is in excellent spirits."

They ate Chinaman that night. His erstwhile leader, Charles Wright, recorded that his pony died of old age precipitated by a bullet. He expressed himself proud to have saved the animal for so long from becoming dog meat, but was now happy to eat him. They made "pony hoosh" and found it sweet and good, though tough. Because their cooking fuel was rationed, they ate the meat semi-raw, which would have ensured a maximum vitamin C content, although they did not know it at the time. "Hoosh" was their name for their daily stew into which pretty much everything was thrown, from biscuits, raisins, curry paste, and pemmican to cocoa powder.

At their camp east of Mount Markham, they were four miles beyond Scott's 1902 "farthest south." Now only Shackleton's group had ever traveled the southerly route they would follow. In 1902, Scott, with some help from dogs, had taken fifty-eight days to reach this point and Shackleton, with only four ponies but far better weather and surfaces, had taken twenty-three days. This time Scott had covered the distance in twenty-nine days and so was still six days behind schedule. Nonetheless, they were at the 83rd parallel, only 420 miles from the Pole, and Scott wrote: "everything looks well if the weather will only give us a chance to see our way to the Glacier."

On December 1, Oates shot his own pony, the fiendish Christopher, who moved at the moment of execution and careered around the camp one last time causing mayhem before Oates could dispatch him. The horse-meat butchery was the job of the dog drivers who, being the fastest movers, had time on their hands. By now everyone could see how the dogs, inferior though they were to Amundsen's Greenland huskies, were superior to pony or man-haul power, at least on the crevasse-free parts of the barrier. Bowers noted that the chances of Amundsen and his 120 dogs having beaten them were looking good.

Wilson's pony Nobby had by this point allowed snowshoes to be fitted to his hooves and Scott wrote: "There is no doubt that these snow-shoes are *the* thing for ponies." The next pony to be shot was Victor. Bowers, his devoted leader, was upset and critical. "[Victor] did a splendid march and kept ahead all day, and as usual marched into camp first, pulling over 450lbs. eas-ily. It seemed an awful pity to have to shoot a great strong animal." Scott's plan of reaching the glacier with the last one of two ponies still in haulage had worked well. The animals, so often criticized as poorly chosen, had done just as well as any others could have, given what was expected of them.

More of their meat should have been preserved and more carefully buried at the depots to avoid deterioration by sunlight. This was the task of Meares and Gerof once the pony group had left each day. There is no way of knowing quite how diligently Meares followed Scott's orders regarding the pony meat. Charles Wright and Cherry-Garrard both grumbled that more of the pony meat should have been stashed at the foot of the Beardmore but they also acknowledged that such laments were all very well with the bene-fits of hindsight. Even the cautious and meticulous Bowers, in charge of ra-tions, said nothing at the time.

Still led by Teddy Evans, the expedition began to cross undulating ice ridges up to twenty-five feet high. To their east, the chaotic outflow of the Beardmore Glacier was clearly visible, spilling out onto the barrier in a se-ries of heavily crevassed waves. Ahead could be seen a rounded-hill feature, strewn with boulders, called Mount Hope, which marked the only passable ramp from the barrier onto the glacier and had been named by Shackleton "the Gateway." In one more half-day's march, they would cross the treach-erous shear-crack zone between barrier and glacier, which could only be done in good visibility. Cherry-Garrard wrote: "It was important that we should have fine clear weather during the next few days when we should be approaching the land. On his previous southern journey Scott had been pre-vented from reaching the range of mountains which ran along to our right by a huge chasm. This phenomenon is known to geologists as a shear crack and is formed by the movement of a glacier away from the land which bounds it." Shackleton had stumbled upon the only possible route onto the Beardmore Glacier and with great boldness had then found his way up its 120-mile, 9,000-foot ascent, riven much of the way by some of the largest impassable crevasse fields and icefalls in Antarctica.

At this point, when Scott least needed it, bad weather set in. Blizzards are to be expected, but not, as one twenty-first-century U.S. atmospheric sci-entist, Dr. Susan Solomon, put it to me, "real humdingers at *that* time and in *that* place." On December 3, Scott and Bowers, on skis, nosed their way forward in nil visibility. They managed ten miles before camping in a blizzard. Scott wrote, "The pony wall blew down, huge drifts collected, and the sledges were quickly buried. It was the strongest wind I have known here in summer." The temperature rose rapidly and both men and ponies were soon sodden with slush underfoot. Bowers, swinging the thermometer, found to his disbelief a recording of 0.6°C.

Scott was depressed. "What on earth does such weather mean at this time of year? It is more than our share of ill-fortune." Oates noted: "I think we shall get to the Pole now, but I think there is a very good chance of the Norskies getting there before us." The blizzard continued for four days and nights: a time of cold, wet misery for men and animals. Teddy Evans wrote: "Another blizzard started, which tore our chances of any great success to ribbons—it was the biggest knock-down blow . . . to date."

And what of Amundsen? While Scott's men waited out the wet blizzard, the Norwegians had already ascended their chosen glacier. They first named it Folgefonni and later the Axel Heiberg, after a sponsor, and found it a very different place from the Beardmore as described by Shackleton. The Axel Heiberg has since been negotiated, by a New Zealand team in 1961–1962, led by Wally Herbert (British) using dog teams, and by an Anglo-Norwegian team in the 1980s, led by a scientist, Monika Kristensen. Neither group had trouble with crevasses, unlike those teams, including my own and Reinhold Messner's, which have since 1912 traveled the Beardmore. The Axel Heiberg icefalls, though steeper than the Beardmore's, are easier to circumvent and Amundsen met good weather and clear visibility at all times when having to find a way around dangerous ice obstacles rather than merely heading south through fog.

Scott had to wait for his four-day blizzard to clear so that he could find his way across the lethal crevasses of the shear crack. But because Amundsen was already up on the plateau, he had moderate weather, nothing like Scott's: Elevation is everything in this region, for the storm in question was what scientists call "upslope." It pushes toward a mountain and runs out of steam after a short climb. The Norwegians were well out of reach of Scott's blizzard.

On December 8, the fourth day of the blizzard, Scott grew seriously worried about fodder for the horses, of which there was just enough for one more day, and for the men who that morning started to consume the special summit rations intended for use only after they had reached the glacier, which was still nine miles to the south. The wind at last seemed to lessen in power, so Scott roused the men. To reach their sledges, they had to dig down through four feet of drifted snow. To see whether a full load could be dragged through the morass of heavy, wet snow, Teddy Evans and his group tried to haul four men sitting on their sledge. With skis, they could shift the load only a yard at a time. Without skis, they merely sank to their knees.

Then they tried to haul a load behind Wilson's pony, Nobby, and he sank to his belly. Wilson felt that the ponies could go no farther and Teddy Evans, although he said nothing, noted in his diary: "I think it would be fairer to shoot them now, for what is a possible 12 miles' help? We could now, pulling 200 lb per man, start off with the proper man-hauling parties and our total weights, so why keep these wretched animals starving and shivering in the blizzard on a mere chance of their being able to give us a little drag? Why, *our* party have never been out of harness for nearly 400 miles, so why should not the other eight men buckle to and do some dragging?"

Oates, on the other hand, told Scott he was sure the ponies could manage another march and reach the Gateway despite the evil surface. So, on December 9, the sodden gear was loaded, Bowers and Cherry-Garrard went ahead to break a trail, and the rest followed as best they could.

On this last pony march, each leader gave his animal half of his own biscuit ration for the day. Cherry-Garrard wrote:

> There was not one man there who would willingly have
> caused pain to a living thing. But what else was to be done—we
> could not leave our pony depot in that bog. Hour after hour we
> plugged on: and we dare not halt for lunch, we knew we could
> never start again. After crossing many waves huge pressure ridges
> suddenly showed themselves all round, and we got on to a steep
> rise with the coastal chasm on our right hand appearing as a great
> dip full of enormous pressure . . . For two hours we zig-zagged
> about . . . Scott joined us . . . Every step we sank about fifteen
> inches . . . Meanwhile Snatcher was saving the situation in snow-

shoes, and led the line of ponies. Snippets nearly fell back into a
big crevasse, into which his hind quarters fell: but they managed
to unharness him, and scramble him out.

At some point, Scott decided to scout parallel with the chasm and they
at last came to a crossing place. Slowly but surely the ponies dragged their
loads up to a point only two miles short of the top of the Gateway ramp. At
this place, according to Cherry-Garrard: "The horses could hardly move,
sank up to their bellies, and finally lay down." A grim Oates despatched the
weary animals with five quick bullets. They named the place Shambles
Camp. Somewhere up at the top of the Axel Heiberg Glacier, Amundsen
shot twenty-two of his dogs and called the site the Butcher's Shop.

Scott had hoped to reach the Gateway with the last pony or ponies at
least six days earlier. He knew that at this point Shackleton had tried to
push on with his one remaining pony, Socks. Without warning, the pony
had disappeared into a hidden crevasse, very nearly taking his sledge leader,
Frank Wild, with him. The vital sledge was rescued but only just. Shackleton wrote: "We lay down on our stomachs and looked over into the gulf but
no sound or sign came to us; a black bottomless pit it seemed to be." Three
days later, Shackleton reached the sheer blue rippled ice above the line of
drift snow from the barrier and then his sledges slid with ease. Scott's blizzard had dumped deep snow much farther up the glacier so, at a time when
he should have made the very best progress, and in midsummer, the curse of
the blizzard's residue stayed with him.

Could Scott have foretold the likelihood of such weather? The only
available record of conditions in that area was Shackleton's and he had ben-
efited from mostly good weather and surfaces around the glacier's base. U.S.
atmospheric scientist Dr. Susan Solomon wrote:

A wet, warm blizzard of such extended duration with winds in
excess of fifty miles per hour has not yet been observed in eight
years of December data at [one] nearby automated weather
station . . . or in fourteen years of December data at [another] . . .
The longest and windiest storm recorded by modern instruments
in this region of the Barrier occurred in December 1995. It lasted

about two days and displayed peak winds of about forty [statute] miles per hour. But Scott and his men were tent-bound while the blizzard dumped heavy snow for four full days and they estimated the wind speed at up to eighty miles per hour. Scott and his men were the victims of bad luck in this exceptionally severe and prolonged storm, which must have been due to a tongue of warm, wet air from the ocean that pushed unusually far across the Barrier.

Scott the fatalist soon emerged; all was not lost. Now was the time for man-hauling. Apart from a four-day deficit of summit rations and a few days' lag behind the optimal schedule, all his plans were going fine. He attributed this state of affairs entirely to Oates.

Wilson exclaimed, "Well! I congratulate you, Titus."

"And *I* thank you, Titus," said Scott.

From that moment, with the ponies gone, Oates's diary lost its carping note against his leader. Perhaps much of his bitching had been a case of attack being the best form of defense. Now that he no longer feared criticism over his dealings with the ponies, he no longer found it necessary to find fault with Scott.

At the top of the Gateway's snow ramp, on December 11, 1911, they made a cache, the Lower Glacier Depot, and from here Scott sent the dog teams back. Their extra help, in towing their loads for some 145 miles and two weeks longer than planned, had helped make the overall Pole plan viable, despite the wet blizzard. They were seven days behind Scott's schedule.

But two weeks extra to the south meant two weeks extra on the return journey too, so Meares and Gerof did not arrive back at Cape Evans until January 5, not December 10, as originally planned. In order to make up extra rations for the two dog drivers, everybody had saved one biscuit per day for some time. Meares also agreed that they would make do without a lunch-halt meal on their way back. Morally this was a handsome gesture, but calorie wise the dog drivers were still better off than the man-haulers and, had Meares delayed his departure from Hut Point by several days, as in Scott's original plan, he would have had those days of man and dog rations on hand to help cope with the extra mileage. Additionally, according to scientist Charles Wright, Meares overfed his dogs too early in the journey, which of course affected the amount of dog food available for the return journey. Wright noted angrily that Meares, a fortnight ahead, had obviously panicked and taken more than his allotted food ration from the depots, despite the easier work of dog-driving.

Scott's summit rations gave each man-hauler a daily total of 4,500 calories. A study by Dr. Mike Stroud, one of Britain's top experts in stress nutrition, showed in the 1990s that Scott's men (and Shackleton's group as well) almost certainly used over 7,000 calories per day during their man-hauling travel. The basis for Mike's scientific program was a series of polar man-haul expeditions of which he was a member over a nine-year period. When I man-hauled across the Antarctic continent with Mike in 1993, his meticulous measurements showed that over a sixty-eight-day period (of our ninety-three-day journey), we burned up a daily average of well over 7,000 calories and lost forty-four pounds of body weight. During our glacial ascent from sea level to 10,000 feet, we burned more than 11,000 calories every day. This was 5,500 calories more than we were eating. (The human body cannot absorb more than 7,000 calories in twenty-four hours, no matter how many calories are being burned.) Our energy use far exceeded any measurements previously reported in scientific literature. For example, levels measured on the Tour de France, one of the world's hardest endurance sporting events, show that the top riders use only about 8,000 calories per day. A typical runner might use 2,500 calories to complete a four-hour marathon.

We man-hauled loads that started out at 485 pounds each and towed them, with no tent days, for ninety-three days. Scott man-hauled for a total of a hundred days (not including tent days) and his sledge load per man was around 180 pounds most of the time. Scott's sledges were often more difficult to haul because his sledge runners were less efficient than our modern versions. He sometimes skied and sometimes walked, as we did. Overall, his calorific deficit would probably have been very similar and equally as devastating as our own.

When Scott set out from the Gateway, his men were fit from pony leading and would have been in top physical shape, apart from Teddy Evans and Bill Lashly (and to a lesser extent, Atkinson), who had man-hauled for over three hundred miles already. Scott may well have suspected that these three

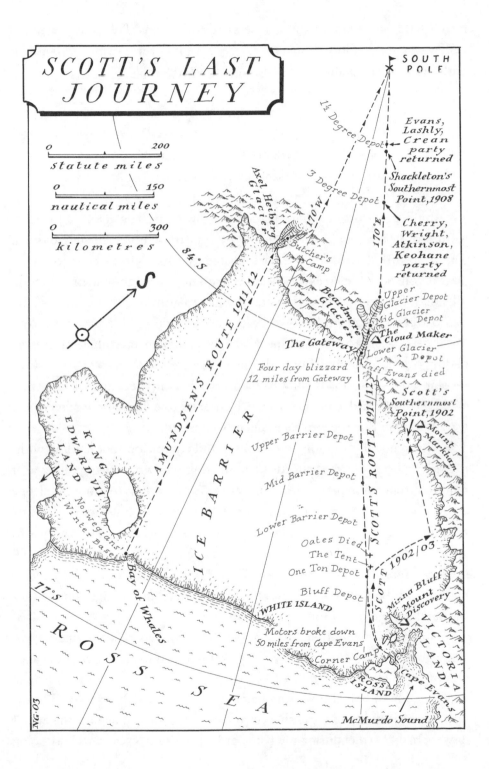

SCOTT'S LAST JOURNEY

SOUTH POLE

0 — 200
statute miles

0 — 150
nautical miles

0 — 300
kilometres

Evans,
Lashly,
Crean
party
returned

1½ Degree Depot

3 Degree Depot

Shackleton's
Southernmost
Point, 1908

170°W

170°E

84°S

Cherry,
Wright,
Atkinson,
Keohane
party
returned

Axel Heiberg Glacier

Butcher's Camp

Upper Glacier Depot

Mid Glacier Depot

△ *The Cloud Maker*

Beardmore Glacier

The Gateway

Lower Glacier Depot

Taff Evans died

Four day blizzard
12 miles from Gateway

Scott's Southernmost Point, 1902

△ *Mount Markham*

KING EDWARD VII LAND

Norwegians Winter Base

Upper Barrier Depot

Mid Barrier Depot

I C E   B A R R I E R

Lower Barrier Depot

Oates Died
The Tent
One Ton Depot

Scott 1902/03

Bluff Depot

Minna Bluff

Mount Discovery

77°S

Bay of Whales

WHITE ISLAND

Motors broke down
50 miles from Cape Evans

V I C T O R I A   L A N D

R O S S   S E A

Corner Camp

Cape Evans

ROSS ISLAND

NG·03

~ *McMurdo Sound* ~

AMUNDSEN'S ROUTE 1911/12

SCOTT'S ROUTE 1911/12

men should not be among those he selected for the final Pole push. From the Gateway, the expedition began the glacier ascent as three teams of four men with five hundred pounds per sledge. They were:

Scott	Teddy Evans	Bowers
Wilson	Lashly	Cherry-Garrard
Oates	Wright	Crean
Taff Evans	Atkinson	Keohane

Any hopes Scott may have nursed that once on the glacial ice the slow torture of heavy snow haulage would disappear were immediately dashed. The deep drift left by the blizzard coated the blue-green ice enjoyed by Shackleton. Scott's men experienced the trudging-through-mud or climbing-hills-of-soft-sand type of nightmare brought to grim reality. Instead of having to wear cramponed boots to keep their grip on bare ice, the men sank knee deep, gasping for breath. Instead of the sliding metal rumble of runners gliding over ice, there was only the heavy silence of reluctant yard by yard resistance of sledge loads sunk to their crossbars in wet snow. These truly awful post-blizzard conditions coincided with the heaviest loads, which were bulky, so that the sledges frequently capsized.

Wilson noted: "Couldn't have gone a mile in this on foot hauling without ski." Cherry-Garrard added: "The starting was worse than pulling as it required from ten to fifteen desperate jerks on the harness to move the sledge at all." At one point, they managed only half a mile in nine hours of heartbreaking toil, constantly stopping to heave the sledges onto one side so as to scrape balled ice off the metal runners. "I have never seen a sledge sink so," Bowers wrote, "I have never pulled so hard, or so nearly crushed my inside into my backbone by the everlasting jerking with all my strength on the canvas band around my unfortunate tummy."

Bathed in perspiration, the man-haulers stripped to their underwear. Their goggles fogged up, so they removed them and many suffered the agonies of snow blindness attacks. Cherry-Garrard wrote that: "our tea leaves, which had been boiled twice and would otherwise have been thrown away, relieved the pain if tied into some cotton and kept pressed against the eyes." Bowers had "been enduring the pains of hell with my eyes as well as doing the most back-breaking work I have ever come up against . . . By sticking plaster over my glasses except one small central spot I shut off most light and I could see the points of my ski, but the glasses were always fogged with perspiration and my eyes kept on streaming water which cannot be wiped off on the march as a ski stick is held in each hand; and so heavy were our weights that if any of the pair slacked a hand even, the sledge stopped." The sun's ultraviolet rays, reflected off the snow, burned not only their corneas but also any exposed skin, especially their lips, which cracked and bled. Their faces became pocked with blisters and scabs.

The tick of the polar summer clock was not merely some convenient indicator of progress: It was the countdown to certain death or narrow survival, and Scott's best way of checking his ongoing status against that clock was Shackleton's progress chart, which Frank Wild had given him in the shape of Wild's own diary records of that journey. Scott's key barrier depots were now in place but, to be sure of a safe return before the killer conditions of winter caught him in the open, he must catch up with the Shackleton schedule.

Scott luckily possessed a rare characteristic, which separated him from most people, the ability to drive himself and his men beyond normal limits of endurance, but short of the point where their health would be endangered. Shackleton and Peary shared this force, as did Livingstone and Columbus. Cherry-Garrard described it in Scott as "the immense shove of the man." Scott led them on remorselessly, eleven and sometimes twelve hours a day. He was, at nearly forty-three, one of the oldest there but his energy seemed limitless. He was annoyed by any delay and impatient with any team that could not keep up.

Over the years of man-hauling in the Arctic and Antarctic, I have found that the best people for any expedition where success depends upon competing against the clock (imposed by the short travel season) are the most naturally competitive individuals. The act of competing, sledge against sledge, hour after hour, day after day, can cause hostility between team members but that is a small price to pay when set against success. The faster and longer a team travels each day, the shorter the period taken to reach the goal. So, although more calories are expended by the greater effort, the shorter the time spent away from base. The fewer days anticipated for a journey, the less food taken, the lighter the sledges, the quicker the journey. In the end, the key to such journeys is speed and the best way to go faster is to foster competitive rivalry within the team.

As with everything in life, it is easy to overdo things. Man-hauling speed may be two miles an hour on flat blue ice, but only half a mile a day in bad-pressure ice or deep soft snow. Sometimes the best speed is a steady plod maintained hour after hour with minimal or no rest stops, but at others, for instance when navigating a crevasse field in good visibility, it may be best to race to reach safe ground before a fog envelops you.

At least two of Scott's team were, like him, natural competitors who hated to be bested physically: Bowers was one and Teddy Evans, sometimes, was another. As the three sledge teams inched their tortuous way up the thirty-mile-wide, nine-thousand-foot-high Beardmore Glacier, a personal race involving stamina and willpower was being played out.

The first team to lag behind and keep Scott waiting was that of Teddy Evans. Scott wrote: "Evans' party could not keep up, and Wilson told me . . . that Atkinson says that Wright is getting played out and Lashly is not so fit as he was." In his tent that evening, Scott asked Teddy Evans what was wrong. Evans naturally pointed out that his team had been man-hauling for four hundred miles farther and five weeks longer than the pony leaders on the same rations. Scott knew and understood this, so he offered to take some of the weight off Evans's sledge, but Evans was proud and declined the offer.

Scott had written to his wife from Cape Evans after one particularly hard man-haul journey that he was holding his own. He must have felt proud and relieved that, after ten years since *Discovery*, days spent onboard ships or at desks, he could still keep up with younger, stronger men. It is easy for a critic to huff and puff that Scott drove his men to exhaustion. They assume he had a reasonable alternative. He could have gone more slowly but that would have increased the risk of running short of supplies and of longer exposure to the vagaries of the weather. I have always found that the best chance of success on a long polar man-haul journey lies in going as fast and as far as possible each and every day.

The strongest of the man-haulers, Bowers thrived on the competition with Scott. He wrote: "Captain Scott got fairly wound up and went on and on . . . my breath kept fogging my glasses, and our windproofs got oppressively warm and altogether things were pretty rotten. At last he stopped and we found we had done 14¾ miles. He said, 'What about fifteen miles for Christmas Day,' so we gladly went on—anything definite is better than indefinite trudging." On one occasion, Bowers's notes show much glee at beating Scott. "Scott fairly legged it, as I expected, and we came along gaily behind him. He could not understand it when the pace began to tell more on his heavy team than on us . . . Of course we need not have raced, but we did, and I would do the same thing every time." To his mother, Bowers wrote: "one gets down to bedrock with everybody, sledging under trying conditions. The character of a man comes out and you see things that were never expected. You get to know each other inside out and respect some more and, unfortunately, some less. I think more highly than ever of our leader . . . [and less highly] of 'Teddy' Evans."

At about this time, one or two others also became critical, at least in their diaries, about Teddy Evans's performance, suggesting that he was a slacker and did not pull his weight except when Scott was watching. Cherry-Garrard's notes for December 14 include a grumpy comment: "Wright wanted to push Teddy Evans down a crevasse. When we dropped the oil cans down we never heard them reach the bottom. It is a pity he didn't."

They passed the 84th parallel. Only 360 miles to go.

Roald Amundsen and his five men reached the Pole that day with the maximum temperature a mild −2°C. They spent three days there ensuring the precise location of the Pole, for they knew the British would be hard on their heels. "Scott will be here sooner or later," Amundsen told his men. "If I know the British rightly they will never give up once they have started, unless forced by something beyond their control. They are too tough and stubborn for that."

If at that point Scott had known the Pole had been reached by the Norwegians, would he have given up? No one will ever know, but to have done so would have been the height of stupidity, for the chances of Amundsen suffering a fatal accident on his return journey were high.

Many years later, expedition groups from around the world, still searching for physical challenges, would remember two things. Amundsen was first to reach the Pole towed there by dog power, and Scott was first by pure manpower. The U.S. scientific station subsequently erected at the Pole is

called the Amundsen Scott South Pole Station in recognition of two great
and very different achievements.

On December 17, still going well, Scott laid the Mid Glacier Depot. He
had abandoned the route taken by Shackleton by moving away from the
shelter of the cliffs. He believed there would be more disturbed ice there
than out in mid-glacier. Parallel with the high ramparts of the Cloudmaker,
a magnificent mountain usually wreathed in clouds of its own homemade
weather pattern, Scott's men negotiated wave after wave of ice ridges, hauling their loads up one side, then sliding at speed down the other. All around
them grinned the mouths of huge crevasses. Not at all a good place for dogs,
they may well have reflected with gratitude.

A further snowstorm interrupted their progress, but luckily not for long
and the hard ice continued, in places so brittle that their boots broke through
the surface crust and jarred their legs and backs as they dropped to the hard
ice eight inches below. The crampons that Taff Evans had fashioned worked
well and helped them to gradually catch up with their ghostly pacemaker,
Shackleton. Every evening Scott carefully compared his distances and times
against the diary that Frank Wild had loaned him, with Shackleton's knowledge, for this very purpose.

One of the Scott critics' favorite lines is that Scott sat Scrooge-like in his
tent each night comparing his progress with that of his "old enemy, Shackleton." This depiction of Scott's rationale in his constant progress checks
combines with the, in my view, unfounded myth of enmity. Teddy Evans
noted: "Of course, we had Shackleton's charts, diaries and experience to
help us. We often discussed Shackleton's journey and were amazed at his
fine performance. We always had full rations, which Shackleton's party
never enjoyed at this stage." Such comparisons are natural. Amundsen was
enormously pleased and wrote in his diary "RECORD" on the day that he
passed Shackleton's most southerly point, and Shackleton himself had constantly checked his progress against his own reference point, the southern
journey of 1902 he had made with Scott and Wilson. His diary included remarks like: "and this latitude we have been able to reach in much less time
than on the last long march with Captain Scott."

After December 17, Scott's daily mileage increased to thirteen and later
twenty-three miles. They began to catch up. At two thousand feet above sea

level, Scott noted: "Our lips are very sore. We cover them with the soft silk plaster . . . We get fearfully thirsty and chip up ice on the march, as well as drinking a great deal of water on halting." Keeping close to the glacier's center, Charles Wright wrote that Scott, gazing up at the great glacier, made the wry comment that somebody would have to be the first to fall through one of the many wicked-looking crevasses and that, very soon thereafter, Scott himself did just that.

Despite the need to make distance and not waste a minute of the day, Scott had a science program to complete and needed to survey the glacier accurately wherever visibility allowed. "[Teddy] Evans and Bowers," he wrote, "are busy taking angles; as they have been all day, we shall have material for an excellent chart." At 5,800 feet, the shoulder of the plateau gradually became visible. Here Cherry-Garrard recorded a huge mass of pressure and noted that the Mill Glacier was both vast and severely crevassed. "There also," he wrote, "seems to be a big series of ice-falls between Buckley Island and the Dominion Range, for the centre of which Scott is going tomorrow."

They were increasingly relieved to see no tracks indicating the Norwegians had preceded them, for they assumed Amundsen would have chosen the Beardmore route. On December 20, at 6,500 feet, they reached the 85th parallel and were only three days behind Shackleton. This was the point at which Scott had to choose which sledge group to send back—a daunting task since nobody appeared openly keen to return. Scott wrote: "I dreaded this necessity of choosing—nothing could be more heartrending." At this point, three hundred miles from the Pole, he had the pick of his entire team to choose from and none seemed to be harboring any injury.

The suggestion of critics that Oates was at this time limping from his old Boer War wound is not borne out by any even thirdhand evidence. He did, however, make an ominous diary entry at that time: "my feet are giving me a lot of trouble. They have been continually wet since leaving Hut Point and now walking along this hard ice in frozen crampons has made rather hay of them, still they are not the worst in the outfit by a long chalk."

Scott made his selection decisions clear to nobody until the last moment. According to Cherry-Garrard's memory years later, he had told Wilson that it was a toss-up between Cherry-Garrard and Oates but, things being close, he would take the older man. Scott knew that many polar men had done well when middle-aged. Admiral Peary, first claimant to reach the North Pole, was fifty-two years old, but he used dogs to pull his sledge. Sir Vivian Fuchs, leader of the first crossing of Antarctica, was fifty, but he traveled in a vehicle cab. Scott himself was nearly forty-three. Cherry-Garrard was disappointed by the news that he must turn back. He had not expected it, and he enjoyed man-hauling. After digesting the unwelcome news: "I said I hoped I had not disappointed him, and he caught hold of me and said 'No—no—no,' so if that is the case all is well. He told me that at the bottom of the glacier he was hardly expecting to go on himself: I don't know what the trouble is but his foot is troubling him, and also, I think, indigestion."

Next to go was Charles Wright, also a young man. Only a few days before, Wilson had been told by his fellow doctor, Atkinson, that, in his opinion, Wright was weakening, or "getting played out" and he had passed this on to Scott. Back at Cape Evans in the early sledging days, Scott had written: "One of the greatest successes is Wright. He is very thorough and absolutely ready for anything. Like Bowers he has taken to sledging like a duck to water and although he hasn't had such severe testing, I believe he would stand it pretty nearly as well. Nothing ever seems to worry him and I can't imagine he ever complained of anything in his life."

When Wright heard the bad news that he must turn back, he was wild with anger. He was convinced that both he and Cherry-Garrard were far fitter than Teddy Evans, their sledge leader. He privately recorded that Scott had been hoodwinked by his second-in-command, who only hauled hard when he was being watched. Wright was furious.

Certainly, if Scott, as latter-day critics suggest, had secretly been jealous of his second-in-command, Teddy Evans, and had therefore wanted to ensure that he was not included in any victorious Pole arrival, he could easily have sent him back at this stage. But Wright and Cherry-Garrard were seemingly weaker than Evans, and both refrained from openly denouncing their sledge leader as the slacker they clearly believed him to be.

Scott recognized Wright's extreme disappointment and tried to make the young Canadian feel better by stressing that he would be the only navigator all the way back to Cape Evans. Wright, in his turn, had noted the previous day that Atkinson was also near the end of his tether. Scott may have noticed this too or maybe the fact that Atkinson, as a doctor, would be more useful back at Cape Evans was the deciding factor. He was also to go back and in fact appeared relieved by this outcome. He had hoped that his friend Oates would be chosen to go back too, Oates having given him the impression of someone "who knew he was done—his face showed him to be and the way he went along." Wishful thinking, perhaps, and Oates himself certainly thought otherwise at the time.

The fourth and last man selected to go back was Patsy Keohane, the chunky petty officer from Cork, who took the decision philosophically, saying only: "Sorry to part with old Crean."

At the Upper Glacier Depot, on December 21, 1911, they laid and marked the last cache before the plateau, changed the groups around, and reloaded the sledges. Now that Scott had a clearer idea of his likely return date, he gave Atkinson new orders regarding the dog teams. By then Scott must have learned that Cecil Meares was considering returning in *Terra Nova* and, if he did, only Gerof would remain as a really competent dog driver. He told Atkinson to "bring the dogs southwards later in the season to meet up with the polar party."

On the last night, Cherry-Garrard wrote: "We had a long talk with the owner in our tent . . . He seemed a bit afraid of us getting hung up, but as he said we had a splendid navigator . . . He also thanked us all heartily for the way we had assisted in the Journey and he should be sorry when we parted."

Wright wrote, having seen no signs of Amundsen on the glacier, that they were very optimistic about their overall chances of Pole priority and that everyone seemed fit—untainted by scurvy. They turned back from 8,000 feet above sea level and 283 miles from the Pole.

THE BLACK FLAG

THE EIGHT REMAINING MEN covered more than ten miles in eight hours. Scott was pleased that his choice had proved right, for Teddy Evans moved well with his new team of Bowers, Lashly, and Crean. "We have weeded the weak spots . . ." Scott noted. "To-morrow we march longer hours, about 9 I hope." They were all on skis most of the time now and using two ski sticks each. They marked each lunch stop with a single snow cairn and each night stop with two. This was to help find their depots.

To avoid the worst upper glacier icefalls experienced by Shackleton where the plateau ice, like water on the lip of Niagara Falls, began its downward flow, Scott headed west at 90° to Shackleton's route. For a while, this proved a successful tactic, but there was no escaping all the crevassed areas. "As first man," Scott wrote, "I get first chance, and it's decidedly exciting not knowing which step will give way . . . we are practically on the summit and up to date in the provision line. We ought to get through." They were pulling 190 pounds each now and they needed to go too fast to be ultra cautious. On December 22, according to Scott, the crevasses were "as big as Regent Street." Scott used his knowledge of ice formation to try to plot a route through the majestic chaos, "a confusion of elevations and depressions," he called it.

In 1993, the first time I had to pick a route through these same icefalls of the upper Beardmore Glacier, I noted my impressions in my diary: "The horizons which now opened to us were awesome; a sprawling mass of rock and ice locked in creeping motion." I had plotted a complex route through or between the nastiest of these features, but of course I was "cheating" in that I used maps and air photographs. Scott had no such help nor did he know that the route he took would not end in some dread cul-de-sac.

Teddy Evans later wrote his impression of the expedition's progress just prior to Christmas, marveling at "the pace of them, the speed of pitching and striking camp, never a second wasted; and how both teams swung together, keeping step, each endeavouring to outpace the other and with every appearance of perfect health. But," he adds, "a close observer, a man trained to watch over men's health, over athletes training, perhaps, would have seen something amiss." Evans wrote this some years after the event, when trying to cast back in his memory for the first symptoms of weakness in the Pole party. He may have given rein to his imagination, for though they were gradually weakening, owing to their daily calorific deficiency, there is no hint in the diaries of the other seven men of any threatening ailments beyond Oates's sore feet.

On December 23, the horizon leveled at last in every direction and Scott wrote: "I trust this may prove the turning-point in our fortunes." They marched fifteen miles and climbed eight hundred feet in eight hours, towing twelve weeks' worth of food and oil. On Christmas Day, 1911, again achieving fifteen miles, they celebrated with a special feast, including plum pudding that neither Wilson nor Scott could finish.

They had traveled for 55 days but only some 140 miles had yet involved man-haul. They ate the summit rations, as tested by Cherry-Garrard on the Cape Crozier winter journey, including eight ounces of butter, twelve of pemmican, and twelve of biscuit daily. The three Crozier men had towed 235 pounds each at the outset and, after conditions of extreme cold throughout their journey, returned after thirty-five days having lost an average of only two pounds in body weight. This is fairly convincing proof that neither the modern-day critics of Scott's rations nor Teddy Evans's suggestion that "something was amiss" could have applied to anybody but the two men, Bill Lashly and Teddy Evans himself, who had by then already man-hauled an extra four hundred miles on standard, not summit, rations.

That day was Bill Lashly's forty-third birthday. He was a few months older than Scott and the grand old man of the party. To celebrate, he tumbled into a fifty-foot-deep crevasse. "Rather a ghastly sight," he noted, "when dangling in one's harness."

The following day involved finding a way through singularly nasty ice-falls. Scott, navigating, wrote: "One cannot allow one's thoughts to wander as others do, and when one gets amongst disturbances, I find it is very worrying and tiring." The strain caused him to snap at Bowers, who somehow managed to break the last hypsometer thermometer they carried in order to tell their altitude, a key part of their survey program and their ability to re-locate depots. Bowers had recently let his pocket watch lose time. Deben-ham later said: "the cause of the watches stopping was [often] forgetfulness, in spite of the last word from tent to tent at night being 'wind watches.'" Luckily Scott's own watch was still accurate, since the precision of their nav-igation depended on the accuracy of their timekeeping.

Had I been Scott, I would not have been at all happy with Bowers, the official navigator, because, without accurate Greenwich mean time, it is impossible to work out accurate longitude. At or near the Pole, this could mean circling around and around, hopelessly confused because all lines of longitude converge at 90°. So, since time and longitude are temporal and geographical measurements based on the same principle, a loss of twenty-six minutes to a watch wearer close to the Pole would only represent a few short steps. At the Pole, after all, you can walk around the world in a sec-ond. On the way back north from the Pole, as the meridians grow farther apart, Bowers's chronometer inaccuracy would be ever more damaging to navigational accuracy (at the equator, each sixty seconds of chronometer er-ror would represent an error of one nautical mile). On Nansen's most fa-mous north polar journey, both he and his sole companion, Hjalmar Johansen, forgot to wind their watches. This was a potentially deadly disas-ter, for they could no longer tell where they were. Somehow Bowers had been careless with his watch and now he had allowed the hypsometer to break. Only a saint would have ignored such clumsiness with two vital instruments and Scott was never in line for canonization. Bowers recorded that he "got an unusual burst of wrath in consequence, in fact my name is mud just at present. It is rather sad to get into the dirt tub with one's leader at this juncture."

The question could be asked, why no spare hypsometer? Scott's method, like Shackleton's, of keeping sledge weights down was to pare away every single nonvital item. In 1993, I did the same; I took no toothbrush to cross the continent. A hypsometer, though relatively light in itself, has to be protected in a sturdy and bulky box. Scott at Cape Evans had to provide enough such instruments to supply each lone sledge group, not just his own, in addition to his two expeditions still working on the Ross Sea coast. Of course he could have carried two of every key item such as a theodolite on each sledge, but overall weights would mount very quickly that way and you have to draw a line somewhere when man-hauling, with no dogs to drag your loads.

For five days, the two teams, free at last from the ever-present danger of crevasses, sped competitively over the high plateau at an altitude of between 9,000 and 10,000 feet. A sinister note had sounded again in the diary of Oates a few days earlier, on December 26. For the second time, he worries in the secrecy of his diary pages about his health. This time he noted: "The back tendon of my right leg feels as if it has been stretched about 4 inches. I hope to goodness it is not going to give trouble." Oates hauled from just behind the leader and navigator, Scott, and did not let on about his leg trouble. Perhaps fortunately for him, Scott's focus was on the other sledge team, which had begun to slow the overall progress. Oates noted: "Scott is very annoyed about the other team's sledge. They must have had a cruel time this week . . . they had a dreadfully heavy day arriving in camp ¾ hour after us . . . Poor devils, they are having a cruel time of it. They have a lighter load than us, but their sledge must have something the matter with it." Either the sledge loading or its runners or its man-haulers were to blame. Or a touch of all three.

Bill Lashly, like Teddy Evans, was far more debilitated than the majority, but like any normal human being in such circumstances, he would be hoping that "the others" were fading as fast as he was. I know the feeling well.

Trying to pin down the cause of the other group's slower pace, Scott switched places with Teddy Evans and immediately found the other sledge more difficult to pull than his own. Suspecting that Lashly might be a weak link, he then switched him with the powerful Taff Evans. This improved matters, but not enough to convince Scott of the basic cause, so he switched the entire teams around and everyone then agreed that there was a problem with Teddy Evans's sledge, not his team. They checked the runners, but these were in good shape. They talked things over and reached the conclusion that Teddy Evans's crew had done up some or all of the sledge-load straps too tightly, thereby forcing the runners out of kilter.

This must have been irritating for Scott, since Teddy Evans's men had sledged for long enough to have sorted out such a basic problem for themselves. Evans admitted as much, for he wrote: "Captain Scott came into our tent and told us that we had distorted our sledge by bad strapping or bad loading. This was, I think, correct, because Oates had dropped his sleeping-bag off a few days back through erring in the other direction and not strapping securely—we meant to have no recurrence and probably racked our sledge by heaving too hard on the straps."

On the barrier, the horses had provided each man with a distraction, as had the scenery and the crevasses of the glacier. But now, the lofty desolation of the polar plateau, devoid of any feature, forced the men in on their own thoughts and weaknesses. Each minute and hour seemed an eternity as ever-repeated anxieties gnawed at the mind and the dull throb of frostbitten toes or fingers vied at each step with the sharper pain of underwear tugging at raw groins. Despite the effects of the altitude, the British were now averaging thirteen miles a day by man-haul on the plateau to the Norwegians' fifteen miles a day with dog teams.

At camp on December 31, Scott was at last able to record: "We have caught up Shackleton's dates." There was still no sign of Norwegian tracks, so hope was high in the hearts of the eight Britons. They could not know that Amundsen that very evening and a hundred miles to their east had passed them on the 87th degree of latitude as they raced back north to the barrier.

That night, Scott laid the first of the plateau caches, Three Degree Depot, 180 miles from the Pole. From here on, speed and light loads were vital. Due to the prevalence of sastrugi (wind-cut ridges like furrows in a plowed field) on this part of the plateau, it is often easier to walk than to ski when man-hauling. When Mike Stroud and I man-hauled the same route in 1993, we often found progress easier off ski than on, even though we towed heavier loads. Scott needed his second team under Evans to travel on for another three days before turning back and, to speed them up, the only weight he could remove from their sledge without some adverse side effect was to leave their ice axes, alpine rope, skis, and sticks at Three Degree Depot, a saving of eighty pounds. Only sixty miles later, at 88°, Scott was to leave all his own group's skis and sticks at the next depot, but then the surface altered radically, so he went back to retrieve them. Scott had written earlier: "It is difficult to know what to do about the ski: their weight is considerable and yet under certain circumstances they are extraordinarily useful." Another problem in such rough sastrugi areas is that sledges are forever capsizing, and anything breakable, like skis or sticks strapped to their tops, is likely to be broken. For many miles on the Beardmore in 1993, Mike Stroud used skis and sticks while I used none and found that I could haul faster than him, although normally, on the flat, he was the faster skier.

Because the cache at the Three Degree Depot allowed lighter sledge loads, Scott's plan to convert both twelve-foot sledges into lighter ten-foot versions could go ahead. Taff Evans and Tom Crean had practiced this modification, but not at nine thousand feet and at −23°C. They completed the job efficiently but at the cost of Taff Evans damaging his hand. One record suggests that he reopened or aggravated an existing wound, others that he suffered a new and deep cut. Either way, he hid the injury with complete success from all the officers, probably because he was hugely eager to reach the Pole and knew that, if injured, he would be sent back.

As soon as the rebuilding of the sledges was done, they all retired to their two tents. For the first time, the tent to be used for the Pole was fixed with a double liner and Teddy Evans was invited in to celebrate the New Year. The petty officers, three good friends, did likewise in the less cramped space of their own tent once they had finished with the sledges. There was clearly no tense atmosphere among Teddy Evans, Oates, Scott, or the other two as they rested and drank tea. Even Oates was chatty and relaxed. Teddy Evans wrote: "He told us all about his home, and his horses . . . He talked on and on, and his big, kind brown eyes sparkled as he recalled little boyish

escapades at Eton . . . At length Captain Scott reached out and affectionately seized him in the way that was itself so characteristic of our leader, and
said, 'You funny old thing, you have quite come out of your shell, soldier!
Do you know we have all sat here talking for nearly four hours? It's New
Year's Day and 1 am!' "

The next day, Teddy Evans's group set out on foot. He recorded that
Scott "and his team never got near us, in fact they actually lost ground." On
January 2, 1912, still on foot, he wrote: "Did 15 miles with ease, but we
were now only pulling 130 lb. per man." On January 3, all Scott's carefully
laid plans came to a critical point. Ration wise he must now, less than 150
miles from the Pole, finish off the carefully planned pyramid system that he
had pioneered in Antarctica.

When Everest was first climbed in 1953, the leader John Hunt gradually whittled away his ace climbers and his Sherpas until, one leg from the
top, he was left with a group of his fittest men. He selected Edmund Hillary
and Tensing Norgay, but nobody, including Hunt, would have been able to
predict until that moment of choice who would figure in that final team.
Hunt had his favorites, no doubt, and he may well have hoped that others
would have been best placed when the moment came. Last-minute changes
might even have forced him to change from a two-man to a three-man summit team.

Similarly, Scott retained the absolute right to select anybody for his Pole
team from the entire company of *Terra Nova*, provided only that they
wished to go. Throughout his time onboard the ship, during his early sledge
travels, and through the long Cape Evans winter, he had made numerous entries in his private diary, pencil sketches of various individuals, some flattering and others pretty rude. Slowly and methodically he was choosing his
Pole men. By the time of the 1911 depot-laying trip, Scott had narrowed his
choice down to all those he took with him as pony leaders and one or two
of the men he had to spare from the science journeys being completed at
that time.

Many Scott observers say that he must have chosen all the final Pole men
just before Christmas 1911, when ascending the Beardmore, because he
wrote their five names and ages on the flyleaf of the new notebook that he
started to use on December 22, 1911. This is in reality no proof at all, since

notes written on flyleaves are not necessarily chronological. He may just as well have made that note on that page weeks after making his selection.

On December 10, and well up the Beardmore, Scott had to decide who to send back out of the twelve men still present. By then he had already noted in his diary: "P.O. Evans, of course, is a tower of strength, but Oates and Wilson are doing splendidly also." This is a fairly late indicator of where Scott's focus was then fixed and can be added to an earlier clue. As soon as the polar winter of 1911 was ended and Scott, raring to go, had set off in mid-September on his Ferrar Glacier jaunt, he had, from everybody available, selected Petty Officer Evans and Bowers. Simpson had gone too but only for a specific scientific purpose. Scott's comments, noted after that excessively cold journey, had included: "the greatest source of pleasure to me is to realize that I have such men as Bowers and P.O. Evans for the Southern journey. I do not think that harder men or better sledge travellers ever took the trail. Bowers is a little wonder."

Just before the start of the polar journey, but still at Cape Evans, Ponting had arranged with Scott to film life in a polar tent. Scott had selected Taff Evans, Wilson, and Bowers to feature in that film. The known clues to Scott's thinking would therefore suggest that the final shortlist for the Pole team would include himself, Oates, Wilson, Bowers, and Taff Evans.

Scott chose his team on one main criterion, and that was his burning desire to reach the Pole, complete certain science work en route, and return to Cape Evans as quickly as was humanly possible. It has been suggested, based on a single secondhand comment (reported years later by Cherry-Garrard and attributed to Wilson), that Scott said he wanted the army represented at the Pole. But there is no other written evidence that he wished his Pole group to be broadly representational of the forces and the lower ranks and so included a token soldier and a token petty officer.

Scott needed above all a good navigator to back up his own well-tested skills. He had used both a sextant and a theodolite in 1903 and did so with a thorough knowledge of the subject. I have spent many years in the polar regions using both instruments and can attest that navigators do not get rusty and they can quickly pick up where they left off, rather like riding a bicycle. The best available navigator by far was Bowers, who was also the highly professional keeper of the expedition's meteorological records. That alone was enough to ensure that Bowers accompanied Scott to the Pole no matter whoever else was chosen.

The next most important component on Scott's list was somebody with sound medical or at least first-aid knowledge so, even if Wilson had not been Scott's great friend, soul mate, and like Bowers a powerful man-hauler, he would have been chosen.

At this point, Scott's selection process is no longer so straightforward. As a man-hauler with many polar journeys sharp in my memory, I can put myself in Scott's *finnesko* and ask myself what attributes I would have re-cruited once the key posts of leader (Scott), navigator (Bowers), and medic (Wilson) were in place. There is but a single clear answer and that is *pulling power,* sheer enduring strength. Who, out of Scott's remaining candidates, would fit this requirement best? Teddy Evans and Lashly? Because of their sterling work with the motorized sledges and the resulting extra four hun-dred miles of man-hauling, their body weight and strength had indisputably dropped well below that of the remaining options, Oates, Taff Evans, and Tom Crean, so I would eliminate them both.

There are those who argue that Scott had other reasons for sending back Teddy Evans. These include a conspiracy theory that Scott plotted Teddy Evans's removal from the Pole team list by putting him in charge of the mo-tors. Scott wrote a letter to his New Zealand–based administrator describ-ing Teddy Evans as "a thoroughly well-meaning little man, but a bit of a duffer outside naval work, and unsuited to be his second-in-command." Nothing here precludes Teddy Evans's suitability for the Pole team, since a well-meaning amateur can make a great man-hauler. Teddy Evans later wrote of receiving Scott's orders to turn back: "I felt very sorry for him [Scott] having to break the news to us, although I had foreseen it—for Lashly and I knew we could never hope to be in the Polar party after our long drag out from Cape Evans." And Bowers recorded: "Poor Teddy—I am sure it was for his wife's sake he wanted to go. He gave me a little silk flag she had given him to fly on the Pole . . . but he had buoyed himself up with the idea of going."

Of the three remaining choices, there was little to choose among them. All three were powerful, but the largest and heaviest were Taff Evans and Oates, at whose side Scott had already pulled all the way up the glacier. Tom

Crean, though as loyal to Scott as was Evans and for just as long, was not, in
Scott's opinion, as powerful as the other two. So, by a narrow margin, he
must go back. Tom Crean never bore a grudge, and his biographer, Michael
Smith, wrote in 2000 that almost sixty years after Crean's own death, his
two daughters recalled that they had never heard their father speak a bad
word against Scott.

Scott's dilemma was now reduced to a choice between two men, both of
whom were powerhouses with whom he worked well. The obvious answer
was to take both.

Did Scott ever suggest that the Pole group could consist of more than
four men? There is no proof of this, but again there is a powerful clue. Although his tents were designed to take four men and his sledges were normally towed by four men, there is a monochrome sketch by Wilson, drawn
shortly before the team left Cape Evans in November 1911, which clearly
depicts *five* men on skis hauling a laden sledge (see fourth picture section).
The angles of each man's pull and the lengths of the tow ropes are clearly
shown in this sketch, as though in a diagram. Wilson virtually never drew
hypothetical scenes or indeed any fictional, imaginative subject matter. He
concentrated on real, detailed images only, so why draw this five-man group
at all if he had not been discussing it with Scott?

Exactly when Scott decided to take five men rather than four is not
something clarified by his diary or any other record. I suspect he waited until the last moment before making up his mind but that he had long since
worked out that five was a workable option and had discussed it with Wilson at least as early as the time of Wilson's sketch of five man-haulers on
one sledge. There is but one clear advantage to five over four men to a sledge
and that is the mathematical fact that far more pulling power is available
without a corresponding increase in weight. Such heavy items as the tent,
the sledge, the navigation, and medical gear do not increase, so their weight
is shared more easily by five than by four man-haulers. Also, from a safety
point of view, Bill Lashly, an engineer with firsthand crevasse experience, believed that a five-man sledge group was optimal for bad crevasse conditions.

There were of course many adverse features to five men in a team, the
most obvious being the confined space of the standard four-man pyramid
tent. Henrik Ibsen once wrote: "A home is where there is plenty of room for

five, although among enemies it seems cramped for two." This well describes the testing conditions in a cold tent with too many inmates, but Scott was focused on success, and, if a certain degree of discomfort was necessary to achieve that end, so be it.

Rations for the Pole group and the other returning group would not be affected. Scott added no one, he merely shuffled the rations between two different groups, his and that of Teddy Evans. Of course Evans's group had the extra nuisance, on the few occasions when they reached a depot, of taking only three-quarters of their original allotment of food and fuel, but this was hardly an onerous task, bearing in mind that there were sixty-mile gaps between depots.

Set against the weight of an extra pair of skis on the sledge, the squash in the tent, and more time spent cooking, the benefits of taking both Oates and Taff Evans were quite clear to Scott. The two factors Scott did *not* know about as he made his final choice were the cut hand of Taff Evans and the state of Oates's foot. Taff Evans knew that success at the Pole would bring him the key to his retirement dream, ownership of a pub in Swansea. He probably thought his hand would heal and would not impede the general progress. Since everyone wore gloves most of the time, it was not difficult to conceal such a wound from Dr. Wilson. Evans kept his hand covered, and Oates, with no visible limp, hauled powerfully at all times.

At no point in any reference to Oates, or by him, during the expedition, was his old war wound or a limp mentioned prior to the day of Scott's final selection. Oates's diary complains about his stretched tendon and that the cold can open up old war wounds but, on the glacier, Oates complained only about his *right* leg, whereas his original bullet wound was in his left. So Cherry-Garrard was quite wrong to assert that "the foot which went must have been on the leg wounded in Africa."

Wilson made no written comment, when selected, but must have been pleased by his inclusion in the Pole team. Only three weeks before, he had written: "whether I shall have the good fortune to be considered strong enough to be one of the final 4 or not—why, I don't know. No one knows yet who they will be." Like the others, Wilson accepted the fact that Scott would, when the time came, present his choice as a fait accompli, not open to discussion.

So, on January 3, 1912, Scott named his four choices: Wilson, Bowers, Oates, and Taff Evans. A doctor, a soldier, a marine, and one other naval man. His old mentor Clements Markham, that great enthusiast of Royal Navy expeditions, is unlikely to have approved.

Four days before making his final selection, when Scott had told Teddy Evans to dump nearly one hundred pounds of gear they would not need, such as ice axes and ropes (because no more crevasses would occur, according to the Shackleton records) and their skis (because heavy sastrugi were forecast by Shackleton), Bowers's skis were left behind. This suggests that Scott was not planning to take a fifth man at that point. It does not suggest that Bowers would not be chosen, because the ski-boot attachments manufactured by Taff Evans were easily adjustable and transferable from person to person. Bowers could easily have taken spells on somebody else's skis.

The team chosen, Scott gave various messages to Teddy Evans to take back to Cape Evans. One, for Meares, updated his previous three instructions on what he wanted the dog teams to do. This last order canceled the previous ones: Meares was to come out and meet Scott between 82° and 83° on the barrier at some time toward the middle of February.

Oates too gave Evans a letter for his mother, confessing: "I am afraid the letter I wrote from the hut was full of grumbles but I was very anxious about starting off with those ponies." He added: "If anything should happen to me on this trip, which I don't think likely, ask for my notebook. I have written instructions on the fly leaf that it is to be sent to you but please remember that when a man is having a hard time he says hard things about other people which he would regret afterwards."

Teddy Evans, Bill Lashly, and Tom Crean followed Scott's group for a few miles toward the Pole to check that their five-man arrangements worked well. Then, on January 4, 1912, they said their farewells.

"I'm afraid, Teddy," Oates said to Evans, "you won't have much of a slope going back, but old Christopher is waiting to be eaten on the Barrier when you get there." Teddy Evans gave three cheers as Scott's men headed away to the south. There were still no signs of any Norwegian tracks, the sun was "warm," and the sky was blue.

So how did the new five-strong team work?

Bowers wrote: "Our party were on ski with the exception of myself: I first made fast to the central span, but afterwards connected up to the toggle of the sledge, pulling in the centre between the inner ends of Captain Scott's and Dr. Wilson's traces. This was found to be the best place, as I had to go my own step." Scott noted: "Bowers has a heavy time on foot, but nothing seems to tire him." And, "It is wonderful to see how neatly everything stows on a little sledge, thanks to Evans. I was anxious to see how we could pull it, and glad to find we went easy enough. Bowers on foot pulls between, but behind, Wilson and myself; he has to keep his own pace and luckily does not throw us out at all." Six days later, Scott added: "Nothing comes amiss to him, and no work is too hard. It is a difficulty to get him into the tent; he seems quite oblivious of the cold, and he lies coiled in his bag writing and working out sights long after the others are asleep."

Bowers, with his short but extremely powerful legs, carried on walking with minimal complaint, no apparent slowing down of the others on their skis, and no damage done to his performance. He remained the strongest of them all, skis or no skis. I know well how long-legged folk (like myself) feel hard done by when watching shorter, stockier-built individuals powering their sledge loads. For thousands of polar miles, I have competed, on and off skis, against Mike Stroud, who has legs that are far shorter and far more powerful than mine. Nonetheless, and at the same time, Mike would opine that I, with my long strides, was the one with the built-in advantage. Bowers was apt to think likewise but seldom bitched about it.

Only two days after taking a fifth man into his tent, Scott stated that cooking times increased by some thirty minutes daily and thus used a lot more fuel. That is, from my experience, an excessive time and can only have been due to an unsettling of the group's tent routine. As Scott's group grew accustomed to their new five-man regime and learned the best ways of coping with the extra man, they would very soon have compensated and, at most, would have added ten minutes per day of extra boiling time. The proof of this is to be found in careful study of the expedition's meteorological register (November 3, 1911–March 12, 1912) found in Scott's death tent and kept meticulously by Bowers. Exact timings of each camp and lunch halt are logged, as is the daily mileage that, with five men in the tent and on the harness, actually improves dramatically overall.

Three days into the journey, Scott wrote: "Our food continues to amply satisfy. What luck to have hit on such an excellent ration! . . . we are very comfortable in our double tent . . . the sleeping-bags remain in good condition . . . It is quite impossible to speak too highly of my companions."

They marched on into the unknown reaches of the plateau, each man wrapped and trapped within himself and silently cursing his sores. The sun never rose or set, but when their day began, its orb lay over their left shoulders, then moved with agonizing slowness until, at midday, they trod upon their own body shadows aimed, like the reverse ends of five compass needles, at the Pole. After noon, and ever more slowly it seemed, their shadows swung around as the sun crept inch by inch toward their right, or western shoulders.

"The marching is growing terribly monotonous," wrote Scott. Their burned lips cracked and bled, cooked by ultraviolet rays and riven by the wind. "I could not tell," wrote Bowers, "if I had a frostbite on my face now as it is all scales, so are my lips and nose." And "it is more tiring for me than the others, as I have no ski. However as long as I can do my share all day and keep fit . . ." Any reader without experience of polar man-hauling, on or off skis, would wonder how on earth the skiless Bowers could possibly have kept up with the others. I have often gone faster than my colleagues when they had skis and I had none, due to the weight of the sledge and the back slip of their skis, especially on an uphill gradient. Wilson, the painter, recorded his impressions: "The worst wind-cut sastrugi I have seen . . . covered with a growth of bunches of crystals exactly like gorse . . . Ice blink all round . . . hairy faces and mouths dreadfully iced up on the march . . . and often one's hands very cold indeed holding ski sticks."

When Cherry-Garrard wrote, years later, of his long-dead comrades, he could tell from their diaries that, on the plateau, they were full of hope, with their goal a mere week's travel ahead and with every chance that they would be the first men in the world to reach the end of the world. "I heard Scott discuss," Cherry-Garrard noted, "the possibility of returning in April; and the Polar Party had enough food to allow them to do this on full rations." Again he stated: "The Polar Party of five men had according to our rations plenty of food either on their sledge or in the depots. In addition they had a lot of pony meat."

On January 6, at 10,500 feet, they came upon unusually bad sastrugi fields, "a sea of fish-hook waves" that made travel on skis impossible. The next day showed no improvement, and their skis, when sledge loaded, were at constant risk of breakage. Scott decided to cache the skis, then the terrain eased so he went back to collect them. They only lost an hour, but Scott had learned his lesson and wrote: "I must stick to skis after this."

Amundsen had made the same mistake when heading for the Pole when he left all his crampons behind at a depot. "Without them," he later wrote, "climbing on sheer ice is supposed to be practically an impossibility. A thousand thoughts raced through my brain. The pole lost, perhaps, because of such an idiotic blunder?"

On January 7, Scott was dismayed to learn that Taff Evans "has a nasty cut on his hand . . . I hope it won't give trouble." Wilson noted: "Evans who cut his knuckle some days ago at the last depot—a week ago—has a lot of pus in it tonight." In 1993, I was fortunate that my co-man-hauler in Antarctica, Mike Stroud, was a doctor who understood how to deal with "polar pus." I remember one evening watching him operate on a swollen abscess on his own foot. I wrote at the time: "I watched with intense admiration as he gave himself two deep injections of Xylocaine anaesthetic and then plunged a scalpel blade deep into the swelling with diagonally crossed incisions. Pus poured out of the wounds and the swelling visibly decreased. Mike then bandaged up his heel and packed away his medical kit. I am not sure whether or not he felt faint but I certainly did."

On January 8, waiting for a blizzard to die down, Scott wrote: "Evans' hand was dressed this morning, and the rest ought to be good for it . . . Evans, a giant worker with a really remarkable headpiece. It is only now I realise how much has been due to him. Our ski shoes and crampons have been absolutely indispensable . . . He is responsible for every sledge, every sledge-fitting, tents, sleeping-bags and harness . . . Now, besides superintending the putting up of the tent, he thinks out and arranges the packing of the sledge." This last comment would indicate that Evans's knuckle wound was not yet bad enough to prevent him from handling frozen gear and lashing straps.

Debenham once described Scott's energy: "Scott had two phrases for good marching and when he said 'Let's leg it' or 'I think we'll step out a bit today' you knew you were in for something unusual in the way of making distance, regardless of weather or any other obstacles." At this point on the plateau with his four strong colleagues, Scott really "legged it." On January 9, they reached 88°25', only ninety-five miles from the Pole, and Scott noted "RECORD" in his diary; "beyond the record of Shackleton's walk. All is new ahead." Three years before to the day, and after an epic journey, Shackleton, Wild, Marshall, and Adams had turned back at about this point and Shackleton noted: "We have shot our bolt . . . Whatever regrets may be, we have done our best." They had beaten Scott's previous record, of which Shackleton had been a part, by nearly four hundred miles. To get this far, they had taken huge risks with their limited rations and with the weather but their luck had just held out.

Years later Shackleton described Scott as "the most daring man I ever knew." They were clearly both daring men who took carefully calculated risks, but Scott, in carrying on all the way to the Pole, was taking far less of a risk than Shackleton took in reaching his "farthest south." At the Pole, Scott could rightly expect that his prelaid supply depots would be more than adequate for his return journey, for he was not to know how many factors, especially utterly unseasonable weather and injuries that two of his men had hidden from him, would interfere with his mathematics. At his turn-back point, Shackleton was fully aware that his supply situation was already stretched to the very limit and that to go any farther south would involve certain death on his return journey.

As Shackleton had once trod south into an unknown land, so now it was Scott's turn. Shackleton had described the feeling: "It falls to the lot of few men to view land not previously seen by human eyes . . . No man of us could tell what we would discover in our march south." Scott kept up the pressure but the snow surface grew worse and worse. "I never had such pulling," he wrote; "all the time the sledge rasps and creaks . . . can we keep this up for seven days? . . . None of us ever had such hard work before."

On January 10, despite "being chary of leaving stores on this great plain," they built a depot, ninety-one miles from the Pole, of a week's rations and anything else they felt they could risk leaving, a hundred pounds in all. For four days, despite their lighter load, they struggled to make good mileage over a dismal surface of blown crystals.

In The Worst Journey in the World, Cherry-Garrard points his finger at crystals as being the man-hauler's greatest enemy. "Time after time," he wrote, "in the diaries you find crystals—crystals—crystals: crystals falling through the air, crystals bearding the sastrugi, crystals lying loose upon the snow. Sandy crystals, upon which the sun shines and which made pulling a terrible effort." Some forty miles from the Pole, on January 12, the diaries begin to show signs of a new discomfort. Scott noted: "At camping tonight everyone was chilled and we guessed a cold snap, but to our surprise the actual temperature was higher than last night, when we could dawdle in the sun. It is most unaccountable why we should suddenly feel the cold in this manner; partly the exhaustion of the march, but partly some damp quality in the air." And two days later, Scott wrote: "Again we noticed the cold; at lunch to-day . . . all our feet were cold, but this was mainly due to the bald state of our finnesko. I put some grease under the bare skin and found it made all the difference. Oates seems to be feeling the cold and fatigue more than the rest of us, but we are all very fit."

"My pemmican," Oates wrote on January 15, "must have disagreed with me at breakfast for coming along I felt very depressed and homesick."

That day, on the verge of triumph, they set off in high spirits. Scott noted: "It is wonderful to think that two long marches would land us at the Pole . . . It ought to be a certain thing now, and the only appalling possibility the sight of the Norwegian flag forestalling ours."

At this point, the five Britons were sure they stood a fine chance of priority at the Pole. The Norwegians must either be behind them or perhaps had suffered some mishap that had forced them to turn back. Otherwise, since all longitudes converged on 90° south, where were their tracks? The Norwegians, they were assuming, had followed the Beardmore route, as they had. After all, Amundsen had studied Shackleton's careful description of his route up the Beardmore just as Scott had. The Beardmore was the only known path to the Pole, and Amundsen's base was sixty miles closer to it than was Scott's. So why should the Norwegians go for the huge uncertainty, the unwarranted risk, of some new, untested route?

The average temperatures plummeted 18° that last week, heralding the end of the short summer at the Pole, but, in the comparative warmth of their congested little tent, their minds were for once not on the cold, for in two short days they should become the first human beings to reach the South Pole. On the morning of January 16, they marched a good, strong seven and a half miles. "We started off in high spirits," Scott wrote after the noon theodolite shot that confirmed there were but eighteen miles to go, "feeling that to-morrow would see us at our destination." At about 2 p.m., on a long downhill stretch and under a cloudless sky, they saw mock suns with great horizontal halos. They were going well.

At 4 p.m. or thereabouts the sharp-eyed Bowers looked up and told the others he thought he could see a cairn. Their hearts must have experienced that awful tug of dread . . . could somebody be ahead of them? But Bowers said it might merely be the sun's rays glinting on oddly angled sastrugi. With their hearts in their throats, I imagine, and not daring to hope, they went on. All eyes must have been fixed on the dread object ahead in the desperate hope it would prove merely a mirage.

"Soon we knew," Scott wrote, "that this could not be a natural snow feature."

The "cairn" coalesced into a black speck and then, smashing all their hopes and dreams, into the blackest of black flags. They reached the flag and saw beside it the drifted-over but still detectable signs of rumpled snow, where a campsite had been, with the disturbance marks of sledge and ski and paw. "This told us the whole story," Scott wrote. "The Norwegians have forestalled us and are first at the Pole. It is a terrible disappointment, and I am very sorry for my loyal companions."

Wilson noted: "The age of the tracks was hard to guess—but probably a couple of weeks, or three or more . . . We camped here and examined the tracks and discussed things." Bowers wrote to his mother: "I am awfully sorry for Captain Scott who has taken the blow very well indeed. We now head for home. You will be glad to hear I have been to this spot I am sure."

The Norwegian trail and theirs were now conjoined but, hoping maybe that Amundsen had somehow missed the Pole itself—his navigation instruments just might have broken (for hope springs eternal)—the Britons took many sun shots and, in Wilson's words, made their own beeline for the Pole. They camped and, constantly checking positions on January 17, marched on different bearings, often into the teeth of a force 6 wind at −30°C. "The coldest march I ever remembered," Wilson wrote. ". . . It was difficult to keep one's hands from freezing in double woollen and fur mits . . . it was a very bitter day."

The sun came out between banks of driving crystal haze and Bowers took sun-altitude shots when he could. "From Amundsen's direction of tracks," Wilson wrote, "he has probably hit a point about 3 miles off . . . but in any case we are all agreed that he can claim prior right to the Pole itself. He has beaten us in so far as he made a race of it . . . We have done what we came for . . . and as our programme was made out." The cold wind that day gave Oates, Evans, and Bowers frostbitten noses and cheeks and Evans's hands were bad enough to cause an hour's delay. They took ten exposures on one roll of film at the Pole. "Mighty cold work," Scott wrote. Bowers took elaborate theodolite readings with many arithmetical calculations. The figures were worked out by Scott and Bowers at their final Pole position of 89°59'14". They left the British flag there.

When the Pole mathematics were scrutinized a year later by Debenham, they were found to contain an error "of ±30" [800 yards] at most," proof positive that Scott's men did reach the Pole.

Scott's oft-quoted words, "Great God! this is an awful place and terrible enough for us to have laboured to it without the reward of priority," contrast with those, thirty-three days earlier, of Amundsen's colleague Bjaaland, "We have attained the goal of our desires and the great thing is that we are here as the first men; no English flag waves." The Norwegians named the polar plateau after their King Haakon VII, unaware that Shackleton had already christened the place after his own king, then they killed and ate one of the dogs that had taken them there. In midsummer, the Norwegians had perfect weather at those times when it mattered most. Amundsen's men reached the Pole on December 14, 1911, but, three weeks later, the icy tendrils of winter were already stirring to greet Scott's arrival there. The Norwegian diaries after the Pole are filled with such comments as "ideal sledging," "beautiful weather," and "eight days of sunshine." Amundsen's expedition to the Pole, planned specifically as a race, was a bold and professional venture with a fine share of good luck and was as successful as any dog-driven journey in history. But decades later, the next men to descend the Axel Heiberg Glacier, a New Zealand team under Briton Wally Herbert, using dogs, wrote, "Amundsen had taken only two photographs and neither photograph showed the icefalls. He had made no maps, left no route sketches. We had no choice but to rediscover a route down the Axel Heiberg."

Scott's expedition, as successful as any man-haul expedition in history, coincided with uniquely bad weather; was not planned as a race, though it was forced too late in the day to try to compete; and achieved a hugely valuable survey and science program. Despite having 60 miles farther to travel overall and 120 miles farther in the debilitating altitude conditions of the plateau, despite the demands of man-hauling and the bad timing of the blizzards, Scott's men had taken only twenty days longer to reach the Pole than the best ski and dog experts in the world. They had come in second in such a race, but given the success of Amundsen's overall deception, it could not have been otherwise.

In the tent that the Norwegians left near the Pole, Scott found a letter addressed to him by Amundsen:

> *Dear Captain Scott,*
> *As you are probably the first to reach this area after us, I will ask you kindly to forward this letter to King Haakon VII. If you can use any of the articles left in the tent please do not hesitate to do so. With kind regards. I wish you a safe return.*
> *Yours truly*
> *Roald Amundsen*

The discarded items referred to included a pair of mittens that Bowers appropriated. Amundsen was sensible in leaving this note, for he and his men could easily die on their return journey; crevasses are no respecters of persons, not even of successful Pole seekers. Gran later wrote: "Neither, at this seriously meaningful time, did Scott express bitter feelings toward Amundsen. On the contrary, he expressed admiration for the effective way the Norwegians had executed the feat." Bowers, who had done his last long stint of "wretched manhauling" without skis, wrote: "I am glad to say I am fit and strong . . . Of course none of us are as strong as we were, and one feels inexpressibly weary at the end of a long march if the surface has been heavy. A good meal and a night's rest, however, and you are as fit as ever. Our ration is an excellent one . . . We have got here and, if ever a journey has been accomplished by honest sweat ours has."

But the journey was only half accomplished. It was as well that none of the five men could see into the future.

INTIMATIONS OF TRAGEDY

"WELL, WE HAVE TURNED our back now on the goal of our ambition," Scott wrote on January 19, 1912, "and must face our 800 miles of solid dragging—and goodbye to most of the day-dreams!"

So they turned north for Cape Evans or, if they were fast enough, *Terra Nova,* which arrived in the Ross Sea the same day they reached the Pole. Both Scott and Amundsen were keen to get their news to the nearest cable-head and both thought they stood the chance of doing so before the other.

Only a Norwegian tent greeted Scott's arrival at the Pole, but, from October 1956, a station was permanently manned there. When I visited the Pole huts with Mike Stroud in 1993, I set up a beacon that bleeped our position straight back to Britain by satellite. We arrived there at 6 p.m. on January 16 and, as we crossed the Pole itself, we were immediately at 6 p.m. on January 17, gaining an instant twenty-four hours in time just as Scott had, precisely eighty-one years before to the day. We stayed at 90° south for one hour in our tent; most of the Pole station inmates were asleep. The windchill factor was suitably –90°C. I altered my compass setting's magnetic variation in readiness for our onward journey to the Beardmore Glacier. Scott's navigator, Bowers, would have done likewise but with a different setting since the magnetic pole is always on the move.

Mike, as part of his research program, weighed us both on his saucer-sized scales. Stripping naked in a four-foot-high, ice-cold tent, to stand on one leg on tiny scales, was briefly humorous until Mike proclaimed that I had lost forty-four pounds in weight, 25 percent of my body weight, in the last sixty-eight days' travel and now had near zero body fat to provide me with insulation against the cold. His own status was similar as, no doubt, was that of Scott's men. We depend on our body fat for our insulation, unlike other primates who rely for their warmth on their fur. We had often felt cold en route to the Pole, but never anything like the real cold we experienced after the Pole on the long, long journey to reach and then descend the Beardmore Glacier.

Only three days out from the Pole, Scott observed: "I think Oates is feeling the cold and fatigue more than most of us." Oates wrote: "One of my big toes has turned black. I hope it is not going to lame me for marching."

That was on January 20, the same day that my own toes, in the same place but all those years later, began to blister badly. I can identify with Oates as I recall the torture of squeezing my feet into my boots. The normal highlight of the day of porridge gruel and coffee at breakfast "were ruined by having to count down the minutes to execution, the moment when I must gingerly draw my socks over the mess of my feet. As the textile hairs brushed against the open nerve ends of the damaged areas, I would grind my teeth together. Then came the unyielding pressure of the boots themselves and the beginning of the twelve-hour ordeal during which I would have only one thing in mind; the moment of release from the boots."

The plateau had not treated me well. Mike described me thus: "He did look old, thin and haggard. Perched upon his bony buttocks, his long legs stretched in front of him were worse than mine, and they ended in those horribly damaged feet. His face was ravaged, almost ancient and hooded lids covered eyes that were somehow dulled. His features were puffed and doughy, and his lips were still scabbed and broken in places. The frost had left its mark. His ears were blistered and beneath one eye was a raw patch where he'd pulled off glasses while they were still frozen on. His hair, thinning a little before we started, was now falling out in tufts."

Wilson wrote: "Our hands are never warm enough in camp to do any neat [sketching] work now the weather is always uncomfortably cold and windy." The ceaseless southerly wind blew at force 4 to 6 all day with an average temperature of −21°C. At first they saw many of the Norwegians' marker cairns, smaller than their own, but soon the two trails diverged. Snowdrifts already covered sections of their tracks and blowing snow formed a haze so that their own marker cairns were often only visible from less than a mile away. All eyes searched constantly for the reassurance of their outward trail, for their vital depots, which, in such featureless and undulating wastes, could otherwise be missed with fatal consequences.

Whenever, at local noon, Bowers could see the sun, he stopped to establish its altitude and work out their latitude. This sounds simple, but some of my coldest polar moments have been spent with a theodolite. If you breathe, the sighting glass mists over with frost. If your eyebrow touches metal, it becomes stuck to it. If your bulky clothing brushes against the tripod, the bubble levels need careful realigning.

Whenever the mainly southerly wind was strong, but not too strong, the five men used their tent floorcloth and a makeshift mast, such as a ski, to provide a sail to help them with the sledge. This was just as well because the dreaded sandlike crystals that made man-hauling hell lay everywhere on the polar plateau. With force 6 winds, the men sometimes had to drag the sledge sideways to prevent overturns when sailing. They managed daily totals of sixteen miles and more, their best so far, but Evans's hands deteriorated further, with five of his fingertips badly blistered.

Now that they were heading north, Scott had a difficult choice to make. He had normally chosen to time his travel hours, when heading south, so that, in the middle of his day, the noon sun was behind him and his shadow therefore pointed due south. To achieve the opposite effect, he would now have to switch twelve hours to "night-time" travel, which would avoid being dazzled by the sun. However, much as Scott would have preferred the night-travel option, he knew that every ounce of warmth must be used to the full, both to conserve body heat and to benefit from the better glide of the runners, and this demanded "day-time" movement. Furthermore, any day-to-night travel switch (usually accomplished by gradual changes over a period of a week, not by halting for twelve hours of precious time) would be accomplished not long before they reached the edge of the plateau where the crevasses began.

Wilson, more prone than the others to suffer from snow blindness, partly because of his sketching duties whenever rock features needed recording, noted on January 25: "Marched on foot in the afternoon as my eyes were too bad to go on on ski . . . Had $ZnSO_4$ and cocaine in my eyes at night and didn't get to sleep at all for the pain." Bowers used Wilson's skis. When the haze of blowing crystals hid the cairns and all signs of their trail were obscured, it was easy to panic. Although it caused delay, they would often unharness and fan out until, to their great relief, somebody found a scrap of the old trail between drifts. Despite such halts, the dazzle, the ever-colder conditions, and with one of the men marching skiless, they nevertheless clocked some spectacular distances on the plateau—nineteen and a half miles, nineteen miles, eighteen miles. They averaged fourteen miles a day man-hauling to Amundsen's fifteen miles a day with dogs. Amundsen traveled in temperatures averaging ten degrees warmer, yet still his men complained of the bitter cold. They were not having to drag their sledges, thus risking sweating, so they could and did wear animal furs with their vastly superior insulative qualities.

Mike and I, in 1993, hauled far heavier loads than Scott's men so we sweated, even at −51°C, and wore even thinner cotton clothes than did Scott's party. Like them, the colder it became, the faster we had to haul to keep our blood circulating. In such circumstances, the last thing you want is one of your team holding you up, because even the briefest halt or slow-down will render your body hypothermic in double-quick time.

Unfortunately, Scott's team, with the Pole less than a week behind them, already had two time bombs ticking. On January 23, Scott noted that Evans was far from well and that "I think Wilson, Bowers and I are as fit as possible under the circumstances. Oates gets cold feet. One way and another, I shall be glad to get off the summit!" As early as January 23, Scott wrote: "There is no doubt Evans is a good deal run down—his fingers are badly blistered and his nose is rather seriously congested with frequent frost bites. He is very much annoyed with himself, which is not a good sign." And, seven days later: "Evans has dislodged two finger-nails tonight; his hands are really bad, and to my surprise he shows signs of losing heart over it."

Since the last pony meat the team had eaten over six weeks before, they had not taken any vitamin C (not that vitamins were then understood), so even small wounds would heal very slowly. Evans may well have refrained from touching the all but raw pony meat anyway, for he was a fussy eater. Back in March 1911, on a minor sledge trip, Debenham had noted, "For supper we had seal liver fried in blubber, excellent. Evans was averse to tasting it as the slightest taste of blubber offends him." Evans's blubber aversion would also have applied to eating seal meat all through the previous winter, putting him in a more vulnerable position to such threats as scurvy.

Because Amundsen's route was longer on the barrier and shorter on the plateau, his men traveled at altitude for less time and mileage than did Scott's group. Man-hauling at altitude is a killer. Of the few dozen scientists who work at the South Pole station, about one every year is evacuated back to sea level because of altitude problems, in extreme cases even cerebral edema, a swelling of the brain. Shackleton's men spent much less time on the plateau than Scott's, but enough to suffer from standard altitude problems such as severe headaches, nosebleeds, and oxygen shortage. All of Scott's men may have been affected by the altitude because the thin air at ten thousand feet near the Pole has the same effect on humans as thirteen thousand feet on equatorial mountains. Dehydration is one such effect, caused by increased respiration and the dry atmosphere. On the plateau, Scott's men received half the oxygen supply they would inhale on the barrier. Their bodies would crave oxygen as their pulses raced and they gasped for breath.

Amundsen's top skier, the national champion of Norway, Olav Bjaaland, declared on the plateau: "I wish to God we were down on the ice-shelf. Here it is hard to breathe and the nights are as long as the Devil." Amundsen himself noted: "The asthmatic condition in which we found ourselves during our six weeks' stay on the plateau was anything but pleasant."

Wilson wrote: "Thin air, low pressure and oxygen deficiency reach a point, at about ten thousand feet, above which even well-fed, fit humans will be affected by altitude 'sickness.' It is best not to exert yourself but, if you must, you will find every movement is an effort." A dog driver exerts far less energy than a man-hauler and the latter constricts his breathing each time he hauls and jerks on his chest harness. In 1993, at 11,000 feet on the plateau, with our by then 350-pound loads frequently jamming in deep sastrugi ruts,

Mike Stroud and I felt we must give up. Mike summed up our feeling of helplessness in the face of the ceaseless bitter wind, the severe dehydration, the bitter cold, and the vast distances still to cover as: "We are running on empty."

First Shackleton, then Amundsen, then Scott—all had to face their time on the plateau and none of them enjoyed it. Scott's group suffered the severe effects for longer and in colder conditions, but they pushed on and still kept to their schedule.

Finding depots, where no land features exist to mark them, depends on a fair degree of luck as well as the ability to direction find. The luck factor consists of good visibility and minimal blizzards creating drifts that bury tracks. Amundsen marked some of his depots laterally with poles at one-mile spaces for ten miles to the west and to the east. I always used three-foot-high minimum snow-block piles. Scott's men built double cairns at each night camp and a single one at each lunch camp. However, when a blizzard arrives at just the wrong moment, there is no way anybody will find either a cairn or a marker pole without actually bumping into it. All tracks, even freshly made ones, will be invisible in a whiteout, so there is little point in taking the extra time and trouble laying out long lines of numbered marker poles. It may sound impressively efficient, but in practice it is usually a waste of time—and time is not readily available when man-hauling.

Scott located all his depots and never ran out of food while still able to travel. On the Beardmore Glacier descent, Scott was twice entangled in major crevasse fields and once had difficulty locating a depot. But he found it without having to turn back. Amundsen, on the far shorter and steeper Axel Heiberg Glacier, seriously missed his bearings twice and missed one of his glacier depots completely, having to send two of his men back to collect supplies when well past the missing depot. However well an expedition marks its outward depots, there will always be great anguish on the return journey through dangerous terrain, since death awaits any team who fails to find a depot.

On January 29, Wilson caught his ski on a rut and bruised his leg badly close by the depot where they had last seen Teddy Evans's team. His leg became swollen and painful, so Wilson went on without skis, lending his to

Bowers as he had some days previously. Bowers picked up his own skis from the depot on the last day of January. There were many deeply cut sastrugi that day, so Oates and Evans found the going easier without skis. Only Scott skied all day, but the group still covered twenty-two miles that day. In 1993, some of our best distances were likewise covered when we walked, although we were both accomplished skiers. This disproves the argument of many Scott critics who suggest that the causes of his tragedy stemmed largely from lack of ski training and from Bowers having to walk, thus delaying the others.

In the tent, Wilson continued his medical care of the others. He noted that: "Titus' toes are blackening and his nose and cheeks are dead yellow. Dressing Evans' fingers every other day with boric Vaseline—they are quite sweet still," he added, referring to a lack of the sickly dead-meat odor that emanates from gangrenous flesh. On an Arctic journey in the 1980s, I was woken one morning by Mike Stroud telling me I must get to a hospital as soon as possible, as the tent smelled of gangrene. He was right and, a week later, back in Europe, I had a skin graft from my thigh to replace the missing flesh on my frostbitten foot.

Mike's hands suffered in a similar way to Taff Evans's a week after we had left the Pole in 1993, and I can understand why Evans was anything but cheerful since I had watched how Mike suffered. At the time I wrote: "Mike's hands had gradually deteriorated since his mitt problems just before the Pole: . . . three of the main finger blisters had burst, the dead skin falling away to reveal raw stumps like red sausages. He continued to handle our evening cooking and turned down my offer to help . . . What pained him most, it seemed, was the removal of his mitts for their wool sometimes stuck to the raw finger flesh."

As the British approached their Three Degree Depot 180 miles from the Pole in the last days of January 1912, Amundsen returned to his base on the Bay of Whales and, fearing Scott might have somehow overtaken him, quickly headed north aboard *Fram* to be sure to reach a cable head to tell the world of his triumph. Scott did not, of course, know that the Norwegians had returned to their base. As far as he was concerned, they may well have died in Antarctica. At no point on their own journey, following their successful attainment of the Pole, could the British assume that the Norwegians would survive, any more than that they themselves would make it back to Cape Evans.

Despite Wilson's leg, a subsequent injury to Scott's shoulder, and the ongoing troubles of Oates and Evans, the group made exceptionally good progress through early February. On February 4, they reached the rim of the plateau and saw the black specks of rocks ahead, the Beardmore Glacier's upper markers. After seven weeks of unrelieved featureless ice, rocky outcrops were a wonderful sight. "It is like going ashore," Scott wrote, "after a sea voyage."

Wilson noted: "Since the last depot we have been having extra food . . . and we are grateful for it." But also: "Evans' fingers suppurating, nose very bad and rotten looking."

Until February 5, one third of the way down the glacier, progress had been swift. Then came a sudden halving of daily distances as Scott recorded that Evans was losing his strength. After three days threading their way through the crevassed ice fields of the Beardmore's southern defenses, they reached their Upper Glacier Depot. Here they found a note from Teddy Evans, who had reached that point without any trouble and at a progress rate almost as fast as their own. Bowers, the rations maestro, was upset when he found they were short of one day's biscuit ration.

Wilson, charged by the absent geologists with collecting certain rock and fossil samples from the Beardmore, began to hanker for rock-hunting forays. On February 8, he sent Bowers off to collect dolerite rock from a nearby outcrop and, on the ninth, all but Evans went out from a camp they made beneath Mount Buckley to locate samples. For a while, they rested in the rare warmth of a windless day. "Coal seams," Wilson noted, "at all heights in the sandstone cliffs and lumps of weathered coal with fossils, vegetable . . . got some splendid things in the short time." Scott wrote: "It has been extremely interesting . . . Wilson, with his sharp eyes, has picked several plant impressions, the last a piece of coal with beautifully traced leaves in layers, also some excellently preserved impressions of thick stems, showing cellular structure."

Despite their rest, which, as Scott pointed out, was good for Evans, they traveled for some part of every day on the glacier. On February 10, with two full days of rations on the sledge, they needed to reach their Mid Glacier Depot in under three days. They did not anticipate any trouble finding it because it lay at the junction of three back bearings from major mountain features. From their rest camp, they aimed toward the towering heights of the Cloudmaker but, with twenty-five miles to go to their food cache, Scott's normally intuitive pathfinding abilities deserted him and the British descended into an icy version of hell. Some excerpts from Scott's diary, coupled with three from other diaries of later attempts to negotiate the same chaotic passage, may give an idea of this devil's own labyrinth.

On the evening of February 10, Scott noted: "We have two full days' food left . . . if the weather doesn't clear by to-morrow, we must either march blindly on or reduce food." In fact, this period of two or three days was, according to Cherry-Garrard, the only period on the plateau or the glacier when Scott's group did not have "their full, or more than their full ration."

In 1993, Mike and I had, by this stage, although badly malnourished like Scott, reduced our food to half rations to extend our remaining travel range. Scott could, of course, have done this, so his position over the next two days was not as desperate (and thus arguably irresponsible) as it might appear.

Once again, Scott's harshest critic was himself. He wrote on February 11: "The worst day we have had during the trip and greatly owing to our own fault." He is referring to the difficult struggle his team experienced in a very dangerous ice field. Of course, since he was navigator, any route that led to trouble was his fault but, in this very same area, the world's most skilled mountaineer later made far worse errors. Reinhold Messner, the great Italian climber of the 1970s and '80s, a past master at threading a way through the worst ice fields in the world, wrote on the Cloudmaker ice field in the 1990s: "You look around and see only crevasses. On a surface of several square kilometres, nothing but upthrust glacier ice and you are in the middle of it with no obvious way out. A false route description given me . . . made us angry. After five hundred metres I believed I had found a fairly safe route. We struggled to the left. We found no way out. This cost a great deal of effort. Like blind men we had run into the middle of the abysses and holes, into a labyrinth of ice towers and crevasses which were more than two hundred metres deep."

Scott wrote: "There were times when it seemed almost impossible to find a way out of the awful turmoil. The irregular crevassed surface giving way to huge chasms closely packed and most difficult to cross." Messner, when close to the Cloudmaker, like Scott, wrote: "We go two miles to get one mile north. From above we have no view of the route. We try to reach the middle of the Beardmore by crossing side-streams. We go three hours with crampons on bare ice and come to a widely shattered ice-fall marked on no map. We get stuck. We go back. In part the crevasses are so big one could put a church inside." Messner had seen air photos of the Beardmore. He had the best available maps of the main danger areas, yet he became hopelessly entangled in the constantly changing crevasse fields together with his German colleague, Arved Fuchs, Germany's most celebrated polar traveler. Scott of course had no maps. He was being harsh with himself to write "greatly owing to our own fault."

After twelve horrendous hours, Scott found a way out. "It was a test of our endurance on the march and our fitness with small supper. We have come through well," he wrote. On February 12, they found marks of their outward trail, which cheered them, but then "by a fatal chance we kept too far to the left . . . arrived in a horrid maze of crevasses and fissures. Divided councils caused our course to be erratic after this, and finally, at 9 p.m., we landed in the worst place of all . . . we decided to camp after a very short supper and one meal only remaining in the food bag. We *must* get there to-morrow . . . Pray God we have fine weather to-morrow." At this point, in Scott's position, I would have switched to half rations. Perhaps he did.

The next day, still in mist, they at last reached the northern edge of the crevasse field and, constantly checking their bearings from the dimly perceived bulk of the Cloudmaker, came upon their depot flag and their vital supplies. A note left there by Teddy Evans suggested that his group had also had trouble finding a way through the Cloudmaker area. Scott promised himself he would in future keep a tighter control on their rations, saving a reserve in case of another such emergency. He also noted of his companions: "Bowers has had a very bad attack of snowblindness, and Wilson another almost as bad. Evans has no power to assist with camping work."

The comment made by Scott while lost in the crevasse zone that most interested me was "Divided councils caused our course to be erratic." After many experiences of navigating in complex, hazardous regions over the years I made the choice that I would never ask for other opinions. This may sound dogmatic or conceited or both, but I had total confidence in my navigating abilities and no confidence in anybody else's and democratic indecision can be lethal. Scott's chief navigator, Bowers, had written of Scott as they ascended the Beardmore a month earlier: "Scott is quite wonderful in his selections of route, as we have escaped excessive dangers and difficulties all along . . . He avoids the sides of the Glacier and goes nowhere near the snow: he often heads straight for apparent chaos and somehow, when we appear to have reached a cul-de-sac, we find an open road."

This praise of Scott's navigational abilities referred to his ascent of the Beardmore, but coming down the glacier was very different. During the time of "divided councils," Wilson grumbled in his diary that they: "plunged into an icefall and wandered about in it absolutely lost for hours and hours" . . . "We ought to have gone west of the big hump" . . . "and we should have missed all today's trouble." And again: "We again had a forenoon of trying to cut corners. Got in amongst great chasms." If Wilson had but tried the options that he favored, he would have found things less simplistic than he thought. As Cherry-Garrard wrote: "One of the great difficulties of the Beardmore is that you saw the ice-falls as you went up and avoided them, but coming down you knew nothing of their whereabouts until you fell into the middle of pressure and crevasses, and then it was almost impossible to say whether you should go left or right to get out." As Shackleton's friend Frank Wild once wrote of the Beardmore ice fields: "It was such an awful place, exactly like a rough sea in appearance."

After their escape from the Cloudmaker ice fields on February 13, 1912, and coming close to the mountains at the glacier's edge, Wilson spent an hour collecting rocks while the others went on ahead to their next campsite. He found at this point samples in which were embedded fernlike fossil leaves. Altogether Wilson and Bowers collected a total of thirty-five pounds in rock samples to be carried over four hundred miles on the sledge.

Shackleton, when he was on the glacier three years earlier, had done likewise. In the light of the horrific experience both groups were later to suffer, was it sensible to spend possibly critical hours and energy collecting and dragging the extra weight of these rocks? If the human cost was great, so was the scientific value of the samples. One of Wilson's Permian leaf fossils was later found to be *Glossopteris,* the plant characteristic of the Southern Hemisphere continent that provided geologists with their first proof that Antarctica was a part of the ancient supercontinent of Gondwana during the Permian Period, some 250 million years ago. If the extra weight of thirty-five pounds in rocks, which included this key fossil, had critically affected Scott's chances of survival, the question "Was it worth it?" would be a more valid one. Although it is vital to keep sledge loads to an absolute minimal weight as a general principle, a thirty-five-pound weight factor shared by three or four man-haulers will not make the difference between life and death.

By February 16, Scott's men were traveling slowly through thick mist but very close to their last cache on the Beardmore, the Lower Glacier Depot. Taff Evans, according to Wilson, "collapsed—sick and giddy and unable to walk even by the sledge on ski, so we camped." Oates, critical by nature, wrote: "It is an extraordinary thing about Evans. He has lost his guts and behaves like an old woman or worse." "[He] is quite worn out with the work and how he is going to do the 400 odd miles we have still to do I don't know." "We could not possibly carry him on the sledge." Scott noted: "Evans has nearly broken down in brain we think. He is absolutely changed from his normal self-reliant self . . . perhaps all will be well if we can get to our depot to-morrow fairly early but it is anxious work with the sick man."

With food for one day only and ten miles from the depot, Scott could not afford further delay. Evans was allowed out of the sledge traces and plodded along in the tracks of the others, gradually losing ground. At first Evans had trouble fixing his ski bindings with his bloody, bandaged, hypersensitive fingers. Hardly surprising. Each subsequent delay to refix them must have made him feel ever more frustrated, impotent, and desperate. At the next halt, there was no sign of Evans, so they all went back for him. "We found him," wrote Oates, "on his hands and knees in the snow in a most pitiable condition. He was unable to walk and the other three went back on ski for the empty sledge and we brought him into the tent where he died at 12.30 am." Scott's description ran: "I was first to reach the poor man and shocked at his appearance; he was on his knees with clothing disarranged, hands uncovered and frostbitten, and a wild look in his eyes. Asked what was the matter, he replied with a slow speech that he didn't know . . . He showed every sign of complete collapse . . . he was practically unconscious, and when we got him into the tent quite comatose. He died quietly . . . It is a terrible thing to lose a companion in this way, but calm reflection shows that there could not have been a better ending to the terrible anxieties of the past week . . . what a desperate pass we were in with a sick man on our hands at such a distance from home."

They left Taff Evans on the ice and no diary mentions details of his burial. Any lingering without hard exertion to keep warm would quickly lead to hypothermia. Either you pull hard or you put the tent up. You do not linger to cover a body that will anyway soon be naturally drifted over in snow. Scott was meticulous in his attention to religious ceremony, and both Bowers and Wilson were deeply religious. Prayers would certainly have been said over Taff Evans's body, but every minute spent standing around would have been a minute too long.

A few hours later, they found their depot without difficulty. The next day, they passed by the Gateway and crossed the great shear crack with no problem in good visibility. At Shambles Camp, where they had shot their last five ponies, they dug up as much of the buried horse meat as they could find, some of which they ate immediately, and felt much stronger than they had for many days.

Why, they all wondered, had Evans, the most powerful man of them all, died so quickly and for no known reason? Historians and medical experts have been wondering and theorizing ever since. Both Scott and Wilson, who watched his slow deterioration closely, believed that his demise had much to do with a severe fall he had suffered two weeks before his death. Their diaries record that he fell into crevasses twice in one day; once only as far as his waist (so he could hardly have hurt his head), but the second time may well have involved a knock on the head that, they believed, had concussed him and caused his subsequent out-of-character and enfeebled personality change. He may, they thought, have suffered some form of brain hemorrhage.

The trouble with any such theory is the lack of any record of a specific head injury to Evans. Scott notes: "Wilson thinks it certain he must have injured his brain by a fall." This suggests some fall unwitnessed by the others.

But in that community, when everybody was clustered about the sledge, there was little chance of anyone falling unnoticed. The only other record is a footnote in the posthumously edited version of Scott's diary, which refers to Evans's mental state as "the result of concussion in the morning's fall." This seems based entirely on the editor's imagination. If Evans had suffered from cerebral edema, an unknown condition at the time, he need not have suffered from any fall, nor would descent to near sea level necessarily have resolved the condition. Expert nutritionist Dr. A. F. Rogers, after meticulous studies of the background of Evans's death, concluded: "The diet consumed by members of Scott's Last Expedition was deficient in calories and vitamins. It contained no Vitamin C . . . at all. The probable cause of death of Chief Petty Officer Edgar Evans, R.N., was a mild head injury insufficient to cause concussion but which caused a subdural haemorrhage in a scorbutic subject and resulted a fortnight later in fatal secondary brain stem haemorrhage." Another medical expert, Canadian Dr. R. C. Falckh, theorized in 1986 that Evans is quite likely to have died of anthrax contracted from the ponies during the winter.

Failure to be first at the Pole may well have meant more to Evans than it did to the others, including Scott, because financially his future was far more dependent on a reasonable level of fame, at least in his native Wales. It is possible this did contribute to his lack of resistance and depressed state, but Evans was by nature a cheerful extrovert, so this seems unlikely. Also, Scott made a pertinent diary note on January 23 that would suggest strongly that Taff's despondency stemmed from the very date of his cut hand, at which point Pole priority still seemed possible. Scott's precise words were that Evans "hasn't been cheerful since the accident." I know well how the least finger injury makes itself painfully felt every waking moment of the day on a polar journey, and Evans's sliced knuckles would have made him anything but cheerful from the start, especially since his were the jobs of sledge stowage and tent erection, which require extensive, dexterous hand work in the cold, often only possible without outer mitts.

Dr. Mike Stroud, now a senior lecturer in the much-respected Institute of Nutrition at Southampton University, has written many learned papers on such topics as "energy expenditure during long periods of endurance exercise with inadequate energy intake." He has himself nearly died on two occasions from hypothermia/hypoglycemia. He wrote me a note in 2003:

> The causes of Evans's death will by its very nature always continue to be speculative. The problem is that you will never be able to quantify the potential contributions from:
>
> a) Vitamin deficiency: scurvy and others.
> b) Frank starvation: ie sheer weight loss: our data suggests that this must have been significant.
> c) Hypoglycaemia/hypothermia: these are both relevant to the Evans case. Weight loss and hypoglycaemia together would have added to the environmental risk.
> d) Some other cause such as the head injury theory.

Scott's scientist Raymond Priestley echoed Cherry-Garrard's repeated opinion that Scott's men had sufficient food at all times up to and beyond the date of Evans's death and that their rations' energy value was sufficient to keep them going. Despite the lack of vitamin C, which we now know was absent from their rations (apart from the small amounts of pony meat they consumed), they had not traveled for long enough without it to have developed the main symptoms of scurvy. Priestley wrote: "Wilson . . . knew the symptoms of scurvy from personal experience; was a conscientious and scientific observer, and did not suggest that visible signs of scurvy had appeared." It takes three months and more for the disease to develop, but Scott's men had consumed vitamin C from lightly boiled pony meat two and a half months prior to Evans's death.

Teddy Evans did nearly die of scurvy on his return journey from the Pole, but nothing can be deduced from this. Priestley wrote that Teddy Evans, who man-hauled much longer than most of his colleagues, "is not a reliable criterion from which to argue about the state of health of his companions." He had been away "in the field" without vitamin C for at least a month longer than all the others.

A great many Scott critics have suggested that Taff Evans suffered an energy loss greater than the others simply because he was a bigger man. Cherry-Garrard was also a proponent of this theory. He wrote: "He was the biggest, heaviest and most muscular man in the party. I do not believe that this is a life for such men, who are expected to pull their weight and to support and drive a larger machine than their companions, and at the same time to eat no extra food. If, as seems likely, the ration these men were eating was not enough to support the work they were doing, then it is clear that the heaviest man will feel the deficiency sooner and more severely than others who are smaller than he."

My own opinion on this is the result of many months spent man-hauling in competition with Mike Stroud. I am a far bigger, heavier man than Mike, yet, after ninety-five days of extreme man-hauling with the same caloric intake, I ended up with far less loss of muscle (which is the key factor, not body weight) than did Mike. Mike Stroud recorded that my lean tissue loss was 4.3 kilograms to his 6.5 kilograms, so my isometric strength in key muscles ended up far greater than Mike's although, at the outset, he was the stronger. Much as I would love to play the card that, being bigger, I should have more food, I simply cannot prove it. One reason for this, as Mike Stroud found from his research, is that a small man, pulling a sledge of equal weight to a big man's sledge, has to work at a higher energy intensity. This principle would hold good when both such men were hauling a single sledge.

Taff Evans's body will have moved several miles out onto the barrier over the past ninety years and will never be found. If it were, however, modern forensics might well be able to ascertain the real reason for his death. He strove hard all the way, and Scott, not knowing of his injury, nor suspecting his decline, could not have chosen a stronger man-hauler.

Scott had reason to be pleased with the expedition's progress the day after Evans's death. That will sound callous from an emotional viewpoint, but I am talking of four people living in fear of their lives. With any one of them slowing the others, their group chances of survival were cut from good to remote. In such circumstances, the death of somebody suffering hugely and bound to die within a few days must be a relief. To pretend otherwise would be hypocritical and Scott was honest in his reaction. "The absence of poor Evans is a help to the commissariat," he wrote and added, "if he had been here in a fit state we might have got along faster."

On such a journey, there was no hope for anyone who could not keep up. Their chances of survival depended on maintaining a certain basic speed, not possible if they had physically to drag any one of their number on the sledge. All they could do was to hope Evans could keep up on skis while they dragged his food and belongings ahead of him. Had Scott been the weak person at that point, the same rules would have applied. Scott summarized the situation: "I take this opportunity of saying that we have stuck to our sick companions to the last . . . In the case of Edgar Evans . . . the safety of the remainder seemed to demand his abandonment, but Providence mercifully removed him at this critical moment." At Shambles Camp on the barrier on February 18, 1912, they discarded their old sledge in favor of a new one left there previously that they loaded with all their gear, including the thirty-five pounds of rocks, plus enough pony meat to last them eight days, and their rations, which included those of the dead Evans.

How were their chances, as viewed in their tent on the night of February 18 at Shambles Camp?

They had come through seven weeks at high altitude on the plateau, a record and an unknown factor when Scott had first laid out his plans. They had then descended the glacier in good time and were back on the barrier ahead of schedule. Gran later summarized their situation: "The way to their meeting place (with the dog teams) was not impossibly long. They were fairly tired but healthy. On the Barrier they might encounter higher temperatures and winds helpful to their sledge sail." Looking back, the initial long haul out from Cape Evans with the heaviest loads and the gradual elimination of the ponies had gone according to plan, as had the desperate haul up the glacier to ten thousand feet. The bitter cold, constant winds, and debilitating altitude effects of the plateau were behind them, as were the nightmare ice fields of the Beardmore. Of the great 1,600-mile challenge, only 400 miles with a single comparatively light sledge load remained. With the benefit of pony meat to boost their health and ample rations at hand, were they justified in believing that the worst was over and that the odds of a successful return were still in their favor?

Cherry-Garrard, with his intricate knowledge of the expedition, summarized their outlook thus: "They had just picked up one week's food for five men: between the Beardmore and One Ton were three more such depôts

each with one week's food for five men. They were four men." The distance
to One Ton Depot was 240 miles, so they had four full weeks of food to
cover 240 miles, which entailed an average of 8.6 miles per day on full rations (but they could extend their rations by saving the Evans ration). On
the flat surface of the barrier at sea level with a light sledge load, 8.6 miles
per day was less than the fifteen miles per day average they had maintained
on the plateau and upper glacier (and less than the average that Teddy
Evans's three-man team had achieved on their return journey over the barrier, despite having to tow Evans on their sledge for six days).

Scott's plans had been based on a 144-day journey and they had taken
112 days so far. To stay on schedule, they had 32 days left to cover the 348
nautical miles to Cape Evans (assuming no help from the dog teams). On
this basis, they must average 10.9 miles per day for 32 days to keep to
Scott's plan, an average far less than for their journey so far. Four hundred
miles of barrier lay ahead of the four men and, by the simple mathematics of
food, time, and distance, the journey looked eminently possible. Survival
was within their grasp.

And what of Amundsen, already the conqueror of the Pole? He was to
spend the rest of his days, despite his great achievements, an aloof and bitter
man constantly in search of new triumphs. He fell out even with his closest
friend and most loyal supporter, his brother Leon, and fought a long and
caustic court battle with him. He never forgave Hjalmar Johansen for his
brief revolt in Antarctica and humiliated him to his suicidal end.

THE GREATEST MARCH EVER MADE

ON FEBRUARY 19, 1912, as Scott's men set out across the barrier, Tom Crean arrived alone at Hut Point. Atkinson was there and with growing apprehension listened to Crean's story. After an exciting but speedy descent of the Beardmore Glacier with Teddy Evans navigating in fine style, he and Bill Lashly had been alarmed by Evans's rapid decline, most probably caused by scurvy. From One Ton Depot, they had towed the apparently dying lieutenant for six days, on the sledge, as far as Corner Camp, where Lashly stayed with him and Crean trekked on alone, a remarkable achievement, for thirty-five miles to Hut Point. Atkinson and Gerof rescued Evans and took him to Hut Point, where Atkinson slowly coaxed him back to life.

When Crean's news spread to everyone at Cape Evans, there were many questions. What of Amundsen? Evans's men had seen no sign of the Norwegians before they had turned back on the plateau. This was great news. What of Scott? He had taken five, not four, men on to the Pole, with plenty of rations. They should make it, Crean thought, as all five were strong men and very fit.

Gran's first reaction on hearing how well everyone had taken to skis was: "They have taken the skis to the Pole, hurrah!" But, when he saw the physical state of Teddy Evans and, to a lesser extent, Crean and Lashly, he was not so happy and wrote: "but from what I had heard it became clear to me that the prospects of our five-man polar party were not so bright as most of the members of the expedition imagined. Evans' frightful return journey was a pointer to what Scott and his men would be bound to undergo."

Back in February 1911, when the expedition had first made camp at Cape Evans, Scott had sent Victor Campbell and five men off with the ship to explore another area. After their chance discovery of the Norwegians in the Bay of Whales, and return to McMurdo Sound, they had been dropped off at Cape Adare. Ten months later, in December 1911, *Terra Nova* picked them up again and repositioned them at another coastal spot to geologize. They expected the ship would come back to collect them in a couple of months. After landing Campbell's team, *Terra Nova* tried to embark an-other group of geologists from the west side of McMurdo Sound. Sea ice prevented the pickup, so this group (Taylor, Debenham, Gran, and Forde) made their own way back around the coast to Cape Evans.

In late February 1912, *Terra Nova* picked up the gravely sick Teddy Evans from Hut Point, as well as eight men from Cape Evans who needed to leave the expedition rather than stay for a second winter. The ship also landed eight mules and some extra dogs that Scott had ordered in readiness for a second attempt on the Pole should that be necessary. The men leaving Antarctica were George Simpson, Herbert Ponting, Griffith Taylor, Raymond Priestley, Bernard Day the motor engineer, Robert Forde, Thomas Clissold the cook, Omelchenko, and Cecil Meares.

Scott's critics like to say that Meares left the expedition a year early because he was in a huff with Scott for making him travel on to the glacier with his dog teams, which was much farther than originally intended. All records, however, indicate that Meares had to return to Britain to sort out the affairs of his father, to whom he was devoted and who had just died.

Atkinson had intended, when he, Cherry-Garrard, Wright, and Keohane had returned to Cape Evans from the Beardmore, that he would head back south to help Scott with Gerof and the dogs on February 20. But, on February 19, after Crean's arrival, Atkinson had to use the dogs to bring back the near-dead Teddy Evans. As the only doctor, Atkinson decided to stay with Evans.

Any sensible expedition leader, like any army officer briefing his men before an operation, will expect to have to alter his original orders and react to changing circumstances. Scott was no different. As the Pole journey un-rolled and as parts went faster or slower than predicted, so he told his mes-sengers, the successive return groups, what his updated requirements were regarding the dog teams. He naturally expected that his *last* orders, those sent back with Teddy Evans, would be faithfully acted upon by his deputy back at Cape Evans. These last orders, which were delivered correctly by Teddy Evans to Atkinson, specified that the dogs, under Meares or Atkin-son, should come out as far as 82° or 83° and beyond the Mount Hooper Depot point. These were clear, sensible orders, which, if acted upon, would plainly have allowed Scott's group and the dog teams to have met up at or near the Mount Hooper Depot in early or mid-March.

With Meares gone, Atkinson, a doctor, concentrated instead on trying his utmost to save Teddy Evans's life, and he succeeded. The task of sending the dogs to meet Scott's returning party in mid-barrier devolved onto Charles Wright, who had dog-driving experience and was a good navigator. Simpson, however, was adamant that since he would be leaving in the ship, the expedition's meticulous meteorological program must be taken over by Wright. This left only Cherry-Garrard, whose dog-driving and navigational skills were at best limited, to take Gerof and the dogs to meet Scott in mid-barrier as he had requested. Sadly, nobody at Cape Evans appreciated the slow progress and damage the cold weather was causing Scott's men.

Should they have been alerted by Teddy Evans's condition, as Gran later suggested, into a full-scale rescue effort? Atkinson was well aware of the symptoms of scurvy. He saw that Lashly and Crean were symptom free and he knew that they, like Scott's team, had consumed more seal meat than Evans. Teddy Evans was clearly the sole scurvy case, due to his extra sledg-ing exertions prior to the Pole journey.

For the dogs to be usefully active in the mid-barrier region, they would need food cached at One Ton Depot, a job Scott had originally detailed to be done by Meares. Because Meares had returned to Cape Evans much later than expected, and had then left in the ship, this task was left undone. On

February 25, 1912, Cherry-Garrard and Gerof left Hut Point with full loads of dog food, twenty-seven days of rations for themselves, and two weeks of rations for Scott.

Terra Nova had to leave Antarctica in early March. After several attempts, she was unable, owing to sea ice, to pick up Campbell's little group, who would have to survive in an ice cave living off seal meat for a year. On Ross Island, eleven men under Atkinson, the new leader, waited anxiously for the return of Cherry-Garrard, Gerof, and Scott's men from the barrier. As far as they knew, Scott was still on or ahead of his original 144-day schedule. If Scott's group, who started from Shambles Camp on February 19, could average thirteen miles per day (less than their average at high altitude on the plateau) over the 240 miles to One Ton, they would meet Cherry-Garrard there between March 3 and 10.

The first day out was not auspicious for the Pole team. The surface conditions were bad, but Scott consoled himself in his diary that their ominously low mileage, only four and a half miles that day, was due to a late start and the heavy drift just off the coastal rim of the barrier. "I sincerely trust," he wrote, "it is only the result of this windless area close to the coast and that, as we are making steadily outwards, we shall shortly escape it." But the next day, they only traveled seven miles and he noted: "Same terrible surface . . . our sledge and ski leave deeply ploughed tracks which can be seen winding for miles behind." They camped for the night of February 20 at the site of the four-day "wet" blizzard that had so delayed their outward journey. Here they searched for more buried pony meat but found none. Scott wrote: "Terribly slow progress but we hope for better things as we clear the land. As usual our trials are forgotten as we camp and good food is our lot."

February 22 saw them approaching, in poor light, a depot. The wind had at last picked up, so they raised their sail and increased their pace. Blown snow covered all tracks and obliterated the line of cairns for a while, but Bowers's sense of direction brought them to the depot and Scott wrote: "Bowers' wonderful sharp eyes detected an old double lunch cairn, the theodolite telescope confirmed it, and our spirits rose accordingly. Tonight we had pony hoosh so excellent and filling that one feels really strong and vigorous again." They covered over eight miles in seven hours without their sail, a pace that was certainly hopeful. They found the Southern Barrier Depot and dug up the head of Oates's recalcitrant old pony Christopher. Oates wrote: "Dug up Christopher for food but it was rotten." Christopher's revenge! Shackleton's men ate rotten pony meat and suffered diarrhea. All the standard rations at this depot were in order but for a shortage of cooking fuel owing to evaporation. "[We] shall have to be *very* saving with fuel," Scott wrote, "otherwise have ten full days' provisions . . . and shall have less than seventy miles to go."

After the Lower Barrier Depot, they pulled clear of the coastal strip, where surfaces seemed to remain deep and sticky whatever the temperature, and started to achieve the good daily distance that Scott had counted on when formulating his original 144-day plan, averaging eleven and a half miles per day.

The planned allotment of fuel for the return journey was two-thirds of a gallon for eight days, the estimated time taken to cover each sixty-three to seventy-mile depot-to-depot stretch, allowing for two full days of bad weather. But the expected march rate was twelve miles per day, so six days between depots was the norm and was achieved by both the teams that returned before Scott's group, neither of whom reported fuel loss at the depots. The fuel allowance was generous, therefore, and had been planned to provide a surplus.

There have been many subsequent theories as to why Scott's cans leaked. On the *Discovery* expedition, Scott's cans had cork bungs. These leaked, especially when sledge loads were jolted and overturned, so by 1911 Scott had switched to using metal screw tops, seated on leather washers. Expeditions by Peary and Amundsen in the Arctic had experienced the same trouble and both men later used silver solder around the caps and along the can seams to prevent fuel loss. To solder over a fuel-can lid is certainly a step I would try to avoid, since the act of cutting it open in extreme cold conditions and with heavy mittens would be just one more devil factor at the moment when hands are at their coldest.

An Amundsen can was located at the base of the Axel Heiberg Glacier fifty-eight years later and had lost no fuel. On the other hand, glaciologist Dr. Charles Swithinbank used U.S.-made four-gallon metal jerricans on his own scientific missions to Antarctica and, in 1962, he once opened such a can at one of his caches and found that the can, "full to the brim with cook-ing fuel when we left, was unaccountably empty. We looked carefully for any hole in the can, but found none. Fortunately we carried a reserve." These U.S. jerricans are used for various fuels all over the world and are nor-mally leak proof.

Of all Scott's depots, only three, all on the barrier, suffered from fuel shortage and not all the cans were affected. In no case was there any ap-parent damage to the can or its cap. Cherry-Garrard later studied the mys-tery in depth. He observed that a wooden case containing eight standard oilcans was dug out of a deep snowdrift at Cape Evans. This case had been there untouched for over a year. When opened, it was discovered that three of the cans were full, three empty, one a third full, and one two-thirds full. The only explanation must have been, Cherry-Garrard believed, that some of the caps' leather washers, shrinking and cracking in response to tempera-ture changes, had allowed the fuel to evaporate, especially at times of warmer temperatures.

Cherry-Garrard commented that such evaporation could be avoided or minimized by stacking oil cans as deep as possible at the base of snow-covered depots and well away from the sun's rays. Scott's men, ignorant of the danger from the sun, used to leave the red oilcans on the top of each de-pot cairn to help make it as conspicuous as possible.

When Gran later visited One Ton Depot, he found rations smelling of cooker fuel, although the fuel cans were stacked on snow well above the ra-tions. This appeared to indicate that, at least on this occasion, pressurized seepage rather than evaporation must have taken place. The hot summer sun could have caused such seepage by vapor expansion in any can not fully topped up and where extreme cold temperatures had cracked its lid washer the previous winter. Some cans probably also leaked from less than perfectly soldered seams.

But what Gran did not know was that the man detailed to man-haul the rations to One Ton had taken rations and fuel already soaked and damaged at Cape Evans. This only became clear to me on reading a later note written by Cherry-Garrard in 1929. "[Simpson] told me that during the recent 'Antarctic' dinner at the Café Royal, Hooper told him . . . that the rations and paraffin tins were damaged: and the rations were soaked with paraffin . . . That he (Hooper) said 'We can't take the food and tins out like this.' To which Nelson replied that 'they had been told to take them out and they must do so!' " This would suggest that the tins may have been damaged off the ship or stacked badly in full sunlight at Cape Evans, not at One Ton. It is also a fine example of how the diary of one witness in 1913 can be contradictory to another sixteen years later. In 1911, food and fuel cans were hand-soldered and were never 100 percent reliable. Modern machine methods solved the problem, but too late for the *Terra Nova* expedition.

Annoying though the fuel shortage must have been to Scott's party, it did not by itself cause any starvation, thirst, or deadly conditions, only additional discomfort. They had to exercise fuel economy by using their cooker only when preparing their meals and never merely for warmth, but they ate exactly what they would have eaten with more fuel. They would, however (as had been the case up on the plateau), have been suffering from the slowly accumulating effects of dehydration through insufficient fluid intake. At no point of the journey was the fuel calculated to provide heat for drying out clothes, so the depot fuel shortage did not affect the state of their clothing in any way.

On February 25, free of the clogging coastal effect on their sledge runners, Scott's men fell back into the fine, swinging ski rhythm they had developed on the plateau. Bowers had at that time kept pace at his own walking speed, but now he too was on skis and no match for Scott, Wilson, and Oates. Scott addressed this point in a critical manner that upset the tough little Scotsman.

Scott, the leader, knew that their only hope lay in making maximum distance whenever on the move. Pulling a sledge in deep or clinging snow does not involve technique because skis cannot be made to glide, but man-hauling on skis does involve synchronized rhythm, with each man achieving his maximum "pull" at exactly the same moment, as in a rowboat. Scott described this as "we are getting into better ski drawing again. Bowers hasn't quite the trick." He naturally tried to point this out to Bowers, who, equally naturally, was dismayed for, as always, he was trying his best. Scott knew this and added: "I never doubted his heart."

Scott's attempts to have his team swing together must have worked, for they managed twelve miles that day, despite the temperature dropping below −29°C for the first time, an ominous sign. They were now in the region well away from the coast and almost out of sight of even the highest mountains. Here was a place they should expect helpful winds from the south, as had Teddy Evans's team a few short weeks before. "Oh! for a little wind," Scott wrote on February 25. But when the winds came, they were mostly from the north and cut into the skin of their cheeks and noses. "Sky overcast at start," Scott wrote, "but able to see tracks and cairn distinct at long distance . . . Very cold nights now and cold feet starting march . . . We are doing well on our food, but we ought to have yet more . . . The fuel shortage still an anxiety . . . Wonderfully fine weather but cold, very cold. Nothing dries and we get our feet cold too often."

Then suddenly, the temperature plunged with a vengeance. From February 25 onward, their thermometer recorded −29°C, from the twenty-seventh, −34.5°C, and, only five days later, −40°C. On the twenty-eighth, Scott wrote: "The sun shines brightly but there is little warmth in it . . . Splendid pony hoosh sent us to bed and sleep happily after a horrid day." There were no complaints about the effectiveness of their sleeping bags.

"Cold night . . . with north-west wind, force 4," Scott noted on the twenty-ninth, "luckily Bowers and Oates in their last new finnesko, keeping my old ones for present . . . The oil will just about spin out . . . [given good weather to the next depot] and we arrive with 3 clear days' food in hand. The increase of ration has had an enormously beneficial result." Despite the strong northerly winds against them, they still managed their daily minimum. Even at these extreme temperatures, with the vicious wind in their face and the constant worry of losing the circulation in their feet, the four men forced their way north.

With cold feet came cold hands, and the temperature inside Scott's tent at night would differ by only a degree or two from that outside. Writing a diary demands fingers unprotected by mittens and, by February, there would have been few fingers left between Scott's men that were not painfully split about the cuticles and nails or raw from burst frost blisters. As early as January 25, Bowers had made his last diary entry, Oates on February 24, and Wilson on February 27. Scott, amazingly, kept going for another month and Bowers maintained the meteorological records meticulously well into March. Survival in extreme cold is a matter of looking after yourself at all times and, as with the principles of hibernation, doing as little as is strictly necessary. Writing a diary does not qualify under that heading.

Well over 99 percent of people have no comprehension of what it is like to be really cold, the kind of deathly cold that comes with the loss of all body fat in the wind-driven, bitterly cold wastes of the polar regions. I have met folks who live in Canada or Minnesota and laugh at the cold. "Oh," they exclaim, "I was working at −40°C last year and it was easy." As like as not, these polar veterans experienced their "cold" wearing adequate clothing, with full stomachs, 18 percent body fat insulation, good health, and a nice warm house to return to.

On the barrier, back in 1908, in similar conditions to Scott's men but a lot nearer his base, Shackleton wrote of suffering from anemomania, literally, wind madness. His colleague, Eric Marshall, carefully monitored their body temperatures and found them to be 2°F under normal. This is a highly vulnerable state to be in. Marshall wrote: "All nearly paralysed with cold." Shackleton agreed. "The end is in sight," he said. "We are weakening rapidly."

In 1993, Mike Stroud and I had man-hauled for over ninety depotless days and reached the same spot as Scott's men on the barrier, where the mountains of the coast at last disappear. At that point, I wrote: "New kind of chisel-hard, hoarfrost surface . . . It is now horribly body-cold. I feel as though naked . . . I have to clasp my arms around my torso and jump [to avoid freezing]." With the sun shining down on us, Mike stumbled and fell over with hypothermia. Like me, and like Scott's men, his body had lost all vestiges of protective fat and he was completely vulnerable to the ever-plummeting windchill. Of our chances of making the last 290 miles to Hut Point, Mike then wrote: "In the ten hours that was the most we could manage, we made only twelve miles. Despite sledges of half the weight with which we had started . . . It was the end of the brief Antarctic summer . . . Even the hauling could no longer drive the chill from our bones. The cold lay heavily in our bodies and weakened us as effectively as venom. We had been crushed by the vastness of our journey, sapped by the weight of our loads, and now our muscles were poisoned by the ice."

At this point, if our modern communications instruments had ceased to work, we would have died on the barrier within two or three weeks. Scott had no such instruments, but, unlike us, he did have a thin lifeline of depots all the way to Hut Point and he did have every reason to expect a relief team with dogs at some point in mid-barrier. He had predicted reaching Hut Point by the end of March. On March 1, with 240 miles to go, he would need an average of only eight miles per day to keep to his plan. That evening he wrote: "very cold last night—minimum −41.5°[F]. We did 11½ yesterday and marched 6 this morning . . . the weather is wonderful. Cloudless days and nights and the wind trifling [but we are] horribly cold. For this lunch hour the exception [with] a bright and comparatively warm sun. All our gear is out drying."

March 2 was a day of reckoning, a day of chilling warnings of what might lie ahead. The only diary still recording events by then was Scott's. "Misfortunes," he wrote, "rarely come singly." At the Middle Barrier Depot, they again found a shortage of oil. "With most rigid economy it can scarce carry us to the next depôt (71 miles away)." The weather changed too, the blue skies clouding over, dark and forbidding as the temperature hovered at −40°C, and, worst of all, Oates announced, to his companions' horror, that his feet were in a bad state.

"Titus Oates," Scott wrote, "disclosed his feet, the toes showing very bad indeed, evidently bitten by the late temperatures." Since Oates had first commented in his diary, a few days after reaching the Pole, that one of his toes was black, eight weeks had passed, during which neither he nor any of the others had ever commented on him limping, nor even that his toes were becoming worse. Nonetheless, Oates must have suffered the pains of hell every time his feet thawed out in the comparative warmth of his sleeping bag.

In 1993, I suffered the same problem, except that in my case, also from the Pole and down the Beardmore, only four of my toes were badly bitten, not all ten. Mike Stroud wrote, when we reached the barrier, "[Ran] could no longer bear the torment without reaction. The swelling on the right foot was now punctured by a deep hole, red, angry, inflamed with pus, and the black and swollen toes of both feet were demarcated by a vivid red line at the base where good tissue fought against the infection. The stench of rotting flesh was added to our already evil body odours."

Oates now took one and a half hours to fit his frostbitten, hypersensitive feet into his frozen *finnesko* in the mornings, valuable time lost to progress.

Wilson slit these hide boots apart to help ease the pain. If my 1993 Antarctic experience taught me a new meaning for the word "cold," it did likewise with "pain." I realized how lucky I had been for fifty years of experiencing comparatively little pain. Broken bones and teeth, torn-off digits, frostbite, and chronic kidney stones had seemed unpleasant at the time. But, those nights in Antarctica, I knew real pain for the first time.

Oates somehow managed to stay harnessed to the sledge and to keep pulling. On March 3, they did ten miles a day, then a little over nine miles on March 4, despite the unremittingly cold temperatures, the ever-greater drag of the snow crust, and the adverse winds. Scott wrote: "We are in a *very* queer street since there is no doubt we cannot do the extra marches and feel the cold horribly." Again: "the wind at strongest, (and from the best quarter), powerless to move the sledge. When the light is good it is easy to see the reason. The surface, lately a very good hard one, is coated with a thin layer of woolly crystals, formed by radiation no doubt. These are too firmly fixed to be removed by the wind and cause impossible friction on the runners. God help us, we can't keep up this pulling, that is certain. Amongst ourselves we are unendingly cheerful, but what each man feels in his heart I can only guess."

The absence of the once-powerful sledger Taff Evans made no difference to the fact that, compared with the time taken by the last two sledge teams to cross the barrier, Cherry-Garrard's and Teddy Evans's groups, Scott's once-vaunted team was advancing like snails. The cause was not the thirty-five pounds of rock samples, nor the pony meat they had taken onboard, but purely the difference in surface conditions.

Teddy Evans's team had but three men to pull their load, yet they had kept up a pace that would have seen Scott safely through to One Ton Depot. And that was so despite Evans's scurvy attack. Even when Crean and Lashly were dragging Evans along on the sledge, they still managed ten miles a day. What ailed Scott's men, their strength assured by ample rations and replenishment vitamin C from the pony meat, was not their own lack of pulling power but the crucial effect of the colder temperatures on the snow as each day passed.

In the immediate vicinity of the coast, where barrier met land, the surface was bad for all the groups whatever the temperature, but once clear of land, the sandy crystal surface caused by the cold grasped and clung only to Scott's runners, for he had come to the barrier a little too late to cope with a rogue year.

The best climbers in the world have died on Everest because, despite their skill, they have had to make their ascent during the brief annual climbing season and, if a severe storm strikes, they will die no matter how good their plan. To have a foolproof plan in such circumstances involves planning not to make the attempt at all. If no ship ever left port to cross an ocean for fear of the unseasonable rogue monster wave, then no skipper would be blamed for a sinking. What is now certain, since the publication of *The Coldest March* by U.S. atmospheric scientist Dr. Susan Solomon in 2000, is that Scott's group was unlucky enough to experience the year of the rogue wave.

Scott's original 144-day plan was based on a meticulous weather chart compiled by expert meteorologist George Simpson, later the director of the Meteorological Office in the United Kingdom. Dr. Solomon stated that Simpson's estimate of the behavior of the barrier weather was "stunning in its accuracy." Charles Wright, who worked under George Simpson at Cape Evans, wrote that Scott's group had been anticipating warmer temperatures as they descended the glacier. He was certain that the unexpected cold weather was the main reason for their death, and he pointed out that Simpson's report (in 1926) confirmed that nobody could have foreseen such weather at that season.

"Simpson's three-volume treatise summarising the meteorological findings of the expedition was published after many years of painstaking analysis, long after Scott was dead. In completing the preface to his great labour in 1919, Simpson wrote: 'Over and over again as point after point was cleared up I have longed to be able to show the result to Captain Scott, for there was hardly a problem of Antarctic meteorology which we had not discussed together.'" But Simpson could not have predicted that extraordinary weather would strike in March 1912, at exactly the time when Scott's party had to make reasonable progress between the barrier depots in order to survive.

The freak weather began at the end of February in fits and starts and was recorded in Bowers's log until March 19. Minimum temperatures day after day were 40°–50° colder than those that Teddy Evans's returning group had experienced on the same route only a month before. The extreme cold froze the blood in fingers and toes and made every action painfully slow. Records now show that almost every daily temperature they logged was between 10° and 20° colder than in an average year. United States weather-recording machines along Scott's barrier route show that, over a fifteen-year period, only one year rivals the severity of the 1912 temperatures.

As the extreme cold set in, Scott's daily distances dropped farther and farther behind those of the other two returning parties, even of scurvy-ravaged Teddy Evans's. Once clear of the mountains and out on the open barrier, Scott had expected a following wind to fill the sledge sail. This had worked well for the other two returning groups, as it had for Shackleton in 1908. But the unseasonal cold snap killed the expected southerly winds. One weather-related problem added fatally to another: the frozen limbs, the painfully slow time taken to make and break camp, the lack of wind, and the killer factor of the snow condition. Scott wrote: "Not the least glide in the world," and, "on this surface we know we cannot equal half our old marches, and that for that effort we expend nearly double the energy." The loose new snow crystals that formed as the temperatures fell acted as a brake on the sledge runners, just as they had on the high plateau a few weeks earlier and just as they do in today's scientific studies of the physical properties of snow.

What Scott's men would have achieved in a normal year, indeed, in nine out of any ten years, on the barrier is not difficult to calculate. Oates would have carried on a great deal farther than he did, certainly well beyond One Ton, until needing to be pulled (as Teddy Evans was) on a sledge. The toes and feet of Scott and Wilson would not have frozen at standard temperatures, possessing new *finnesko* as they did. Even without southerly winds, they would have continued to achieve the fifteen miles per day average they were previously managing and which had been performed by the other two groups at that stage. At such a rate, they would have reached One Ton on March 4 when Cherry-Garrard was there. He did not leave until March 10. For the last 130 miles to Hut Point, an average of only six miles per day would have seen them safely home.

The new meteorological records demonstrate unarguably why Scott could not in 1912 have foreseen such exceptional weather. It had seemed perfectly safe to Simpson to travel on the barrier until the end of March. American scientists in the 1990s have established beyond a doubt that

March 1912 saw abnormally cold and unrelenting temperatures on the barrier at exactly the time and place where Scott's men slowed and died. For three straight weeks, temperatures were 10°C below average, conditions that have been repeated only once in the last thirty-eight years.

The response of the ignorant critic who has never mounted an expedition is: "Oh, but surely he should have expected the worst and not been surprised by a bad winter." I have planned expeditions in hot and cold deserts based on likely weather behavior patterns, but always hoping to avoid the catastrophe of a hurricane, major sandstorm, or flood. Scott was hit by just such a freak event, before which his team's ongoing progress was at a rate that would have taken them safely home.

On March 3, 103 miles to the north of Scott, Cherry-Garrard and Gerof reached One Ton Depot and made camp. Two days later, not knowing this, Scott wrote of Oates's condition:

> Our fuel dreadfully low and the poor Soldier nearly done. It is
> pathetic enough because we can do nothing for him; more hot
> food might do a little, but only a little, I fear. We none of us
> expected these terribly low temperatures, and of the rest of us
> Wilson is feeling them most; mainly, I fear, from his self-
> sacrificing devotion in doctoring Oates' feet. We cannot help each
> other, each has enough to do to take care of himself. We get cold
> on the march when the trudging is heavy, and the wind pierces our
> worn garments. The others, all of them, are unendingly cheerful
> when in the tent. We mean to see the game through with a proper
> spirit, but it's tough work to be pulling harder than we ever pulled
> in our lives for long hours, and to feel that the progress is so slow.
> One can only say "God help us!" and plod on our weary way,
> cold and very miserable, though outwardly cheerful. We talk of all
> sorts of subjects in the tent, not much of food now, since we
> decided to take the risk of running a full ration. We simply
> couldn't go hungry at this time.

Through the next two dark and pain-filled days, Oates somehow kept his place at the traces and the group managed nine and a half and then six and a half miles, which took them to within eighty miles of Cherry-Garrard, Gerof, the dogs, and plentiful supplies of food and fuel. On March 6, with Oates still man-hauling and six and a half miles done, Scott wrote: "If we were all fit I should have hopes of getting through, but the poor Soldier has become a terrible hindrance, though he does his utmost and suffers much, I fear." The next morning, Scott added: "One of Oates' feet *very* bad this morning; he is wonderfully brave. We still talk of what we will do together at home . . . One feels that for poor Oates the crisis is near, but none of us are improving . . . We are only kept going by good food . . . I should like to keep the track to the end."

Only six and a half miles were achieved on March 7, the day that, from the Hobart cable head, Amundsen announced his triumph to the world.

On March 6, Scott wrote: "Poor Oates is unable to pull, sits on the sledge when we are track-searching . . . He makes no complaint, but his spirits only come up in spurts now, and he grows more silent in the tent." Then, on March 8, a significant entry. "Have to wait in night foot gear for nearly an hour before I start changing, and then am generally first to be ready. *Wilson's feet giving trouble now*, but this mainly because he gives so much help to others." That lunchtime they camped only eight and a half miles away from Mount Hooper Depot, the last provisions cache before One Ton Depot, past the barrier's midpoint and a place where they could reasonably expect the dog teams to be waiting, or at least for them to have stocked supplies.

In London, Kathleen Scott was uneasy after hearing Amundsen's victory news. Her little son, Peter, said to her, "Amundsen and Daddy both got to the Pole. Daddy's stopped working now." Kathleen wrote that she was lonely, that the young people didn't care and the old people didn't feel. When Nansen heard the news, he was, as his personal diary clearly shows, anything but happy but, in public, he praised and congratulated Amundsen.

In Antarctica, as their likely plight became more apparent, Scott and his companions must have thought increasingly of their only hope of salvation from Cape Evans: the dog teams. On March 7, Scott wrote: "We hope against hope that the dogs have been to Mt. Hooper; then we might pull through. If there is a shortage of oil again we can have little hope." On March 10, after reaching that depot, Scott wrote: "Oates' foot worse. He has rare pluck and must know that he can never get through. He asked Wilson if he had a chance this morning, and of course Bill had to say he didn't know. In point of fact he has none. Apart from him, if he went under now, I doubt whether we could get through. With great care we might have a dog's chance, but no more . . . Poor Titus is the greatest handicap . . . Poor chap! it is too pathetic to watch him: one cannot but try to cheer him up."

The reason for Scott's pessimism in this entry was the discovery at the Mount Hooper Depot that the dogs had never arrived there. Not only did the cache show no signs of restocking, but even the standard provisions that did await them were less than expected. In such circumstances, I would have felt close to despair. The provisions left by the previous return groups were less than the amount planned by Bowers, either due to others having taken more than their share of the provisions, or due to further seepage. Scott noted bleakly: "Shortage on our allowance all round. I don't know that anyone is to blame. The dogs which would have been our salvation have evidently failed. Meares had a bad trip home I suppose . . . It's a miserable jumble."

There are two ways of looking at this "miserable jumble." One is that Scott was entirely to blame for not anticipating correctly every eventuality over the entire 1,600-mile journey. The other is that he had to make his plans using likely estimates for his own and three other separate groups as best he could and it only needed a touch of bad luck to throw out of kilter whatever plans he made. Cherry-Garrard summed up Scott's dilemma. "To estimate even approximately at what date a party will reach a given point after a journey of this length when the weather conditions are always uncertain and the number of travelling days unknown, was a most difficult task . . . A week one way or the other was certainly not a large margin. A couple of blizzards might make this much difference."

Scott's original 144-day plan was rightly pessimistic and allowed for surplus provisions to cope with slow progress. The person at Cape Evans responsible for whatever relief Scott might eventually need was Atkinson, because his senior, Teddy Evans, was by then nearly dead with scurvy. Atkinson had originally expected Scott's return date to be at the end of March, or even early April. Scott's original plan, like all the best-laid plans of mice and men, was surely liable to alter and Atkinson had received Scott's clear last set of orders from Teddy Evans, which naturally contradicted the original plans. Atkinson was a surgeon in the Royal Navy. He was a sensible, thinking man, not an automaton. He did not obey orders that made no sense, nor did the scientists with him at Cape Evans.

Scott had clearly stated his preference that the dogs should be used as little as possible so that they could be conserved for the next year's sledging program. But nobody in their right mind would use this as a pretext for not using the dogs if lives were at risk and a rescue team was needed. Over the years to come, however, individuals accused of not doing enough to save Scott's men did just that to protect their own reputations.

What orders did Atkinson give Cherry-Garrard? They were verbal and only Cherry-Garrard ever wrote them down. He did so years later, by which time he was already feeling unfairly blamed for not doing enough to save Scott's men, including his great friends Wilson and Bowers. There is a possibility that Cherry-Garrard may have interpreted his orders from Atkinson in a way that would excuse his decision to wait at One Ton Depot rather than to venture on farther south to Mount Hooper Depot or beyond. He remembered his orders as requiring him "To travel to One Ton Depot as fast as possible and leave the food there." The next order was: "If Scott had not arrived at One Ton Depot before me I was to judge what to do." Cherry-Garrard then added two further points, which are not orders per se but were clearly meant as guidance by Atkinson to help him judge what to do. One point was that "Scott was not in any way dependent on the dogs for his return," the other that he had given "particular instructions that the dogs were not to be risked in view of the sledging plans for next season."

When Cherry-Garrard and Gerof arrived at One Ton Depot on March 3, with all the dogs in good condition, they unloaded the Pole party's stores and waited there as long as Cherry-Garrard felt they sensibly could. Gerof was sick, dog food was strictly limited, and for four days the weather remained too bad to travel. "On the two remaining days I could have run a day farther south and back again, with the possibility of missing the party on the way. I decided to remain at the Depot where we were certain to meet."

Although there was no spare dog food, Cherry-Garrard could have gone southward along the line of cairns to the Mid-Barrier Depot (as Scott's last and so most pertinent message, via Teddy Evans, had clearly requested). The potential to do this lay in Cherry-Garrard's ability to kill dogs for dog meat, but he chose not to do so on the grounds that, as far as he knew, Scott had plenty of provisions and was probably still ahead of schedule. After all, Teddy Evans had last seen Scott at 87° 32' S, ahead of schedule and going strongly for the Pole. Also, Scott had made clear his wishes to retain the dogs for future work. Cherry-Garrard wrote: "My orders on this point were perfectly explicit; I saw no reason for disobeying them." The "orders is orders" syndrome.

It might be argued that Cherry-Garrard was overcomplacent about Scott's status, since he was witnessing the extreme temperatures of the barrier that autumn and knew they were far lower than those predicted by Simpson, upon which Scott's travel plan was based. But, as revealed by Cherry-Garrard's physical collapse upon his return to Hut Point, he was himself in a feeble state, having participated in the polar support group to the upper reaches of the Beardmore and other demanding journeys. His inner instincts would, subconsciously at least, have warned him against further southerly travel in those inhuman conditions. And his only companion, the dog-aware Gerof, was showing signs of an alarming illness, including semiparalysis. Yet was not Cherry-Garrard's duty to do all he could, using his own initiative, to help Scott's team? He could go farther by killing some of his dogs.

After all, Cherry-Garrard's inner voice must surely have nagged, whether they had reached the Pole or not, one of Scott's team might have suffered an injury, causing delay to the others, who would thus need extra supplies at least as far back as the mid-barrier depot. So, kill a dog or two and go on south for a few days? A risk worth taking, surely, just in case his good friends were in trouble? Scott's orders regarding the retention of dogs for the "next season's sledging programme" were made when he planned to make another Pole attempt if the first one failed. He would also need dogs for various scientific journeys, but he was expecting new dogs and mules on *Terra Nova* before then. Cherry-Garrard could well have argued that, since there was a good chance anyway that no second Pole attempt would be needed, he could clearly kill some of his dogs to give all possible help in case Scott's men were in trouble.

Cherry-Garrard did, after all, appreciate that Scott's own orders were not written in stone. He wrote: "In this sort of life orders have to be elastic: and Scott's were. They were complicated, elastic and excellent."

Long after Scott's death, the men who might have been able to save him lived on and many reached positions of prominence. All of them, naturally, presented their memories of Scott's demise and the reasons for it from a personal point of view. Scott's defense relied only on those letters and diaries he wrote as he died slowly and horribly with the bodies of his close friends lying frozen beside him.

Cecil Meares left Antarctica not knowing whether or not the Pole team might sorely need his expertise with dogs. If I had been him, when he later heard of Scott's end, I would have felt misgivings about my early departure. Perhaps he did, for he felt the need for self-justification and, together with Oates's mother, the need to find fault with Scott. Cherry-Garrard could have gone looking for Scott beyond One Ton Depot without the need to kill dogs if Meares had, as Scott had asked, made a journey to lay out dog food at One Ton.

Why didn't he? Because, it is said by Scott critics, he had been made to take his dogs onto the Beardmore, 140 miles farther than originally planned, and so had returned to base too late to make the dog-food journey. This is questionable, for he was back at base by January 5, and, even allowing a two-week rest, he could have set out to One Ton by January 20. This would have given him plenty of time to do a round-trip to One Ton and still be back at base by mid-February, and able to catch the ship.

So was Meares to blame, or Atkinson or Cherry-Garrard in any way? Or should we revert to the standard response . . . Scott, as leader, was at fault whatever the various factors? One viewpoint to consider must surely be that of Cherry-Garrard, biased though it may be, for he spent forty years worrying about the issue.

Why did Cherry-Garrard feel he should not kill dogs and carry on south for a few days using his initiative? He may have known he was dangerously weak. His journal comments: "A few days after reaching Hut Point, I collapsed and was very ill." He was very reliant on Gerof, the Russian dog driver, of whom he wrote: "He went so far as to say his right side was useless." Later, back at Hut Point, he wrote: "I get back to Hut Point and save

Demitri's life." But then he adds: "Demitri immediately recovers. Atkinson considered he had been malingering." A year later, Cherry-Garrard added: "On our arrival in New Zealand Demitri stated to the Press that he had wished to go on from One Ton but that I had prevented him." After the Second World War, when Cherry-Garrard was mentally unstable, he wrote, as late as 1948: "Now I know that Scott's taking on the dogs 300 extra miles . . . 3 extra weeks made it impossible that his original order could be carried out." But he could have known that from Scott's clearly worded order to Simpson sent back with Bernard Day in 1912.

Some *Terra Nova* survivors believed that Meares had been ready at Cape Evans to take his dogs to resupply One Ton as ordered when he had seen the ship arrive in the bay and so stayed at base. The "ship" turned out to be a mirage. In 1938, Cherry-Garrard put this to Simpson, who replied: "That's quite possible . . . I would not altogether blame Meares; he wanted to get home and did not want to miss the ship. And of course there was no fear of a disaster then." Cherry-Garrard noted:

> I am afraid it is becoming clear that the not laying of this depot by Meares was more or less deliberate. I have always had a feeling that Meares let the whole show down in some rather indefinite way: I have also had the feeling that he got off very lightly . . .
>
> Meares proved himself a coward when he refused to go down the crevasse which Scott told him to do on the Depot Journey. Some of Scott's decisions not to take dogs to the Pole may have been really that he knows that Meares was not much good!
>
> As we now know he [Meares] took some of the food of the 3 returning parties from the depots or depot. Then, not having taken out the most urgent rations, which was done by a manhauling party, he failed to take out anything else, including the dog food.

Years later, Charles Wright was clear that Meares should have been sent and not Cherry-Garrard. Meares and Gerof had arrived back at base with the dogs on January 5, so they were well rested when Cherry-Garrard set out, despite their staying with Scott for 140 miles farther than was originally planned. There are many individuals involved with what Scott termed a "miserable jumble," and all have produced their own versions of what prompted their action or inaction at the time. Scott did not apportion human blame nor did he accept it. He identified instead a series of unpredictable mishaps, the chief of which was the freak weather that defied Simpson's meticulously worked-out predictions.

On March 10, the last day of Cherry-Garrard's vigil at One Ton, a blizzard struck Scott's men and forced them to camp after traveling only a few hundred yards. Oates still hauled away on his half-dead feet. If a miracle had whisked him away to Britain that very day, his feet would have been amputated but his legs probably saved. Scott wrote: "Titus Oates is very near the end, one feels. What we or he will do, God only knows. We discussed the matter after breakfast; he is a brave fine fellow and understands the situation, but he practically asked for advice. Nothing could be said but to urge him to march as long as he could."

When the blizzard cleared on the eleventh, they marched nearly six miles, a mileage below the rate that might avoid death for them all. Oates still did his bit in the traces at −38°C, but that day his fingers froze to a condition of uselessness, at which point, like Taff Evans before him, he became a true liability to the others. He was now more burdensome than the thirty-five pounds of rock samples, for they did not use up provisions or cause hours of delay. That day, Bowers decided he could no longer make the great effort required to continue the meticulous meteorological records he had kept since the start of the expedition. Wilson's physical state had deteriorated to the point where, at the end of the day, he could not bend down to detach his ski bindings. On the twelfth, Oates was "not pulling much," but they again managed seven miles with "the cold intense . . . Not a breath of favourable wind."

Scott worked out that, with travel hours cut down by the long delays spent nursing Oates, fingerless for dressing or even feeding himself, they could at best make six miles per day and they had food for six days; so they might just manage thirty-six miles. One Ton Depot was forty-eight miles away. An overlap of only twelve miles without provisions sounds little enough, but, in such conditions, it would be likely to kill the four men.

At this stage, even the tightest-lipped Briton might have been excused for contemplating available options for a more dignified exit. To wait in the tent for a lingering death might take many nightmare days and nights, watching one another perish inch by inch, but always with the hope, however faint, of the approaching howl of dogs sent out from Cape Evans. Death on the trail, and they *say* death is painless in the snow, might sound beguiling to those who have not tried it, but I for one would choose it as a very last resort.

Each of Scott's sledging groups carried in their medical box enough opiate tablets to provide each man with a quick way out should life become unbearable. Scott wrote: "I practically ordered Wilson to hand over the means of ending our troubles to us so that any one of us may know how to do so. Wilson had no choice between doing so and our ransacking the medicine case. We have 30 opium tabloids apiece and he is left with a tube of morphine."

On March 13, they woke to find a strong wind blowing from the north with a temperature close to −40°C, a windchill factor of over −90°C. They sensibly stayed in their tent most of the day, each with the means to die in his pocket. For men who preferred to defecate in a blizzard *outside* the tent, rather than face embarrassment within, each must have decided they would sooner swallow and die out in the snow rather than subject their comrades, cheek by jowl, to their death throes. The first person to contemplate such thoughts must surely have been Oates, whose world was, and long had been, filled not with mere pain but with agony such as few people will ever experience.

A surge of renewed hope arrived on March 14, along with a long-awaited southerly breeze, such as should have predominated on that part of the barrier. God knows how they prepared Oates even to don his outdoor gear, or how they broke camp and stowed their sledge, but they did, and at −42°C at noon, they made good another few miles before the wind veered round and forced them to camp. Wilson was in a bad way, so Scott and Bowers erected the tent by themselves. Inside the tent, Scott, the only diarist, wrote: "Truly awful outside the tent. Must fight it out to the last biscuit." He was obviously not contemplating his opium, but what were the others' thoughts on suicide?

Wilson, a man of the strictest moral principles, was strongly against something that was contrary to the Ten Commandments, which accounts for his reluctance to hand out the opium. In the early stages of the *Terra Nova* expedition, he had told Taylor, who asked, "What are we to do if one of the party breaks his leg?," that "you will have to make a more or less permanent camp . . . and wait there until you are relieved, or until the leg is usable again." But he had changed his philosophy on the ethics of such sledging dilemmas over the years. A decade before, after the *Discovery* voyage, Wilson had told a journalist that, according to an old code of honor among polar explorers, anyone who fell sick on a journey and so caused a grave risk to his companions should "walk out."

Bowers was perhaps the most straightforward of the group, as morally bound as Wilson and intensely loyal. He had said he was "Scott's man to the last," and he clearly meant it. No opium for Bowers. Yet he had, during the darkest days of the Crozier winter journey, discussed the matter with Cherry-Garrard, who later wrote: "[Bowers] had a scheme of doing himself in with a pick-axe if necessity arose, though how he could have accomplished it I don't know: or, as he said, there might be a crevasse and at any rate there was the medical case. I was horrified at the time: I had never faced the thing out with myself like that." Cherry-Garrard did, however, later resolve his own philosophy on the subject, for he wrote: "if you break your leg on the Beardmore you must consider the most expedient way of committing suicide, both for your own sake and that of your companions."

Ponting later wrote of the same question he had put to Oates at Cape Evans in 1911. What should a man do if injured and a burden to his mates? Oates had emphatically replied that a pistol ought to be carried and that "if anyone breaks down he should have the privilege of using it."

Did Scott feel that Oates should take his opium to help the others stand a faint chance of survival? If so, when did Scott start to feel that way? There is absolutely no proof one way or the other of Scott's thoughts on the topic and only he could have known what conflicting thoughts and hopes went through his mind in those long, desperate days and nights of suffering, of despair, then hope, and again further despair. It has been suggested that from the very moment Scott found the Norwegian flag at the Pole, his morale plummeted and he contemplated a glorious suicide rather than a glum return. Such conjecture does not fit with Scott's character or with any of the known facts. Furthermore, if he intended suicide, why continue to push himself and his men to the limit on the homeward journey?

Bowers wrote to his mother: "Our sick companions have delayed us till too late in the season which has made us very short of fuel and we are now out of food as well." He clearly believed that, had Taff and Oates plunged into crevasses rather than lingered on, the survivors might have made it. But this observation, shared elsewhere by Scott, does not constitute a philosophical statement on suicide.

After March 14, Scott began to make his diary entries only intermittently and with confused dates. There is nothing written on the fifteenth, but for March 16 or 17 Scott noted:

> Lost track of dates . . . the day before yesterday, poor Titus
> Oates said he couldn't go on; he proposed we should leave him in
> his sleeping-bag. That we could not do, and we induced him to
> come on, on the afternoon march . . . he struggled on and we
> made a few miles. At night he was worse and we knew the end
> had come . . . He slept through the night before last, hoping not to
> wake; but he woke in the morning—yesterday. It was blowing a
> blizzard. He said, "I am just going outside and may be some time."
> He went out into the blizzard and we have not seen him since.

That was on March 16. Gran, who later searched for Oates's body, was subsequently to recount his own hypothesis of what happened: "That day a terrible storm ensued. The Barrier stood boiling and the temperature was around −40°C. In the evening Oates crawled out of his sleeping-bag and used his remaining strength to force himself out of the tent door. Scott let him take this desperate step. To stop Oates would have been to engage in torture, and commit an inconsiderate action toward Wilson and Bowers."

Oates left his split *finnesko* behind. With useless fingers, he would have been unable to untie the lashings of the door funnel or "force himself out of the tent door." Somebody must have done it for him. With a blizzard outside, the bunched up "door" material would have been carefully lashed and the ties frozen into a hard knot, difficult enough to untie with fit fingers. Once Oates was outside, those inside would have tied the door back up instantly to exclude blown snow and the loss of any warmth that might be trapped within the tent.

In the blast of the blizzard, seeing nothing, smelling nothing, and hearing only the wind roar, Oates would not have been able to complete the simplest of acts with his "frozen meat" hands, with or without mittens. Even the taking of opium tablets from pocket to mouth would have been impossible. If he did take his tablets, he must have done so in the tent, unnoticed, or at least unremarked on, by the others. He may have wished to undo his clothing to die more quickly but even that would have been beyond the power of his fingers. Within the space of ten minutes, it is likely that his physical sufferings would have died away as nerve endings froze from the extremities to the core. Thought processes too would have fallen fast into oblivion as the mind and the spirit of Titus Oates left Antarctica, bound perhaps for the stables of Gestingthorpe, in Essex. He was thirty-two years old.

Not long before he left the tent, Oates turned to the man who had cared for him so well for so long, Wilson, and asked him to give his diary to his mother; also, when Wilson could, to assure her that her son had loved her to the last. Wilson wrote to Mrs. Oates, in his diary, but by way of a letter.

This is a sad ending to our undertaking. Your son died a very noble death, God knows. I have never seen or heard of such courage as he showed from first to last with his feet both badly frostbitten—never a word of complaint or of the pain. He was a great example. Dear Mrs Oates, he asked me at the end, to see you and give you this diary of his—You, he told me, are the only woman he has ever loved.

Scott also wrote a letter to Mrs. Oates, praising her son's great qualities. In his diary, he noted: "We knew that poor Oates was walking to his death . . . the act of a brave man . . . we all hope to meet the end with a similar spirit, and assuredly the end is not far."

Two hours after Oates had left the tent, they roused themselves, for the wind must have dropped, and they toiled a few more tortuous miles, carrying Oates's sleeping bag and *finnesko* to the cairns that marked the next pony-camp site. Here they left them, as well as their camera and theodolite, now useless, unlike the thirty-five pounds of rock samples that were considered to be of great value, especially by their collector Wilson. On March 18, the three men hauled their load to within twenty-one miles of One Ton, but during the day Scott lost all feeling in three or four of the toes of his right foot. Self-critical, as usual, he put this down to neglect, but it did not stop the group doing a fine march of ten miles the following day, reaching to within eleven miles of One Ton when stopped by another blizzard. Without the delaying factor of Oates, their distance traveled had increased.

Bowers wrote to his mother on or about March 22: "I am still strong and hope to reach this one [the depot] with Dr. Wilson and get the food and fuel necessary for our lives. God alone knows what will be the outcome of the 22 miles march . . . but my trust is still in Him and in the abounding Grace of my Lord and Saviour whom you brought me up to trust in and who has been my stay through life . . . There will be no shame however and you will know that I have struggled to the end."

Wilson wrote to his wife on about March 22 also. "Birdie and I are going to try and reach the Depôt 11 miles north of us and return to this tent where Captain Scott is lying with a frozen foot . . . I shall simply fall and go to sleep in the snow . . . All is for the best to those that love God, and oh, my Ory, we have both loved Him with all our lives . . . We have struggled to the end and we have nothing to regret. Our whole journey record is clean . . . The Barrier has beaten us—though we got to the Pole."

The plan for this two-man foray, described in Scott's diary on March 21 as a "forlorn hope," was short-lived and, a day later, Scott wrote: "Blizzard as bad as ever—Wilson and Bowers unable to start—to-morrow last chance—no fuel and only one or two of food left—must be near the end. Have decided it shall be natural—we shall march for the depôt with or without our effects and die in our tracks." At this point, all three men were planning to make a dash for the depot.

There is no clue at all as to why they made and then abandoned these two plans, but in such a position, wild ideas chase one another through your head. Just when one seems best, the weather outside the tent changes and another course of action seems preferable. With no fuel left on March 21, for the first time and with extreme low temperatures everywhere except inside their sleeping bags, they must all have realized they could not make another day's sledging. There was nothing to drink save snow, which further depleted their remaining body-core warmth. They had reached that point where their ability to haul their laden sledge for the twelve hours minimum to reach One Ton was no longer viable.

Wilson, or more likely Bowers, who was clearly stronger than Wilson, probably suggested trying for the depot with the sledge empty apart from their sleeping bags. The tent was their heaviest item. Scott, who could not go fast with his dead foot, could stay in the tent while they tried to race the sledge to the depot, collect food and fuel, and race back. Scott would indeed have felt this a "forlorn" plan, but did not hold out against it. The two men then dashed off their farewell letters to their loved ones while waiting for the wind to die.

But the wind did not die, and so Wilson and Bowers very sensibly stayed put. Both had already recognized in their letters that a tentless journey in such conditions would likely prove a suicide mission. Wilson, six days before, had been too weak to help Scott and Bowers erect the tent and found it difficult even to undo his own skis. On March 21 or 22, he wrote to his parents that, "two of the 5 of us are already dead and we three are nearly done up." Wilson's spirit may have been willing to try for One Ton but his physical state would clearly have rendered such an effort unlikely to succeed.

Nonetheless, an attempted foray to One Ton by Bowers alone might have proved worthwhile in principle, since the dog teams might have been waiting there, intending to go no farther, as Cherry-Garrard had been twelve days earlier. The wind blew constantly from the west-southwest, so their sail would not help. And this wind continued to blow for several more days. While it blew, light ski and sledge tracks could quickly disappear overnight, so Bowers and Wilson both stayed in their bags. If they were all going to die, they might as well die together. If they died outside, as Oates had, with the tent on their sledge, nobody would find their bodies and nobody would ever know if they had reached the Pole.

Scott's diary comment of March 22 (or 23), that all three of them would go on to the depot together and die on the trail, thus came to nothing and from that day on they would have eaten nothing and slaked their thirst only with snow melted in their mouths. Imperceptibly, inside their bags, life would have ebbed away.

On March 27, Atkinson and Keohane man-hauled out onto the barrier in a last-ditch attempt to locate the Pole party. They gave up on March 30 and turned back to spend another winter at Cape Evans. They were both fit and healthy men with fresh equipment and, most important, unhindered by severely frost-damaged fingers or toes, yet they could not last more than thirty-five miles on the barrier.

There is no question in my mind, after thirty years, on and off, of travel in polar blizzards, that neither Bowers nor Wilson (with or without Scott) would have survived the prevailing conditions for more than a few hours without a tent during the likely period of the blizzard, March 21–23. So they lay in their sleeping bags with only their own ever-decreasing body heat to keep them alive. Without food or fuel, they would weaken rapidly, so that by the time the wind lessened to what Scott, on March 29, described merely as "a continuous gale," they would have been too frail to set out.

Ever since reaching the barrier a month earlier, the fuel shortage had meant drinking less than was advisable, and dehydration has a seriously weakening effect that is cumulative. The longer you lie in a freezing tent listening to the wind outside, the more difficult it can be to rouse yourself to face the elements, even to sit up in your bag, let alone to struggle with the door lashings that bring down showers of frost shavings from the tent lining and set you biting your lips to prevent you screaming as your raw-ended fingers touch the material and blood stirs in your damaged feet.

There is no evidence that the three men ever looked outside the tent again after March 23. They had no need to defecate, for they would by then be starving and dehydrated.

If Bowers had wished to continue alone, and had been strong enough, he would have done so. He was loyal to Scott, but he was every bit his own man. Just as Crean skied on alone to save Teddy Evans, so too would Bowers, had he believed there was the faintest chance of saving Scott and Wilson. The previous year, when adrift on the floes, Bowers had ignored Scott's pleas to leave the ponies and save himself. Only when he could see that there was no hope for the ponies did he obey orders and seek safety.

There is also no evidence to suggest that either Bowers or Wilson stayed in the tent owing merely to some self-sacrificing loyalty to Scott, nor that he would have wanted them to. All that is known is that the three men died to-

gether in their tent without heat, food, or water. Scott's last diary entry was
on what he believed to be March 29, at which time his thinking was still
crystal clear and his writing rock solid.

> Every day we have been ready to start for our depôt 11 *miles*
> away, but outside the door of our tent it remains a scene of
> whirling drift. I do not think we can hope for any better things
> now. We shall stick it out to the end, but we are getting weaker, of
> course, and the end cannot be far. It seems a pity, but I do not
> think I can write more. R. Scott

In all his expedition diaries, Scott often mixed "I" with "we" when referring only to himself, so this hardly serves as a clue as to whether, on
March 29, he was alone or not. Either way, he was the last to be keeping a
diary.

That Scott should have had the mind and the strength to think and write
clearly for at least six or seven days in such circumstances, after all food and
heat were finished, shows, above all, to repeat Cherry-Garrard's words, "the
immense shove of the man." His last written words reflect his ongoing
worry that he was leaving the dependents of the expedition's dead without
means. "Last entry. For God's sake look after our people."

He was clear in his own mind that the disaster, which killed his companions and was about to kill him, was his fault because the expedition was
his project. In a letter to Wilson's widow, he wrote that her husband had expressed "never a word of blame to me for leading him into this mess." All
his adult life, Scott had worried about his ongoing ability to earn enough to
keep his mother, sisters, and, more recently, his wife and son living well.
Now he felt responsible too for the dependents of "our people." He did not
have a rock-solid religious faith like Bowers and Wilson, but he seems to
have believed more strongly than your average agnostic that there was a
God, whom he invoked in his last plea for the care of those left behind.

The person most likely to know exactly why the three men died was the
naval surgeon Atkinson, who eight months later found their bodies. After
looking for telltale outward signs of scurvy, he stated unequivocally that

none of the bodies showed visible evidence. "Ah," say the Scott detractors, "but he would say that, wouldn't he, in order to save the expedition's good name!" At the time, scurvy was the sign of a badly managed voyage.

If Atkinson's official report is discounted as inaccurate by those determined that scurvy killed Scott's men, how do they account for the fact that Wilson, the most scrupulously honest man on God's earth, never once described symptoms of scurvy in any of the five men before or after the Pole? On the *Discovery* expedition, Wilson noted each and every scurvy symptom in Scott, Shackleton, and himself.

"But," say those who believe that scurvy killed Scott's men, "Teddy Evans had it, so why not the others?" Evans himself explained that apparent anomaly by pointing out that for seven weeks prior to the team's departure from Cape Evans, he had been involved in survey work and depot-laying trips, during which he ate sledge rations, whereas the others had, at base, eaten fresh meat daily.

Back in England, old *Discovery* hands corresponded about the *Terra Nova* expedition. They remembered Scott, Wilson, and Shackleton returning from their far shorter southern journey raddled by scurvy. "I would bet one hundred to one," Skelton wrote to Hodgson, "on the scurvy business being the primary cause." Scurvy was an easy answer but, on the evidence, the wrong one. Evans had completed four hundred more miles of man-hauling than the men of the Pole group. He also stated clearly that Scott, Wilson, and Bowers had died of "exposure and weakness."

Charles Wright, who observed the bodies, was convinced that they had perished from the twin causes of starvation and the cold. Roald Amundsen, studying Scott's expedition over a year later, wrote: "Scott and his companions died on the way back from the Pole, not because they were broken by our earlier arrival, but on account of hunger, because they were not in a position to obtain sufficient food."

Nutritionists have for many years tried to find out if Scott's rations may have weakened his men. The results of Mike Stroud's analysis of our 1993 man-haul experience show that we did not consume enough calories and that we were on a starvation diet, as were Scott's men. Both we and they would have taken more food if we could have, but simple logistics prevented us from doing so. Mike summarized his opinion of Scott's rations as vitamin deficient, containing too much protein and, like ours, energy inadequate. His rations, more substantial than those of Shackleton in 1908, would nonetheless have been more adequate for the journey had he not run into freak weather conditions on the barrier.

One known deficiency in the summit rations (not recognized at the time) resulted from the daily loss of four hundred calories by the altitude difference between the plateau and sea level, where the Crozier ration trials took place. Another suspect was vitamin deficiency. In Scott's day, neither he nor anyone else understood the science of vitamins. Unfortunately for him, vitamins were discovered soon after his death and a generation of specialists seized upon Scott to demonstrate their newborn vitamin-deficiency theories without full access to the *Terra Nova* facts. Successive generations then grew up believing that scurvy or other vitamin deficiencies killed Scott.

Once Scott's men reached the base of the Beardmore, having achieved excellent distances to that point (Taff Evans's delay notwithstanding), they consumed plenty of undercooked pony meat containing enough vitamins B and C to have saved them from scurvy or pellagra, another likely vitamin-deficiency disease. If the Pole team had traveled for four months without fresh meat, some of them may have then begun to suffer the first symptoms, but this did not happen. Food was only responsible for the death of Scott's men through its absence at the end. Every ounce of food, but for "a little sugar and a small bag of tea leaves," had been used up long before death came to the three men.

Did they die by their own hand through taking opium or morphine? Dr. Atkinson's report stated: "I can testify certainly that they all died natural deaths. This I can do on the facts. I don't think men ever died a nobler death." Cherry-Garrard was told in 1930 that, when the medical chest of Scott's group was investigated, "the morphia and opium tubes were found empty and that the hypodermic syringe was full." This would indicate that Wilson had not injected himself and that all the pills had been handed out to the individuals. Neither Wilson nor Bowers favored suicide, which they considered a mortal sin, and Scott's manner of death was by no means indicative of a peaceful opiate-inspired exit. When Gran saw Scott's body, he wrote: "It was a horrid sight . . . It was clear he had had a very hard last minutes. His skin was yellow, frostbites all over." Gran is here describing skin damage that must have occurred prior to death.

On March 18, Scott wrote: "We have the last *half* fill of oil in our primus and a very small quantity of spirit—this alone between us and thirst." Yet he was still alive and using his diary eleven days and nights later, since his last diary entry was dated March 29. Twelve letters he had written were found either on the floor of the tent beside him or within the body of his diary. Some of the letters were written at lunch stops during the days before the final camp; one was dated March 16, another March 24, but most have no date. For eight terrible days, almost as dark inside the frosted double lining of the drifted tent as during the eight sunless nights, anyone who survived lived on without food or liquid, heat or light.

Is it possible, without speculation, to learn anything of what happened between them in their living tomb before the last of them died?

When Scott wrote his letter to James Barrie over a number of hours, even days, the three men were all still alive. His words give a clue as to their interaction as they lay awaiting death. Far from considering that their mission had failed, they were rightly proud of their unique man-haul achievement. "We have done the greatest march ever made and come very near to great success . . . We are in a desperate state, feet frozen, etc. No fuel and a long way from food, but it would do your heart good to be in our tent, to hear our songs and the cheery conversation as to what we will do when we get to Hut Point. *Later*—We are very near the end, but have not and will not lose our good cheer."

Scott's letter to his wife was written in stages, at first at lunch stops when still traveling and, later, over the nine days in the tent. One isolated sentence in mid-letter reads: "You must understand that it is too cold to write much." In another letter, he notes: "Excuse writing: it is –40°F and has been for nigh a month." He talks about their son, Peter:

> *I had looked forward to helping you bring [Peter] up . . .*
> *Make him interested in natural history if you can . . . I must write*
> *a little letter for the boy if time can be found, to be read when he*
> *grows up. The inherited vice from my side of the family is*

indolence—above all he must guard, and you must guard him, against that. I had to force myself into being strenuous, as you know—had always an inclination to be idle. My father was idle and it brought much trouble.

He talks about Kathleen remarrying.

You know I cherish no sentimental rubbish about re-marriage. When the right man comes to help you in life you ought to be your happy self again—I wasn't a very good husband, but I hope I shall be a good memory. Certainly the end is nothing for you to be ashamed of . . . I shall try to write more later—I go on across the back pages . . . I have written letters on odd pages of this book. Will you manage to get them sent . . . Dear, you will be good to the old mother . . . also keep in with Etty and the others . . . I haven't time to write to Sir Clements, tell him I thought much of him, and never regretted his putting me in command of the "Discovery."

Bowers and Wilson, debilitated by starvation, dehydration, and exposure, appear not to have fought against the inevitable. When their hearts stopped beating, Scott was left alone. He was forty-three years old, the age of today's top long-distance endurance racers, so it makes medical sense that he outlasted all the younger men.

Today's polar trophies go to those who reach their goals by the toughest means, unsupported by outside contrivances, be they dogs or snow machines. Scott, on this basis, had achieved more than Amundsen. In the latter half of the twentieth century, great geographical challenges were taken on, first by the "easy" way, using every means available, and then by the difficult purist route. Thus Everest, in the 1950s, was climbed by a mass assault with teams of Sherpas and oxygen cylinders and, in the 1980s, by that toughest of all climbers Reinhold Messner, alone and aided by nought but his own physical power and iron will.

One member of Amundsen's great Pole team, Helmer Hanssen, said: "It is no disparagement of Amundsen and the rest of us when I say that Scott's achievement far exceeded ours . . . Just imagine what it meant for Scott and the others to drag their sleds themselves, with all their equipment and provisions to the Pole and back again. We started with 52 dogs and came back with eleven, and many of these wore themselves out on the journey. What shall we say of Scott and his comrades, who were their own dogs? Anyone with any experience will take off his hat to Scott's achievement. I do not believe men ever have shown such endurance at any time, nor do I believe there ever will be men to equal it."

For decades, Scott's own countrymen appreciated what he and his men had done, even though nobody could really grasp the enormity of their achievement without going to hell and almost back as they had. So far you have read about Scott and what happened to him. He left behind his reputation, as each of us will, and what follows traces the twisted path of what happened to that reputation.

❧ 18 ❧

THE LEGACY

ATKINSON, LEFT IN COMMAND of the thirteen men remaining for a second winter at the Cape Evans base, expected Scott back from the Pole by March 27, 1912, and by the end of the month, when there was still no sign of him, Atkinson and his men began to fear the worst. And not just for Scott, since Victor Campbell's five-man team, cut off by ice when *Terra Nova* had tried to collect them, was languishing somewhere along the barren, hostile coast to the west with no hut and only six weeks' worth of food to last through the winter.

When travel again became possible, Atkinson had to decide which group to search for first. Campbell's men might have survived in an ice cave if they had killed enough seals, but Scott's group must surely be dead on the lifeless barrier or deep down a Beardmore crevasse. Atkinson had manpower enough only to mount one search journey at a time and, putting the decision to the vote, he found that all but one of his men were keen to search for Scott first. Campbell could travel back, given reasonable luck, and a shipborne search remained a possibility, whereas, if Scott was never found, all records of his journey would be lost forever.

The decision made, Atkinson settled down to run Cape Evans on the lines laid down by Scott. The packing-case wall between officers and men stayed where it was and camp routines were not changed. The Australian Frank Debenham noted that once again it was Crean who kept up the spirits in the dwindling mess-deck section of the hut, adding: "This second year the scenery has lost much of its beauty to us, the auroras are cheap and the cold rather colder—companions rather too well known—[but] I am a peaceable man and seem to get along with most people."

There were others, touched by the aurora that winter, who showed the first chinks in their armor. Their extreme experiences had begun to unhinge them. In Campbell's cave, wallowing in blubber filth, Petty Officer George Abbott suffered a gradual mental breakdown and, at Cape Evans, Cherry-Garrard began in subtle ways a slow descent into a void of gloom and bitterness that would last his lifetime and include periods of partial insanity. Nonetheless, the book that he later wrote would partly shape Scott's image-to-be. That winter, beside so many empty bunks and ever alert to the ghostly sound of *finnesko* on ice outside the door, Cherry-Garrard brooded. Could he have, should he have, gone farther than he did to look for Scott?

He was often irritated by Scott's replacement as leader. Atkinson could do no right. Cherry-Garrard was angry when asked to collect seal meat. He wrote: "It is all I can do not to speak out sometimes . . . There is not a dangerous or hard job which has ever been done down here that I have not done—depôt journey, ponies on the sea ice, winter journey, southern journey, unloading ship, dog journey to south—work till an inevitable breakdown which has given me such hell this winter as I hope never to suffer again."

When the time to travel came again in November, Atkinson set out along the old cairn line over the barrier with ten of the others and enough provisions hauled by the eight mules and all available dogs to take them to the top of the glacier and back. Their only aim was to ascertain the fate and find the records of their leader and their friends.

Eleven miles beyond One Ton Depot, on November 12, 1912, Canadian Charles Wright veered right, for he had glimpsed something odd in the snow, which turned out to be the tip-off. He had seen the tip of Scott's tent just showing above a drift. They dug out the tent and the nearby sledge with great care. Thomas Williamson, who had been with Scott on *Discovery* and *Terra Nova*, noted: "I shed a few tears and I know the others did the same. It came as a great shock although we knew we should meet this sort of thing . . . I felt I could not look . . . but when at last I made up my mind I saw a ghastly sight . . . Captain Scott's face and hands looked like old alabaster, his face was very pinched and his hands terribly frostbitten . . . Their sufferings must have been terrible . . . We called the place Sorrowful Camp."

Charles Wright recorded that Atkinson read aloud passages from Scott's diaries that summarized what had happened to the Pole party; how they had reached the Pole on January 18 only to find the Norwegians had been there on December 17 by way of a different glacier; how Taff Evans and later Titus Oates had died. Atkinson had then said prayers and read a lesson from the burial service. Cherry-Garrard noted in his own diary: "and there with the floor-cloth under them and the tent above we buried them in their sleeping-bags—and surely their work has not been in vain." One by one, each of the men knelt in the entrance of the death camp. Cherry-Garrard wrote: "That scene can never leave my memory."

Searching the clothes of the dead men for their diaries and chronometers, they had to move Scott's frozen arm. Outside, Gran heard a noise. "It was something breaking," he wrote. "It was Scott's arm."

They noted that the tent had been well pitched and nothing inside was disorganized. They took away all that they could for the dead men's next of kin and the rock samples for geological analysis. Among the items from the tent listed by Atkinson were all the opium tablets and a vial of morphine. They also took the records on which Scott's reputation would rest, his notebooks and the two rolls of film that Bowers had exposed. Gran sketched a diagram in his diary of how the bodies lay and sent it a year later to Kathleen. In it he notes that only Wilson's head was by the door end of the tent; the opposite description to Cherry-Garrard's of the death scene. Either man may have been wrong, but Cherry-Garrard had spent many a dark time in such a tent with Bowers, Scott, and Wilson, on previous journeys, so he was more likely to have been correct.

They built a twelve-foot snow cairn by the tent, the cloth walls of which they lowered over the three bodies. They sang "Onward Christian Soldiers,"

Scott's favorite hymn, and then searched to the south for Oates. They found his sleeping bag but no signs of his body. They left a cairn where he may have died with a cross and a note saying: "Hereabouts died a very gallant gentleman, Captain L.E.G. Oates of the Inniskilling Dragoons. In March 1912, returning from the Pole, he walked willingly to his death in a blizzard to try and save his comrades, beset by hardship. This note is left by the Relief Expedition of 1912." Cherry-Garrard signed this note.

For him, Scott's diary was of tragic import, for it revealed that Scott had been a mere sixty-three miles from One Ton Depot on March 8 when he, Cherry-Garrard, was waiting there. In three days, he could have reached them with the dogs. If only he had known! Now that he did know, the implications would haunt and unhinge him until his own death in 1959.

Gran, known to Oates as "the Norskie," skied back to Hut Point wearing Scott's skis to be sure that they went *all* the way. He wrote on the journey back: "I think of Scott, I think of Amundsen. I have learned that something called friendship exists. I have come to know men willing to sacrifice themselves for their country and for their convictions."

Better news awaited the eleven men on their return to Hut Point, for Campbell's group had found their own hazardous way back, alive if not exactly kicking. In 1913, *Terra Nova* came back. Teddy Evans, fully recovered and as bouncy as ever, was onboard as a passenger. He yelled down from the deck: "Are you all well?" When he and the ship's crew learned that all was far from well, their shock and later their sorrow killed their mood of happy anticipation. The flags and bunting came down and the ship's carpenter, Francis Davies, built a nine-foot-high memorial cross. This was erected on Observation Hill, which today overlooks the American polar metropolis of McMurdo station on one side of its promontory and the New Zealand–run Scott Base on the other. The names of the five dead men are inscribed on the cross, along with words from Tennyson: "To strive, to seek, to find and not to yield."

On February 12, back in New Zealand, Atkinson sent cables from Timaru to the relatives of the dead and to the Central News Agency in London, with which the expedition had an exclusive contract. The next day, the Lyttelton harbormaster came to the ship and the men discovered the impact of their news on the waiting world. Cherry-Garrard wrote: "We landed to find the Empire—almost the civilized world, in mourning. It was as though they had lost great friends."

Scott's mother and sisters had now lost the third and last man of their immediate family, their beloved Con. Kathleen did not hear the news along with the rest of the world, for she was at sea on her way to meet Scott when he returned, as expected, to Lyttelton with *Terra Nova*. She had no idea that she was already a widow of eleven months' standing. Early in March of the previous year, the media had briefly mistaken Amundsen's victory news and the London headlines had screamed: "Scott at South Pole. Brilliant Victory." Messages of congratulations had poured in to Kathleen, even after her heart had sunk a day later with the amended news that, as far as the triumphant Amundsen knew, Scott had not reached the Pole. There had been no suggestion that Scott was in trouble, but Kathleen had remained uneasy.

An *Evening Standard* reporter who attended the memorial service held at St. Paul's Cathedral for Scott and his men wrote, "[I doubt if St. Paul's] ever contained a congregation so profoundly moved as that which gathered there today." The crowd at St. Paul's for their memorial service was greater even than that for the *Titanic* dead the previous year; 1,340,000 copies of a special edition of the *Daily Mirror*, a record, were sold. The reporter continued that in reporting the event he could not forget "one who is still ignorant of the frightful tragedy, that hapless woman, still on the high seas, flushed with hope and expectation, eager to join her husband." Her ship's captain finally received the wireless message on February 19 and handed her the news of the tragedy. Her outward display of strength over the months ahead masked a very real anguish.

In New Zealand, Atkinson handed her all Scott's journals and a batch of his letters to her. Back home she became Lady Scott on the grounds that Scott, like Shackleton before him, would have been knighted, in his case as knight commander of the bath. She wrote in her private diary: "All these long weary days . . . always only his pain—his mental agony—boring into my brain . . . all the different aspects of it come to me one by one. How one hopes his brain soon got numbed and the horror of his responsibility left him, for I think never was there a man with such sense of responsibility." She took her own responsibility to him seriously. Although she married again, she remembered Scott's hopes for their son, Peter, that he should become interested in the outdoor world. By the time Peter himself died in 1989, he had become a world-famous evangelizing conservationist and had helped save many wildlife species from extinction.

One of Scott's last letters was headed "Message to the Public." This gave his thoughts on the reasons for the disaster and ended:

> *We are weak, writing is difficult, but for my own sake I do not regret this journey, which has shown that Englishmen can endure hardships, help one another, and meet death with as great a fortitude as ever in the past. We took risks, we knew we took them; things have come out against us, and therefore we have no cause for complaint, but bow to the will of Providence, determined still to do our best to the last. But if we have been willing to give our lives to this enterprise, which is for the honour of our country, I appeal to our countrymen to see that those who depend on us are properly cared for.*
>
> *Had we lived, I should have had a tale to tell of the hardihood, endurance, and courage of my companions which would have stirred the heart of every Englishman. These rough notes and our dead bodies must tell the tale, but surely, surely, a great rich country like ours will see that those who are dependent on us are properly provided for. R. Scott*

The country responded to this blatant plea for a fund for the bereaved by raising the sum of £75,000 (£3.4 million). After grants had been made to the relevant dependents, the residue was used to publish the scientific results and to found the Scott Polar Research Institute in Cambridge, which today is an undisputed world center of polar research. Frank Debenham was its founder and for many years its director.

The messages of respect or sympathy included one from Robert Peary, the U.S. explorer: "They died like Englishmen, fighting against the most abnormal conditions, and meeting their death after a dogged struggle worthy of the highest traditions of their profession." And, reported in the *Daily Mail,* "It is a splendid tragedy—a splendid epic, written like many another British epic dotted over the globe in a language which every creed and race and tongue of man can understand." U.S. presidents past and future, Theodore Roosevelt, Wilson, and Taft, added their condolences, and Germany's great polar explorer Wilhelm Filchner wrote: "The scientific notes and observations that have been saved promise to yield a valuable contribution to our knowledge of the Antarctic, in the exploration of which Great Britain has taken a prominent part. This fresh sacrifice will be painfully felt beyond the Channel and throughout the world."

The greatest of the French polar explorers, Dr. Jean Charcot, wrote in *Le Matin*: "Scott has conquered the Pole. The public, ill-informed, will say that he reached his goal only second; but those who know—Amundsen and Shackleton, I am sure, among the first—will say that it was Scott who opened the road to the Pole and mapped out the route; and a halo of glory, shedding a reflecting glow upon his country, will surround his name." He added: "Scott would not turn aside from his scientific programme . . . It is quite another thing with Amundsen. He is not a scientist. He is rather bent on setting up a record. If one wishes to pronounce the one greater than the other, the preference must go to him who surrounds this magnificent result with the greatest number of discoveries and scientific observations."

Amundsen, lecturing in the United States, wrote: "I am unwilling to believe the report is true. I was reported to have perished, so was Shackleton. Scott was a brave man, one whose first thought was for the safety of his men. He took no thought of his own danger or comforts. I am grieved beyond measure at the report."

The celebrated Swedish explorer Sven Hedin added: "Immortal glory rises round the name of the greatest Antarctic explorer of all times. He has reached his goal. He has served his science. He has sacrificed his life. He has honoured his country again. As in Franklin's days, England has conquered the first place in a desperate fight for knowledge, and in the pantheon of heroic deeds the British nation may be proud of such sons."

A more down-to-earth Norwegian comment came much later from Tryggve Gran: "No polar explorer of historical stature has escaped blunders. Nansen, Peary, Amundsen, Shackleton, Ross, Borchgrevink—all of them messed up one way or the other, and others followed them, but they were able to overcome their mistakes. Scott was the unlucky one. His false step brought him a catastrophe, but also glory." "In the history of the great voyages of discovery these two (Scott and Amundsen) will always stand side by side—so different in character, so alike in their indomitable courage. They belong among the ranks of men like Leiv Eriksson, Columbus, Magellan, Stanley, Livingstone, Peary and Gagarin. We Norwegians have always felt ourselves closely bound to Great Britain. Robert Falcon Scott strengthened the links tighter than ever before."

Polar explorers from France, Norway, Australia, and the United States subsequently honored Scott by naming prominent Antarctic features that they discovered after him, eight place names in all.

At home, Shackleton seemed genuine in his ongoing praise of his erstwhile leader. On first hearing of the Norwegians' triumph, he had told the press: "I would not in any way detract from the merit of Amundsen's achievements for he has accomplished a brilliant march. But Scott's is a much bigger expedition and he had a great deal of general scientific work to do."

The media were not interested in the scientific aspects of the Scott tragedy. For them, the event would sell hundreds of thousands of newspapers worldwide. They would ensure that Scott and his men, especially Oates, became national, if not international, symbols. "Nothing in our time," declared the *Manchester Guardian* in February 1913, "has touched the whole nation so instantly and so deeply as the loss of these men." Fleet Street was still realizing the benefits of hugely increased circulation figures from the *Titanic* disaster only ten months before. Here was another equally heroic saga. The papers ran and ran the story from every conceivable angle. They were filled with it for at least two weeks and still printing related enlargements, commentary, and letters six months later. Reporters hounded the three-year-old Peter Scott and a full-page color photo was printed of him, sitting naked by the sea looking innocent and forlorn, entitled "Portrait of Master Peter Scott."

The Educational Council had Scott's story read in schools to 750,000 schoolchildren, many of whom are alive today. A few teachers, either through ignorance or enthusiasm, told their charges that Scott had been the first to reach the Pole. This was quickly seized on by the Norwegian press. The public responded to the whole saga with a national outpouring of grief, not as spontaneously as that which ninety years later followed the death of Diana, Princess of Wales, but on as personal a level. Scott's death was a year old by the time it became public knowledge and there was no television to dramatize the event, yet the impact was still large.

The story was not of a victory but of courage in adversity, the true stuff of legends. The main images were Oates stumbling from the haven of the tent into the icy blast to die for his friends, and of Scott, Bowers, and Wilson lying in the tent for up to eight days with no food or water at −40°C, yet refusing the opiate option.

Of course it helped that they died. Tales of martyrdom spring only from death. Douglas Mawson mounted a hugely ambitious Antarctic expedition immediately after the Scott, Shackleton, and Amundsen epics. His story was one of great success in terms of geographic and scientific discoveries, as well as personal bravery against huge odds. But he missed out on lasting fame, even in his native Australia, partly because he went on to die naturally in old age, not advisable from a PR point of view.

The Scott story broke in February 1913, a year before the Great War, and at a time of singular national gloom. The "unsinkable" *Titanic*'s sinking had emphasized Britain's waning prowess. Dismay and self-doubt were everywhere on display. The story of Scott's men served to bolster confidence when it was most needed. A country that could produce such men should hold its head high. For a time, the story of their deaths banished from the front pages all such depressing topics as Trades union power, coal strikes, suffragette militancy, home rule for Ireland, the threat of a socialist people's budget, and German imperialism.

It was, of course, all a matter of interpretation by the media. The papers told their readers how to view Scott. Not as a polar amateur beaten by a professional rival, not as a hugely successful scientific coordinator, not as a great leader and explorer, but above all as a man who could inspire his countrymen to triumph over adversity, including death. Such was the power of the press. By the 1880s, sensationalism rather than accuracy was the key to selling newspapers. Henry Stanley, the "journalist explorer" who traveled to Africa to find Dr. Livingstone, summed up the situation by saying that accuracy was no longer wanted because the public preferred action and adventure to the often less titillating truth.

By the 1890s, just before Scott first appeared on the scene, explorers were in demand as public speakers in British theaters and concert halls. Society lionized them and bought their latest books. Children's books about explorers proliferated. Early photographers joined expeditions hoping for fame, and advertisements for everything from soup to shoes featured explorers' portraits, as did collectors' cards in cigarette packets. The public had become hero hungry.

When in 1908 Scott was planning to head south again, the Arctic, as we have seen, had become a battleground between two great U.S. explorers, Peary and Cook. Each was backed up by a newspaper sponsor: Commander (later Rear Admiral R.E.) Peary and the *New York Times* versus Dr. Frederick Cook, championed by the *New York Herald*. When in 1909 Cook claimed the Pole a year before Peary, their respective newspapers declared open war.

When news of the Scott tragedy broke, the world media were ready and waiting. This was a story with *all* the right ingredients. As U.S. historian and editor Beau Riffenburgh cynically commented, had Peary and Cook not fought each other's claims or had Scott lived, there would have been far less interest in all three. As it was, their relevant press coverage ensured them a mythic status, which would endure for a century, maybe more. "And certainly," in Riffenburgh's words, "for the vast majority of the newspapers in the United States and England, this kind of ennoblement . . . and its consequent sensationalized story was far more important than a scientific result or the conquest of some unknown land." And so, when Scott died in 1912, having reached the South Pole, he became revered worldwide, eclipsing for a while the fame of Shackleton, who died in 1922 having failed to achieve the Pole or his other major goal, the crossing of Antarctica, but whose popularity was to peak again when the next century celebrated his *Endurance* journey.

Heroes on pedestals of popularity have long been prey to the professional character assassin and, once they are dead, they can be attacked at will without fear of litigation and thus without need to worry overmuch about historic reality. Within days of *Terra Nova*'s arrival in New Zealand on February 13, 1913, and the news of Scott's death, rumors began to circulate. The vultures of the press had discovered a corpse and they sensed that there must be bad smells. These included mention of a row between Scott and Teddy Evans.

As early as February 15, a *Daily Mail* reporter wrote:

Commander Evans, in an interview with me, firmly declined, "speaking as a naval officer," to be drawn into any discussion of "the wicked rumours and conjectures" which have been in circulation.

"I don't want to give a defence," he said, "where no defence is needed. As to the allegations of dissension in the party, I went against the doctor's advice to the Antarctic to see Scott through. Does that look like dissension?"

Regarding "the shortage of fuel, for which I cannot account," mentioned in Captain Scott's diary, Commander Evans stated that the depots were untouched by the supporting parties on their return northward after accompanying the Southern Party part of the way to the Pole. There was evaporation of the oil owing to the leather washers of the tins, and as supplies were cut so fine, this made a considerable shortage.

Commander Evans characterised the rumours that Petty-Officer Evans went mad as cruel, scandalous, and without foundation. Petty-Officer Evans behaved admirably.

Captain Scott left instructions that no search parties should leave the base to look for him.

Commander Evans declares that it was humanly impossible for the base party to save Scott and his comrades.

All the members of the expedition describe the rumours of dissensions and of the tapping of depots as "dastardly lies" emanating from irresponsible people.

Some members of the expedition state that in consequence of the wild and baseless stories which have been circulated, they quite expect that a searching inquiry into the whole expedition will be ordered.

Lord Curzon, the president of the Royal Geographical Society, requested just such an inquiry in order to clear the dead Scott's name. It never took place, but critics of Scott have been conducting their own investigations ever since, many of which today are still based on unfounded rumors produced from thin air back in February 1913. These include the stories that Oates's feet had dropped off before he died, that Taff Evans had been dragged for many miles, insane, on a sledge, and that sixty-one members of the team had died.

One myth, which fooled me for two years, was that of Scott's last biscuit. A collection of Scott memorabilia was to be auctioned in 2000 and I was asked by the Antarctic Heritage Trust to help with the bidding, to keep the items in Britain. The cheapest item in the auction catalog was described as "a biscuit found in Scott's tent," so I agreed to bid for it by phone. The bidding went crazy, fueled by foreign collectors, and the biscuit finally cost me just under £4,000. Some of the other items fetched over £60,000. The biscuit never reached my home, where we keep biscuit-eating dogs, but was preserved and kept by the National Maritime Museum at Greenwich.

Fascinated as to why, dying of starvation, Scott's men had not eaten this last biscuit, I made inquiries as to its provenance. In December 2002, Scott's daughter-in-law, Lady Philippa Scott, told me she had found a suitcase long kept by her husband, Sir Peter Scott, in a London bank, which had been left to him by Kathleen Scott and which contained the "Scott relics." These must have been taken from the death tent by Atkinson and given to Kathleen. One of the items was a solitary sledge biscuit. Checking through the reference books, I found an entry on page 90 of *South: the Race to the Pole*, a National Maritime Museum 2000 publication, which stated: "It is well known that Scott, Wilson and Bowers were almost out of food when they died, only a single bag of rice and one or two biscuits being reclaimed from their tent." I checked with the book's author, who said the origin of this information was a book by Professor Robert Feeney of the department of food at the University of California. In February 2003, I heard from Professor Feeney, who wrote: "Unfortunately I cannot help you with a reference for the phrase you requested . . . In my book there was no such phrase. The editors [of *South*] added many pictures and a new table. Maybe they added the phrase."

So I probably paid nearly £4,000 for a biscuit that came back from Scott's *Terra Nova* belongings but not from his tent. I had fallen for one of the many Scott myths and (in studying his story, private letters, numerous files in museums and private collections, and 112 relevant books) I have discovered a great many more myths of a far more damaging nature, most of them promulgated by just one man, ex-journalist Roland Huntford, but believed today by millions worldwide.

Back in 1913, the *Terra Nova* survivors and friends formed a committee to handle publicity and finances. Teddy Evans was a major player under the chairmanship of Lord Curzon, the venerable Royal Geographical Society president. They gave Scott's journals to the editor of his *Discovery* book, Leonard Huxley, an erstwhile schoolmaster, to prepare for publication. Contrary to another rumor, there is no proof of interference by Kathleen with the editing process. Cherry-Garrard, already smarting from gossip that he could have saved Scott, wrote: "The Committee (Curzon) meant to hush everything up. I was to be sacrificed." He suspected that this book committee had instructed Huxley to whitewash Scott. If such instructions ever existed, Huxley hardly obeyed them, for the finished work, *The Personal Journals of Captain Scott,* was released (as speedily as possible) in 1913 and contained a great many self-critical comments by Scott, some of which would probably have been removed had Scott edited the journals himself, as he intended. The original private journals are on display at the British Museum, with copies available to the public, so it is not difficult to compare the original with the Huxley edited version.

Over a period of thirty-five years, I have written several books about my own expeditions, based largely on my own private diaries. I recorded for myself every raw impression of each fresh experience, mood, and observation, which would include my letting off steam about my colleagues at times, when I was frustrated, upset, or merely depressed. During one expedition in the Arctic in the mid-1970s, I made critical notes about the men traveling with me to help select those most suitable for a major expedition I was planning. When I later used that diary as the basis for my book *Hell on Ice*, I edited out my more acerbic comments on team members. If I had died and my diary had been edited by a third party, I would certainly have wanted him/her to make just such cuts in the text and I would not describe such editing as whitewashing.

Leonard Huxley did edit out many, probably seventy, such personal remarks by Scott, but retained most of Scott's self-criticism, which forms the basis of much anti-Scott commentary up to the present day.

To my mind, Scott overdoes his own self-doubt, almost indulging in self-flagellation. Cherry-Garrard wrote: "he had a habit of self-criticism." Before leaving England in 1901 he wrote to Nansen, as though to a father confessor, with his innermost thoughts of his own inadequacy: "I am distinctly conscious of want of plan—I have a few nebulous ideas centreing round the main object, to push from the known to the unknown, but I am quite prepared to find that such imaginings of inexperience are impracticable and that hasty and possibly ill-conceived plans must be made on the spot. Thoughts such as these cannot but show me how very much I am removed from the illustrious men who have led successful polar ventures hitherto." Once his expeditions had set out, Scott's diary became his father confessor, as indeed it had been since he was a teenager, and his day-to-day notes often accentuate his black moods. Scott was under contract to write a book, as are most leaders of major expeditions, so of course he intended to use the notes, but not as they stood. Huxley would appreciate that and would need to second-guess the dead Scott as he did his editing work. Cherry-Garrard summed up the situation accurately: "Scott's diary, had he lived, would merely have formed the basis of the book he would have written."

I have noted some of the self-deprecating passages with which Scott damned himself and which Huxley chose not to edit. They point to a very poor whitewash job, if such was indeed the Curzon committee's intent. Such passages include: "Not a single article of the outfit had been tested; and amid the general ignorance that prevailed, the lack of system was painfully apparent in everything"; "It is already evident that had the rollers been metal cased . . . they would now be as good as new. I cannot think why we had not the sense to have this done"; "Cooking for five takes a seriously longer time than cooking for four, perhaps half an hour on the whole day. It is an item I had not considered when re-organising." These are all disarmingly honest and absolutely damning comments, which Scott would surely not have repeated had he done his own final editing. I do not believe that Scott doctored his diary to cater to the eventuality of his dying in harness. Perhaps he should have done so? Certainly, in thirty years of completing expeditions in remote regions, I have always kept diaries that I intended to use to help me write subsequent books, and I never groomed the text with death in mind. I was aware that I might die but felt it to be highly unlikely. Scott, in my opinion, wrote his day-to-day observations, comments, and critiques of himself and others exactly as he felt them at the time, and assuming that he would be able to edit them prior to their appearing in print.

In his dual biography of Scott and Amundsen, Huntford claims that "[Scott's] instincts were to evade responsibility and shift the blame," ignoring the many official diary entries where Scott shoulders the blame, often, in my opinion, wrongly, for much that goes wrong. Ponting, in the winter of 1911, asked Scott if he had started on a book. "He said he would leave that until he got home and his Journal was to be used merely as notes, to be elaborated later into his official account." Having used up all his own savings, Scott's main hope of paying off expedition debts rested on producing a narrative at the journey's end, first for the press and then for a book.

Until a few miles from One Ton Depot, and certainly up to the point when he reached the Mount Hooper depot, there was always a very real hope of relief, as requested, from the dog teams. So, until then, Scott would have carried on with his diary as an aide-mémoire, pure and simple. Only when death became a near certainty in the last two weeks could he have written his words directly for posterity, and by that time he was concentrating on his letters; there is very little in the diary itself at that point. All that was important to him was summarized in his Message to the Public, which he must have written while he still had the power of clear and rational thought and fingers that could firmly grasp a pencil to produce sharp, legible script.

Scott had been trained since a teenage midshipman to keep meticulous and consistent naval logs, he read a great deal, and his prose was neither complex nor contrived. He wrote wonderful English under awful circumstances.

Scott critics later deplore "the ossification of Scott as supreme national hero [that] was already under way, brilliantly choreographed by him from his deathbed." They accuse him of writing his last letters while "looking over his shoulder at an unseen audience, concerned more with his reputation than his actions," of starting to "sculpt out his post-expedition image in his journal entries," and of "preparing his alibi . . . to seek immolation in the tent . . . to snatch a kind of victory out of defeat." The self-critical entries already referred to make a mockery of such theories. In the secret tribunal of his mind, Scott allowed himself no mercy. His restless and critical nature shows through honestly in his death notes, as though demanding critical controversy in the years to come, not "ossification as a national hero," nor "concern with his reputation."

The *Terra Nova* book, *Scott's Last Expedition,* Huxley's edited version of Scott's diaries, remains a classic and a truly absorbing read nine decades on. When it was published, the British, like many other nations, were threatened by the immense power and naked aggression of Germany, at a time when aerial bombardment and new machine guns meant enhanced killing potential. Thousands of individuals would be required, a year after they heard of Scott's death, to walk forward into a hail of bullets. Scott's story helped to inspire such individuals. A German war propagandist would surely have preferred Scott and Oates alive rather than the powerful figures of inspiration they were in death.

Herbert Ponting lectured about the expedition for ten months before the war. His films of the *Terra Nova* venture were copied and sent to France to be seen by over one hundred thousand officers and men. The senior forces chaplain thanked him: "The intensity of [your story's] appeal is realised by the subdued hush and quiet that pervades the massed audience of troops while it is being told. We all feel we have inherited from Oates and his comrades a legacy and heritage of inestimable value in seeing through our present work." That work included sixteen thousand men killed in a single day and hundreds of thousands maimed. Subsequent British cynics forget all those of their countrymen in two world wars who needed help and found it through the examples of their contemporary heroes, such as Scott and his men.

As thousands of heroes were dying daily on the western front, it might well be thought that all memories of Scott's tent would vanish like some long-ago theatrical event, fine at the time but forgotten. But the Scott story was not merely some extension of the original war jingoism, the Rupert Brooke quotes, or the voice of the schoolboy who rallies the ranks. Scott and Oates provided real strength and an image of the human ability to endure, which lonely men could and did summon up to fight their inner fear and weakness. As Cherry-Garrard later wrote just before the Second World War: "Birdie . . . died in a tent on the Great Ice Barrier twenty-six years ago . . . Since then ten million men have been killed . . . and you might have thought that the cumulative tragedy of it all would have swamped what they did. But there is something in this story which lives through unimaginable miseries and horrors; partly as an example, as I believe: and partly as a help. And this is a time when decent sane men and women want help."

Everyone has their breaking point, but, as Cherry-Garrard wrote: "That was the glory of those men whom we found lying in that tent; they never broke." When Kathleen's papers were filed after her death in 1947, they included sheaves of letters from soldiers thanking her dead husband for his example, which had so helped them in their hours of need.

As a high-profile survivor of *Terra Nova*, Cherry-Garrard too received many letters for many years and not just from soldiers. "They say—deeply moved—it is an inspiration," he wrote. "They write from the ends of the earth: from hospitals and operations and great trials—that the story of these men has helped." "I have heard discussions," he added, "of their failure. The same men would have discussed the failure of Christ hanging upon the Cross: or of Joan of Arc burning at the stake . . . [but] I know, and you know, that by the more important standards of success and failure they never failed . . . The world is full of the efforts of human beings to leave something behind them when they die . . . yet [Scott and his men] have left something behind—in men's minds."

Tryggve Gran said, emerging from the death tent: "They died having done something great—how hard must not death be having done nothing."

Scott's popularity only proved lasting, say his detractors, because the government used his story as war propaganda to encourage cannon fodder to "die as Scott had," covering up any blemishes. Roland Huntford, for instance, introduces his book *Scott and Amundsen* with a Liddell Hart quote: "It is more important to provide material for a true verdict than to gloss over disturbing facts so that individual reputations may be preserved." This at once suggests to the reader that Huntford is a scrupulous investigator about to reveal disturbing truths about Scott long suppressed by the establishment. Not only was no officially inspired monument to Scott ever raised in London at that time, but no government document has ever been found by generations of searchers suggesting any government-inspired initiative to use Scott to help gird the nation's loins. When Scott's journals were published, no ministry of propaganda reprinted thousands or even hundreds of copies to distribute. No one sent *Terra Nova* survivors far and wide to lecture to the troops.

Because Scott and his men became emblems of national pride and motivation to millions throughout the years of slaughter in the Great War, certain details of Scott's death were highlighted and treated with reverence. One such was the fact that Scott himself died last. To me it matters little who died first or last of these three brave friends, but I hate to see history crudely distorted just for the pleasure of pulling down a hero from his pedestal.

Six men looked at the frozen bodies when the death tent was discovered and some clues to the last days of Scott, Bowers, and Wilson can be gleaned from their written memories. Gran wrote: "Captain Scott lay in the middle, half out of his sleeping bag, Bowers on his right, and Wilson on his left but twisted round with his head and upper body up against the tent pole. Wilson and Bowers were right inside their sleeping bags. The cold had turned their skin yellow and glassy, and there were masses of marks of frost-bite. Scott seemed to have fought hard at the moment of death, but the others gave the impression of having passed away in their sleep." William Lashly noted that: "it looked very much like Captain Scott being the last survivor, it must have been a dreadful time for him to wait for death." Charles Wright had noted in his journal that, on opening the tent, they found the three bodies of Scott, Wilson, and Bowers and they agreed that Scott must have died last with his arm over Wilson's body and his diary beside him.

The reason for their belief that Scott was the last to die was explained by Tom Crean: "When I entered *I found Wilson and Bowers were tied up in their bags, but poor Scott was not, proving that he had died last and been able to fasten up the bags of the others.* They had all died as proper English gentlemen, although they were given the necessary medicine with which to take their own lives if they so desired." The practical Crean, who had always helped Taff Evans and Bill Lashly design and modify all the sledging gear, knew the details of the sleeping bag ties, some of which could not be fixed from inside. To him, therefore, the fact that these ties had been fastened on the bags of Bowers and Wilson was proof that Scott died last. Crean wept and later said of Scott: "I must say I have lost a good friend."

Cherry-Garrard wrote: "Bowers and Wilson were sleeping in their bags.

Scott had thrown back the flaps of his bag at the end. His left hand was stretched over Wilson, his lifelong friend . . . Near Scott was a lamp formed from a tin and some lamp wick off a finnesko. It had been used to burn the little methylated spirit which remained. I think that Scott had used it to help him to write up to the end. I feel sure that he had died last—and once I had thought that he would not go so far as some of the others. We never realized how strong that man was, mentally and physically, until now." Atkinson, the doctor, writing the official report, noted: "Captain Scott had died last, and had died when partly out of his bag with his arm resting on Doctor Wilson [who] had died quietly in his bag, and was asleep when he passed away . . . Lieutenant Bowers had evidently also died in his sleep. Extensive cold had caused their death and also lack of food."

Only Cherry-Garrard noted that Bowers, on Scott's right, lay with his feet to the door, unlike the other two. Since Bowers was famous for his snore and for weeks had climbed in and out of the tent for navigation purposes, he had probably been sleeping that way around for months. To confuse the issue, Gran drew a sketch of the death scene showing Wilson, not Bowers, with his feet to the door. But Cherry-Garrard is more likely to be right. He wrote: "I went over Bill's body . . . |It| was dreadfully hard to feel and it was most difficult to locate the chronometer in his vest pocket next the skin—quite terrible."

In an undated note to Mrs. E. A. Wilson, Scott wrote: "If this letter reaches you, Bill and I will have gone out together. We are very near it now and I should like you to know how splendid he was at the end—everlastingly cheerful . . . His eyes have a comfortable blue look of hope . . . I can do no more to comfort you than to tell you that he died as he lived, a brave, true man—the best of comrades and the staunchest of friends. My whole heart goes out to you in pity."

There can be little doubt from this letter, and the fact that Scott started but did not finish some letters to his own close family, that Wilson died before Scott. To Bowers's mother Scott wrote: "I write when we are very near the end of our journey, and I am finishing it in company with two gallant, noble gentlemen. One of these is your son. He had come to be one of my closest and soundest friends . . . As the troubles have thickened his dauntless spirit ever shone brighter and he has remained cheerful, hopeful and indomitable to the end. The ways of Providence are inscrutable, but there must be some reason why such a young, vigorous and promising life is taken. My whole heart goes out in pity for you."

From this it would seem as though Bowers too died before Scott, but we cannot be sure just from this evidence since, like newspapers that prepare the obituaries of the famous long before they die, Scott may have done likewise.

To his friend, the *Peter Pan* playwright James Barrie, Scott wrote: "We have had four days of storm in our tent and nowhere's food or fuel. We did intend to finish ourselves when things proved like this, but we have decided to die naturally in the track." This would suggest, given that they had been stormbound since late on March 19, that Scott wrote this when Bowers and Wilson were still alive, on March 24. His last diary entry was dated March 29.

One detail of the death tent suggests that Bowers might have survived Scott, which led to questions being raised about everyone's truth. Charles Wright found a message written on the back of one of Scott's letters, in Bowers's handwriting, saying: "The diary of Wilson is to be found in his satchell and in the instrument box are 2 of his sketchbooks. H. R. Bowers."

When in 1979 Scott's main detractor, Roland Huntford, sought out this note and could not locate it, he invented a conspiracy theory that the Scott Polar Research Institute in Cambridge had "suppressed" it. In 2003, I, in my turn, approached the institute and a friend of mine went there to find the elusive note. After much investigative help from Bob Headland, the chief archivist, the relevant letter was found in a frame but with the Bowers note on the invisible side. The ancient frame was taken apart and there, sure enough and unsuppressed, was Bowers's scribble on the back of Scott's letter. The letter had no date but had been written by Scott inside his diary, then torn out, prior to his writing several others, one of which notes: "we are pretty well done—four days of blizzard just as we were getting to the last depôt." An indication that it was written, like the Barrie letter, on March 24, when all three men were still alive.

When three men survive in a tent for many days, they do not all sleep at the same time. Once, in 1981, I was forced to stay in a three-man pyramid tent on the plateau and two hundred miles from the Pole for seventeen days and nights. None of us was frostbitten and we spent most of that interminable time in our sleeping bags. What I remember most is how time lost all meaning. You would wake to find the others sleeping; each of us soon developed different sleeping patterns. Add the pain of frostbite, extreme cold, starvation, and dehydration and the most likely scenario would have been that Wilson, near the end, asks Bowers—perhaps at a time when Scott was asleep—to make a note to the effect that his, Wilson's, papers were to be found in the instruments box on the sledge. Bowers would have reacted by reaching across to the sleeping Scott's pencil and diary and inscribing Wilson's message therein (neither he nor Wilson was keeping diaries or weather records, so neither would have had pencils or paper at hand over the period when this note is likely to have been penned). It is more likely that Bowers would make the note at the time Wilson asked him to than some days later.

Soon afterward, Wilson dies. At some later point, Bowers dies. Then Scott writes the letters to their next of kin. He eventually hastens his own death by half-opening his sleeping bag to lose the protection of his last faint body warmth. If, when Scott did this, Bowers had still been alive and sufficiently able to make and sign the Wilson note in firm handwriting, he would surely, being the deeply religious man that he was and devotedly loyal to Scott, have also laid Scott's body in a dignified position, closed his eyes, and placed his outstretched arm at rest. Bowers's scribble merely adds to the evidence that Wilson died first; it has no bearing on the existing evidence that Scott died last.

What exactly constitutes failure depends upon how you or I wish to define such an artificial concept. If all your life you strive for a goal, whether it be finding a cure for cancer or running a mile in three minutes, have you failed if some other human, three weeks before you, also finds the cure or runs the mile? Did Scott fail because, like Mallory on Everest, he died without returning to base? Hardly. Before setting out, he stated to the press: "We may lose our lives. We may be wiped out." Shackleton and Amundsen were to die on ventures that failed, Amundsen on an air rescue mission for a crashed Arctic balloonist, and Shackleton of a heart attack on a voyage back to Antarctica. Scott died on one of his expeditions having successfully reached his goal. Scott's 1940 biographer, George Seaver, put Scott's expedition work into context.

Scott himself wrote: "It might be said that it was James Cook who defined the Antarctic Region, and James Ross who discovered it." Seaver adds: "But it was Scott who penetrated it." *Terra Nova* survivors did not see their venture as a failure. Charles Wright stated that the expedition had been a triumph over adversity, with the men succumbing to bad weather and bad fortune but not to their own weakness. Cherry-Garrard said: "Scott's reputation is not founded upon the conquest of the South Pole. He came to a new continent, found out how to travel there, and gave knowledge of it to the world: he discovered the Antarctic and founded a school. He is the last of the great geographical explorers."

For sixty years, Scott's unquestionable achievements were acknowledged worldwide, especially by his own country. The circumstances of his death and the magnetic effect of his prose established him as the leading national hero in the field of polar endeavor. Then, in the late 1970s, Roland Huntford's anti-Scott book, *Scott and Amundsen,* rewrote history. His largely fictional version of Scott became accepted as reality and turned respect into derision. Scott's resulting removal from the pantheon of polar heroes caused a vacuum that was quickly filled by Scott's old sledging mate Ernest Shackleton.

A book by the American writer Caroline Alexander, *The* Endurance: *Shackleton's Legendary Antarctic Expedition,* appeared in 1998 and was rapturously received worldwide. It led to a number of filmmakers plumbing the treasure trove of dramatic movie footage and photos taken by Shackleton's talented cameraman, Frank Hurley. This provided great television viewing and material for exhibitions.

Kenneth Branagh starred in a $35 million drama, IMAX featured a highly impressive Shackleton movie, numerous mini-documentaries focused on the Irish explorer's successes, and a Shackleton exhibit at the American Museum of Natural History in New York City opened with a quarter of a million visitors. Shackleton mania had arrived, and the explorer soon became an icon for good leadership.

American explorer Jared Diamond, accepting the version of Scott spun by Huntford and the spate of parroted books and films that followed, wrote in *Discover* magazine: "Now, with Huntford's reappraisal of Scott, there are much broader lessons for all of us." The *Wharton Leadership Digest* raved about Shackleton as a leader of men and was able to emphasize his achievements all the better for being able to compare them with the Scott of Huntford's imagination.

One example of the Shackleton hyperbole was the myth that he "never lost a man," whereas, in reality, three of his key men did die in Antarctica, partly due to inadequate administrative planning. Another example is the notion that Shackleton's projects were successful and Scott's were not. The truth is that Scott reached the Pole and Shackleton did not. Shackleton's most famous achievement was surviving a failure. His ambitious attempt to cross Antarctica ended in disaster before even reaching the coastline. In *South,* Shackleton's account of the last voyage of *Endurance,* he took the credit for most if not all key decisions, understating the essential role played by the amazing Frank Worsley, a navigational genius without whom all Shackleton's men would surely have perished. The result of this increasingly popular perception of Shackleton and Scott was that it soon became quite difficult to find anyone, even in polar circles, whose opinions were not influenced by the Huntford fiction.

I have organized and led polar expeditions on and off for over thirty years and would find the Scott school of leadership infinitely preferable to that of Shackleton. Nonetheless, both were great men in their separate ways, and neither alone would have garnered the great results that their joint work achieved.

In 1938, Louis Bernacchi wrote, "Owing to the great discoveries of Ross, Biscoe, Balleny, Weddell, Scott, Shackleton, Mawson and other British explorers, we now own a silent empire in the extreme south, the territorial rights of which are likely to be of high importance in the future, just as similar rights in the extreme north have proved valuable to Canada and to Soviet Russia. Our title to our Antarctic Dependencies must not in the future be questioned by an unfriendly Power."

Scott was one of the long list of British explorers who could have given Britain territorial rights to the South Pole. Fortunately, political ambitions gave way to scientific interest and, by the late 1950s, fifty-two research stations were manned all around the Antarctic continent by some twelve countries. Scott, who successfully liaised with German and Swedish scientists and tried to persuade Amundsen to do similar work with him, would have been pleased by the way things have worked out. He showed the way to such cooperation.

With Skelton, Day, and Barne, Scott pioneered the design and early trials of tracked snow vehicles, which eventually proved far superior to dogs for work in Antarctica and which helped defeat the German armies by the introduction of British tracked "tanks" in 1917, only five years after Scott's tracked machines so nearly proved successful on the barrier.

Ironically, perhaps, of all the nations operating in Antarctica, including the Norwegians, the British were the last to give up using dog teams alongside tracked vehicles. I remember my 1981 expedition's ski plane flying two husky bitches from a British base to mate with New Zealand dogs 1,600 miles away to avoid interbreeding in two of the continent's last four working teams.

Equally ironic must be the fact that, in the twenty-first century, modern expeditions vie with one another to complete journeys of physical toil. Journalists who castigate Scott for using men rather than dogs will in their very next article belittle a modern polar traveler for seeking any outside help beyond his or her own unaided manpower. Scott would either be amused or bemused.

In 1993, Mike Stroud and I man-hauled across the Antarctic continent with no outside support. Dogs could not have done that journey without resupply, so we proved that humans are more efficient self-contained transportation systems than dogs. But, vis à vis the relative performances of Scott's men and Amundsen's dogs, our achievement proves nothing because both their groups used depot systems and such outside support gives dogs the edge over men.

When the Second World War came so swiftly after the slaughter of the First, Cherry-Garrard's *The Worst Journey in the World* was listed by the National Book Council in London as recommended reading for troops. He received many letters once again, saying how the story of Scott and Oates had helped men face danger and fear through that later war. Britain did not win World War II by herself but, in the summer of 1940, she did stand alone to save the rest of Europe from falling to the Nazis. Goebbels's propaganda was strident and compelling, but the British held firm because they still believed in themselves and they still had values of the sort exemplified by the likes of Scott. His achievement was that, through what he did and how he wrote about it, he touched the imagination of his country, as did Churchill, and helped his countrymen to achieve their finest hours.

Scott never planned the manner of his death, but when it had become inevitable, he was determined to face it head on. "After all," he wrote in the frozen tent, "we are setting a good example to our countrymen, if not by getting into a tight place, by facing it like men when we were there."

Jeremy Paxman, in his 1998 book *The English,* says: "Certainly, the war and its immediate aftermath are the last time in living memory when the English had a clear and positive sense of themselves." After that epoch, Paxman suggested, and up to the present: "*any* public display of national pride is not merely unsophisticated but somehow morally reprehensible . . . No one stands for 'God Save the Queen' anymore." Paxman goes on to quote Orwell. "In left-wing circles it is always felt that there is something slightly disgraceful in being an Englishman, and that it is a duty to snigger at every English institution, from horse-racing to suet puddings." Orwell could have added Scott to his list, except that he was writing in 1948 and Scott had not yet become a target. Such was the simple strength of his message that Scott had retained a position of respect with the majority of the public and, the same year that Orwell wrote of suet puddings, Ealing Studios brought out their massively popular *Scott of the Antarctic,* with John Mills in the title role, an epic still remembered with emotion by the over-sixties.

Scott's reputation had stood proud through two world wars and would remain so for another three decades. But Britain was changing her attitude to her past and it took one man alone to sow the seeds that, to many minds, metamorphosed Scott from hero to fool.

THE LAST WORD

WHY WRITE ABOUT DEBUNKERS at all? Why feel compelled to attack lies told about dead men? When I told Wally Herbert, Britain's greatest living polar explorer, who wrote a biography of Robert Peary, that I would be writing this book, he responded: "I must warn you, from my own unpleasant experience, of the dangers of getting involved in historical controversy. It is the egos of those historians and journalists on both sides of the debate that this [Peary] controversy is all about. The practicalities of travelling across the polar pack are simply ignored. I have learnt the hard way that those who do not want to hear will not listen. No matter what your polar credentials are, the hacks will spit at you in print—indeed they delight in doing so for it makes them feel important. You'll be in for a bruising experience. They will personally attack you in order to discredit your opinion. So, is it worth it?"

I think so.

The debunking of the famous, past and present, has been going on forever and in every land but, given an international debunking-challenge trophy, I think the British would do well. We treat it as a skill, and publishers

57. A typical Antarctic phenomenon, the parhelion, photographed by the author in 1979 on the Antarctic plateau.

58. Mike Stroud, during our Antarctic continental man-haul crossing in 1993, approaching a crevassed area of the Beardmore Glacier.

59. Scott's men probing a crevasse; all three men are separately harnessed to their sledge to minimize the dangers.

60. In 1979, we traveled through 900 miles of intermittent sastrugi. Those in this photograph average two feet in height, with the furrow between each "wave" approximately six feet wide. When traversing such areas, it is often best to man-haul without skis.

61. One of Amundsen's dog teams on the plateau in 1911.

62. I took this photograph of Mike Stroud on the plateau, a twelve hours' man-haul from the Pole, shortly before he suffered a hypothermia attack at a temperature of −68°C windchill.

63. Mike Stroud some twenty miles from the Gateway, at the base of the Beardmore Glacier. Although our sledges were comparatively light by this point, the soft snow conditions made for very heavy man-hauling. It was much worse for Scott's men due to the crossbars between their sledge runners.

64. In 1969, I contemplate finding a route to begin the first recorded descent of Briksdals Glacier, in central Norway. Such lethal unstable areas can be found in many parts of the Beardmore Glacier and caused Scott's men (and others) a great deal of heartache.

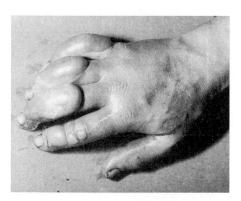

65. This frostbitten hand belongs to Dr. Edward Atkinson and, though serious, did not result in amputation.

66. In 2000, I was forced to submerge my hand in the North Polar Sea for three to four minutes to rescue sinking life-essential equipment. A week later, I had frostbite in five fingers, which resulted in partial amputations five months later.

67. The sketch by Edward Wilson indicating that long before setting out, Scott contemplated taking five, not four, men on the final Pole journey.

68. At the South Pole, a photograph taken on January 18, 1912.
Left to right: Wilson, Scott, Evans, Oates, and Bowers.

69–73. "Taff" Evans (top left) died first on the glacier. Not long afterward Oates (top right) could no longer carry on. Only eleven miles from their main resupply depot, Wilson (right), Bowers (bottom left), and Scott died in their tent. The date of their death is generally accepted as March 29, 1912, the date of Scott's last diary entry, but no one can know for sure, and it is possible that Scott may have survived until March 30.

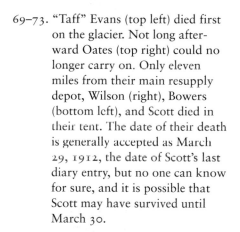

74. The men of *Terra Nova*, on hearing of the tragedy, erected this cross above Hut Point in memory of their dead friends. It stands there today.

will pay top rates for a reasonably convincing demolition job on even a mediocre "celeb," providing their legal department, in these litigious times, has rid the book of all nonprovable defamations. The big debunking book is assured of high sales figures in Britain because denigration is part of our national character, along with talking ourselves down, and, another aspect of the same tendency, our love of feeling "up against it." Huge military victories are never debated with such gusto as narrow escapes where a few Brits turn the tables on superior forces. Dunkirk, Agincourt, and Rorke's Drift are fine examples.

One motive for debunking is political. In 1698, radical Whig politicians who wished to "purify" Oliver Cromwell's image commissioned the writing of a brilliant forgery purporting to be the memoirs of one of his generals. This book successfully fooled everyone until the late twentieth century. A single book misled even the most erudite historians for three centuries. The grandfather of twentieth-century British debunking is Lytton Strachey, who at about the time of Scott's death left Cambridge and started writing a collection of condensed exposés of famous Victorians. His targets included the public-school system, imperialism, liberalism, and the sort of religious evangelism that assured men and women of heavenly grace in the trenches because God hated the Hun. The subjects of Strachey's *Eminent Victorians* included such icons of the day as Gordon of Khartoum and Florence Nightingale. "Everyone knows the popular conception," Strachey wrote, "of Florence Nightingale. The saintly, self-sacrificing woman . . . the Lady with the Lamp . . . the vision is familiar to all. But the truth was different." This was shocking indeed to the establishment of his day, but the book would now merely be seen as ultramild and wittily cynical.

If Strachey was a punchy little terrier nipping at venerable trouser-legs, he set the pattern for a succession of rottweilers. His advice to future biographers was: "It is not [the biographer's] business to be complimentary, it is his business to lay bare the facts of the case, as he understands them." Strachey shunned direct interviews, straight chronological storytelling, or research confined to the shelves of libraries. "If the biographer is wise," he wrote, "he will adopt a subtler strategy. He will attack his subject in unexpected places; he will fall upon the flank, or the rear; he will shoot a sudden, revealing searchlight into obscure recesses, hitherto undivined. He will row out over that great ocean of material, and lower down into it, here and there, a little bucket, which will bring up to the light of day some characteristic specimen, from those far depths, to be examined with a careful curiosity."

Another rationale for debunking, perhaps the simplest of all motives, is finding someone else to blame. Successive representatives of the Fletcher Christian and William Bligh families, down through the generations, have indulged in this. The struggle to adjust their forebears' reputations still goes on. It started with Christian's first cousin, the then lord high chancellor of England, who used his influence to paint the actually humanitarian Bligh as a sadist of the worst order, thereby justifying cousin Christian's mutinous behavior. Later, as was to happen with Captain Scott in the film *The Last Place on Earth* (and with William Wallace in *Braveheart*), the movie industry became involved and persuaded the world that a whole new set of dramatic "facts" that emanated from the relevant scriptwriter's imagination were historical events. By the 1930s, Bligh was established worldwide as a brute and Fletcher Christian as a hero figure played successively by Errol Flynn, Clark Gable, and (a slim) Marlon Brando.

The scale of human suffering in the First World War demanded that blame be allotted. The war produced a hundred thousand heroes and, since somebody had to take the blame for all the slaughter, a hundred new villains too, all of them ripe for the penetrating attentions of rottweiler reincarnations of Strachey, many as yet unborn when the war ended. The standard suspects for the carnage were lined up; some were politicians but most were the likes of Haig and his generals, all of whom, it seems, were unintelligent and vain, whereas their German counterparts were good to their troops and shrewd to boot. The fact that they lost and the British side won is explained away by Uncle Sam's arrival (albeit only for the last seven months of a five-year war). Never let it be said that historic facts get in the way of a determined denigrator.

Another handy candidate to blame for the horror of it all was, of course, the British class system: eggheaded Ruperts leading flocks of yokels to certain death on feudal lines. Forget the fact that, alone of the armies, the British had an ex-ranker as their overall boss and an officer corps far more socially elastic than the French or Germans. The post-traumatic shock of a million dead prevented a balanced verdict. Myths were established that soon became facts. Radicals blamed imperialism and the class system. Cynics rubbed the public's noses in the pointlessness of it all, especially when Hitler popped up a short while later.

The focus on who to blame for the First World War was diffused by the Second but returned with a vengeance in the 1960s with a plethora of books, plays, and films stressing futility and incompetence, like *Oh! What a Lovely War,* which, for most of Britain, became the reality of the Great War. Or, perhaps, it summarized more accurately a quite different reality, the mood of the British in the 1960s and their readiness to soak up whatever facts the media fed them.

By the 1970s, there was a growing interest in biographies written with character assassination as their main motive. To gain a lucrative contract with your publisher, especially for a first biography, you had to produce a real killer, a principle that still holds. Here are a couple of random examples. In 2002, a critic reviewing the reviews of Fiona MacCarthy's book on Byron wrote that it was a "sad comment on our culture," that a major biography such as this "has little to say about what made Byron a great poet," while "devoting several hundred pages to proving that he was a closet homosexual." Another critic, reviewing reviews of a biography of the author Anthony Burgess, by Roger Lewis, quoted Philip Hensher: "It's some time since I read a book so exhilaratingly lacking in human charity as this one. [The book may] grow less and less convincing through the sheer volume of insult [but it is] deplorably enjoyable." The critic went on: "His book is not so much a conventional biography as a hostile and extended critique of the novelist both as a person and as a writer [which accuses him along the way of] sado-masochism, reckless parenting, tightness with money . . . it's true that character assassination does make for livelier copy than hagiography, but what's entertainingly malicious in a short article becomes tedious at book length."

Both Byron and Burgess were of course dead and could refute nothing that MacCarthy and Lewis cared to write about them. Such writing may be summed up as a supreme form of cowardice. The great advantage for the dedicated debunker in attacking the reputation of a dead targeted figure is, of course, that you can make up as many vaguely believable lies as you like, and, though you may deeply offend surviving relatives, there is nothing they or anybody else can do about it.

Captain Robert Scott's biographers have been many and varied. I give a list of most of them at the back of this book. But we can already see that by the 1970s, the time was ripe for a massive Scott debunk. The mood of the seventies scorned anyone seen as an old-style hero, in particular a Briton with a stiff upper lip. Character assassinations had become major sellers. Scott debunkers would benefit enormously from the fact that the socially acceptable moral and value standards of Victorian society were so utterly different from what is considered politically correct and fashionable thinking today. These two ways of thinking are almost unrecognizable, so it is very easy to present individuals like Scott as representative of much that is politically unacceptable today and to forget that he must be judged only as a human being of his times. None of us, after all, would want to be posthumously measured against a totally inappropriate set of values, yet that is exactly what Scott's modern detractors have done.

During the years after the expedition, various books were written, by Teddy Evans, Priestley, Cherry-Garrard, Taylor, and Ponting. Clements Markham also wrote about Scott's polar achievements and all six books were "polite" about him.

Cherry-Garrard published his famous book, *The Worst Journey in the World,* in 1922, ten years after his abortive attempt to relieve Scott. This was not a biography of Scott but an exciting story about the *Terra Nova* venture, told by Cherry-Garrard but heavily influenced by his friend and neighbor George Bernard Shaw and his wife, Charlotte. Neither Cherry-Garrard nor George Bernard Shaw was interested in religion; both hated war but loved literature and the act of writing. They spent many contented hours together at their country homes wandering their grounds and discussing Scott. Shaw decided that he disliked Scott, whom he had never met, intensely, but he enjoyed the company of Scott's widow, Kathleen.

In a letter to Kathleen, Shaw described his input in persuading Cherry-Garrard to expand *The Worst Journey* beyond a mere description of events and to discuss personalities, especially Scott's: "I never met Con, and had only a derived personal interest in him through you. He was only a figure in a tragedy for me: I had no idea what manner of man he was. Cherry's book brings him to life and makes him therefore much more interesting. But bringing a hero to life always involves exhibiting his faults as well as his qualities. Cherry describes Con as he was without criticising him. But I, of course, make criticisms."

Shaw had a penchant for stirring up trouble among his various friends and he did his best to create sparks between Kathleen and Cherry-Garrard for a while after *The Worst Journey* was published. For thirty-six years, Cherry-Garrard chewed over the minutiae of the *Terra Nova* expedition with Shaw until Cherry-Garrard died, still clearheaded, at ninety-two. Until the end, Shaw continued to impress on Cherry-Garrard how *he* was not to blame. Scott's death, Shaw opined, was entirely self-inflicted.

Shaw's imagination worked many a new angle into all aspects of the long-ago tragedy, even suggesting to Cherry-Garrard that Scott had abandoned Taff Evans and had later sat staring at Oates until he left the tent, forced by his leader to commit suicide. This was a typically George Bernard Shaw piece of mischievous fiction that did little harm at the time but would later be added to the anti-Scott mythology as hard fact. Shaw labeled Scott as the "most incompetent failure in the history of exploration," an opinion that was reflected in a long, updating "postscript" that Cherry-Garrard added to his 1951 reissue of *The Worst Journey*.

In the end, Shaw himself tired of or at least recognized some of his own less-endearing traits. He wrote of his own cynicism: "you chaff and sneer and taunt them for not doing the things you daren't do yourself. And all the time you laugh! laugh! laugh! eternal derision, eternal envy, eternal folly, eternal fouling and staining and degrading, until, when you come at last to a country where men take a question seriously and give a serious answer to it, you deride them for having no sense of humour, and plume yourself on your own worthlessness as if it made you better than them."

Cherry-Garrard lived most of his life haunted by the death of his colleagues and was very fortunate in his late marriage to a girl, many years his junior, who cared for him loyally through long years of illness, depression, and periods of psychotic delusion, shot through, fortunately, with patches of contentment and enthusiasm. Whether Shaw's friendship really helped him is not clear.

In 1928, Gordon Hayes, a Worcestershire vicar who had studied at Cambridge and had, as his full-time hobby, an avid interest in polar history, produced the first constructive criticisms of Scott's Pole journey. He complained to Dr. Hugh Mill (a past friend of Scott and a huge fan of Shackleton), during a ten-year correspondence, that of all the *Terra Nova* survivors who had said they would help his Scott research, only Ponting and, to a lesser extent, Priestley had done so. His attack on Scott included the points that he should have used dogs, was a bad planner and organizer, traveled too late in the season, was inclined to depression, suffered from and died of scurvy, and that the *Terra Nova* research repeated the *Discovery* work.

Debenham summarized the Hayes book: "His whole criticism . . . reads perilously like a vast expansion of the words 'Scott was a fool not to use dogs and that it was faulty organisation not to have done exactly as Amundsen did.'" Yet of Amundsen Hayes merely noted: "We must now summarize the obvious criticism of Amundsen's enterprise. This, to be perfectly frank, is its uselessness." Four years later, Hayes wrote another book about Antarctic exploration, *The Conquest of the South Pole,* which was uncritical of Scott and said of him: "Captain Scott must have been a man after God's own heart, for his most noble quality was his unselfishness . . . [He was] both a sensitive and a modest man . . . noted for an iron determination and self-reliance. He was, at the same time, impulsive and temperamental, and thus had a varied and interesting character."

Despite these relatively mild critiques by Hayes and Cherry-Garrard, Scott's image remained that of an explorer of whom the British could be as proud as they were of Livingstone. The first approved biography of Scott, the proofs of which were read by Kathleen, was released in 1929, a fairly anodyne affair with new access to private letters between Scott and Kathleen. George Seaver in 1940, Frank Debenham in 1959, Harry Ludlam in 1965, Reginald Pound in 1966, and L. B. Quartermain in 1967 all added new aspects to the Scott story through original research into journals, letters, and archives, but nothing likely to cause Scott to stir in his tent. In 1974, a book by Peter Brent delved a touch deeper and tried to introduce a harsher judgment of Scott, more in tune with other biographers of the 1970s who by then were giving their subjects the full X-ray treatment. But still

Scott retained his seeming immunity from the ever-circling literary vultures and would-be assassins.

In 1974, Roald Amundsen's reputation received a severe jolting by a fellow Norwegian. Kåre Holt called his book *The Race* a novel, but nonetheless the Norwegian polar establishment took grave offense. With a Norwegian debunker taking vicious potshots at national hero Roald Amundsen, the scene was set for Scott's long-overdue assassination by a fellow Englishman. He was about the only high-caliber hero still perched on his pedestal. Others, shot down almost monthly by the mid-seventies, included Albert Schweitzer, Winston Churchill, and V. I. Lenin.

The year 1977 produced two interesting new Scott biographers quite likely to deal the death blow. Certainly David Thomson tried hard and was as critical as was possible within the constraints of retaining his own objectivity. He emphasized every possible flaw in Scott's performance and persona but, in my view, he failed to ruin a dead man's reputation. Elspeth Huxley's Scott biography that year involved a good deal of new material and sold well. She scrutinized Scott with the eye of a shrewd and professional biographer who had over thirty books to her name. In the end, she decided that Scott was "anything but the simple, straightforward sailorman . . . that he may once have seemed to be" but was a hero nonetheless.

Then, in 1979, Roland Huntford's *Scott and Amundsen* was published. A year later, when I reached the South Pole for the first time, I spent four days there helping the denizens with the dishwashing in their canteen. I chatted to many of the overwintering scientists and was interested to hear their views on various explorers, including Scott. They mentioned this new book. Did I know about it? Apparently the whole story about Scott the polar hero was a British imperialist plot, and this Huntford guy had exposed it as such. I meant to buy the book on returning home but forgot.

In the mid-eighties, I was reminded about it by an unusual source, Mrs. Raisa Gorbachev, to whom I was making a presentation in Moscow. I did then buy the Huntford book and watched the video (of which, more later). Both contained information that I found questionable but I enjoyed them purely as entertainment. The Huntford book was very well written, in the style of an exciting novel, and, not being well versed in polar history at the time, I was impressed by Huntford's lengthy acknowledgments and lists of references.

In 1993, I man-hauled across the Antarctic continent with Mike Stroud, and, in 1997, quite by chance, I saw the Central TV film again. This time it rang a very different bell.

My own experience as a polar explorer, leader, and man-hauler had deepened. Recovering from frostbite in 2000, I made detailed notes on the book and began to read all the books I could get hold of about Amundsen and Scott, some 112 in all. I became slowly aware of the magnitude of the change wrought on Scott's reputation—indeed, this interpretation of Scott had spread so widely as to become the accepted view. Once my own polar work convinced me that there was something profoundly wrong in Huntford's book, I determined to try and return Scott to his rightful place in the history of exploration.

The reason this matters so much, and the reason I've devoted so much time and effort to this quest, is because up to this day, *Scott and Amundsen* is used as *the* Scott reference book. New biographies of Scott, since Huntford's, use his quotes and text. He is generally accepted as the world's number one polar biographer, and much of his book is now treated as history.

His image of Captain Scott in *Scott and Amundsen* has radically changed the world's concept of Scott. By the time a new edition of the paperback was published in 1999, Paul Theroux was writing of Scott in his introduction as "insecure, panicky, humorless . . . a bungler . . . always self-dramatizing." For a snapshot of Roland Huntford's attitude to his main protagonists, it is interesting to compare the index entries for Scott and Amundsen. Under "characteristics" for Amundsen, we have: "animals, love of; leadership, capacity for; magnetism; modesty; physical fitness; rectitude, sense of; sensitivity; sexual reticence; short sight; single-mindedness; stoicism; vanity." Scott's "charactistics" entry reads: "absentmindness; agnosticism; command, unsuitability for; criticism, refused to accept; depression, bouts of; emotionalism; impatience; improvisation, belief in; inadequacy, sense of; insecurity; insight, lack of; irrationality; isolation; jealousy; judgement, defective; leadership, failure in; literary gifts; panic, readiness to; recklessness; responsibility, instinct to evade; sentimentality; vacillation."

The question that I increasingly wanted an answer to was: How did

Huntford manage to convince his readers that his version of Scott was the correct one?

First, Huntford presented himself as a man with practical snow and ice experience, but shows his ignorance of polar regions with statements like: "[At] about –40°C . . . each breath burns like fire." I have man-hauled at –50°C and have never experienced this Huntford phenomenon. He writes too that Amundsen's man Stubberud, being a house builder, knew how to dig large snow grottos "without the risk of the roof collapsing." Most expeditions that winter in Antarctica, including mine, dig such grottos to store gear or as work rooms. You don't need a house builder.

Huntford wrote of Scott as "incapable of the specialized interplay of arms, torso and legs [at] . . . the heart of cross-country skiing. [Scott] struggled awkwardly . . . squandering energy with every step . . . [He] was ill-suited to bear the strains of Polar travel." In fact, Scott, over a succession of polar journeys, was to prove himself eminently well suited to polar travel and by far the best individual man-hauler of the age. I have taught army teams to cross-country ski using the interplay of limbs that Huntford mentions and I have also man-hauled heavy sledges for thousands of miles on skis. I can confirm that Huntford, for whatever reason, seems to have missed the point: Good skiing techniques are utterly irrelevant to heavy man-hauling.

Scott is castigated for his use of man-made clothing materials, not furs, even though polar experts know that man-haulers would be unable to move in furs. They would perspire too much. For man-hauling, even at –50°C, it is best if you wear lightweight cotton clothes, otherwise your sweat is trapped and freezes on your skin as your body cools. Furs are only correct for dog drivers—the dogs are the ones exerting themselves.

Huntford states: "Scott forced the pace. He covered thirteen miles a day, not far short of Amundsen's fifteen . . . on the march for nine or ten hours, hauling heavy weights . . . Dragging 200 pounds per man up to 10,000 feet was inhuman enough." It is not inhuman for a leader like Scott to set such a man-haul pace, it is standard practice and remains so today. Nine or ten hours is the norm. Two hundred pounds is a comparatively light load and ten thousand feet happens to be the average height of the polar plateau.

Huntford alludes many times to Scott battling with Shackleton as "with an imaginary foe." He suggests that Scott kept comparing his progress with that of Shackleton, "the ghostly rival," in order to "sneer" at Shackleton. Having completed many expeditions over terrain where some predecessor has been, I know that the most natural and satisfying activity each day is to compare progress with that of the previous traveler. This does not involve "sneering," merely checking progress against some known yardstick. Polar explorer Vivian Fuchs said of Huntford's book: "It is one man's interpretation, and his inexperience of the conditions he is writing about clearly makes him incompetent to judge them."

Second, Huntford tapped into the mood for late-twentieth-century mea culpa breast-beating, by Britons feeling guilty about their colonial past, by directly relating Scott to that legacy. "Scott," he emphasizes, "came from a rich and mighty empire, albeit in decline; Amundsen from a small, poor country, with a sparse and scattered population." Another plus for the Norwegian, since the British love the underdog! Huntford returns to his refrain, that "Scott personified the glorious failure which by now had become a British ideal. He was a suitable hero for a nation in decline." He describes Amundsen as an upper-class Viking whose deeds were synonymous with Norway's emergence as an independent state and Scott as a middle-class brewer's son personifying the British national decline. The year 1870, two years after Scott's birth, he calls the "start of the collapse of British power. If Scott's birth had been chosen as a symbol, it could scarcely have been better timed."

Huntford emphasizes matters of class. "Scott had the nervous uncertainty of the ambitious middle class faced with a natural aristocrat" and again, "The appearance of an upper-class captain of Dragoons in a middle-class enterprise was an interesting prospect." Scott never writes of class matters, but, in segregating his officers from his men, causes Huntford to write: "Scott . . . ran her under Naval discipline with rigid segregation of officers and men." There is, in fact, no evidence of rigidity. The hut's library, kept in Scott's room, was open to everyone; all games and sports were played together. Scott wrote that, apart from messing and sleeping in the winter hut, "it is an advantage on such an expedition as ours that all should share the same hardships and, as far as possible, live the same lives."

Third, Huntford sometimes gets ahead of the evidence—as he has said,

"One has to interpret now and then." In a BBC *Nationwide* television interview, he explained his description of Scott trying to force Oates out to his death as being based on his, Huntford's, "intuition." When Sara Wheeler interviewed him for her 1996 book, *Terra Incognita,* she asked if he ever hankered to go south, since his polar descriptions were so good. He replied: "No. These are landscapes of the mind, you see." So even his scenery descriptions are intuitive. In 1972, the *Times Literary Supplement,* reviewing his book on Sweden, commented: "His book is interpretive rather than informative: a more dispassionate account might have been more convincing." Wayland Young, in the magazine *Encounter,* wrote of *Scott and Amundsen* that Huntford "was satisfied, not by any documentary evidence, not even by a contemporary hint or allusion or expectation; he was satisfied by his own understanding . . . [This] is not the procedure of a scholar; to be satisfied by those means that a man long dead was a villain . . . is the procedure of a novelist."

Fourth, Huntford damned Scott in the eyes of his readers through selective omission. He quotes, but rarely from the hundreds of diarists with good things to say about Scott in order to balance the quotes he frequently uses from the few critical diarists. In this book, I use both.

Huntford announced to the Norwegian reviewers of his book that he had "discovered that Scott had falsified his diary of the *Discovery* expedition. He altered his diaries. They later got lost. I found them with a branch of the family and was first to compare them with the published account . . . I am not alone to react against our historic cover-up, the dangerous myths we have invented to cultivate our glorious [English] reputation." To *Aftenposten,* and referring to *Scott's Personal Journals,* Huntford admitted that these diaries had not been altered by Scott but that "the establishment" covered up for Scott, "and that is exactly what we suffer from in England." Huntford adds: "I have found more than seventy large omissions," mostly "spiteful things [Scott wrote] about those he was responsible for."

Already discussed in this book is the obvious reason for the seventy omissions Huntford refers to, all of which would have been made by Scott had he lived, since they were mostly his private notes, good and bad, about his men and never intended to go further. Huntford's pointed comments about explorers' use of their diaries often seems contradictory. He brands

Scott as dishonest for omissions and for "tampering with the record," in using much, but not all, of his diary material. Yet when Huntford gives examples of similar omissions in Amundsen's *The North West Passage,* he says
Amundsen is "selective" but "in what he tells there is no tampering with the
record." Although Huntford constantly uses Armitage's twenty-year-old
anti-Scott mutterings, he says of an equivalent critic of Amundsen: "This is
reconstruction after brooding, and is unlikely to be the whole truth."

Throughout his book, he almost entirely ignores the scientific aspect of
Scott's expeditions that involved far more man hours of work and travel
than his Pole-journey travels ever did. Yet science was Scott's main purpose.
His critic Cherry-Garrard makes crystal clear that the expedition's devotion
to science was genuine. Cherry-Garrard, Scott, and the rest also stated that
their other main aim was to reach the Pole.

The thirty-five pounds of rocks Scott carried were, in Huntford's words,
"a pathetic little gesture to salvage something from defeat at the Pole." If
Scott and his men had been first at the Pole, does Huntford believe they
would have left the rocks behind? The British Museum (natural history)'s
official report on the expedition's research stated: "The heroic efforts of the
Polar Party [in collecting the rocks] were not in vain. They have laid a solid
foundation; [which] . . . will stimulate their successors to provide material
for the superstructure [of the continent]." Many decades later, this material
furnished scientists with their first proof not only of profound changes in the
earth's climate but in its very shape and structure. Huntford further claimed
that such rocks were unnecessary, as Shackleton "had already done most of
the work." In fact, Scott's specimens revealed the age of the Beacon sandstone and the key to the origin of Antarctica, whereas Shackleton's did not.

Oates provides Huntford with his most potent ammunition, and Huntford is clearly an Oates fan. On the other hand, Huntford has openly stated
that he "can't *stand* Wilson," no doubt because Wilson is a very critical,
very honest man whose comments on Scott are mostly favorable. Huntford
mentions to readers of *Scott and Amundsen* that new material had fallen
into his hands, including the last letters of Captain Oates, which had been
unavailable to previous authors. He also told his publishers that this should
be stated in the publicity material being sent out with the book. This suggests that *he* had unearthed the letters. In fact, the coauthor of a proposed

book on Oates, Sue Limb, had already been shown all these letters by Oates's surviving sister, Violet. All Oates's letters had been jealously guarded by his mother, Caroline, who had ordered them all to be destroyed on her death. Violet had secretly copied many of them just before their destruction, and, because she liked Sue Limb, made them available to her in 1963. Frank Debenham, who had introduced them, wrote to her with key advice about Oates and his letters: "you will have to depend more on circumstantial evidence, what he said and did, than what he wrote down. His character will only appear from his deeds and not from his words."

Huntford seems to have ignored that advice, just as he ignored Oates's own advice when, recognizing his own tendency to overcriticize, he wrote to his mother: "please remember that when a man is having a hard time he says hard things about other people which he would regret afterwards." Sue Limb, in her Oates book, took this to heart and wrote: "Oates's hard comments about Scott are vital to an understanding of the situation. His regrets are no less important."

Oates confided to Wilson in the death tent that his mother was the only woman he had ever loved. This love was more than reciprocated. Caroline Oates never recovered from the blow of his death. She slept every night in his bedroom, dressed for the rest of her life only in black, and bitterly attacked those who wrote biographies of Oates, however favorable, including Stephen Gwynn and Louis Bernacchi. She hated Kathleen Scott and felt that Captain Robert Scott was the sole reason for her son's death, choosing to forget that Oates had joined Scott fully aware that he might die. Had not Scott said in public: "We may get through, we may not. We may lose our lives. We may be wiped out." For years, Mrs. Oates would invite Meares, Debenham, and Atkinson to her London flat for dinner and would grill them about Scott. She prompted them with her belief that Scott had driven her son to "the extremities of suffering." Huntford adds: "Mrs. Oates . . . was perhaps going too far when she called Scott [her son's] 'murderer.'" He gives no reference for this phrase: It appears nowhere in the only collection of Mrs. Oates's letters to be itemized in Huntford's source list. I checked with Oates's biographer Sue Limb, who told me: "I'm fairly sure I must have told Huntford [in 1978] that I had the impression that Mrs. Oates considered Scott was responsible for her son's death, but asked him not to quote it." Sue Limb was right to caution Huntford over this, as such secondhand quotes, apparently from the grief-bitter mother of Oates, were not exactly reliable.

The obsessive Mrs. Oates, bitter and aggressive to the end, died alone at age eighty-three in her great country house with parts of every room swathed in black. She wrote that Atkinson had said: "Captain Scott would be very rude and not behave well and then be very friendly and try to make it up." She added that Meares had told her that "there used to be great trouble and unhappiness. Captain Scott would swear all day . . . and the worst was it was not possible to get away from the rows." Anger and blame are well recognized stages of grief. Judging from her diaries, Mrs. Oates had no emphatic religious inclinations and would not have been likely to accept her beloved son's death with pride as a selfless act of sacrifice for his colleagues and country.

Whether or not this old lady's memories were genuine recordings of comments from Atkinson and Meares, Huntford uses them as evidence that the *Terra Nova* expedition "had evidently been in a state of demoralisation, not to say incipient mutiny." On the earlier expedition's southern journey, Huntford claims actual mutiny—"This was the almost inevitable moment of mutiny"—using the Armitage tale of twenty years later, for which there seems to be no shred of evidence. Many such expeditions do cause enormous strain between members but, then and now, the time when such hostility is most obvious to third parties is always the moment the expedition returns to civilization. When Scott, Shackleton, and Wilson returned to their ship, observed by well over a dozen keen diarists, all the evidence points to the fact that the three of them were getting along extremely well. As Shackleton's diary also recounts, which in no way supports Huntford's suggestion of friction (let alone mutiny) on the southern journey.

Other serious claims by Huntford for which there is apparently equally scant evidence include the concept that the navy would not have allowed any good man to go on the *Discovery* expedition, as war was in the offing. So Markham was coerced into accepting a "dull lieutenant with mediocre prospects" because there were no alternatives. War was fifteen years away, and Scott was at that time recommended, on his merits, for promotion to captain.

Roland Huntford comments on the Meterological Office's report of the *Discovery*'s work: "The elementary error of confusing true and magnetic compass bearings had been made, and the wind observations were thus largely worthless." What he does not report is that in 1904, the Meteorological Office admitted that the mistake was theirs.

Huntford also claims: "From the start he [Scott] had led Evans to believe that he would go to the Pole." I can find absolutely no evidence for this. He also claims that Scott had decided to "break Evans so as to ease the task of sending him back." According to the Australian polar scientist Dr. Phillip Law: "There is absolutely no justification for [this] statement . . . It is a despicable concoction."

As we have seen, Huntford further claims Scott tried "to force Oates out to his death" and on television offered his "intuition" as evidence. With Oates dead, Scott is next accused of persuading Wilson and Bowers "to lie down with him and wait for the end." Wayland Young, Kathleen Scott's son by her second marriage, commented in *Encounter* that there was not a shred of evidence for the Huntford "deduction." It had been agreed that Bowers and Wilson should leave Scott and try for the next depot if the weather eased . . . but it didn't.

Huntford introduced homosexuality and adultery by turning Markham into a leering old queen and Kathleen into a shameless adulteress involved with Nansen in a Berlin hotel during her husband's Pole trip. Both accusations were levied without, it seems, a vestige of hard evidence. Both the people he libeled were dead. Huntford damns Markham from the start, stating: "Though married, with a daughter, Markham was a homosexual. He sometimes went south to indulge his proclivities safe from criminal prosecution. He liked earthy Sicilian boys." Huntford draws this conclusion, he says, from Markham's own diaries. From Markham's innocent comments about a trip to Sicily with his wife, Huntford draws his interpretation that Scott's patron must have been homosexual. Huntford has no source for this other than Markham's own diaries. But Markham wrote them while fully aware that they would be donated to a learned society—so, open to inspection—at a time when homosexuality was illegal and a taboo subject.

Huntford claims that Kathleen was bisexual, a feminist, a calculating adventuress, and past a desirable age when Scott married her. In reality, she was antifeminist, and when Scott proposed, she was being hotly pursued by two well-known suitors. He also claims that: "Nansen and Kathleen Scott had been having a love affair . . . It was consummated in a Berlin hotel." In Berlin, Kathleen actually stayed with American friends and with her cousin, an attaché at the British embassy there. Huntford also states that at that time she marked in her diary when her periods were due. This proves nothing, since she made such entries all her life. He also states that Nansen wrote of looking at a sofa on which she had lain.

Nansen undoubtedly had very strong feelings for her; Huntford's main basis for the adultery charge are Nansen's letters to Kathleen—hers to him do not survive. Nansen's letters are in the Cambridge University Library, as well as two other letters in which Kathleen convincingly denies any affair with Nansen. Writing to her son in 1938, she says of Nansen's letters: "I think if anyone read *carefully* they would see it was *not* an affaire *à out-rance* . . . I was a completely faithful wife—only I was not going to throw aside such a divine friendship . . . You know he was a very grand person. I am entirely proud of my friendship." Huntford chose to ignore this evidence, as it would have contradicted his allegation. Huntford denied to the press that he had ever read the letters: "I seem to have missed the letters," he said, despite having had them photocopied on June 3, 1976.

There are also allegations about Scott's own sex life. Huntford suggests that Scott went absent without leave from the navy for eight months due to an affair with a married woman. "But what happened at this time is obscure. Admiralty records are incomplete; they have almost certainly been pruned. There is the hint of an irregular trip home, the protection of a superior officer, and a cover-up." Exact details of actual postings can be unclear, but no more so in Scott's record than in that of any other officer. This seems to have led to Huntford's surmise that one such gap can only have been explained by an extramarital affair. His point—that "they have almost certainly been pruned"—suggests some kind of cover-up for which there is absolutely no evidence.

Huntford presses his case by his constant comparison of Scott with Amundsen. The reader soon forgets that Scott was not Norwegian and was responsive to a very different set of traditions. Sporting-background skills and national constraints on the two men were utterly different. To present a dual biography as an account of two men on an equal footing, striving for the same goal for the same reasons, is a clever but ultimately artificial exercise, having little basis in reality—though it works well in making for a very readable book. Huntford portrays the whole event as merely a straight race between two adventurers. The true picture was summed up in 1985 by Dr. David Drewry, chancellor of Hull University, who said: "It would be simpleminded to regard this chapter of polar endeavour as a pure race."

Did Huntford practice conscious deceptions to achieve his dramatic aim of completely changing the world's attitude toward Scott? I can only present the evidence I have gained from my research and let readers of this book make up their own minds. His fellow biographer Elspeth Huxley frequently met Huntford in the Scott Polar Institute while researching her own biography. According to a record of a telephone conversation with Sir Peter Scott (now among the Scott papers in Cambridge), she said of Huntford: "He was always spitting venom! I think he's crackers . . . [He was] animated by a burning hatred of your father . . . [and] he had this extraordinary kink . . . He was convinced that there was some scandal in his [Scott's] naval career and the last time I saw him I asked whether he had found it. He said, 'No, but I shall.'" Huxley also told him of Huntford's assertion that Captain Scott "was the sort of man who would have been an Admiral if he had survived and sent thousands of men to their deaths in the first World War."

For years before his book came out, staff at the Scott Polar Research Institute would say to visitors: "Oh, that's Roland Huntford. He's writing a great book about Scott." Huntford wrote to the children and other relatives of the Scott team on the institute-headed paper imprinted with the name of Dr. G. de Q. Robin, then director of SPRI. I have a copy of one such letter sent to the nephew of Edward Wilson in November 1978, asking permission to quote from Wilson's diaries. SPRI's present librarian has confirmed to me that "Roland Huntford had no official position within the institute and was simply a regular user of the library and archives. He had no right to use institute-headed paper." Some of the recipients of these Huntford letters, assuming from the letterhead that SPRI was behind him, gave their permission. Wilson's great-nephew, Dr. David Wilson, told me that when it became known that the letters were written on Huntford's initiative alone, it was too late. The hitherto good relationship between some of the recipients and the institute was already damaged: "The result was that few of the po-lar families trusted researchers again; indeed some of the families placed strict controls upon their archives as the result."

Huntford opened his long list of acknowledgments in the original edi-tion of his Scott book by expressing his thanks to Dr. Robin, the SPRI's di-rector. The institute's reaction to the book was such that Huntford, for a time after its publication, was not welcome there.

When Huntford first asked Peter Scott to let him see his father's private papers, he wrote that his intention was: "to achieve a dispassionate presen-tation of the evidence." His words reassured Peter Scott, who gave him full access to the private papers in his home at the Slimbridge Wildfowl Centre. Huntford wrote to Peter Scott in March 1978, by which time he had fin-ished the draft of his book, saying: "May I take the opportunity of thanking you for your generous help." Peter Scott wrote back: "I'm glad that your book is now finished and feel sure that it will add usefully to the under-standing of my father's character . . . I am ready, as I told you earlier, to per-mit publication of those documents . . . over which I retain publication rights. This is all in the spirit of our original conversation in which you as-sured me that your book was not going to be a debunking exercise." The book was duly published with, in the acknowledgments, glowing thanks to Peter Scott, which indicated that Captain Scott's own son fully approved of the book's contents.

Peter Scott immediately brought a court action against Huntford and is-sued a statement to the press: "Mr Huntford came to me with an introduc-tion from Messrs Hodder & Stoughton and, since they were also my own publishers and I had known them for some years, I naturally gave Mr Hunt-ford both my confidence and access to papers of my father and mother on condition that his book would not be a debunking exercise, since so many writers seem nowadays to indulge in character assassination of our national heroes once they can no longer defend themselves or seek redress. What he told me of his intentions only strengthened my confidence." Peter Scott then read the book and found that Huntford "had seriously and to my mind des-picably maligned my father and also my mother in the way he dealt with the evidence I had made available to him . . . In his 'acknowledgements,' Mr Huntford 'thanks' me for my help, which I regard as an insult."

Huntford, through his lawyers, replied to Peter Scott's lawyers that his book did not contain debunking items that were unfair. Their response was: "Apparently your client considers the book a fair biographical study and as such one to which our client would have given his approval and assistance, when he alleges bisexuality on the part of Sir Peter's mother, when he doubts her claims to virginity at the time of her marriage and when he refers in the most offensive terms to the alleged circumstances of Sir Peter's conception." The court action was settled against Huntford, who agreed to pay costs and to apologize. Perhaps, unsurprisingly, there is no mention of this case anywhere in Huntford's current paperback edition.

Wayland Young wrote: "I object to Roland Huntford's book as a son, because he maligns my mother and her first husband; as an owner of archives because I gave him access to them and he misused them; and as an (occasional) historian because he has dishonoured that essential calling and put its raw materials at risk, not only for himself but for others."

After *Scott and Amundsen*, Huntford began to research another biography. On November 20, 1979, a letter from the then director of the Royal Geographical Society appeared in *The Times*: "you published a letter from Mr Roland Huntford in which he uses the Royal Geographical Society as his address . . . his letter was sent without any authorization from the Society . . . our past President, Lord Shackleton . . . assures me that neither has the Shackleton family commissioned any biography of his father." Some years later, after the success of the Scott book, Huntford approached the family of Fridtjof Nansen, another intended subject. Nansen's next of kin was Marit Greve, his granddaughter, married to Tim Greve, the author of a two-volume biography of Nansen and the director of the Nobel Institute in Oslo. Tim Greve refused Huntford any access to the Nansen private papers; when Greve died in 1986, Huntford repeated his request, this time to his widow, and was again turned down.

Scott and Amundsen would always have been a partial book with a "one-note" attitude to Scott, very hurtful and painful to those involved in, or connected to, a great polar expedition, but it would have been of little importance had it not received so much coverage and if its influence had not been so lasting. A number of subsequent Scott biographers refer constantly to *Scott and Amundsen,* or praise Huntford's scholarship. *The Observer* voted the 2000 paperback reprint of *The Last Place on Earth* their "Paperback of the Week," and their reviewer, Caroline Boucher, wrote a single sentence that summed up the reaction to Scott of hundreds of thousands of readers worldwide: "Reading this book made my blood boil at the pigheaded arrogance of the man."

On the other hand, a more critical analysis did also emerge. Francis Spufford, author of *I May Be Some Time,* wrote: "Huntford's assault on Scott was so extreme it plainly toppled over into absurdity." The *Contemporary Review* observed: "Huntford, a journalist rather than a trained historian, can be criticised for his mis-use of evidence and subjectivity. His book cites an impressive range of source material, but in places the list flatters to deceive . . . His chief preoccupation was to write a good and controversial story for marketing reasons, as evidenced by his squeezing of certain material to fit his thesis." Not surprisingly, the *Polar Record* was equally unimpressed: "An account by an admirer of Amundsen who appears to have a paranoid dislike of Scott . . . another 'debunking' book typical of this age . . . If an unfavourable quotation is not available, the author disparages Scott by 'reading between the lines' or if this is not possible, he uses his imagination to construct the thoughts of Scott and his men . . . I refer to Huntford's determination to make the book readable, to embellish it with ideas unsupported by evidence."

Tryggve Gran's daughter, Ellen McGhie, wrote to the *Daily Telegraph*: "Huntford has seen fit to draw extensively, for his character assassination of Scott, on a diary published in Norway in 1915 by my father, Tryggve Gran. I recently translated this diary for the National Maritime Museum and it appears to have been dredged by Mr Huntford for anything that could conceivably be interpreted as derogatory to Scott and, by contextual manipulation, attributed to him opinions he did not express."

Was Scott the "horrid man" Huntford suggests, the inept, selfish risk taker portrayed in his book? He does not sound like a character that any sensible person would follow on one, never mind two, long polar expeditions. Yet the Huntford book converted millions into believing in a negative image of Scott. I wrote to Huntford and asked if I could interview him for this book. He declined, saying: "It is perfectly clear that we are on opposing sides." I asked people whom I knew had worked alongside Huntford in the

SPRI archives over many years what they knew about him. Without exception, everybody I asked had the impression that Huntford's father was some English colonial gentleman given to romantic travels in pre-Soviet Russia, had married there, and moved to Cape Town, where Roland was born. The result was a young Englishman with romantic parentage. Huntford has told interviewers that "my mother was Russian and my father was a colonial— but he spent, as far as I know, a lot of time in Russia. Before the Revolution." He told Dr. Charles Swithinbank, the Cambridge-based glaciologist, that "his father was an Army officer and his mother was from Russia." On the jacket flaps of his books, we learn that he was born in South Africa in 1927, graduated from Cape Town University in 1947, and went to Imperial College, London. He took a post with the UN in Geneva in 1959, and was a journalist for *The Spectator.* In 1961, he became *The Observer*'s winter-sports correspondent in Scandinavia and the Alps, where he gained firsthand experience of Nordic skiing and of training and driving dog sleds.

In the 1960s, Huntford was taken on by the late Chris Brasher of *The Observer* as a sports correspondent and, later, as that paper's man in Scandinavia. He sent his publisher, for use on the Scott book cover, a photo of himself with a dog and sledge. He explained that the dog was his pet, which he had trained to pull a sledge in a suburban forest. The author biography in the publicity brochure proclaimed, with Huntford's approval, that he was "amply qualified to comprehend the subject of polar exploration," describing him as a "linguist, cross-country skier, mountaineer and dog-driver."

Apart from establishing that he wrote for *The Observer,* I failed to verify anything in the biography on his original book jacket. Then I discovered that Huntford had changed his name from Horwitch when he was thirty-two. His parents were a Lithuanian émigré named Sam Horowitz and the granddaughter of another Lithuanian émigré, Isaac Asherson, living in South Africa. Huntford broke with everything his father represented. His father was a mild man; he became a harsh critic. His parents were happy in South Africa. They were proud of their name and their heritage; he appears to have cut himself off from both.

When asked about his time at Imperial College, Huntford replies: "Oh, I left in disgrace . . . but that's another story." He states: "Quantum mechanics was my great interest. I was a bit fed up with London at that time,

which is an emotion I've never quite lost." When asked about his time with
the UN, Huntford replied that he acquired for them "an abiding contempt
and loathing." What did he think about Sweden? His second wife, of over
thirty years, is Swedish and he lived there for twelve years. The jacket blurb
of a book he wrote about Sweden, *The New Totalitarians,* boasts that he
makes the country sound like "the nearest example in the modern world to
the societies envisaged by George Orwell." Asked if, since he hates the likes
of Scott, loathes the UN, and detests the Swedish government, does Huntford consider himself a rebel, he replied: "Yes, you're right."

When asked in 2002 about his current thoughts on Scott, he replied: "I
think he was a horrible man and a bully. A really horrid man. And the navy
thought so too . . . his brother officers didn't like him. And the admiralty
didn't like him . . . he only got promotion through his family influence because his sister married the financial secretary to the admiralty . . . And I believe he may have had syphilis, which may have changed his personality."

Leif Mills, the Anglo-Norwegian biographer of Frank Wild, told me he
believed Huntford's motive in championing Amundsen was that: "he fell
into the trap of being more Norwegian than the Norwegians and that may
explain some of his attitude to Scott." Huntford developed an affinity with
the Norwegians as a super-race in terms of snow and ice travel. He may
have translated his admiration for Amundsen "into unnecessary and somewhat unfair criticism of some of the English explorers."

The former librarian of the Scott Polar Research Institute, Harry King,
said that Huntford, fresh from his years in Stockholm, wanted to smarten
himself up in Scandinavian eyes by producing a hagiographic biography of
Amundsen and, subsequently, another on Nansen. But his publishers told
him the British public had no interest in Amundsen and he should therefore
include Scott alongside the Norwegian.

The Scott of Huntford's book has now spread worldwide in movie for-
mat and is available in video form. It has become the popular truth. Dr. Susan Solomon, viewing the video in the South Pole station television lounge,
wrote: "Once such seeds were sown, Scott's mistakes grew to assume legendary proportions, radically transforming the figures of all of the men of
Scott's fatal expedition from heroism and tragedy to folly and even farce."
The script for that film, a Central TV production based on Huntford's biog-

raphy, was by Trevor Griffiths, a writer with a self-confessed political agenda. In his book *Judgement over the Dead*, Griffiths says he first looked at Huntford's story purely in terms of its relevance to current political events—"the present struggle," as he put it. "Maybe one could feel the build-up to the Falklands in advance . . . some recrudescence of imperialist ideology . . . During the Falklands crisis . . . I have never seen so many Union Jacks and flagwaving and bullshit talking in my life . . . This was [all over again] the Scott myth and its proximity to the Great War." Griffiths explained other aspects of the project: "One has to be fairly factual . . . about what actually took place . . . We [needed our actors] to cohere as representatives of a class in action—an imperial class in action."

The film was promoted around the world as "a gripping 7-episode film drama series [which] tells the true story of that legendary contest and the men behind the myth." As late as 2000, the video was still being shown at U.S. science stations in Antarctica as a key part of the polar induction program of the U.S. National Science Foundation, and described as an important part of South Polar history! And yet this "documentary" includes sequences of Markham fondling a pretty young Scott's knee, of Kathleen being carried naked to Nansen's hotel bed, of Atkinson telling the scientists to lie about Scott's death, of Scott using filthy language to his men. He was, in fact, known to not use even mild bad language. When a similar film with a foul-mouthed Scott was shown in Norway, Tryggve Gran was still alive. He wrote to the filmmakers, saying: "Scott never said anything like it . . . Scott was the last man in the world to use bad words."

After the Central TV film, the myth of Scott's self-serving incompetence continued to spread. Charles Lagerbom, a teacher who had visited Scott's hut by cruise ship, wrote an eminently readable biography of Henry Bowers, *The Fifth Man*. An American, Lagerbom's attitude shines through with prose like: "the Empire's spastic evolution towards Commonwealth" and "the glories of imperialism and the British Empire were drilled annually into little heads: these manufactured little imperialists then grew up and kept the empire alive and strong."

The year 1999 produced a rash of Scott-bashing books, including *The Rescue of Captain Scott* by Don Aldridge, which also relies on Huntford. In reviewing this book, Judy Skelton wrote: "The author tries to give his book every appearance of a scholarly work. It is packed with quotations, many from primary sources, each with a detailed reference to the original. Unfortunately the work is seriously flawed and cannot sustain this scholarly image. There are errors of fact and the majority of quotations I checked against original sources were found to be inaccurately reproduced, in a significant number of cases sufficiently so as to lay the author open to charges of deliberate misrepresentation." And reviewer T. H. Baughman from the University of Oklahoma wrote of the Aldridge book: "Too bad the tragedy of Antarctic historiography continues in the guise of works such as this one."

The National Maritime Museum in Greenwich held a major public exhibition in 2000 celebrating Scott and Amundsen's South Pole journeys and brought out a book at the same time called *South—the Race to the Pole*. The authors did not intend to be biased either way, but, presumably because of a lack of time for original research, seem inevitably to have leaned heavily on Huntford.

Two excellent books appeared in the first two years of this century, *Antarctica Unveiled* by David Yelverton and *The Coldest March* by Dr. Susan Solomon, both producing new historical and scientific facts to do away with the myth that Scott was merely an incompetent complainer. American scientists in the 1990s have established beyond doubt that March 1912 saw abnormally cold and unrelenting temperatures on the barrier at exactly the time and place where Scott's men slowed and died. For three straight weeks, temperatures were 10°C below average, conditions that have been repeated only once in the last thirty-eight years. According to Huntford, however, the weather in March 1912 around the time of Oates's death was "not exceptionally low for the season of the year."

Huntford and those of like mind tend to brand any book that is not entirely critical of Scott as sycophantic. No doubt they will write this book off on the same grounds. They will accuse me of wishing to identify with Scott. Nothing could be further from the truth. I would want to write about anyone whose life and work had been traduced as Scott's has been. As I have explained, my natural empathy is with Oates, at least up to the point where he joined *Terra Nova*.

Cherry-Garrard once wrote: "It is difficult for those who have never been to the Antarctic to write about it." To the best of my knowledge, Roland

Huntford has never been there, nor has he any experience of leading men, of survival in the cold, or of organizing a huge endeavor into the unknown.

I want to end my book with some words from those who knew Scott personally:

> He was a thoroughly cheerful and good natured man, a trifle impatient at times.
>
> —*Thomas Hodgson*

> Sound in his judgement and just in his criticisms he was always quick to appreciate and generous in praise.
>
> —*Herbert Ponting*

> He wouldn't ask you to do anything he wasn't prepared to do himself.
>
> —*Assistant Stoker Bill Burton*

> [Scott] had achieved something great for his country, for his family, and indeed [morally] for the whole of mankind . . . We Norwegians have always felt ourselves closely bound to Great Britain. Robert Falcon Scott strengthened the links tighter than ever before.
>
> —*Tryggve Gran*

> He is thoughtful for each individual and does little kindnesses that show it.
>
> —*Edward Wilson*

> I loved every hair on his head. He was a born gentleman and I will never forget him.
>
> —*Tom Crean*

Whether, having read this book, you believe me or you believe the denigrators' versions of Scott is, of course, entirely your choice. Either way, Scott, Bowers, Wilson, Oates, and Evans still lie frozen in the ice, as they have since the day their journey ended. They alone know the truth.

APPENDIX I: MEMBERS OF THE *DISCOVERY* EXPEDITION, 1901–1904

OFFICERS

Commander Robert F. SCOTT, RN	Leader (director of scientific staff)
Lieutenant Albert B. ARMITAGE, RNR	Second-in-command (navigator)
Lieutenant Reginald SKELTON, RN	Chief engineer (photographer)
Lieutenant Charles W. R. ROYDS, RN	First lieutenant (meteorologist)
Lieutenant Michael BARNE, RN	Second lieutenant
Sub-Lieutenant Ernest H. SHACKLETON, RNR	Third lieutenant (*invalided after first season*)
Sub-Lieutenant George F. MULOCK, RN	Third lieutenant (surveyor) (*replaced Shackleton in 1903*)

CIVILIAN SCIENTIFIC STAFF

Dr. Reginald KOETTLITZ	Surgeon, botanist, entomologist
Dr. Edward A. WILSON	Assistant surgeon, zoologist, artist

Louis C. BERNACCHI	Physicist and magnetician
Thomas V. HODGSON	Marine biologist
Hartley T. FERRAR	Geologist
Dr. H.R. MILL	*(left ship at Madeira)*
Dr. George MURRAY	*(left ship at Cape Town)*
Horace BUCKRIDGE	Laboratory assistant
	(joined at Cape Town)

SHORE PARTY CREW
(* returned after first season)

Warrant Officer James DELLBRIDGE, RN	Second engineer
William HUBERT	Donkeyman
Ldg. Stoker William LASHLY, RN	Chief stoker
	(trained in ballooning)
Ldg. Stoker Arthur QUARTLEY, RN	
Ldg. Stoker Thomas WHITFIELD, RN	
Stoker William PAGE, RN*	
Stoker Frank PLUMLEY, RN	*(joined at Simonstown)*
Warrant Officer Frederick DAILEY, RN	Carpenter
Shipwright James DUNCAN, RN	Carpenter's mate
Warrant Officer Reginald FORD, RN	Chief steward
Lance Corporal Arthur BLISSETT, RM	Steward
Private Gilbert SCOTT, RM	Steward
Clarence HARE	Assistant steward*
Henry BRETT	Cook*
Charles CLARK	Assistant cook and baker
Petty Officer 1st Cl. Thomas FEATHER, RN	Boatswain
Petty Officer 1st Cl. David ALLAN, RN	Assistant boatswain and quartermaster

Petty Officer 1st Cl. William MACFARLANE, RN	Quartermaster*
Petty Officer 1st Cl. William SMYTHE, RN	Quartermaster (*disrated to able seaman in New Zealand; rating restored 1903*)
Petty Officer 1st Class Jacob CROSS, RN	Assistant zoologist
Petty Officer 2nd Cl. Thomas KENNAR, RN	Acting quartermaster
Petty Officer 2nd Cl. Edgar EVANS, RN	
AB (Able seaman) Arthur PILBEAM, RN	Leading seaman
AB James DELL, RN	
AB William HEALD, RN	(*trained in ballooning*)
AB William PETERS, RN*	
AB Thomas WILLIAMSON, RN	
AB James WALKER	
AB Frank WILD, RN	
AB Thomas CREAN, RN	(*joined at Christchurch*)
AB George CROUCHER, RN	(*joined at Simonstown*)
AB Ernest JOYCE, RN	(*joined at Simonstown*)
AB William WELLER	Dog handler (*joined at Christchurch*)
AB George VINCE, RN	(*joined at Simonstown; drowned after cliff fall in Antarctic, 1902*)
AB Jesse HANDSLEY, RN	(*joined at Port Chalmers*)

OTHERS WHO DID NOT GO SOUTH

Hugh MILLER	Sailmaker (*discharged unfit in NZ*)
Job CLARK	Laboratory assistant (*discharged at Cape Town*)
Sydney ROPER	Cook (*discharged in NZ*)
Albert DOWSETT	Steward (*discharged in NZ*)

AB Henry BAKER, RN   (*deserted in NZ*)
AB Charles BONNER, RN   (*killed by fall from mast in NZ*)
AB John WATERMAN, RN   (*discharged with syphilis at Cape
                                       Town*)

AB John MARDON   (*discharged at Cape Town*)
AB James MASTERTON   (*discharged at Cape Town*)
AB Robert SINCLAIR   (*joined at Cape Town; deserted at
                                       Port Chalmers, NZ, after funeral
                                       of Bonner*)

APPENDIX II: MEMBERS OF THE *TERRA NOVA* EXPEDITION, 1910–1913

SHORE PARTY
*(*died on expedition)*

OFFICERS

Commander Robert F. SCOTT, CVO, RN*	Leader
Lieutenant Edward R. G. R. EVANS, RN	Second-in-command
Lieutenant Victor L. A. CAMPBELL, RN	Leader of northern party
Lieutenant Henry R. BOWERS, RIM*	In charge of stores
Captain Lawrence E. G. OATES, * (army)	In charge of ponies
Surgeon Edward L. ATKINSON, RN	Main party surgeon, parasitologist
Surgeon George LEVICK, RN	Northern party surgeon

SCIENTIFIC STAFF

Dr Edward A. WILSON*	Chief scientist and zoologist
George C. SIMPSON	Meteorologist
T. Griffith TAYLOR	Geologist
Thomas V. HODGSON	Marine biologist
Edward W. NELSON	Biologist
Frank DEBENHAM	Geologist
Charles S. WRIGHT	Physicist
Raymond E. PRIESTLEY	Northern party geologist
Apsley CHERRY-GARRARD	Assistant zoologist
Cecil H. MEARES	In charge of dogs
Bernard C. DAY	Motor engineer
Lieutenant Tryggve GRAN, RNN	Ski expert
Herbert G. PONTING	Photographer (*returned after first season*)

SHORE PARTY MEN

Chief Stoker William LASHLY, RN	
Petty Officer 1st Cl. Thomas CREAN, RN	
Petty Officer 1st Cl. Edgar EVANS, RN*	
Petty Officer 1st Cl. Robert FORDE, RN	
Petty Officer 1st Cl. Patrick KEOHANE, RN	
Petty Officer 1st Cl. Thomas WILLAMSON, RN	
Petty Officer 1st Cl. George ABBOTT, RN	Northern party
Petty Officer 2nd Cl. Frank BROWNING, RN	Northern party
A. B. Harry DICKASON, RN	Northern party
W. ARCHER, RN (Rtd)	Chief steward
Thomas CLISSOLD, RN (Rtd)	Cook

Frank HOOPER, RN (Rtd)	Steward
Anton OMELCHENKO	Groom
Demetri GEROF	Dog driver

SHIP'S PARTY

(excluding men discharged before first voyage south)

OFFICERS AND SCIENTISTS

Lieutenant Harry I. L. PENNELL, RN	Captain
Lieutenant Henry F. de RENNICK, RN	First officer
Lieutenant Wilfred M. BRUCE, RNR	Second officer
C.E.R.A. 2nd Cl. William WILLIAMS, RN	Chief engineer
E.R.A. 3rd Cl. William A. HORTON, RN	Second engineer
E.R.A. 2nd Cl. James WEBB	Third engineer *(first voyage south only)*
Ldg Shipwright Francis E. C. DAVIES, RN	Carpenter
Asst. Paymaster Francis R. H. DRAKE, RN (Rtd)	Meteorologist
Dennis G. LILLIE	Biologist
James R. DENNISTOUN	In charge of mules *(first voyage south only)*

CREW

Alfred CHEETHAM, RNR	Boatswain
Petty Officer 1st Cl. William HEALD, RN (Rtd)	
Petty Officer 1st Cl. Frederick PARSONS, RN	

Petty Officer 2nd Cl. Arthur
   BAILEY, RN
Leading Seaman Arthur BALSON,
   RN
AB William KNOWLES   *(first voyage south only)*
AB Joseph LEESE, RN
AB William MACDONALD
AB Mortimer McCARTHY
AB William McLEOD
AB Robert OLIPHANT   *(first voyage south only)*
AB James PATON
AB James SKELTON
AB Charles WILLIAMS
OS Petty Officer John MATHER,
   RNVR
OS P. BRADLEY
OS W. COPP   *(first voyage south only)*
Stoker Petty Officer Robert   Leading stoker *(died in accident*
   BRISSENDEN, RN   *in NZ)*
Acting Leading Stoker Edward   Leading stoker *(after Brissenden's*
   McKENZIE, RN   *death)*
Leading Stoker Bernard STONE, RN   *(first voyage south only)*
Stoker 1st Cl. William BURTON,
   RN
Fireman W. KELLY   *(first voyage south only)*
Fireman Charles LAMMAS   *(first voyage south only)*
Fireman Angus McDONALD
Fireman Thomas McGILLON
Steward W. NEALE

❧ ACKNOWLEDGMENTS ❧

My thanks to David Yelverton for his knowledge, advice, and facts from his excellent book *Antarctica Unveiled*. To Celene Pickard and Robert Headland for their patience, expertise, time, and interest. Likewise, Pamela Stevenson. A thousand thanks to Gina Rawle for all the long hours and midnights of careful and tortuous work. To Philippa Harrison and Maggie Body for their unequaled expertise and dedication. To Rupert Lancaster for his professionalism and patience. As always, my thanks to Ed Victor for making the book possible.

For reading and correcting the original text, as well as their time and knowledge:

David Wilson, Jonathan Shackleton, Judy Skelton, Sue Limb, Marit Greve, Geoffrey Hattersley-Smith, Philippa Scott, Ellen McGhie, Charles Swithinbank, Mike Stroud, Susan Solomon, Muriel Finnis, Ann Savours Shirley, Barbara Debenham, Gill Blenkinsop.

Also for the following publishers, authors, and organizations for allowing me to use quotes from their books and resources: June Back, David Drewry, Robert Feeney, Marit Greve, Wally Herbert, Harry King, Charles Lagerbom, Katherine Lambert, Sue Limb, Ellen McGhie, Leif Mills, William Mills, Diana

Preston, the Royal Geographical Society, Philippa Scott, the Scott Polar Research Institute, Judy Skelton, Michael Smith, Susan Solomon, Mike Stroud, Charles Swithinbank, Wayland Young (Lord Kennet), David Wilson, and David Yelverton. Extracts from *Captain Scott—The Full Story* by Harry Ludlam, reprinted by permission of W. Foulsham & Co. Ltd; extracts from *The Worst Journey in the World*, reprinted by permission of Angela Mathias; extracts from *A First-Rate Tragedy* by Diana Preston, reprinted by permission of Constable & Robinson Ltd; extracts from *"Birdie" Bowers of the Antarctic, Edward Wilson of the Antarctic*, and *Scott of the Antarctic* by George Seaver, reprinted by permission of John Murray (Publishers) Ltd; extracts from *Terra Incognita* by Sarah Wheeler, published by Jonathan Cape, reprinted by permission of The Random House Group Ltd. To Philippa and Falcon Scott for allowing me access to their private papers.

Thanks to the following organizations that have been so helpful with their resources:

Bedford County Library; British Antarctic Survey (David Walton, John Hall, Chris Rapley, and Nick Cox); Cambridge University Library; Dexcrest Ltd; Imperial College Archives; Minehead Library (Sarah Lander and Sue Rutt); Norsk Polarklubb; Royal Geographical Society; The Scott Polar Research Institute; The Captain Scott Society; Wootton Library, Bedfordshire.

Also for help, support, advice, and time, all those below:

Anna Jacobson-Amundsen, Mary Bates, Gervase Belfield, Kevin Bloot, Chris Brasher, Lawson Brigham, Juliet Brightmore, Joyce Burnett, Martha Calderon, Peter Carter-Ruck, Mike Curtis, John Deverell, David Drewry, Robert Feeney, Jill Firman, Karen Geary, Hermann Gran, Natalie Harrison, David Harrowfield, Tim Haskell, Wally and Marie Herbert, Don Hewitt, Justin Hobson, Kelly Jones, Mike Kantey, Harry King, Michael Kobold, Monica Kristensen-Solås, Katherine Lambert, Fergus Lawler, Mary Lynch, Lucy Martin, Angela Mathias, Hilary McEwan, Tom and John McGhie, Neil McIntyre, Peter Meadows, Roger Mear, Peter van der Merwe, William Mills, Sarah Newton, Greg Paterson-Jones, Lucia van der Post, Stephen Pritchard, Alan Rankin, Johnnie and Jacquie Rathfelder, Mike, Gemma, and Kate Rawle, Anne and Arthur Rivett, Gary Rolfe, Juan and Daniel Romero, Frances Savić, Shirley Sawtell, Michael Scott, Sergey Shevchenko, Michael Smith, Geoff Somers, Vernon Squire, Robert Stephenson, Mike Stroud, Robert Swan, Mike Tarver, Gordon Thomas, David Vaughan, Peter Wadhams, Mary Wakefield, Godfrey Waller, Graham Ward, Gritta Weil, Rolf Williams, Clive Woodman, Joanna Wright, Sian Wynn-Jones, Wayland Young, and, finally, to my wife, Ginny, for putting up with everything when the book took over.

None of the above named necessarily support or agree with any of this book's text.

Every reasonable effort has been made to acknowledge the ownership of the copyrighted material included in this volume. Any errors that may have occurred are inadvertent, and will be corrected in subsequent editions provided notification is sent to the author. All attempts at tracing the copyright holder of *Scott of the Antarctic* by Elspeth Huxley and *Scott of the Antarctic* by Reginald Pound, published by Weidenfeld & Nicolson, were unsuccessful.

❧ PICTURE ACKNOWLEDGMENTS ❧

Courtesy Antarctic Meteorological Research Center, Space Science and Engineering Center, University of Wisconsin-Madison: 33 (satellite image of the calving of icebergs in May 2000). © Corbis: 1 (Betterman), 74 photo Ann Hawthorne. © Bryn Campbell: 40, 41, 46, 50. © Ranulph Fiennes: 38, 39, 43, 48, 54, 57, 60, 66. © Virginia Fiennes: 45. © Howell, Fiennes, Stroud: 52, 53, 55, 58, 62, 63. © Hulton Arhives/Getty Images: 2. © National Maritime Museum, London: 44. © Robert Powell: 64. © Royal Geographical Society: 3–32, 34–37, 42, 47, 49, 51, 59, 61, 65, 68–73. © Robert Swan: 56. Courtesy David M. Wilson: 67.

✥ BIBLIOGRAPHY ✥

Aldington, Richard, *Lawrence of Arabia*, Collins, 1955.
Aldridge, Don, *Rescue of Captain Scott*, Tuckwell Press, 1999.
Alexander, C., *The Endurance*, Alfred A. Knopf, 1999.
Amundsen, R., ed. R. Huntford, *The Amundsen Photographs*, Hodder & Stoughton, 1987.
Anderson, V., *The Last of the Eccentrics*, Hodder & Stoughton, 1972.
Armitage, Albert B., *Cadet to Commodore*, Cassell, 1925.
Armitage, Albert B., *Two Years in the Antarctic*, Bluntisham Books, 1984.

Bainbridge, Beryl, *The Birthday Boys*, Duckworth, 1991.
Baughman, T. H., *Pilgrims on the Ice*, University of Nebraska Press, 1999.
Bernacchi, L. C., *Saga of the "Discovery,"* Blackie & Son, 1928.
Bernacchi, L. C., *To the South Polar Regions*, Hurst & Blackett, 1901.
Bickel, Lennard, *Shackleton's Forgotten Men*, Thunder's Mouth Press, 2000.
Bickel, Lennard, *Mawson's Will*, Stein & Day, 1977.
Bowman, Gerald, *From Scott to Fuchs*, Evans Brothers, 1958.

Brent, Peter, *Captain Scott and the Antarctic Tragedy*, Weidenfeld & Nicolson, 1974.

Cameron, Ian, *Antarctica: The Last Continent*, Cassell, 1974.

Cherry-Garrard, Apsley, *The Worst Journey in the World* (first pub. 1922), Chatto & Windus, 1951, Picador, 1994.

Crawford, Fred D., *Richard Aldington and Lawrence of Arabia*, Southern Illinois University Press, 1998.

Debenham, Frank, *In the Antarctic*, John Murray, 1952.

Debenham, Frank, ed. June D. Back, *The Quiet Land*, Bluntisham Books, 1992.

Dowswell, Paul, *True Polar Adventures*, Usborne, 2002.

Dunnett, H. M., *Shackleton's Boat*, Neville & Harding, 1996.

Evans, Edward (Mountevans), *South with Scott*, William Collins, 1952.

Evans, Edward (Mountevans), *The Antarctic Challenged*, Staples Press, 1955.

Feeney, Robert E., *Polar Journeys*, University of Alaska Press, 1997.

Fiennes, Ranulph, *Mind over Matter*, Sinclair-Stevenson, 1993.

Fiennes, Ranulph, *Hell on Ice*, Hodder & Stoughton, 1979.

Fiennes, Ranulph, *To the Ends of the Earth*, Hodder & Stoughton, 1984.

Fisher, M. & J., *Shackleton*, Barrie Books, 1957.

Fuchs, Sir Vivian, *Of Ice and Men*, Anthony Nelson, 1982.

Ganeri, Anita, *Perishing Poles*, Scholastic, 2002.

Godsell, Philip H., *Arctic Trader*, Robert Hale, 1951.

Gran, Tryggve, *The Norwegian with Scott* (first pub. 1915 in Norwegian), HMSO, 1984.

Gran, Tryggve, *Kampen om Sydpolen* (50 Years Polar Remembrance), translated by Gordon Thomas, 1961.

Griffiths, Trevor, *Judgement over the Dead*, Verso, 1986.

Gwynn, Stephen, *Captain Scott*, Bodley Head, 1929.

Hanssen, Helmer, *Voyages of a Modern Viking*, George Routledge & Sons, 1936.

Hayes, J. Gordon, *Antarctica*, Richards Press (first pub. 1928).

Hayes, J. Gordon, *The Conquest of the South Pole*, Keystone Library, 1936.

Heacox, Kim, *Shackleton the Antarctic Challenge*, National Geographic, 1999.

Herbert, Wally, *A World of Men*, Eyre & Spottiswoode, 1968.

Holt, Kare, *The Race*, Michael Joseph, 1976.

Huntford, Roland, *Scott and Amundsen*, Hodder & Stoughton, 1979.

Huntford, Roland, *The Last Place on Earth*, Atheneum, 1986.

Huntford, Roland, *Shackleton*, Atheneum, 1986.

Huntford, Roland, *The New Totalitarians*, Allen Lane, Penguin Press, 1971.

Huntford, Roland, *Nansen*, Duckworth, 1998.

Huntford, Roland, ed., *The Sayings of Henrik Ibsen*, Duckworth, 1996.

Huxley, Elspeth, *Scott of the Antarctic,* Pan Books, 1979.

Huxley, Elspeth, *Peter Scott*, Faber & Faber, 1993.

Jones, A. G. E., *Antarctica Observed*, Caedmon of Whitby, 1982.

Jones, A. G. E., *Polar Portraits*, Caedmon of Whitby, 1992.

Keir, David, *The Bowring Story*, Bodley Head, 1962.

King, Peter, ed., *Scott's Last Journey*, HarperCollins, 1999.

Lagerbom, C.H., *The Fifth Man—Henry R Bowers*, Caedmon of Whitby, 1999.

Lambert, Katherine, *"Hell with a Capital H,"* Pimlico, 2002.

Lansing, Alfred, *Endurance*, Hodder & Stoughton, 1961.

Lashly, William, ed. Ellis, *Under Scott's Command*, Victor Gollancz, 1969.

Law, Phillip, *Antarctic Odyssey*, Heinemann, 1983.

Limb, Sue, and Cordingley, Patrick, *Captain Oates: Soldier and Explorer,* Leo Cooper, 1982.

Lopez, Barry, *Arctic Dreams*, Macmillan, 1986.

Ludlam, Harry, *Captain Scott*, Foulsham, 1965.

Markham, C., *Antarctic Obsession*, Bluntisham Books, 1986.

Markham, C., *The Lands of Silence*, Cambridge University Press, 1921.

Mawson, ed. F. and E. Jacka, *Antarctic Diaries*, Unwin, 1988.

Mear, Roger, and Swan, Robert, *In the Footsteps of Scott*, Jonathan Cape, 1987.

Mill, H. R., *The Life of Sir Ernest Shackleton*, William Heinemann, 1924.

Mill, H. R., *Siege of the South Pole*, Alston Rivers, 1905.

Mills, Leif, *Frank Wild*, Caedmon of Whitby, 1999.

Nansen, Fridtjof, *Farthest North*, Tandem, 1975.

National Maritime Museum, *South, the Race to the Pole*, Cambridge University Press, 2000.

Neider, Charles, *Edge of the World*, Cooper Square Press, 2001.

Niven, Jennifer, *The Ice Master*, Macmillan, 2000.

Norman, Andrew, *T. E. Lawrence, Unravelling the Enigma*, Central Publishing, 2001.

Paxman, Jeremy, *The English*, Penguin, 1999.

Ponting, Herbert, *The Great White South*, Duckworth, 1950.

Pound, Reginald, *Scott of the Antarctic*, World Books, 1968.

Preston, Diana, *A First Rate Tragedy*, Houghton Mifflin, 1999.

Riffenburgh, Beau, *The Myth of the Explorer*, Belhaven Press, 1993.

Rose, Jonathan, *The Edwardian Temperament*, Ohio University Press, 1986.

Royds, Charles, *Diary*, T. Roger Royds, 2001.

Savours, Ann, ed., *Scott's Last Voyage*, Book Club Associates, 1975.

Savours, Ann, *The Voyages of the Discovery*, Virgin Books, 1992.

Scott, Robert Falcon, *Scott's Last Expedition* (Personal Journals), Universal-Tandem, 1973.

Scott, Robert Falcon, *Voyage of the "Discovery,"* Vols. I and II, Smith Elder, 1905.

Seaver, George, *"Birdie" Bowers of the Antarctic*, John Murray, 1947.

Seaver, George, *Edward Wilson of the Antarctic*, John Murray, 1950.

Seaver, George, *Scott of the Antarctic*, John Murray, 1940.

Shackleton, Ernest, *The Heart of the Antarctic*, Heinemann, 1932.

Sheffield, Gary, *Forgotten Victory*, Headline, 2002.

Simpson-Housley, Paul, *Antarctica*, Routledge, 1992.

Smith, Michael, *An Unsung Hero—Tom Crean,* Collins Press, 2000.

Smith, Michael, *I Am Just Going Outside*, Spellmount, 2002.

Solomon, Susan, *The Coldest March*, Yale University Press, 2001.

Spufford, Francis, *I May Be Some Time,* Faber & Faber, 1996.

Stewart, Douglas, *The Fire on the Snow* (radio play), Angus & Robertson, 1958.

Strachey, Lytton, *Eminent Victorians,* Penguin, 1986.

Stroud, Mike, *Shadows on the Wasteland,* Jonathan Cape, 1993.

Stroud, Mike, *Survival of the Fittest,* Jonathan Cape, 1998.

Swithinbank, Charles, *An Alien in Antarctica,* 1997.

Taylor, Griffith, *With Scott: The Silver Lining,* Smith, Elder, 1997.

Thomson, David, *Scott's Men,* Allen Lane, 1977.

Wheeler, Sara, *Terra Incognita,* Jonathan Cape, 1996.

Wheeler, Sara, *Cherry,* Jonathan Cape, 2001.

Wilson, Edward, ed. Ann Savours, *Diary of the "Discovery" Expedition, 1901–4,* Blandford Press, 1975.

Wilson, Edward, *Diary of the "Terra Nova" Expedition, 1910–12,* Blandford Press, 1972.

Wilson, D. M., and Elder, D. B., *Cheltenham in Antarctica,* Reardon Publishing, 2000.

Worden, Blair, *Roundhead Reputations,* Allen Lane, 2001.

Worsley, Frank A., *Shackleton's Boat Journey,* Folio Society, 1975.

Worsley, Frank A., *Endurance,* W. W. Norton, 1999.

Wright, Charles S., *Silas,* Ohio State University Press, 1993.

Yelverton, David E., *Antarctica Unveiled,* University Press of Colorado, 2000.

Young, Louisa, *A Great Task of Happiness,* Macmillan, 1995.

❧ NOTES ON THE SOURCES ❧

SPRI—Scott Polar Research Institute
BAS—British Antarctic Survey
RGS—Royal Geographical Society

Oates's letters to his mother, Caroline Oates, are kept at SPRI, MS 1317.
Bowers's letters to his mother, Emily Bowers, are kept at SPRI, MS 1505.
Kathleen Scott's diaries are kept at the Cambridge University Library.
R. F. Scott's diary is at the British Museum, but SPRI has it on microfilm.
Most newspaper cuttings have been obtained from SPRI and BAS.

Where only an author's name is quoted, the title of the book is detailed in the
   bibliography.

Chapter One. *Markham's Grand Design*

1 "I dislike Scott intensely," Oates, letter to Caroline Oates, Oct. 11–28,
   1911

1 "I am Captain Scott's man," Bowers, letter to Emily Bowers, Nov. 1, 1911

1 "he is one of the best," Bowers, December 1910, as quoted in Cherry-
Garrard, p. 55

1 "The Captain is a splendid leader," Bowers, letter to Emily Bowers,
Oct. 27, 1910

2 "There is nothing," Seaver, *Edward Wilson of the Antarctic*, p. 266

2 "He is thoughtful," Seaver, p. 84

2 "I have known him now," Cherry-Garrard, p. lix

3 "To have been born English," Paxman, p. 66

3 "we happen to be," ibid., p. 66

3 "Ask any man," ibid., p. 1

4 "Should anyone possess," Preston, p. 11

6 "dragged like ploughs," Mackinnon, C. S., *The British Man-hauled Sledging
Tradition*, Dept. of History, University of Alaska

6 "There will never be any more," ibid.

10 "the very best man," Pound, p. 19

11 "I was much struck," Markham, *The Lands of Silence*, pp. 447–48

Chapter Two. *Torpedo Lieutenant Scott*

13 "We frequently robbed orchards," Munday, R., letter to Peter Scott,
June 4, 1943, Scott family papers

13 "His temper never lasted," Ludlam, p. 13

15 "zealous and painstaking" and "promising," Huxley, *Scott of the Antarctic*,
p. 25

15 "intelligent and capable," ibid., p. 26

16 "This slow sickness," Scott, diary entry between Dec. 1889 and Apr. 1890

16 "a young officer of promise," Gwynn, p. 15

17 "his romantic nature," Huxley, *Scott of the Antarctic*, p. 31

17 "on a bitter March morning," Pound, p. 20

17 "precisely in the same position," Ludlam, p. 22

18 "At present," Scott, letter to Kathleen O'Reilly, Aug. 3, 1899, Provincial
Archives, Victoria, B.C.

18 "I was more than ever impressed," Markham, *The Lands of Silence*,
p. 447

18 "He is just the fellow," Huxley, *Scott of the Antarctic*, p. 36

20 "I was just sitting down," Markham, *Antarctic Obsession*, p. 13

20 "had no urge," Huxley, *Scott of the Antarctic*, p. 37

20–21 "I felt that the," "I have to feel," "I undertook the expedition,"
  Fiennes, *Mind over Matter*, pp. 24–26

21 "relinquishing," Pound, p. 30

22 "I have my eye on," Huxley, *Scott of the Antarctic*, p. 52

Chapter Three. *Order Out of Chaos*

24 "wild professors" and "howling cads," Markham, diary entries, Feb. and
  Mar. 1901, RGS Archives. CRM 1/14

25 "I must have," Markham, *Antarctic Obsession*, p. 14

26 "and we were friends" and "if anyone, could bring," Huxley, *Scott of the
  Antarctic*, p. 55

26 "always followed in Arctic exploration," Markham, speech at the launch of
  Discovery, reported in *Dundee Advertiser*, Mar. 22, 1901

27 "The main object," Markham, *The Lands of Silence*, p. 452

27 "England has not maintained" and "it is abroad," Scott, *The Voyage of the
  "Discovery,"* Vol. I, p. 409

30 "performed their contract," etc., Skelton, SPRI, MS 342/1/1

30 "From a very early date," Lashly, p. 13

31 Wright, Charles, "With Scott in Antarctica," *The Canadian Magazine*, 1974

32 "I went to see Scott," Armitage, *Cadet to Commodore*, p. 130

Chapter Four. *Through the Pack Ice: 1901–1902*

39 "Murray is excellent," report of the Ship Sub-Committee, Nov. 29, 1899.
  RGS Archives AA 5/2/19

39 "Goodbye old chap," Huxley, *Scott of the Antarctic*, p. 71

39 "With his quick brain," Bernacchi, *Saga of the "Discovery,"* p. 212

40 "all but his temper," Pound, p. 49

41 "bad-tempered," ibid., p. 49

41 "He is very definite" and "no fear," ibid., p. 50

41 "and made a very poor job," "He said that at my age," and "He was going
  to add sugar," ibid., p. 55

41 "These 'brown studies,' " Bernacchi, *Saga of the "Discovery,"* p. 211

41 "his sense of right," ibid., p. 212

42 "One of his weaknesses," ibid., p. 211

42 "affected him quickly," ibid., p. 211

43 "I had anticipated," Scott, RGS, AA 12/1/13: Nov. 28, 1901, p. 10

43 "as big a sea," Wilson, *Diary of the "Discovery" Expedition*, Nov. 26, 1901, p. 81

44 "there has been a great deal of fighting," SPRI, 342/1/1: Mar. 12, 1901

Chapter Five. *Nudging the Great Barrier: 1902*

48 "He was near a ton in weight," Wilson, *Diary of the "Discovery" Expedition*, July 1, 1902

48 "we came thoroughly to enjoy," Scott, *The Voyage of the "Discovery,"* Vol. I, p. 131

49 "There was a . . . heavy swell," Wilson, *Diary of the "Discovery" Expedition*, Jan. 22, 1902, p. 105

49 "The exploring party reported," SPRI 972: Jan. 20, 1902

51 "an exceedingly dangerous," Wilson, *Diary of the "Discovery" Expedition*, Feb. 4, 1902, p. 111

52 "At this time," Scott, *The Voyage of the "Discovery,"* Vol. I, p. 202

53 "but necessities are often hideous," Seaver, *Scott of the Antarctic*, p. 49

55 "Eyes are turned towards," Scott, *The Voyage of the "Discovery,"* Vol. I, p. 213

Chapter Six. *Dogs, Skis, and Men*

56 "a wretched specimen," Scott, *Diaries*, Feb. 10, 1902, SPRI MS 352/1/2 *Diaries*

58 "The ski boots," Wilson, *Diary of the "Discovery" Expedition*, Feb. 19, 1902, p. 116

59 "Do not even attempt," Herbert, Wally, letter to R. Fiennes, May 2, 1976

60 "It was undeniable cruelty," Neider, p. 91

60 "a combination of horses and dogs," Gran, *50 Years Polar Remembrance*

60 "In recent times," Geoff Somers, letter to R. Fiennes, 2002

60 "Polar exploration without ski," Sverdrup, Otto, *Nyt Land*, H. Aschenhough & Co., 1903, Vol. I, pp. 19/20

61 "We have been trying," Scott, *The Voyage of the "Discovery,"* Vol. II, p. 88

62 "Another thing," ibid., p. 88

62 "I am bound to confess," ibid., Vol. I, p. 229

65 "Thank God," Yelverton, p. 134

Chapter Seven. *The First Winter*

68 "everything was wrong," Scott, *Voyage of the "Discovery,"* Vol. I, p. 273

68 "That we were eventually able," ibid., p. 273

70 "Men don't improve," Wilson, *Diary of the "Discovery" Expedition*, Aug. 13, 1902, p. 171

70 "helped to preserve an atmosphere" and "of infinite benefit," Huxley, *Scott of the Antarctic*, p. 101

71 "You can see nothing," Wilson, *Diary of the "Discovery" Expedition*, July 18, 1902, p. 163

71 "The Skipper is endlessly," Huxley, *Scott of the Antarctic*, p. 103

72 "We are not angels," SPRI, 972: Aug. 24, 1902

72 "we are treated," Baughman, p. 134

72 "the Captain was quite," Huxley, *Scott of the Antarctic*, p. 101

73 "These little troubles," SPRI, 753: May 31, 1902

77 "We will go," Wilson, *Diary of the "Discovery" Expedition*, June 12, 1902, p. 151

77 "I am inclined," Scott, *The Voyage of the "Discovery,"* Vol. I, p. 515

78 "when one thinks," SPRI, 654/1: Sept. 26, 1902

78 "None of them were," Wilson, *Diary of the "Discovery" Expedition*, Oct. 3, 1902, p. 195

Chapter Eight. *The Southern Journey: 1902–1903*

81 "Should I not return," Armitage, *Two Years in the Antarctic*, p. 144

81 "Shackle started," Wilson, *Diary of the "Discovery" Expedition*, Nov. 6, 1902, p. 212

81 "Confident in ourselves," Scott, *The Voyage of the "Discovery,"* Vol. II, p. 23

83 "Shackleton in front," ibid., p. 33

83 "the most eerie sound," Griffith Taylor, "How I Survived the Scott Ordeal," *Cavalier Magazine*, 1961, SPRI

85 "Today I have been trying," Scott, *The Voyage of the "Discovery,"* Vol. II, p. 54

85 "well in hand," Wilson, *Cheltenham in Antarctica*, p. 66

85 "The amount of shouting," Wilson, *Diary of the "Discovery" Expedition*, Nov. 30, 1902, p. 220

85 "The coast we are making for," ibid., Nov. 27, 1902, p. 218

85 "Snow grains falling," ibid., Dec. 1, 1902, p. 220

85 "in preparing our hot stuff," ibid., Dec. 2, 1902, p. 220

86 "Our hunger is very," ibid., Dec. 18, 1902, p. 226

86 "We have decided now," ibid., Dec. 19, 1902, p. 226

87 "It is a moral cowardice," Scott, *The Voyage of the "Discovery,"* Vol. II, p. 92

87 "Poor Wilson has had," ibid., p. 73

88 "We argued, however," ibid., p. 73

88 "we have had the unlooked," Wilson, *Diary of the "Discovery" Expedition*, Dec. 28, 1902, p. 229

89 "luckily it all remained," Scott, *The Voyage of the "Discovery,"* Vol. II, p. 84

90 "I sprang up," ibid., p. 99

90 "I think we could all have wept," ibid., p. 104

91 "Shortly after their return," Huxley, *Scott of the Antarctic*, p. 134

91 "During the winter, Wilson," ibid., p. 134

92 "Armitage is a peculiar chap," Skelton, *"Discovery" Journal*, Sept. 11, 1902, SPRI

92 "I think Armitage's character," Huxley, *Scott of the Antarctic*, p. 137

92 "All the crocks I," ibid., p. 137

93 "On January 15 I broke down," Fisher, p. 79

93 "I say Shackles, how," Preston, *A First Rate Tragedy*, p. 68

94 "had it out with Scott," Seaver, *Edward Wilson of the Antarctic*, p. 114

94 "The Captain and I," Wilson, *Diary of the "Discovery" Expedition*, Jan. 23, 1903

94 "during these three months," Gwynn, p. 70

94 "the relief ship, *Morning*," Wilson, *Diary of the "Discovery" Expedition*, Feb. 3, 1903, p. 244

95 "I turned in," Mill, *The Life of Sir Ernest Shackleton*, p. 79

95 "we had plodded with," *The Voyage of the "Discovery,"* Vol. II, p. 125

97 "Mr Shackleton's breakdown," Huxley, *Scott of the Antarctic*, p. 133

97 "I hear it is true," ibid., p. 134

97 "It is with great reluctance," Scott, certificate for E. H. Shackleton, RGS

98 "Fortunately my appointment," Armitage, *Cadet to Commodore*, p. 131

98 "Mr. E. H. Shackleton," Pound, p. 89

98 "we went on very slowly," Huxley, *Scott of the Antarctic*, p. 134

Chapter Nine. *Lost on the Plateau: 1903–1904*

103 "in my opinion his," Royds, diary, May 30, 1903, p. 252

103 "Armitage applied to," Wilson, *Diary of the "Discovery" Expedition*, July 18, 1903, p. 271

104 "My appointment," Armitage, *Cadet to Commodore*, p. 131

105 "I was told," ibid., p. 133

105 "I received valuable assistance," ibid., p. 157

105 "did not allow the matter," ibid., p. 155

106 "Two years now since," Wilson, *Diary of the "Discovery" Expedition*, July 16, 1903, p. 271

106 "Hundreds of thousands," ibid., April 29, 1903, p. 256

106 "On looking at her," ibid., Aug. 15, 1903, p. 282

107 "Every Tuesday for dinner," ibid., Sept. 1, 1903, p. 287

107 "I can imagine nothing," ibid., Sept. 7, 1903, p. 289

108 "If he can do it," Huxley, *Scott of the Antarctic*, p. 163

108 "The gravity of this loss," Scott, *The Voyage of the "Discovery,"* Vol. II, pp. 239–40

109 "a rule of thumb," ibid., p. 274

109 "the prospect which lay," ibid., p. 253

111 "We all know each other," Yelverton, p. 264

111 "The worst time for," Scott, *The Voyage of the "Discovery,"* Vol. I, pp. 473–74

112 "the sledges have grown," ibid., p. 474

112 "There must be no," ibid., p. 475

112 "Once the hoosh," ibid., pp. 479–81

113 "It is very trying work," ibid., pp. 488–89

114 "With these two men," Scott, *The Voyage of the "Discovery,"* Vol. II,
    p. 259

115 "Half an hour before," ibid., pp. 280–81

116 "Well, I'm blowed," ibid., p. 285

116 "It is certainly," ibid., p. 293

116 "What a splendid," ibid., p. 290

117 "Few dog parties," SPRI, *Polar Record*, Vol. V 37/38, 1949, p. 316

117 "He takes the cake," Royds, letter to P. Aldrich, Feb. 12, 1903, MS
    582/1–2: D

117 "Few of our camping," Scott, *The Voyage of the "Discovery,"* Vol. II,
    p. 265

117 "no class of men," Preston, p. 73

119 "I feel more disgusted," Ludlam, p. 91

119 "the utterly unnecessary," Scott, letter to Admiral Sir Arthur Moore,
    1904, SPRI MS475/3/1–2: D

120 "A glorious sight met," Scott, *The Voyage of the "Discovery,"* Vol. II,
    p. 347

120 "Scott was terribly excited," Preston, pp. 78–79

121 "About lunch time," Wilson, *Diary of the "Discovery" Expedition*,
    Feb. 17, 1904, p. 340

121 "Mulock was on watch," ibid., p. 340

Chapter Ten. *A Promise Broken*

123 "My dear Captain Scott," Yelverton, p. 326

123 "a very jolly evening," Markham, diary entry, Sept. 15, 1904, reported in
    the *Geographical Journal* 24/4: Oct. 1904, RGS, p. 384

123 "felt they could do anything," *Geographical Journal*, 24/4: Oct. 1904,
    p. 384, SPRI

124 "The inference is," Fisher, p. 69

125 "I want to marry you," Young, p. 88

126 "I suppose the world does," ibid., p. 241

126 "He may be a genius," ibid., p. 241

128 "My Dear Shackleton," Scott, letter to Shackleton, SPRI, 1456/23/1:
    Feb. 18, 1907

129 "I feel sure with," ibid.

129 "I don't want to be," Scott, letter to Shackleton, SPRI, 1456/23/2: Feb. 18, 1907

129 "I think you ought," SPRI 1456/26: Feb. 28, 1907

130 "I had always a wish," letter from Shackleton to Sir Clements Markham, Mar. 8, 1907, SPRI MS 22: D

130 "the sacrifice you are making," SPRI 1456/23/4: Mar. 26, 1907. The date March 26 on this was probably a misprint for March 16, as it is acknowledged in Shackleton's letter of March 23

130 "To make everything clear," SPRI MS 25: D, Shackleton's letter to Scott, May 17, 1907

132 "he hasn't got the guts," Marshall, diary, Jan. 24, 1908, RGS

132 "I have been through," Shackleton, letter to his wife, Jan. 26, 1908

132 "There can be no doubt," Huxley, *Scott of the Antarctic*, p. 187

133 "it is my intention," R. Amundsen, letter to F. Nansen, Aug. 22, 1910

133 "I am very, very busy," Pound, p. 148

134 "this comprehensive and important," Bernacchi, *Saga of the "Discovery,"* p. 114

136 "confusedly and insecurely," Preston, p. 100

136 "we grow to better understanding," Scott, letter to Kathleen Scott, Nov. 1, 1908

136 "he was full of enthusiasm," Scott, letter to Kathleen Scott, Nov. 28, 1908

136 "I'm obstinate, despondent," Scott, letter to Kathleen Scott, as quoted in Young, p. 104

136 "laziness, untidiness, touchiness," Preston, p. 100

137 " 'I think,' he said," Huxley, p. 215

137 "Unqualified congratulations on," Ludlam, p. 123

138 "Bravo!," ibid., p. 124

138 "I never saw anyone," Huxley, *Scott of the Antarctic*, pp. 216–17

138 "In the immediate future," Ludlam, p. 124

139 "A general feeling of relief," Marshall's diary entry for Aug. 12, 1908, Mills, p. 68

140 "I thought you would like," Mills, *The Life of Sir Ernest Shackleton*, p. 159

141 "The English nation," R. Amundsen, letter to J. Scott Keltie, Mar. 25, 1909, RGS

144 "There was not room," Ludlam, p. 125

145 "write or speak to him," R. F. Scott, letter to Skelton, Mar. 21, 1910,
    SPRI MS 342/28/65
146 "with him [Scott]," Preston, p. 222
146 "entirely friendly," Ludlam, p. 134
146 "the race," ibid., p. 135
146 "The main objective," Huxley, *Scott of the Antarctic*, p. 218
147 "£40,000 is needed," *The Times*, Sept. 13, 1909
147 "It's no good talking," Pound, p. 179

Chapter Eleven. *The Race Begins: 1910*

150 "She was the largest," Preston, p. 114
150 "I shall never forget," Evans, *South with Scott*, p. 6
152 "There is no real reason," Huxley, *Scott of the Antarctic*, p. 230
152 "Shackleton was five weeks," Taylor, p. 241
154 "no happiness but," Scott, *Personal Journals*, Aug. 29, 1911, p. 309
154 "We got sick of each other," Pound, p. 243
155 "I am very disappointed," Simpson, letter to Professor Schuster, SPRI
    1122/1/2: Nov. 1, 1901
155 " 'Simpson,' wrote Wilson," Wilson, *Diary of the "Terra Nova"
    Expedition*, July 5, 1910, p. 18
155 "One thing which never fails," Thomson, p. 149
155 "I did not like Dr. Wilson," Mawson, p. 53
156 "spends all his time," Thomson, p. 151
156 "If only they will leave," Seaver, *"Birdie" Bowers of the Antarctic*, p. 111
157 "a fat little man," Preston, p. 108
157 "What a silly," Evans, *South with Scott*, p. 8
158 "man with brains," Smith, *I Am Just Going Outside*, p. 88
158 "I told Scott I," *Daily Telegraph,* quoting Colonel Yardley of the
    Inniskilling Dragoons, Feb. 15, 1913
158 "The job is most suitable," Oates, letter to Caroline Oates, Jan. 1910
158 "I'm Oates," Evans (later Lord Mountevans), "My Recollections of a
    Gallant Comrade," *The Strand Magazine*, Dec. 1913
158 "we never for a moment," Limb and Cordingley, p. 95
160 "We waited," Tryggve Gran, *Fra Tjuagutt til Sydpolfarer*, Ernst G.
    Mårtensen, p. 178

160 "Could Scott have beaten," Gran, *50 Years Polar Remembrance*, Forlag, 1974

160 "a hurry and scurry," Gran, *Slik var Det*, Gyldenal Norst Forlag, 1945, p. 75

161 "Dear Sir," Pound, p. 181

161 "You shall go to," Kathleen Bruce, letter to R. F. Scott, quoted by Louisa Young, p. 98

161 "a very very clever woman," Preston, p. 98

161 "ready to strike," Pound, p. 184

162 "He was not an alarmist," Ludlam, p. 133

162 "If nothing is heard," Pound, p. 193

162 "No one else," Preston, p. 123

163 "The bunkers," Wilson, *Diary of the "Terra Nova" Expedition*, June 6, 1910, p. 16

163 "the coal is now," ibid., Oct. 27, 1910, p. 60

163 "In this fashion," Solomon, p. 62

164 "The Skipper has decided," Oates, letter to Caroline Oates, Nov. 23, 1910

164 "Scott hits it off well," Seaver, *"Birdie" Bowers of the Antarctic*, p. 161

165 Wright, Oct. 2, 1910, p. 27

165 "If the voyage," Gran, *The Norwegian with Scott*, pp. 13–14

165 "Beg leave to inform you," Fram Museum, Oslo

165 "The *Fram* goes direct," *Daily Mail*, Feb. 11, 1913

165 "While Captain Scott," Ludlam, p. 147

166 "I do not belong," Amundsen, R., *Gjennem Luften til 88° Nord*, Gylkdendal Norsk Forlag, 1925, p. 20

167 "Unknown," Gran, *50 Years Polar Remembrance*

167 "[Amundsen] is going to," Huxley, *Scott of the Antarctic*, p. 242

167 "so considerably altered," Pound, p. 202

168 "Bloody Norskies," Oates, letter to William King, Nov. 13, 1910

168 "It will make us look," Oates, letter to Caroline Oates, Nov. 23, 1910

168 "[Amundsen's] proceedings," Thomson, p. 183

168 "He is a good fellow," Scott, *Personal Journals*, Jan. 20, 1911, p. 104

169 "rather sickening," Smith, *I Am Just Going Outside*, p. 119

169 "Meares is reluctant," Scott, *Personal Journals*, p. 4

170 "Scott has been kicking up," Oates, diary, Nov. 23, 1910

170 "I have now ordered," ibid., Nov. 28, 1910

170 "Dear Mother," Oates, letter to Caroline Oates, Nov. 17, 1910

170 "Oates was anxious," Seaver, *"Birdie" Bowers of the Antarctic*, p. 164

171 "Dear Mother, *the ponies*," Oates, letter to Caroline Oates, Nov. 23,
     1910 (author's italics)

171 "Victor . . . Narrow chest," Oates, diary, undated

172 "From the first," Cherry-Garrard, *Annotated Journals*, 1910

172 "a shallow man," Wheeler, *Cherry*, p. 79

173 "Teddy Evans climbed down," Cherry-Garrard, *Annotated Journals*

173 "Nobody likes her," Bowers to May Bowers, Nov. 28, 1910, SPRI

173 "Dear Mother, Mrs Scott," Oates, letter to Caroline Oates, Nov. 23, 1910

173 "Evans' tantrums," Scott, Kathleen, diary, Nov. 29, 1910

173 "May it never be known," Bowers to Emily Bowers, Dec. 7, 1910

173 "anyone to see him sad," Young, p. 117

173 "for tea in the stern," ibid., p. 117

173 "personally I had a heart," Evans, *South with Scott*, pp. 29–30

174 "If you could look down," Gwynn, pp. 170–71

Chapter Twelve. *Near Disaster: 1911*

176 "wondering what the," Wilson, *Diary of the "Terra Nova" Expedition*,
     Dec. 1, 1910, p. 65

176 "risk nothing and do," Gwynn, p. 173

176 "It makes me feel," Limb and Cordingley, p. 103

177 "a full gale," Ponting, p. 14

177 "I am afraid it's," Cherry-Garrard, p. 53

177 "Seems a primitive," Debenham, *The Quiet Land*, Dec. 3, 1910, p. 12

177 "Thus were we driven," Taylor, p. 41

178 "on the weather rail," Cherry-Garrard, p. 57

178 "A dog was drowned," Scott, *Personal Journals*, Dec. 2, 1910, p. 11

178 "actually lifting," Evans, "My Recollections of a Gallant Comrade,"
     The Strand Magazine, December 1913

178 "I was drenched," Oates, letter to Caroline Oates, Nov. 1910

178 "Not a word," Scott, *Personal Journals*, Dec. 7, 1910, p. 16

178 "Scott himself working," Evans, *South with Scott*, p. 34

180 "Captain Scott was," Gwynn, p. 173

181 "I have never thought," Cherry-Garrard, *Journal*, Dec. 11, 1910, SPRI

181 "Dr. Wilson then," Debenham, *The Quiet Land*, Dec. 15, 1910, p. 26

181 "is like a slug," ibid., Dec. 12, 1910, p. 24

181 "our patience was," Evans, *South with Scott*, p. 42

181 "penguin stews and 'hooshes,'" ibid., p. 44

182 "To Scott any delay," Limb and Cordingley, p. 105

182 "I can imagine," Scott, *Personal Journals,* Dec. 30, 1910, pp. 56–57

182 "Huge icebergs crept," ibid., p. 57

183 "It is rather a surprising," Scott, *Personal Journals*, p. 45

183 "we three talked," Scott, *Personal Journals*, Dec. 7, 1910, p. 15

183 "their ignorance is colossal," Oates, letter to Caroline Oates, Jan. 22, 1911

183 "Oates is unremitting," Scott, *Personal Journals*, Dec. 28, 1910, p. 51

184 "Talking to Capt. Scott," Debenham, *The Quiet Land*, p. 31

185 "Comfortable quarters for," Scott, *Personal Journals*, p. 65

186 "What the ice gets," F. A. Worsley, *Endurance*, p. 4

186 "Indefinite conditions," Young, p. 105

186 Wright, p. 77

186 ibid., p. 77

186 "Scott . . . himself came," Cherry-Garrard, p. 104

186 "between the way," Priestley, letter from Cape Adare, undated, SPRI

187 "astonished," Smith, *I Am Just Going Outside*, p. 128

187 "'Oates,' he wrote," Scott, *Personal Journals*, Jan. 7, 1911, p. 80

187 "a more unpromising lot," Oates, notes on the ponies, SPRI

187 "might have proved," Smith, *I Am Just Going Outside*, p. 129

187 "The dogs are getting," Scott, *Personal Journals*, Jan. 6, 1911, p. 78

187 "we found the old," Wilson, *Diary of the "Terra Nova" Expedition*,
    Jan. 27, 1911, p. 99

188 "Everyone declares that," Scott, *Personal Journals*, Jan. 6, 1911, p. 78

188 "any definite information," R. F. Scott to J. J. Kinsey, Jan. 22, 1910, SPRI
    MS 701/8/13–34: D

191 "I can't stand," Oates, letter to Caroline Oates, Jan. 31, 1911

191 "would fifty times," Oates, letter to Caroline Oates, Jan. 22, 1911

192 "If we had more," Scott, *Personal Journals*, Feb. 3. 1911, p. 121

192 "raging chaos," Cherry-Garrard, p. 116

192 "Scott's tent was a," Preston, pp. 141–42

192 "Fight your way," Cherry-Garrard, p. 116

192 "all our ponies were," ibid., p. 116

193 "It taught us the nature," Scott, *Personal Journals*, Feb. 14, 1911, p. 133

193 "The incident is deplorable," ibid., pp. 133–34

193 "We are five," ibid., Feb. 13, 1911, p. 132

194 "Oates proposed to Scott," Gran, *Fra tjuagutt til sydpolarfarer [From kid to south polar explorer]*, 1974, Oslo, Ernst G. Mårtensens Forlag

194 "It would have been," Scott, *Personal Journals*, Feb. 15, 1911, p. 135

194 "Oates is certainly," Smith, *I Am Just Going Outside*, p. 140

195 "It was not expected," Cherry-Garrard, p. 127

195 "I was running," Wilson, *Diary of the "Terra Nova" Expedition*, Feb. 21, 1911, p. 105

195 "Scott told Meares," Cherry-Garrard, *Annotated Journals*

196 "I feel that a man," Cherry-Garrard, *Journal*, Dec., 1911

196 "Up to this day," Cherry-Garrard, *Annotated Journals*

196 "Well, if they are," Lambert, pp. 47–48

197 "all seemed charming," Wilfred Bruce, letter to Kathleen Scott, quoted by Anderson, p. 203

197 "Curses loud and deep," ibid., p. 203

197 "heavy arguments . . . ," ibid., p. 203

197 "It is very unfortunate," Lambert, p. 50

197 Wright, p. 81

198 "We must at all costs," Huxley, *Scott of the Antarctic*, p. 262

199 "Every incident," Scott, *Personal Journals*, Feb. 22, 1911, p. 147

199 "For an hour or so," Cherry-Garrard, p. 132

200 "By Jove," Cherry-Garrard, *Annotated Journals*

200 "Scott in the tent," ibid.

200 "We spent a very," Evans, *South with Scott*, p. 77

200 "One thing only fixes," Scott, *Personal Journals*, Feb. 22, 1911, p. 147

201 "If you have a destination," Shaw to Norman, Oct. 4, 1915, British Library, Add. MS. 50562, fols, pp. 92–93

201 "As for Amundsen's," Wilson, *Diary of the "Terra Nova" Expedition*, Feb. 22, 1911, p. 107

201 "was so genuinely upset," Bowers, diary letter undated, SPRI

201 "If we reach the Pole," Gran, *The Norwegian with Scott*, p. 63

201 "I think Amundsen's enterprise," Gran, *50 Years Polar Remembrance*

201 "Now every effort," Scott, *Personal Journals*, Mar. 1, 1911, p. 150

202 "The plan was," ibid., Feb. 28, 1911, p. 150

202 "Meares and I," Wilson, *Diary of the "Terra Nova" Expedition,* Feb. 28, 1911, p. 108

204 "My orders were," Cherry-Garrard, p. 142

204 "misunderstood their orders," ibid., p. 142

204 "Crean . . . who had," ibid., p. 142

204 "Crean drank his," Pound, p. 232

204 "It was 2 pm," Cherry-Garrard, pp. 143–44

205 "At 5 am I woke," Wilson, *Diary of the "Terra Nova" Expedition,* Feb. 28, 1911, p. 110

Chapter Thirteen. *The Worst Journey: 1911*

208 "After some hours," Cherry-Garrard, pp. 145–46

208 "I sent a note," ibid., p. 146

208 "Oh I just kept going," SPRI, Polar Record, 3 (17): 78–79 (1939)

209 "The Killers were too interested," Cherry-Garrard, p. 147

209 "[Scott] . . . was too relieved," ibid., p. 148

209 "Captain Scott was so pleased," ibid., pp. 148–49

210 "While supper," ibid., p. 149

210 "The hardest jump," ibid., pp. 150–52

212 "there was an open," ibid., pp. 160–61

213 "Six hours earlier," Bowers, diary letter, undated, SPRI

213 "no one in the world," Cherry-Garrard, Chatto & Windus, p. 582

213 "We lost 6 ponies," Limb and Cordingley, p. 120

213 "Our party is split up," Gran, *The Norwegian with Scott,* Mar. 1, 1911, p. 64

213 "Scott was the one," ibid., p. 68

213 "Inside it is dark," ibid., p. 68

213 "The way thoughts," Wilson, *Cheltenham in Antarctica,* p. 88

213 "We spent . . . our evenings," Cherry-Garrard, p. 164

214 "Scott and Wilson," ibid., pp. 166–67

214 "I was closer to Scott," Griffith Taylor, "How I Survived the Scott Ordeal," *Cavalier Magazine,* 1961, SPRI

214 "This life . . . is quite interesting," Gran, *The Norwegian with Scott,* p. 73

214 "Some of our party," Evans, "My Recollections of a Gallant Comrade," *Strand Magazine,* December 1913

214 "We wonder what," Wilson, *Diary of the "Terra Nova" Expedition*, Mar. 5, 1911, p. 115

214 "On top of all," Cherry-Garrard, p. 163

215 "In choosing the site," Scott, *Personal Journals*, Apr. 13, 1911, p. 178

216 "Here we have come," Wilson, *Diary of the "Terra Nova" Expedition*, Apr. 13, 1911, p. 121

216 "a male, very fat," ibid., Apr. 3, 1911, p. 119

216 "It was a good piece of work," Evans, *South with Scott*, p. 92

216 "We gladly started off," ibid., p. 93

216–17 "it seemed folly," Pound, p. 237

217 "the snow hid everything," Cherry-Garrard, p. 175

217 "If ever there was," Griffith Taylor, "How I Survived the Scott Ordeal," *Cavalier Magazine*, 1961, SPRI

217 "Opinions were varied," Debenham, *The Quiet Land*, p. 92

217 "to ensure Taylor's safety," Cherry-Garrard, p. 176

217 "truly awful," Gran, *The Norwegian with Scott*, p. 76

217 "I roused the party," Scott, *Personal Journals*, Apr. 13, 1911, p. 176

217 "We reached some stranded icebergs," Gran, *The Norwegian with Scott*, p. 78

219 "Our expedition to," Gran, *50 Years Polar Remembrance*

220 "The presentation was followed," Gran, ibid.

220 Wright, p. 138

221 "the cab-horse," Limb and Cordingley, p. 129

221 "I am . . . . very disappointed," Debenham, *The Quiet Land*, pp. 124–25

222 "disgusted," Smith, *I Am Just Going Outside*, p. 157

222 "no love lost," ibid., p. 158

223 "From what I see," Oates, letter to Caroline Oates, Oct. 24–31, 1911

223 "Myself, I dislike," ibid., Oct. 24–31, 1911

223 "having a 'first class,'" Smith, *I Am Just Going Outside*, p. 133

223 "please remember that when a man," Oates, letter to Caroline Oates, Oct. 24–31, 1911

223 "think from what I say that Scott," ibid., Jan. 22, 1911

224 "Meares is excellent to a point," Scott, *Personal Journals*, Feb. 22, 1911

224 "the genius of," Debenham, "Scott 1912—An Expedition in Harmony," *Geographical Magazine*, 1962

224 "We got on very well," Limb and Cordingley, p. 127

224 "Priestley and I," Lambert, p. 79

224 "I feel rather a beast," ibid., p. 79

225 "Nothing is so important," Fiennes, *Mind over Matter*, p. 231

225 "It was made clear," ibid., p. 234

226 "Meares is the wanderer," Debenham, *The Quiet Land*, p. 126

226 "It was interesting," Wilson, *Diary of the "Terra Nova" Expedition*,
    May 22, 1911, p. 130

226 "The old bull lay," Lambert, p. 37

227 "But indeed the whole time," Scott, *Personal Journals*, Jan. 20, 1911, p. 103

227 "The ski bindings," Gran, *50 Years Polar Remembrance*

227 "We were using," Wilson, *Diary of the "Terra Nova" Expedition*, June
    27, 1911, p. 141

228 "Scott was playing," Taylor, p. 236

228 "If you felt," Cherry-Garrard, p. 199

229 "Scott, who always," ibid., pp. 204–5

229 "If then I say," ibid., p. 230

230 "We are, with," Debenham, *The Quiet Land*, p. 127

230 "Captain Oates," ibid., p. 41

230 "He worries me," Pound, p. 236

230 "Scott was a man," Gran, "With Scott's Last Expedition," *Observer
    Magazine*, Mar. 31, 1974

231 "The thought of," Sverre Hassel, diary, Aug. 13, 1911, University
    Library, Oslo

232 "He also impressed upon," Wilson, *Diary of the "Terra Nova"
    Expedition*, June 25, 1911, p. 136

232 "the biggest scientific," Wilson, *Cheltenham in Antarctica*, p. 89

232 "Another new departure," Scott, *Personal Journals*, June 20, 1911, p. 252

233 "This winter travel," ibid., June 27, 1911, p. 262

233 "They are the best," Wilson, *Diary of the "Terra Nova" Expedition*,
    June 27, 1911, p. 142

233 "Antarctic exploration is," Cherry-Garrard, p. 304

235 "I for one," ibid., p. 242

236 "Wilson is very thin," Scott, *Personal Journals*, Aug. 2, 1911, p. 283

237 "It was all," Cherry-Garrard, p. 315

237 "Everyone was out," Debenham, *The Quiet Land*, p. 117

238 "suddenly there was," Gran, *The Norwegian with Scott*, p. 208

238 "I am fully alive," Pound, pp. 55–56

Chapter Fourteen. *The Dangerous Glacier*

239 "[The] utmost thing on his," Gran, *50 Years Polar Remembrance*

239 "If you people want to suffer," Gran, *The Norwegian with Scott*, Sept. 6, 1911, p. 122

240 "I never met such," Huxley, *Scott of the Antarctic*, p. 279

240 "a remarkably pleasant and instructive," Scott, *Personal Journals*, Oct. 1, 1911, p. 320

240 "At the breakfast table," Amundsen, diary, Sept. 17, 1911, University Library, Oslo

241 "The whole journey there," Debenham, *The Quiet Land*, pp. 102–3

242 "I don't know whether it is possible for men," ibid., p. 104

243 "I do not believe," Cherry-Garrard, p. 595

244 "It is trying," Pound, p. 254

244 "Rather a horrid day today," Young, p. 134

244 "Hooper accompanied Lashly's car," Evans, *South with Scott,* p. 166

245 "the motors advanced the necessaries," ibid., p. 173

245 "No praise could be too great," Ponting, p. 266

245 "Knowing in what respects," ibid., p. 266

245 "The general design seemed," Cherry-Garrard, p. 332

246 "You're young," Gran, "With Scott's Last Expedition," *Observer Magazine*, Mar. 31, 1974

248 "While the sun is shining," Seaver, *"Birdie" Bowers of the Antarctic*, p. 233

248 "The weather was about," ibid., p. 232

248 "It is curious," Cherry-Garrard, p. 349

248 "When eating snow he," Scott, *Personal Journals*, Aug. 10, 1911, p. 294

248–49 "It is satisfactory," Scott, diary, Nov. 5, 1911

249 "Scott told me today," Oates, diary, Nov. 1911

249 "The Soldier thinks," Scott, *Personal Journals*, Nov. 12–13, 1911, p. 361

249 "if only these wretched old cripples," Oates, diary, Nov. 12, 1911

250 "Scott realises now," Oates, diary, Nov. 18, 1911

250 "Just a note from the Barrier," Scott, letter to Kathleen Scott, Nov. 24, 1911

251 "ponies doing fairly well," Cherry-Garrard, *Annotated Journals*

251 "Meares . . . has just come up," Scott, *Personal Journals*, Nov. 25, 1911, p. 369

251 Wright, p. 201

251 "A year's care," Cherry-Garrard, p. 346

251 "He was a game little devil," Oates, diary, Nov. 28, 1911

252 "Altogether things look," Scott, *Personal Journals*, Nov. 29, 1911, p. 374

252 Wright, p. 203

252 "everything looks well," Scott, *Personal Journals*, Dec. 2, 1911, p. 376

252 "There is no doubt," Scott, *Personal Journals*, Dec. 1, 1911, p. 375

252 "[Victor] did a splendid march," Cherry-Garrard, p. 351

253 Wright, p. 203

253 "It was important," Cherry-Garrard, p. 350

253 "real humdingers at *that* time," Susan Solomon, e-mail to R. Fiennes

254 "The pony wall blew down," Scott, *Personal Journals*, Dec. 3, 1911, pp. 376–77

254 "What on earth does such weather," Scott, *Personal Journals*, Dec. 5, 1911, p. 379

254 "I think we shall get," Oates, diary, Nov. 29, 1911, p. 146

254 "Another blizzard started, which tore," Evans, *South with Scott*, p. 184

255 "I think it would be fairer," ibid., p. 186 (author's italics)

255 "There was not one man," Cherry-Garrard, p. 361

256 "The horses could hardly move," ibid., p. 360

256 "We lay down on our stomachs," Shackleton, p. 185

256 "A wet, warm blizzard of such," Solomon, p. 178

257 "Well! I congratulate you," Cherry-Garrard, p. 362
     Wright, p. 235

260 "Couldn't have gone," Wilson, *Diary of the "Terra Nova" Expedition*, Dec. 12, 1911, p. 217

260 "The starting was worse," Cherry-Garrard, p. 367

260 "I have never seen," Seaver, *"Birdie" Bowers of the Antarctic*, p. 242

260 "our tea leaves," Cherry-Garrard, p. 367

260 "been enduring the pains," ibid., pp. 366–67

262 "Evans' party could not," Scott, *Personal Journals*, Dec. 10, 1911, p. 386

262 "Captain Scott got fairly wound up," Bowers, diary, Dec. 25, 1911

263 "Scott fairly legged it," Cherry-Garrard, pp. 179–80

263 "one gets down to bedrock," Bowers, quoted in Pound, p. 268

263 "Wright wanted to push," Cherry-Garrard, *Annotated Journals*

263 "Scott will be here sooner or later," Ludlam, p. 190

264 "Of course, we had Shackleton's," Evans, *South with Scott*, p. 195

264 "and this latitude," Mills, p. 80

265 "Our lips are very sore," King, Dec. 17, 1911, p. 141

265 Wright, p. 220

265 "[Teddy] Evans and Bowers," Scott, *Personal Journals*, Dec. 19, 1911, p. 398

265 "There also," Cherry-Garrard, p. 376

265 "I dreaded this necessity," Scott, *Personal Journals*, Dec. 20, 1911, pp. 398–99

265 "my feet are giving me," Oates, diary, Dec. 19, 1911

266 "I said I hoped I had not disappointed him," Thomson, p. 268

266 "getting played out," Scott, *Personal Journals*, Dec. 10, 1911, p. 386

266 "One of the greatest successes," Scott, *Personal Journals*, Oct. 1911, p. 338

266 Wright, p. 221

266 Ibid., p. 221

267 "who knew he was done," E. L. Atkinson, quoted by Cherry-Garrard, diary, Apr. 4, 1912

267 "Sorry to part with," Patrick Keohane, diary, Dec. 21, 1911, SPRI

267 "bring the dogs southwards," Lagerbom, p. 166

267 "We had a long talk," Cherry-Garrard, p. 398

267 Wright, p. 213

Chapter Fifteen: *The Black Flag*

268 "We have weeded," Scott, *Personal Journals*, Dec. 22, 1911, p. 401

268 "As first man," King, p. 144

268 "as big," Solomon, p. 192

269 "a confusion of elevations," Scott, *Personal Journals*, Dec. 22, 1911, p. 402

269 "The horizons which now opened," Fiennes, diary

269 "the pace of them," Seaver, *Scott of the Antarctic*, p. 161

269 "I trust this may prove," Scott, *Personal Journals*, Dec. 23, 1911, p. 403

270 "Rather a ghastly sight," Huxley, *Scott of the Antarctic*, p. 290

270 "One cannot allow," ibid., p. 290

271 "got an unusual burst," Bowers, diary, Dec. 27, 1911, SPRI

271 "The back tendon of," Oates, diary, Dec. 26, 1911

271 "Scott is very annoyed," ibid., Dec. 28–29, 1911

272 "Captain Scott came into," Evans, *South with Scott*, p. 204

272 "We have caught up," Scott, *Personal Journals*, Dec. 31, 1911, p. 409

273 "It is difficult," Solomon, p. 194

273 "He told us all," Preston, p. 176

274 "and his team," Evans, *South with Scott*, p. 205

274 "Did 15 miles," ibid., p. 206

275 "P.O. Evans, of course, is," Scott, *Personal Journals*, Dec. 10, 1911, p. 386

275 "the greatest source of pleasure," ibid., Oct. 1, 1911, p. 325

276 "a thoroughly well-meaning," Preston, p. 159

276 "I felt very sorry for him," Evans, *South with Scott*, p. 206

276 "Poor Teddy—I am sure," Huxley, *Scott of the Antarctic*, p. 292

277 "A home is where there," Ibsen, p. 20

278 "the foot which went," Cherry-Garrard, *Annotated Journals*

278 "whether I shall have the," Pound, p. 267

279 "I am afraid the letter," Oates, letter to Caroline Oates, Jan. 3–4, 1912

279 "If anything should happen," ibid., Oct. 8–24, 1911

279 "I'm afraid, Teddy," Evans, "My Recollections of a Gallant Comrade," *The Strand Magazine*, Dec. 1913

279 "Our party were on ski," Cherry-Garrard, pp. 514–15

280 "Bowers has a heavy time," Scott, *Personal Journals*, Jan. 7, 1912, p. 416

280 "It is wonderful to see," ibid., Jan. 4, 1912, p. 412

280 "Nothing comes amiss," ibid., Jan. 8, 1912, p. 417

280 "Our food continues to amply," ibid., Jan. 7–8, 1912, p. 416

281 "The marching is growing," ibid., Jan. 9, 1912, p. 418

281 "it is more tiring for me," Bowers, diary, Jan. 4, 1912, SPRI

281 "The worst wind-cut sastrugi," Wilson, *Diary of the "Terra Nova" Expedition*, Jan. 6–7, 1912, pp. 229–30

281 "I heard Scott discuss," Cherry-Garrard, p. 427

281 "The Polar Party," ibid., p. 434

282 "a sea of fish-hook waves," Scott, *Personal Journals*, Jan. 6, 1912, p. 414

282 "I must stick to skis," Jones, *Polar Portraits*, p. 288

282 "Without them . . . climbing on sheer ice," Amundsen, sledging diary, Dec. 1, 1911, University Library, Oslo

282 "has a nasty cut," Scott, *Personal Journals*, Jan. 7, 1912, p. 416

282 "Evans who cut his knuckle," Wilson, *Diary of the "Terra Nova" Expedition*, Jan. 7, 1912, p. 230

282 "I watched with intense admiration," Fiennes, *Mind over Matter*, p. 119

282 "Evans' hand was dressed," Scott, *Personal Journals*, Jan. 8, 1912, p. 416

282 "Scott had two phrases," Debenham, *In the Antarctic*, p. 41

282 "beyond the record," Scott, *Personal Journals*, Jan. 9, 1912, p. 418

282 "We have shot our bolt," Shackleton, p. 210

283 "the most daring man," Kathleen Scott, diary, June 14, 1911

283 "It falls to the lot," Shackleton, Jan. 26, 1908, p. 172

283 "I never had such pulling," Scott, *Personal Journals*, Jan. 11, 1912, p. 419

283 "being chary of leaving stores," ibid., Jan. 9, 1912, p. 418

284 "Time after time," Cherry-Garrard, p. 517

284 "At camping tonight," Scott, *Personal Journals*, Jan. 12, 1912, p. 420

284 "Again we noticed," ibid., Jan. 14, 1912, p. 422

284 "My pemmican," Smith, *I Am Just Going Outside*, p. 203

284 "It is wonderful," Scott, *Personal Journals*, Jan. 15, 1912, p. 423

285 "We started off," ibid., Jan. 16, 1912, p. 423

285 "Soon we knew," ibid., p. 423

285 "This told us the whole story," ibid., Jan. 16, 1912, p. 423

285 "The age of the tracks," Wilson, *Diary of the "Terra Nova" Expedition*, Jan. 16, 1912, p. 231

285 "I am awfully sorry," Seaver, *"Birdie" Bowers of the Antarctic*, p. 250

285–86 "The coldest march I ever," Wilson, *Diary of the "Terra Nova" Expedition,* Jan. 17, 1912, p. 232

286 "From Amundsen's direction of tracks," ibid., Jan. 17, 1912, p. 232

286 "of ±30" [800 yards]," "Survey in Antarctica," *Scottish Geographical Magazine* 1924, p. 216

286 "Great God! this is," Scott, *Personal Journals*, Jan. 17, 1912, p. 424

286 "We have attained," Bjaaland Olav, *Antarctic Diary*, 1910–1912

287 "Dear Captain Scott, As you," Limb and Cordingley, p. 157

287 "Neither, at this seriously meaningful time," Gran, *50 Years Polar Remembrance*

287 "I am glad to say," Seaver, *"Birdie" Bowers of the Antarctic*, pp. 250–51

Chapter Sixteen. *Intimations of Tragedy*

289 "Well, we have turned," Scott, *Personal Journals*, Jan. 18, 1912, p. 426

290 "I think Oates is feeling," ibid., Jan. 20, 1912, p. 428

290 "One of my big," Oates, diary, Jan. 25, 1912

290 "were ruined by having," Fiennes, *Mind over Matter*, p. 166

290 "He did look old, thin," Stroud, *Shadows on the Wasteland*, p. 147

291 "Our hands are never," Wilson, *Diary of the "Terra Nova" Expedition*, Jan. 19, 1912, p. 236

292 "Marched on foot," ibid., Jan. 25, 1912, p. 237

292 "I think Wilson, Bowers," Scott, *Personal Journals*, Jan. 23, 1912, p. 430

292 "There is no doubt," ibid., Jan. 23, 1912, p. 430

292 "Evans has dislodged," ibid., Jan. 30, 1912, p. 434

293 "For supper we had," Debenham, *The Quiet Land*, p. 88

293 "I wish to God," Fiennes, *Mind over Matter*, p. 162

293 "The asthmatic condition," Preston, p. 189

293 "Thin air, low pressure," Fiennes, *Mind over Matter*, pp. 161–62

295 "Titus' toes are blackening," Wilson, *Diary of the "Terra Nova" Expedition*, Feb. 4, 1912, p. 240

295 "Mike's hands had," Fiennes, *Mind over Matter*, p. 194

296 "It is like going ashore," Scott, *Personal Journals*, Feb. 8, 1912, p. 441

296 "Since the last depot," Wilson, *Diary of the "Terra Nova" Expedition*, Feb. 4, 1912, p. 239

296 "Evans' fingers suppurating," ibid., Feb. 5, 1912, p. 240

296 "Coal seams," ibid., Feb. 8, 1912, p. 241

296 "It has been extremely," Scott, *Personal Journals*, Feb. 8, 1912, p. 440

297 "We have two full days' food," ibid., Feb. 10, 1912, p. 442

297 "their full," Cherry-Garrard, p. 545

297 "The worst day we have had," Scott, *Personal Journals*, Feb. 11, 1912, p. 442

297 "You look around," Fiennes, *Mind over Matter*, pp. 198–99

298 "There were times when," ibid., p. 205

298 "We go two miles," ibid., p. 205

298 "greatly owing to," Scott, *Personal Journals*, Feb. 11, 1912, p. 442

298 "It was a test of," ibid., p. 443

298 "by a fatal chance," ibid., Feb. 12, 1912, p. 443

298 "Bowers has had," ibid., Feb. 13, 1912, p. 444

299 "Scott is quite wonderful," Seaver, *"Birdie" Bowers of the Antarctic*, p. 244

299 "plunged into," Wilson, *Diary of the "Terra Nova" Expedition*, Feb. 12, 1912, p. 242

299 "We ought to have gone," ibid., Feb. 5, 1912, p. 240

299 "We again had," ibid., Feb. 6, 1912, p. 240

299 "One of the great difficulties," Cherry-Garrard, p. 538

299 "It was such an awful place," Mills, p. 84

300 "collapsed—sick and giddy," Wilson, *Diary of the "Terra Nova" Expedition*, Feb. 16, 1912, p. 243

300 "It is an extraordinary," Oates, diary, undated

300 "[He] is quite worn out," ibid., Feb. 15, 1912

300 "We could not possibly," ibid., Feb. 16, 1912

300 "Evans has nearly broken," Scott, *Personal Journals*, Feb. 16, 1912, p. 446

300 "We found him," Oates, diary, this entry is dated February 18, although Evans's death occurred on February 17

300 "I was first," Scott, *Personal Journals*, Feb. 17, 1912, p. 446

301 "Wilson thinks it certain," ibid., Feb. 17, 1912, p. 447

302 "the result of concussion," Rogers, Allan F., "The death of Chief Petty Officer Evans," *Practitioner*, 1974, SPRI

302 "The diet consumed," ibid., pp. 11–12

302 "[Evans] hasn't been cheerful," Scott, *Personal Journals*, Jan. 30, 1912, p. 435

303 "The causes of Evans's death," Dr. Mike Stroud, letter to R. Fiennes, Jan. 3, 2003

303 "Wilson . . . knew the symptoms," Priestley, R. E., "The Scott Tragedy," *Geographical Journal*, October 1926, SPRI, p. 342

303 "is not a reliable criterion," ibid., p. 342

304 "He was the biggest," Cherry-Garrard, p. 544

304 "The absence of poor Evans," Scott, *Personal Journals*, Feb. 19, 1912, p. 449

305 "I take this opportunity," ibid., March 16–17, 1912, p. 462

305 "The way to their," Gran, *50 Years Polar Remembrance*

305 "They had just picked," Cherry-Garrard, p. 545

Chapter Seventeen. *The Greatest March Ever Made*

308 "They have taken," Gran, *The Norwegian with Scott*, p. 175

308 "but from what I had heard," ibid., p. 177

310 "I sincerely trust," Scott, *Personal Journals*, Feb. 19, 1912, pp. 448–49

310 "Same terrible surface," ibid., Feb. 20, 1912, p. 449

310 "Terribly slow progress," ibid., p. 449

310 "Bowers' wonderful sharp eyes," ibid., Feb. 23, 1912, p. 450

311 "Dug up Christopher for food," Oates, diary, Feb. 24, 1912

311 "[We] shall have to be," Scott, *Personal Journals*, Feb. 24, 1912, p. 451

312 "full to the brim," Swithinbank, p. 92

312 "[Simpson] told me," Cherry-Garrard, *Annotated Journals*

313 "we are getting into better ski," Scott, *Personal Journals*, Feb. 25, 1912, p. 452

313 "I never doubted his heart," ibid., Feb. 25, 1912, p. 452

314 "Oh! for a little wind," ibid., Feb. 25–26, 1912, p. 452

314 "The sun shines," ibid., Feb. 28, 1912, p. 454

315 "All nearly paralysed," Fiennes, *Mind over Matter*, p. 192

315 "The end is in sight," ibid., p. 192

315 "New kind of chisel-hard," ibid., p. 165

315 "In the ten hours," Stroud, *Shadows on the Wasteland*, p. 162

316 "very cold last night," Scott, *Personal Journals*, Mar. 1, 1912, p. 454

316 "Misfortunes," ibid., Mar. 2, 1912, p. 455

316 "Titus . . . disclosed his feet," ibid., Mar. 2, 1912, p. 455

316 "[Ran] could no longer bear," Stroud, *Shadows on the Wasteland*, p. 163

317 "We are in a *very* queer street," Scott, *Personal Journals*, Mar. 2, 1912, p. 455

317 "the wind at strongest," ibid., Mar. 3, 1912, p. 455

317 "the crucial effect," Solomon, p. 235

318 Wright, p. 373

318 "Simpson's three-volume treatise," Solomon, p. 113

319 "Not the least," Scott, *Personal Journals*, Feb. 19, 1912, p. 448

319 "on this surface," ibid., Mar. 8, 1912, p. 459

319 "American scientists in the 1990s," Solomon, pp. 294, 296, 297, and BAS meteorological data, McMurdo Sound, 2000–2002

320 "Our fuel dreadfully low," Scott, *Personal Journals*, Mar. 5, 1912, p. 457

321 "If we were all fit," ibid., Mar. 6, 1912, p. 458

321 "One of Oates' feet," ibid., Mar. 7, 1912, p. 458

321 "Poor Oates," ibid., Mar. 6, 1912, pp. 457–58

321 "Have to wait," ibid., Mar. 8, 1912, p. 458

321 "Amundsen and Daddy," Young, p. 148

321 "We hope against hope," Scott, *Personal Journals*, Mar. 7, 1912, p. 458

321 "Oates' foot worse," ibid., Mar. 10, 1912, p. 459

322 "Shortage on our allowance," ibid., Mar. 10, 1912, p. 459

322 "To estimate," Cherry-Garrard, p. 427

323 "To travel to One Ton Depot," ibid., p. 430

323 "If Scott had not arrived," ibid., p. 430

323 "On the two remaining days," ibid., p. 433

324 "My orders," ibid., p. 434

325 "In this sort of life," ibid., Chatto & Windus, p. 589

325–26 "A few days after," "He went so far as to say," "I get back to Hut
     Point," "Demitri immediately recovers," and "On our arrival in New
     Zealand," all from Cherry-Garrard, *Annotated Journals*

326 "Now I know," ibid.

326 "That's quite possible," ibid.

326 "I am afraid it is becoming clear," ibid.

327 "miserable jumble," Scott, diary, Mar. 10, 1912

327 "Titus Oates," Scott, *Personal Journals*, Mar. 11, 1912, p. 460

327 "not pulling much," ibid., Mar. 12, 1912, p. 460

328 "I practically ordered," ibid., Mar. 11, 1912, p. 460

328 "Truly awful," ibid., Mar. 14, 1912, p. 461

329 "What are we to do," Taylor, p. 443

329 "you will have to make," ibid., p. 443

329 "[Bowers] had a scheme," Cherry-Garrard, p. 537

329 "if you break your leg," ibid., p. 596

329 "if anyone breaks down," King, p. 186

330 "Our sick companions," Bowers, letter to Emily Bowers, March 1912

330 "Lost track of dates," Scott, *Personal Journals*, Mar. 16–17, 1912,
     pp. 461–62

330 "That day a terrible storm ensued," Gran, *50 Years Polar Remembrance*

331 "This is a sad ending," Smith, *I Am Just Going Outside*, p. 226

331 "We knew that poor Oates," Scott, *Personal Journals*, Mar. 16–17, 1912, p. 462

332 "I am still strong," Seaver, *"Birdie" Bowers of the Antarctic*, p. 262

332 "Birdie and I," Seaver, *Edward Wilson of the Antarctic,* pp. 293–94

332 "forlorn hope," Scott, *Personal Journals*, Mar. 21, 1912, p. 463

332 "Blizzard as bad as ever," ibid., Mar. 22–23, 1912, p. 463

333 "two of the 5 of us," Wilson, *Diary of the "Terra Nova" Expedition*, p. 247

334 "a continuous gale," Scott, *Personal Journals*, Mar. 29, 1912, pp. 463–64

335 "Every day we have been ready to start," ibid., p. 464

335 "the immense shove of the man," Cherry-Garrard, p. 390

335 "Last entry," Scott, *Personal Journals*, Mar. 29, 1912, p. 464

335 "never a word of blame," ibid., p. 470

336 "I would bet," Skelton, letter to Hodgson, Mar. 26, 1913, SPRI

336 "exposure and weakness," *Daily Mail*, Feb. 14, 1913

336 Wright, p. 344

336 "Scott and his companions," R. Amundsen, *Mitt Liv som Polarforsker*, Gyldendal Norsk Forlag, 1927, p. 69

337 "a little sugar," SPRI, MS 761/8/11

337 "I can testify certainly," Edward Atkinson, MS 761/8/11, SPRI

337 "the morphia and opium," Cherry-Garrard, *Annotated Journals*

338 "It was a horrid sight," Huxley, *Scott of the Antarctic*, p. 305

338 "We have the last *half*," Scott, *Personal Journals*, Mar. 18, 1912, p. 463

338 "We have done the greatest," Scott, letter to J. M. Barrie, *Personal Journals*, pp. 471–72

338 "You must understand," Scott, *Personal Journals*, p. 475

338 "Excuse writing: it is −40°F," ibid., p. 473

338 "I had looked forward," Gwynn, pp. 221–22

339 "You know I cherish," ibid., pp. 221–23

339 "It is no disparagement," Ludlam, p. 227

Chapter Eighteen. *The Legacy*

342 "This second year," Debenham, *The Quiet Land,* p. 143

342 "It is all I can do not to speak out," Cherry-Garrard, *Annotated Journals*

342 Wright, p. 345

343 "I shed a few tears," SPRI, *Polar Record,* Vol. 14, No. 88, 1968, pp. 33–39

343 Wright, p. 346

343 "and there," Cherry-Garrard, pp. 496–97

343 "That scene can never," ibid., p. 497

343 "It was something," Gran, in *Scott's Last Journey,* BBC 2, Mar. 19, 1972

344 "Hereabouts died a very gallant," Scott, *Personal Journals,* p. 468

344 "I think of Scott," Gran, *The Norwegian with Scott,* p. 219

344 "Are you all well?," Cherry-Garrard, p. 584

344–45 "We landed to find," ibid., p. 593

345 "[I doubt if St. Paul's]," Pound, pp. 299–300

345 "All these long weary," Young, p. 158

346 "We are weak," Scott, *Personal Journals,* p. 477

346 "They died like Englishmen," *Nottingham Evening Post,* Feb. 12, 1913

346 "It is a splendid tragedy," *Daily Mail,* Dec. 11, 1913

347 "The scientific notes," Filchner, *Nottingham Evening Post,* Feb. 12, 1913

347 "Scott has conquered," Charcot, *Daily Mail,* Feb. 12, 1913

347 "Scott would not turn aside," Charcot, *Sheffield Independent,* Mar. 8,
    1912

347 "I am unwilling," Amundsen, *Daily Mail,* Feb. 11, 1913

347 "Immortal glory rises," Hedin, *The Times,* Feb. 13, 1913

347 "No polar explorer," Gran, *50 Years Polar Remembrance*

347 "In the history," Gran, *Kampen om Sydpolen,* Ernst G. Mortensens, 1961

348 "I would not," Shackleton, *Daily Telegraph,* Apr. 2, 1912

350 "And certainly . . . for the vast majority," Riffenburgh, p. 199

351 "Commander Evans," *Daily Mail,* Christchurch, Feb. 15, 1913

352 "It is well known," *South: The Race to the Pole,* National Maritime
    Museum, p. 90

352 "Unfortunately I cannot help you," Robert Feeney, e-mail to R. Fiennes,
    Feb. 24, 2003

353 "The Committee (Curzon)," Cherry-Garrard, *Annotated Journals*

354 "he had a habit," Cherry-Garrard, Chatto & Windus, p. 595

354 "I am distinctly conscious," Scott, letter to Fridtjof Nansen, Nov. 2, 1901, University Library, Oslo

354 "Not a single article," Scott, *Voyage of the "Discovery,"* Vol. I, p. 229

354 "It is already evident," Scott, *Personal Journals*, Oct. 27, 1911, p. 346

354 "Cooking for five," ibid., Jan. 5, 1912, p. 414

355 "[Scott's] instincts," Huntford, *The Last Place on Earth*, p. 156

355 "He said," King, p. 118

355 "the ossification of Scott," Lambert, p. 184

355 "looking over his shoulder," Huntford, *The Last Place on Earth*, p. 421

355 "sculpt out his post-expedition image," Lagerbom, p. 176

355 "preparing his alibi," Huntford, *The Last Place on Earth*, p. 507

356 "The intensity of," Ponting, p. 292

356 "Birdie . . . died in," Seaver, *"Birdie" Bowers of the Antarctic*, p. xi

357 "That was the glory," ibid., p. xix

357 "They say—deeply moved," ibid., p. xx

357 "I have heard discussions," ibid., pp. xix–xxi

357 "They died having done," Huxley, *Scott of the Antarctic*, p. 305

358 "Captain Scott lay," Gran, *The Norwegian with Scott*, p. 216

358 "it looked very," SPRI, letter from Lashly to R. Skelton, Jan. 18, 1913, MS 324/23/1–5; D, SPRI

358 Wright, p. 346

358 "When I entered," Crean, letter to Captain R. H. Dodds (author's italics) as quoted by Smith, *An Unsung Hero*, p. 172

358 "I must say I," Crean, letter to J. Kennedy, Jan. 1913, SPRI

358 "Bowers and Wilson were," Cherry-Garrard, pp. 497–98

359 "Captain Scott had died last," Atkinson, "Account of Events Concerning Southern Party," MS 761/8/11, SPRI

359 "I went over Bill's body," Cherry-Garrard, *Annotated Journals*

359 "If this letter reaches," Scott, *Personal Journals*, p. 470

359 "I write when we are," ibid., pp. 470–71

360 "We have had four days," ibid., p. 472

360 "The diary of Wilson," MS 175; D, SPRI

360 "we are pretty well done," Scott, *Personal Journals*, p. 474

361 "We may lose," Ludlam, p. 151

361 "It might be said," Seaver, *Scott of the Antarctic*, p. 39

362 C. Wright in *Radio Times* interview, Mar. 16, 1972

362 "Scott's reputation," Cherry-Garrard, Chatto & Windus, pp. 593–94

363 "Owing to the great," Bernacchi, *Saga of the "Discovery,"* p. 201

365 "After all . . . we are setting," Scott, *Personal Journals*, p. 473

365 "Certainly, the war," Paxman, p. 2

365 "*any* public display," ibid., p. 12

365 "In left-wing circles," ibid., p. 12

Chapter Nineteen. *The Last Word*

366 "I must warn you," Wally Herbert, letter to Ranulph Fiennes, Feb. 19,
      2002

367 "Everyone knows," Strachey, p. 111

367 "It is not [the biographer's] business," ibid., p. 10

367 "If the biographer is wise," ibid., Preface

369 "sad comment," Duncan Wu, *The Independent*

369 "It's some time," Philip Hensher, *The Spectator*, Nov. 30, 2002

370 "I never met Con," letter from G. B. Shaw to K. Scott, Mar. 23, 1923,
      Bernard Shaw: Collected Letters III, ed. Dan Laurence, p. 817

371 "most incompetent failure," G. B. Shaw, letter to Lord Kennet, Feb. 21,
      1948

371 "you chaff and sneer," Rose, p. 197

372 "His whole criticism," F. Debenham, letter to the editor of the *Geographi-
      cal Journal*, July 1928

372 "We must now summarize," Hayes, *Antarctica*, p. 180

372 "Captain Scott must have been," Hayes, *The Conquest of the South Pole*,
      p. 128

373 "anything but the simple," Huxley, *Scott of the Antarctic*, Preface

375 "[At] about –40° C," Huntford, *The Last Place on Earth*, p. 332

375 "without the risk," ibid., p. 355

375 "incapable of the specialized interplay," ibid., pp. 168–69

375 "Scott forced the pace," Huntford, *The Last Place on Earth*, p. 438

375–76 "with an imaginary foe," ibid., p. 397

376 "It is one man's interpretation," Vivian Fuchs, review of *Scott and
      Amundsen* in *Geographical Journal*, Vol. 146, p. 273

376 "Scott . . . came from a rich," Huntford, *The Last Place on Earth*, p. 25

376 "Scott personified," ibid., p. 524

376 "start of the collapse," ibid., p. 119

376 "Scott had the nervous uncertainty," ibid., p. 308

376 "The appearance of," ibid., p. 260

376 "Scott . . . ran her under," ibid., p. 156

376 "it is an advantage," Scott, *The Voyage of the "Discovery,"* Vol. I, p. 300

377 "One has to interpret," Huntford, *Encounter*, Vol. 54, No. 5, May 1980, p. 17

377 "intuition," ibid., p. 17

377 "No. These are landscapes," Wheeler, *Terra Incognita*, p. 59

377 "His book is interpretive," *Times Literary Supplement*, June 2, 1972

377 "[Huntford] was satisfied," Wayland Young, *Encounter*, Vol. 54, No. 5, May 1980, p. 18, SPRI

377 "discovered that Scott," Carl Gråndahl, *Aftenposten*, 1980, translated by Gordon Thomas

377 "and that is exactly," ibid.

377 "I have found more than," ibid.

377 "spiteful things," ibid.

378 "tampering with the record," Huntford, *The Last Place on Earth*, p. 187

378 "selective," ibid., p. 189

378 "in what he tells," ibid., p. 189

378 "This is reconstruction," ibid., p. 530

378 "a pathetic little gesture," Huntford, *The Last Place on Earth*, p. 521

378 "The heroic efforts," British Museum (Natural History), *Natural History Reports*, 1914

378 "had already done most of the work," Huntford, *The Last Place on Earth*, p. 521

378 "can't *stand* Wilson," Wheeler, *Terra Incognita*, p. 141

379 "you will have to depend," Limb and Cordingley, p. 12

379 "please remember," Oates, letter to Caroline Oates, Oct. 24–28, 1911

379 "Oates's hard comments," Limb and Cordingley, p. 139

379 "We may get through," Pound, p. 203

379 "the extremities of suffering," King, p. 172

379 "Mrs. Oates . . . was perhaps going too far," Huntford, *The Last Place on Earth*, p. 523

379 "I'm fairly sure," letter from Sue Limb to R. Fiennes, Mar. 16, 2003

380 "Captain Scott would be," Huntford, *Shackleton*, p. 361

380 "there used to be great trouble," ibid., p. 361

380 "had evidently been," ibid., p. 361

380 "This was the almost inevitable," Huntford, *The Last Place on Earth*, p. 170

380 "dull lieutenant," ibid., p. 133

381 "The elementary error," ibid., p. 229

381 "From the start he," Huntford, *The Last Place on Earth*, p. 170

381 "break Evans . . . so as to ease," ibid., p. 439

381 "There is absolutely no justification," review of *Scott and Amundsen* by P. Law 60: *Overland* 82, 1980, p. 60

381 "to force Oates out," Huntford, *The Last Place on Earth*, p. 507

381 "to lie down with him," ibid., p. 507

381 "Though married," ibid., p. 126

382 "Nansen and Kathleen Scott," ibid., p. 510

382 "I think if anyone read *carefully*," K. Scott quoted in *Encounter*, Vol. 54, No. 5, May 1980, p. 14, SPRI

382 "I seem to have missed the letters," Huntford, *Encounter*, Nov. 1980, p. 126

382 "But what happened," Huntford, *The Last Place on Earth*, p. 122

382 "they have almost certainly," ibid., p. 122

383 "It would be simpleminded," D. Drewry, letter to *The Times*, Feb. 16, 1985

383 "He was always spitting venom," Elspeth Huxley, telephone conversation with Peter Scott, Aug. 19, 1979, Cambridge University Library, A400 Scott Papers

383 "was the sort of man," ibid.

383 "Roland Huntford had no official position," William Mills, letter to R. Fiennes, Jan. 13, 2003

384 "The result was," David Wilson, letter to R. Fiennes, May 26, 2003

384 "to achieve a dispassionate," Huntford, letter to Peter Scott, Apr. 21, 1978

384 "May I take the opportunity," Huntford, letter to Peter Scott, Mar. 21, 1978

384 "I'm glad that your book," Peter Scott, letter to R. Huntford, Mar. 28, 1978

384 "Mr Huntford came to me," *Daily Telegraph,* report of press statement, Sept. 19, 1979

384 "had seriously and to my mind," ibid., Sept. 19, 1979

385 "Apparently your client," Peter Scott's lawyers to R. Huntford's lawyers, Sept. 1979

385 "I object to Roland Huntford's book," Wayland Young, *Encounter,* Vol. 54, No. 5, May 1980, p. 19, SPRI

385 "you published a letter," John Hemming, *The Times,* Nov. 20, 1979

386 "Reading this book," Caroline Boucher, *The Observer*

386 "Huntford's assault on Scott," Francis Spufford, *Daily Telegraph,* Oct. 6, 2001

386 "Huntford, a journalist," P. Beck, *Contemporary Review,* Vol. 250, No. 1452, 1987, SPRI

386 "An account by an admirer," Dr. Gordon Robin, *Polar Record,* 19 (123), 624–6, SPRI

386 "Huntford has seen fit," Ellen McGhie, *Daily Telegraph,* Oct. 17, 1979

386 "horrid man," Huntford, transcript of an interview, 2002, R. Fiennes's personal papers

386 "It is perfectly clear," Huntford, e-mail to R. Fiennes, June 3, 2003

387 "my mother was Russian," Huntford, transcript of an interview, 2002, R. Fiennes

387 "his father was an Army officer," Charles Swithinbank, telephone conversation with R. Fiennes, Dec. 16, 2002

387 "born in South Africa," Huntford, jacket flap of *The New Totalitarians*

387 "Oh, I left in disgrace," Huntford, transcript of an interview by Gordon Thomas, 2002

387 "Quantum mechanics," Huntford, transcript of an interview, 2002

388 "an abiding contempt," ibid.

388 "the nearest example," Huntford, front jacket flap of *The New Totalitarians*

388 "Yes, you're right," Huntford, transcript of an interview, 2002

388 "I think he was a horrible man," ibid.

388 "he fell," Leif Mills, letter to R. Fiennes, Feb. 24, 1998

388 "Once such seeds were sown," Solomon, p. xvi

389 "the present struggle," Griffiths, pp. ix–xxxiv

389 "a gripping 7-episode film drama," *The Last Place on Earth* press packet

389 "Scott never said anything," Gran, *Observer* magazine, Mar. 31, 1974

389 "the Empire's spastic evolution" and "the glories of imperialism,"
Lagerbom, pp. 221–22

389 "The author tries to give," Judy Skelton, review in *Antarctic*, Vol. 18,
No. 1, 2000, of *The Rescue of Captain Scott* by Don Aldridge

390 "Too bad the tragedy," T. H. Baughman, review of *The Rescue of Captain
Scott* by Don Aldridge, *Polar Record*, 37 (200)

390 "For three straight weeks," Solomon

390 "not exceptionally low," Huntford, *The Last Place on Earth*, p. 499

390 "It is difficult," Cherry-Garrard, Chatto & Windus, p. 582

391 "He was a thoroughly cheerful," Hodgson, MS 1181, SPRI

391 "Sound in his judgement," Ponting, p. 162

391 "He wouldn't ask you to do," Bill Burton in *Scott's Last Man,* National
Radio documentary, New Zealand, Feb. 29, 1987

391 "[Scott] had achieved something," Gran, quotes from *Slik van Det* and
Kampen om Sydpolen as reported in Ellen McGhie's letter to the *Daily
Telegraph*, Oct. 17, 1979

391 "He is thoughtful," Wilson, letter to his parents, Seaver, p. 84

391 "I loved every hair on his head," Crean, undated letter to Peter Scott, SPRI